Telecourse Study Guide

**English Composition
Writing for an Audience**

The Annenberg/CPB Telecourse

Peter Berkow

for use with
**A Community of Writers
A Workshop Course in Writing**

Peter Elbow and Pat Belanoff

Mc
Graw
Hill

Boston   Burr Ridge, IL   Dubuque, IA   Madison, WI   New York   San Francisco   St. Louis
Bangkok   Bogotá   Caracas   Kuala Lumpur   Lisbon   London   Madrid   Mexico City
Milan   Montreal   New Delhi   Santiago   Seoul   Singapore   Sydney   Taipei   Toronto

McGraw-Hill Higher Education

A Division of The **McGraw-Hill** *Companies*

Telecourse Study Guide for use with
A Community of Writers: A Workshop Course in Writing
Peter Elbow and Pat Belanoff

This telecourse study guide was developed for use by students enrolled in the Annenberg/CPB telecourse, *English Composition: Writing for an Audience.* This telecourse consists of 26 half-hour video programs broadcast on PBS, this *Telecourse Study Guide,* the McGraw-Hill textbook, *A Community of Writers: A Workshop Course in Writing,* telecourse edition by Peter Elbow and Pat Belanoff, and a *Telecourse Faculty Guide.* A package of the telecourse edition of *A Community of Writers, WebWrite!,* an online peer-review program, and the *Telecourse Study Guide for use with A Community of Writers* is available at a discounted price. For more information, contact your McGraw-Hill representative.

English Composition: Writing for an Audience is produced by Peter Berkow and Anita Berkow.

The Annenberg/CPB Project
Funding for *English Composition: Writing for an Audience* is provided by the Annenberg/CPB. Annenberg/CPB, a partnership between the Annenberg Foundation and the Corporation for Public Broadcasting, uses media and telecommunications to advance excellent teaching in American schools. Other notable series funded by Annenberg/CPB include *A Biography of America, Destinos, In Search of the Novel, Literary Visions,News Writing, Voices & Visions,* and *The Western Tradition.*

1 2 3 4 5 6 7 8 9 0 DOC/DOC 0 9 8 7 6 5 4 3 2 1
ISBN 0-07-251017-X
www.mhhe.com

Telecourse Study Guide

English Composition: Writing for an Audience

Produced by Peter Berkow and Anita Berkow

The Annenberg/CPB Telecourse

This telecourse consists of 26 half-hour video programs broadcast on PBS. This *Telecourse Study Guide* is for use with the McGraw-Hill textbook, *A Community of Writers: A Workshop Course in Writing,* by Peter Elbow and Pat Belanoff. There is also a *Telecourse Faculty Guide* to accompany *A Community of Writers.*

    English Composition: Writing for an Audience may be used as a video resource for classes, libraries, and media centers or as a telecourse for distant learners. For further information, please call the phone numbers listed here.

Colleges, universities, and other educational institutions may

PURCHASE THE PROGRAMS ON VIDEOCASSETTE

Purchase the programs on videocassette for use in the classroom or media center. For more information, call **1-800-LEARNER** or visit the Annenberg/CPB Web site at <www.learner.org> and search on *English Composition: Writing for an Audience.*

Curriculum Package: $389

- 26 half-hour video programs on 13 cassettes
- Right to duplicate one set of videos

Two half-hour programs on one cassette: $39.95

All prices are good in the United States only. For information about additional video duplication rights, call **1-800-LEARNER**. For a list of distributors outside the United States, visit <www.learner.org> or fax your inquiry to 1-802-864-9846.

LICENSE THE TELECOURSE

License the use of *English Composition: Writing for an Audience* as a complete college-credit telecourse for distant learners beginning in spring 2001 or acquire an off-air or off-satellite taping license through the PBS Adult Learning Service. For more information, call 1-800-257-2578 or visit the Adult Learning Service Online at <www.pbs.org/als>.

- Telecourse License: $500 per semester plus $20 per student
- Off-Air Taping License: $200 per series
- Off-Satellite Taping License: $300 standard fee; $200 for Adult Learning Satellite Service Associates

Dedication and Thank You

This book should start off with a thank-you to more than two hundred instructors, writers, students, and everyday working folks who participated in the telecourse project. At the top of the list is our advisory board. All five members are respected composition instructors and active participants in the Conference on College Composition and Communication (CCCC). They also helped shape the instructional design of this course with advice and feedback throughout the five years we spent developing and testing this project. More than fifty other composition instructors took the time to talk to us on camera and share their instructional techniques. They are all among the best composition instructors in the country, and we are fortunate to have their views in the course.

The telecourse also features views from dozens of the best novelists, essayists, and journalists in the country. All were generous enough to share their writing techniques without charge to the Public Broadcasting System (PBS) or Annenberg/CPB. This is rather extraordinary, considering that many of them earn $5,000 to $20,000 for a speaking engagement. The only payment promised these professional writers was the satisfaction of knowing their insights will help many thousands of students learn about writing.

Another thank-you should go out to the celebrities who made cameo appearances in the program and the everyday folks who volunteered to share how they use writing in the working world.

The students who appeared in the television series deserve our gratitude, and we should acknowledge about five hundred students (of all ages) at Shasta College in Redding, California, who took variations of the telecourse during our testing and evaluation phase. We should thank our daughter, Wysteria Berkow, plus her many friends who made our happy home Teen Central while we worked on this project. They were all about thirteen years old when we did our first interviews for the PBS series. As we approached the final editing stages, we gained insight into one very important segment of our audience: the eighteen-year-olds who, like them, are just entering colleges and universities across the country. Certainly, we learn as much from them as they do from us. In another decade (or less), they'll be the ones passing on the ideas.

For patience and guidance on the project, we thank the editorial team at McGraw-Hill, including Lisa Moore, Magaret Manos, and Laura Barthule.

Finally, we extend a heartfelt appreciation to Mark Zempel, Michael Bertsch, and Hilda Moskowitz Goodman. All made significant contributions to this manuscript.

Anita Berkow and Peter Berkow
January, 2001

Brief Contents

Contents

This program previews the entire telecourse, showing how the classroom is a natural link to – and actually part of – the "real world." Students also meet the people who will help them master the goals of this English composition course, including educators, everyday folks who use writing on the job, well-known authors, and first-year writing students from colleges and universities across the nation. The program foreshadows many of the issues in the sequence "Thinking/Writing Strategies."

This program introduces the "Writing Process" sequence – invention, drafting, and revision – with the most basic problem in English composition: How does a writer start "inventing" ideas? When an instructor says, "Write about anything you want to write about," some students panic; the process of selecting a topic and narrowing it down is intimidating. Other writers have the opposite challenge: an instructor or boss selects the topic, and the student or employee has to find a unique angle. This program helps students grapple with both of these problems.

Many writing contexts require strong, accurate descriptions. Featured examples include a police officer's arrest report, a music critic's magazine story, an engineer's technical description of metal-cutting techniques, and scene-setting and character development in the work of novelists Sue Grafton, Tom Robbins, and Joseph Wambaugh. Students, instructors, and writers of many types share their observations about what makes good description and offer tips on describing well.

Good writing comes from good reading. English instructors including Mike Rose (UCLA) and Joe Harris (editor of the *CCC Journal*) explain how reading is part of the writing process. Teachers, students, and writers including literary great Ernest J. Gaines and science fiction author Kevin J. Anderson describe how they translate their joy of reading into better writing. Students also learn ways to make the transition from reading for pleasure to deciphering academic texts.

5: NARRATIVE WRITING 67

This program shows the relationships among narrative writing, personal writing, and academic writing. The skills of good storytelling are examined, and English composition instructors discuss the link between successful academic writing and good narrative writing. A variety of contexts in which writers need strong narrative skills, both in the workplace and in school, are presented. Science fiction author William Gibson, mystery writer John Morgan Wilson, literary novelist Charles Johnson, and others share their advice on how to tell a good tale.

6: VOICE 81

We use different voices when we talk to a police officer, a lover, a parent, or a rival. Writers also shift language, attitude, and tone when their audience changes. A student might use different writing "voices" on an English composition essay, an advanced biology lab report, and a pre-law exam. In this program, students, instructors, and writers, including Pulitzer Prize-winning journalist Richard Aregood and novelist David Guterson, dissect both the esoteric and the mechanical aspects of creating a writer's voice.

7: PROCESS ANALYSIS 95

This program provides examples of "process analysis/how-to" writing in action, from a marine biology student showing how to reproduce a scientific experiment to football coach Bill Walsh explaining a lineman's technique to Steve Shanesy, editor of *Popular Woodworking*, explaining how to stain a walnut table.

8: REVISION 107

This program explores the process of macrorevision – looking at the whole work – and offers a variety of strategies to help the student writer revise. Experienced writers, including Emmy Award-winning scriptwriter David Mills (*NYPD Blue* and *ER*) and humorist Dave Barry, share their views about revision and their techniques for revising. Students also hear from other students and instructors, including Santi Buscemi (Middlesex County College) and Beverly Moss (Ohio State University).

9: WRITING UNDER PRESSURE 123

The skills learned in an English composition course can be used successfully in timed-writing situations ranging from essay exams and term papers in other academic courses to writing documents under deadline on the job. Students learn how to quickly adapt the processes of invention, drafting, and revision and find links between rhetorical strategies and real-life writing challenges in these high-stakes situations.

10: FREEWRITING AND GENERATING 135

This program looks at ways to generate ideas and overcome writer's block, with advice from a variety of people, including Dr. Peter Elbow (University of Massachusetts), who is an authority on freewriting; Chitra Divakaruni (Foothill

Community College), who is both a novelist and an English composition instructor; Pulitzer Prize-winner Frank McCourt; science fiction writer Kim Stanley Robinson; keyboardist and lyricist Thomas Dolby; and actor Kevin Dorff of the Second City comedy troupe.

A variety of writers and instructors, ranging from Chip Bayers of *Wired* magazine to Cynthia Selfe of Michigan Technical University, discuss how computers are changing the way we read, research, organize, draft, and revise our written documents. Also explored is collaborative writing through computer networks in the context of distance-learning environments.

Every writer has his or her own strategy for organization – and most of these strategies work equally well. This program explores different prewriting strategies, including outlining, clustering, and listing, as well as organization at three levels: thesis, topic sentence, and paragraph. Writers and instructors – including humorist Tom Bodett, composition instructor John Lovas (national chair of TYCA, the Two-Year College English Association), and screenwriter Peter Farrelly (cocreator of the film *There's Something About Mary*) – discuss a variety of methods for organizing text.

Comparison and contrast can be useful thinking strategies during the invention and drafting stages of composition. A musicologist, a marine biologist, and a police officer, among others, show how these strategies – combined with critical thinking, persuasive writing, narrative writing, and other strategies introduced throughout this course – work well in a variety of contexts.

Students, instructors, and professional writers demonstrate how the revision process often starts out – and sometimes works best – in a group setting. This can work for both macrorevision (looking at the whole work) and microrevision (examination at the sentence level). Viewers observe a federal judge and her clerks, a group of students, and a team of journalists to see how the whole can be greater than the sum of its writers.

Definition is used in a variety of writing contexts, from "defining yourself in the world" to technical definitions used in engineering and science courses. Definition is examined not in isolation, but as an aspect of all other writing tasks: in argument, process analysis, and narrative writing, and in invention, drafting, and revision. Film producer Michael Moore and radio host Rush Limbaugh spar about the definition of *welfare*.

16: COLLABORATION   223

This program shows how many people whose work involves writing can learn, research, draft, and revise as a team – creating better documents. Instructors, students, and professionals including actors and writers from Mad TV, a federal judge and her assistants, a pair of science fiction novelists, and writers in academic settings share strategies for successful collaboration.

17: PERSUASION   239

In this program, students consider the art of persuasion and learn how it is similar to and different from formal academic argument. Composition instructors, political activists, journalists, students, advertising executives, and others discuss techniques for persuading and influencing people to change their actions or views. Featured are author and "culture jammer" Kalle Lasn of *Adbusters* magazine and Jeff Goodby, originator of the "Got Milk?" ad campaign.

18: READING AS A THINKER   255

How can students learn to read challenging college textbooks – not just in English composition but in any course? How can you learn how to "own" the words in a dense text by challenging some of the author's ideas and agreeing with others? How do you summarize and paraphrase an author's words and then state new ideas synthesized from his or her words and your own thoughts? How does reading become part of the thinking strategy of every writer? This program answers those questions and more.

19: ARGUMENT   271

The formal argument is the basis for most academic papers, including term papers and research papers. Students learn about the process of writing a simple statement (a main claim, thesis, hypothesis, or focus sentence) and supporting it with evidence. Featured writers and academics include political science instructor George Wright (California State University) and composition instructor Betsy Klimasmith (University of Washington).

20: QUOTES AND CITATIONS   291

Most instructors consider plagiarism a crime. It's a difficult academic task to find the balance between unethically "borrowing" another writer's words and artfully incorporating them into your own work, giving the proper credit. This program explains several crucial skills: how to properly summarize, paraphrase, quote, and use citations from the stylebooks of the Modern Language Association (MLA) or the American Psychological Association (APA) in academic work and other writing. Viewers learn from people as diverse as U.S. District Judge Helen Gillmor, writer-musician David Ellefson (Megadeth), and English composition instructor Thomas Fox (California State University, Chico).

21: RESEARCH   307
Doing college research can be seen as joining an ongoing conversation among academics. Students get advice from librarians and instructors on such research issues as how to evaluate evidence obtained from the popular press, peer-reviewed academic journals, and Internet sources. They also learn how research is valuable during each stage of the writing process: choosing a topic, narrowing a topic to a thesis, and developing the thesis into an argument. Filmmaker Michael Moore and novelist Tom Robbins note the value of research beyond school.

22: EDITING: SENTENCES   327
This program helps students correct their own writing weaknesses, with a special emphasis on diagnosing problems with sentence structure. Students learn to identify and correct common problems: misplaced modifiers, comma splices, fragments, run-on sentences, nonparallel construction, and other mistakes that can make otherwise coherent writing confusing. Frank McCourt, Geoffrey Philp (Miami-Dade Community College), and Teresa Redd (Howard University) are among those who offer instruction.

23: CRITICAL THINKING   339
Students and instructors contemplate the concept of critical thinking, from how it affects the relationship among students, their textbooks, and their instructors to its importance in good reading and writing. Students learn how to recognize logical fallacies (with the help of Al Franken and Rush Limbaugh), "read" a variety of situations critically, and apply the process to writing. Contributing instructors include Akua Duku Anokye (University of Toledo), Robb Lightfoot (Shasta College), and Cynthia Selfe (Michigan Technical University).

24: EDITING: WORD CHOICE   355
In this program, students learn how to recognize and correct errors in word choice, such as pronoun-antecedent disagreement, subject-verb disagreement, homonym confusions, and other errors that obscure the clarity of a final draft. The featured instructors and writers include Sue Grafton, Betsy Klimasmith, Santi Buscemi, and humorist and grammar expert Dave Barry, known internationally as "Mr. Language Person."

25: WRITING ACROSS THE DISCIPLINES   369
On a college campus, different departments emphasize different writing styles. How does a student learn to apply the skills learned in English composition to assignments in engineering, political science, nursing, art, agriculture, or chemistry courses? This program introduces a variety of contexts for applying the writing processes and rhetorical strategies learned in an English composition course to situations across the curriculum – effectively summarizing the entire telecourse.

This program helps students proofread for problems with language mechanics. Students study the importance of correcting mistakes that could ruin the credibility of an otherwise excellent paper and learn strategies for identifying punctuation errors. Michael Bertsch, Patricia Scully, Santi Buscemi, and Dave Barry give advice.

Appendix

Introduction to the Telecourse

Writing, that crucial act of communication, usually occurs with an audience in mind. *English Composition: Writing for an Audience* is a new telecourse and video series that introduces basic writing principles and strategies, with the goal of helping students learn how to put words together to communicate something to an audience.

Throughout the 26 half-hour programs, students meet a wide array of people whose work involves writing, either peripherally or centrally: authors, journalists, musicians, judges, humorists, professors, composition instructors, nurses, engineers, scientists, celebrities, and athletes. They discuss how they write with their specific audiences in mind, showing students how writing techniques are used in the "real world" and how composition skills can be useful in many different situations.

English Composition: Writing for an Audience can be used as a college-credit course to fulfill composition requirement. Instructors can customize instruction to emphasize either thinking/writing strategies or the writing process – or to combine both approaches. Odd-numbered programs address thinking/writing strategies; even-numbered programs cover the writing process

The 13 programs that focus on thinking/writing strategies offer a view of what some composition instructors call rhetorical modes and others call genres. Within on-the-job and classroom contexts, they show how research papers, arguments, narratives, definitions, and other strategies are used in combination with critical thinking skills to communicate. These programs also examine how composition techniques can be used when students are writing under pressure or across disciplines.

The 13 programs that focus on the writing process examine various writing techniques, showing composition as a continuous process of invention, drafting, rewriting, and proofreading. These programs cover freewriting, organizing devices, revision, collaboration, peer feedback, and editing. This sequence also shows how developing an awareness of voice, reading as a writer, reading as a thinker, and using quotes and citations affect the composition process.

The curriculum design for *English Composition: Writing for an Audience* was guided by Peter Berkow – a working writer, composition instructor, and creator of the Annenberg/CPB telecourse *News Writing* – and by an advisory board of respected specialists in composition theory.

Taking the telecourse

Find out the following information as soon after registration as possible:

- The books have been required by your instructor.
- If and when an orientation session has been scheduled.
- When *English Composition: Writing for an Audience* will be broadcast in your area.
- When course examinations are scheduled. (Mark these on your calendar.)
- Whether any additional on-campus meetings have been scheduled. (Plan to attend as many sessions, seminars, and other meetings as possible.)

To learn the most from each unit:

1. Before you view the television program, read the *Telecourse Study Guide*. Pay particular attention to the "Learning Objectives," "Introduction," and "Before Viewing" sections for each instructional unit.

2. Read the textbook assignment given to you by the instructor or recommended by the *Telecourse Study Guide*. Some students prefer to read the "Viewing Guide" for each instructional unit before watching the program.

3. View the program, keeping the learning objectives in mind. Be an active viewer. Many students find that taking notes in a double-entry notebook while viewing the program is helpful. There may be several opportunities for you to watch and review the program. If you have access to library tapes or personal copies, you may find that multiple viewings reveal additional levels of understanding.

4. Read the "After Viewing" section of the *Telecourse Study Guide*, and review the "Viewing Guide" section to reinforce concepts and expand on what you have seen.

5. Attend class discussions or complete journal assignments. If you are attending via a distance-learning environment or virtual classroom, the class discussions may be in the form of an asynchronous forum or bulletin board discussion thread. Your journal may be in the form of a threaded discussion. Some instructors prefer a journal that is written by hand in a bound notebook. Your instructor's first-day handout will explain the criteria for attendance.

6. Complete the exercises assigned by the instructor. These exercises will be from the *Telecourse Study Guide*.

7. Complete the multiple-choice "Quick Review" at the end of each *Telecourse Study Guide* chapter, even if it is not assigned by the instructor. These reviews are designed to help reinforce the main concepts in each unit.

8. Complete any writing and reading assignments made by your instructor.

9.   Seek as much feedback as possible from your instructor and your peers.

10.   Keep up with the course on a weekly basis. Each unit of the telecourse builds upon knowledge gained in previous units. Stay current with the programs and readings. Make a daily checklist and keep a calendar, noting scheduled activities. Be sure to block out time for viewing, reading, and writing. Most instructors expect students to do the equivalent of two hours of coursework for every hour of classroom time. Students who commit that amount of time to a college course usually succeed; those who try to get by with the minimal amount of effort often suffer.

11.   Stay in touch with your instructor. You should have your instructor's mailing address, e-mail address, phone number, office hours, and telecommuting (or call-in) hours. Most instructors like to hear from their students and willing to guide you through the learning process. Your instructor should be willing clarify any questions you have about the course, so don't hesitate to ask.

12.   Save your work; keep electronic backups and hard copies. Too often, students trust a computer or floppy disc to store the only copy of an important assignment, only to have the data disappear. Keep a portfolio of your work and save the instructor's feedback. Portfolios of your work may be used for end-of-term evaluation. You may be asked to show revisions along with the original drafts that include suggestions made by the instructor.

Coordinated books

THE TEXTBOOK

A telecourse edition of *A Community of Writers: A Workshop Approach to Writing* by Peter Elbow and Pat Belanoff (ISBN: 007-249-9257) has been created for use with the PBS series, *English Composition, Writing for an Audience*, from Annenberg/CPB. This groundbreaking guide to writing is known for addressing students as writers as it challenges students to develop their skills by writing often, by exploring their own writing process, and by sharing their writing with others. In *A Community of Writers*, Elbow and Belanoff emphasize that writing is a social process through a practical workshop approach; the textbook's flexible modular organization makes it easy to use with the video programs of the Annenberg/CPB telecourse, *English Composition, Writing for an Audience*. Before writing *A Community of Writers*, Peter Elbow wrote two other influential books about writing, *Writing Without Teachers* and *Writing with Power: Techniques for Mastering the Writing Process*. He also served for four years on the Executive Council of the Modern Language Association and was a member of the Executive Committee of the Conference on College Composition and Communication. Pat Belanoff has been both president of the State University of New York's Council on Writing and a member of the College Steering Committee of the National Council of Teachers of English.

THE TELECOURSE STUDY GUIDE

The *Telecourse Study Guide* for use with Peter Elbow and Pat Belanoff's *A Community of Writers* provides the student with exercises and activities that integrate the Annenberg/CPB's *English Composition: Writing for an Audience* telecourse with the material in Peter Elbow and Pat Belanoff's groundbreaking guide to writing (ISBN: 007-251-017-X). The telecourse study guide is written by Peter Berkow, producer of the Annenberg/CPB telecourse, *English Composition: Writing for an Audience*.

Each chapter of the *Telecourse Study Guide* includes the following:

- **Introduction to the Topic**, providing insight into how the unit will be approached
- **Learning Objectives**, introducing key instructional goals in a clearly defined list
- **Before Viewing** sections, which give student suggestions related to their viewing of the video program and consider how students may already be familiar with the topic at hand
- **While Viewing** sections, highlighting key points and subtleties to watch for
- **After Viewing** sections, which invite students to use what they have learned both in and out of the classroom
- **Viewing Guide**, exploring each program in detail. It includes advice from the instructional designers and summaries of the best quotations from the teachers and notables in the program Goals and learning objectives from each unit are also reinforced
- **Exercises**, designed for continued exploration of the subject
- **Quick Review**, capping off each unit with succinct multiple-choice questions

THE TELECOURSE FACULTY GUIDE

The *Telecourse Faculty Guide* to Accompany Peter Elbow and Pat Belanoff's *A Community of Writers* is a handbook for instructors teaching the Annenberg/CPB telecourse, *English Composition: Writing for an Audience* (ISBN: 007-251-0188). The faculty guide is written by Peter Berkow, producer of *English Composition: Writing for an Audience*. In it, he provides a diverse selection of activities, exercises, and discussion prompts to integrate *A Community of Writers* with the Annenberg/CPB telecourse, *English Composition: Writing for an Audience*. Each chapter of the *Telecourse Faculty Guide* includes the following:

- **Unit Overview**
- **Learning Objectives**
- **Video-Related Discussion Points and Questions**, a thorough section highlighting key elements of the video programs, with specific visual and time cues. This section suggests activities for both traditional classroom environments

and distance-learning situations, including two-way television and online learning communities

- **Related Exercises** that specifically coordinate the textbook and the video programs. These exercises include transcripts from key moments in the program for study and analysis, as well as additional exercises designed to help students master concepts delivered in the video presentation

- **Focus Questions** to stimulate class discussion

- **Self-Evaluation and Peer Feedback Form**, which helps instructors guide their students in self-analysis and peer analysis in each lesson

- **Additional Reading**, coordinating key points from the video program with samples of writing in the textbook

- **Faculty Forum Discussion** closes each chapter with insights from a different composition instructor, who shares techniques for teaching the topic of each chapter. These same faculty forum discussion essays will be used to kick off related Internet discussions by faculty members using this telecourse at the telecourse Web site: www.englishcomposition.com <http://www.englishcomposition.com>

ADDITIONAL RESOURCES

A Community of Writers is supplemented by an Online Learning Center at <http://www.mhhe.com/elbow>.

WebWrite! is an interactive peer-review program that allows students to post papers online, read comments from their peers and instructor, discuss, and edit. An online demonstration is available at <http://www.metatext.com/webwrite> (ISBN: 007-244-9934).

PageOut is a course Web site development center, hosted by McGraw-Hill, that enables instructors to build a course online. To find our more about PageOut, contact your local McGraw-Hill representative for a quick consultation or fill out the form at www.mhhe.com/pageout <http://www.mhhe.com/pageout>.

Peter Elbow and Pat Belanoff s *A Community of Writers: A Workshop Approach to Writing, telecourse edition* for use with the *PBS series, English Composition: Writing for an Audience, from Annenberg/CPB*, the *Telecourse Study Guide* for use with *A Community of Writers*, and *WebWrite!* is available as a package at a discounted price (Package ISBN: 007-412-6792). For more information, contact your local McGraw-Hill representative.

Who's Who in the Telecourse

KEVIN J. ANDERSON
Science fiction author, best known for creating "X-Files" novels and novels based on *Star Wars* characters. Anderson also writes novels built around characters of his own invention, with co-author Doug Beason.

AKUA DUKU ANOKYE
Associate professor of English, and the director of the composition program, at the University of Toledo, Ohio.

RICHARD AREGOOD
Pulitzer Prize-winning editorial writer, formerly of the Philadelphia Inquirer, currently editor at the Star-Ledger, New Jersey.

WHITLOW AU
Chief scientist of the Marine Mammal Research Program, at the Hawaii Institute of Marine Biology, and author of *The Sonar of Dolphins.*

DAVE BARRY
Pulitzer Prize-winning, syndicated humor columnist. As a youth, Barry taught grammar to hordes of corporate humanoids learning to write "clear" memos and reports so they could better scam the rest of us. Barry won UPI's Most Consistent Hair Award in 2001. He also dabbles in fiction.

CHIP BAYERS
One of the original producers for *HotWired* Internet magazine, Bayers is currently a writer and senior editor at *Wired* Magazine, San Francisco, CA

PAT BELANOFF
Past president of the SUNY Council on Writing, Belanoff is the co-author of *A Community of Writers;* she is an associate professor of English at State University of New York, Stony Brook.

Telecourse Study Guide

KATHLEEN BELL
Director of the composition program at the University of Central Florida, and author of *Developing Arguments: Strategies for Reaching Audiences.*

PETER AND ANITA BERKOW
Peter and Anita Berkow are co-producers of 46 television programs for PBS television, including the award-winning Annenberg/CPB telecourse *News Writing*. Peter Berkow is currently a full-time distance-learning specialist and composition instructor at Shasta College, Redding, CA. Anita Berkow is an editor, videographer, and producer of video documentaries.

MICHAEL BERTSCH
Composition instructor, Butte College, California, Bertsch sits on several statewide technology-in-learning committees. He is also vice president of research and development and chief envisioner for www.belearning.com.

SARAH BLAKESLEE
Research librarian and information technology expert at California State University, Chico.

TOM BODETT
Known for his humorous commentaries broadcast on National Public Radio, Bodett is author of *End of The Road* and other collections of short stories. Host of the PBS video series, *America's Historic Trails*, he penned the companion guide for the series and recently wrote *Williwaw!,* an adventure novel for kids.

TIM BOUSQUET
Reporter, editor, publisher, circulation manager, and defense attorney for the *Chico-Examiner,* Chico, California, Bosquet runs one of the last American one-man newspapers – a town crier and political advocate for his community.

T. CORAGHESSAN BOYLE
The award-winning author of novels and collections of short stories, including *The Road to Wellville* and *A Friend of the Earth,* Boyle is a professor of English at the University of Southern California, in Los Angeles.

xxii

DUFF BRENNA

Author of *The Holy Book of the Beard*, and winner of the Associated Writing Programs Novel Award for *The Book of Mamie*. A one-time Wisconsin dairy farmer, Duff Brenna teaches English literature, and creative writing at California State University in San Marcos.

STEVEN BROWNING

Composition instructor, University of Washington.

EDNA BUCHANAN

A winner of the Pulitzer Prize for her hard news journalism work covering crime for the *Miami Herald*, Buchanan is also the author of several crime novels starring newspaper reporter Britt Montero.

SANTI BUSCEMI

The author of composition textbooks including *The Basics* and *75 Readings Plus,* Buscemi is a Professor of English at Middlesex County College, Edison, New Jersey.

SANDRA CARPENTER

Editor of the *Artist's Magazine*.

BARBARA CASTRO

Social activist, Chico Peace Center, California.

SHARON CASEY

Organic produce vendor who lives in the Sierra Nevada mountains.

THOMAS CLARK

Former editor of *Writer's Digest*, Clark is the author of *Queries and Submissions*.

DEBBIE COBB
Former reporter and assignment editor, Cobb is currently news director for KHSL-TV, Chico, CA.

MO COLLINS
Actress and writer on the Fox comedy television show *Mad TV*.

DAVE DALEY
Professor of Agriculture, California State University, Chico.

CHITRA DIVAKARUNI
Author of the best selling novels, *The Mistress of Spices* and *Sister of My Heart*, Divakaruni teaches composition at Foothill College, Los Altos Hills, California. She has won several awards for her writing, including the American Book Award from the Before Columbus Foundation.

THOMAS DOLBY
A ground-breaking musician, composer, and songwriter, Dolby is currently working with interactive computer software. Dolby is known for pioneering computer/keyboard composition techniques and recording many hit songs, including "Blinded Me With Science" and "Aliens Ate My Buick."

KEVIN DORFF
A comic writer, director, and performer, Second City comedy club, Chicago, Ill. Currently, Dorff is a staff writer for the Conan O'Brien Show.

GLEN DOWNEY
Composition instructor, University of British Columbia, Canada

PETER ELBOW
Director of the writing program at the University of Massachusetts in Amherst, the co-author of *A Community Of Writers*, as well as author of several other groundbreaking books including *Writing Without Teachers*, Elbow is a nationally recognized innovator in composition theory.

DAVID ELLEFSON
Bassist for the rock group Megadeth, and the author of *Making Music Your Business: A Guide For Young Musicians,* Ellefson is also a columnist for *Bass Player* magazine.

JAMES ESH
Veterinarian writer and editor, Esh edits a quarterly veterinary journal in Northern California.

PETER FARRELLY
Screen writer and director, along with his brother Bobby Farrelly. They are responsible for movies such as *Dumb and Dumber* and *There's Something About Mary*. Peter's novels include *The Comedy Writer* and *Outside Providence*.

THOMAS FOX
English instructor and director of the writing center at California State University, Chico, as well as an active participant in various committees for the Conference on College Composition and Communications. Fox is also a member of the advisory board for this telecourse.

AL FRANKEN
Comedy writer and political satirist, best known for his Emmy Award-winning work on NBC's *Saturday Night Live*. Franken is the best-selling author of *Rush Limbaugh Is a Big Fat Idiot* and *Why Not Me?*

J. JOAQUIN FRAXEDAS
Author of the novel *The Lonely Crossing of Juan Cabrera,* Fraxedas is also an attorney in Orlando, Florida

ERNEST J. GAINES
Author of several books, including *The Autobiography of Miss Jane Pittman* and *A Lesson Before Dying*. Gaines has won dozens of awards and honors, including the National Book Critics Award. He is a professor in the English department at the University of Southwestern Louisiana.

ELIZABETH GEORGE
The author of best-selling mystery/suspense novels including *In The Presence of the Enemy*. George is the winner of the Anthony and Agatha Awards for mystery writing.

JUDGE HELEN GILLMOR
U.S. District Judge, state of Hawaii.

LOREN GOERING
Goering is a U.S. Park Ranger who demonstrated the Benjamin Franklin
Printing Press in Philadelphia, Pennsylvania.

DAVID GUTERSON
Guterson is a former high school English teacher, and novelist, best
known for his novel *Snow Falling on Cedars*, the winner of the
PEN/Falkner award. He is also author of several other novels and
collections of short stories.

WILLIAM GIBSON
Has won every conceivable award for his best selling science fiction
novels, including the Hugo and Nebula awards. Gibson is best known for
inventing the term "cyberspace." His works include the short-story
collection *Burning Chrome* and the novel *Neuromancer*.

JEFF GOODBY
Is an advertising executive in San Francisco, known for award winning
television ads, including the "Budweiser Lizards" and the "Got Milk?"
campaign.

ARIEL GONZALEZ
Composition instructor, Miami-Dade Community College.

SUE GRAFTON
America's favorite mystery novelist, Grafton is best known for her alphabet
series starring detective Kinsey Milhone. Grafton has won many awards for
her writing, and continues to keep the nation anticipating her next book.

KAY HALASEK
Assistant Professor of English, and Director of first year writing programs,
Ohio State University.

JOE HARRIS
Associate professor of English and director of the Center for teaching, learning, and writing, Duke university; former editor of the journal *College Composition and Communication*; member of the advisory board for this telecourse.

CARL HIAASEN
Award-winning investigative journalist and columnist for the Miami Herald, as well as prolific author of action packed novels of humor and intrigue, Hiaasen is known for his books *Tourist Season* and *Stormy Weather*.

VICTORIA HINDES
Grant researcher and writer, Shasta College, CA, and the director of the Northern California "Gear-Up" program.

DR. THOMAS HILGERS
Director of the writing program, University of Hawaii.

RICHARD HOLETON
English instructor, Stanford University, Holeton is also the author of *Composing Cyberspace: Identity, Community, and Knowledge in the Electronic Age*.

MARK IBANEZ
Is an award winning sportscaster at KTVU-TV Oakland, and author of the book *Mark's Remarks*.

CHARLES JOHNSON
Winner of the National Book award for his novel *Middle Passage*, Johnson has published scholarly work, criticism, essays, screenplays, and five novels. He is also a revered writing instructor at the University of Washington who can claim David Guterson among many of his prized students.

MILES JORDAN
Music critic, *Jazz Times* magazine.

Telecourse Study Guide

PAT KILBANE
Actor on the Fox comedy television show *Mad TV*.

SCOTT KING
Writer for the Fox comedy television show *Mad TV*.

BETSY KLIMASMITH
Is a composition instructor at the University of Washington.

CHARLES KURALT
The late Emmy award-winning CBS correspondent, host and producer of the televised series *On The Road*, was also the author of many best-selling books.

KALLE LASN
Founder and editor of *Adbusters* magazine and author of *Culture Jam: The Uncooling of America,* Lasn is also the director of the Vancouver-based political action group, the Adbusters Media Foundation.

GREG LIGGINS
A news reporter and anchor, formally of KTVU-TV, Oakland, CA. Liggins currently works at WTTG in Washington, D.C.

ROBB LIGHTFOOT
Speech and debate instructor, Shasta College, Redding, CA.

RUSH LIMBAUGH
America's best-known syndicated conservative radio commentator, and self-proclaimed "servant of humanity," Limbaugh publishes a newsletter and is the author of several best-selling books about American politics, including *The Way Things Ought To Be* and *See, I Told You So*.

xxviii

JOHN LOVAS

English instructor at De Anza College, Cupertino, California, author, past chair of TYCA (the Two-Year College English Association) and the 2001 National Chair of CCCC (the Conference on College Composition and Communication), Lovas is also a member of the advisory board of this telecourse.

CHRIS LOWE

A student at the time of his interview, is currently an assistant professor at California State University, Long Beach. He teaches biology, animal behavior, and ichthyology classes.

MIN-ZHAN LU

English instructor, Drake University, and active participant in CCCC (the Conference on College Composition and Communication), she is also a member of the advisory board for this telecourse.

MARIA MADRUGA

Composition instructor and director of the writing center at Shasta College in Redding, CA.

ROCKY MAFFIT

Maffit is a touring percussionist and musicologist, and the author of the book *Rhythm And Beauty*.

AMY MAKI

News editor for KTVU television and documentary filmmaker, Maki is the writer/producer of *The Aftermath of Apartied*.

JOHN MERZ

Chair, board of directors, Sacramento River Preservation Trust.

FRANK MCCOURT

High school English teacher for more than 27 years before writing his Pulitzer Priz- winning memoir *Angela's Ashes*, McCourt is also the author of the novel *'Tis*, and a successful playwright and essayist.

BEVERLY MOSS
Associate professor of english, and director of the writing center, Ohio State University.

MICHAEL MOORE
Author of popular political books, including *Downsize This*, Moore is the director and producer of *Roger and Me,* the most-watched documentary film in recent history. He is also the creator of the television series *TV Nation* and *The Awful Truth*.

DAVID MILLS
Award-winning scriptwriter for the television series *NYPD Blue* and *ER*.

ELAINE MAIMON
Provost, and professor of English, Arizona State University, West.

HIMILCE NOVAS
A Cuban-born writer and history instructor at the University of California, Santa Barbara, Novas has written several non-fiction books, including *Everything You Need to Know About Latino History*. Her works of fiction include *Mangos, Bananas, and Coconuts: A Cuban Love Story*.

GORDY OHLIGER
Musicologist and "banjo-ologist," Ohliger is a California Arts Council grant recipient several years running. He is known internationally for his historical and entertaining presentations of American culture, through the music made decades ago.

SHARON OWEN
Writing center tutor, Shasta College, Redding, CA

ALDRICH "PAT" PATTERSON, JR.
Psychologist and instructor at California State University, Chico

JANICE PERITZ
Composition instructor at Queens College, City University of New York.

DONALD PHARR
Composition instructor at Valencia Community College in Orlando, Florida.

GEOFFERY PHILP
Composition instructor at Miami-Dade Community College. Philp is the author of several novels and collections of short stories, including *Uncle Obadiah and the Alien*."

TERESA REDD
Former editor at Time/Life books, Redd is currently a composition instructor at Howard University, where she is the director of the writing across the curriculum program. She is also on the executive board of CCCC (the Conference on College Composition and Communication) and on the editorial board of CCC (College Composition and Communication).

MARK REYNOLDS
Professor of composition, Jefferson Davis Community College and editor, TETYC (Teaching English at the Two Year College).

DENNIS RICHMOND
Anchor for the evening news at KTVU-TV in Oakland, CA.

TOM ROBBINS
Well-known novelist. His work includes *Jitterbug Perfume, Even Cowgirls Get the Blues,* and, most recently, *Fierce Invalids Home From Hot Climates*.

KIM STANLEY ROBINSON
Popular science fiction author, noted for his Mars trilogy, *Red Mars*, *Green Mars*, and *Blue Mars,* Robinson won the Hugo and Nebula awards for best science fiction novel three years in a row.

KUULEI RODGERS
Graduate student, marine biology, University of Hawaii.

MIKE ROSE
Member of the UCLA graduate school of education faculty and instructor for the UCLA writing program. He is also the author of several books that have inspired Composition instructors across the nation, including *Lives On The Boundary* and *Possible Lives*.

PETER RUBIE
Writer, editor, and literary agent, NY.

RAY RUMMEL
Rummel is an engineering professor at California State University, Chico.

JOE SATRIANI
Considered by many to be the best instrumental rock guitarist alive today, Satriani also manages an often-visited Web site, and uses the Internet to communicate with his many fans.

PATRICIA SCULLY
English teacher, Pleasant Valley High School, Chico, CA.

STEVE SCOTT
Scott is a news reporter for WLS radio in Chicago, Illinois.

CYNTHIA SELFE
Composition instructor, Michigan Technological University, National Chair 1998–99 Composition Conference, College Composition and Communications. Selfe is also on the advisory board for this telecourse.

STEVE SHANESY
Editor and publisher of *Popular Woodworking* magazine and An avid woodworker, Shanesy writes many of the articles in his own magazine.

JULIA SHOVEIN
Nursing Professor, California State University, Chico.

EMILY SPIVEY
Comedy writer for the Fox television show *Mad TV*. Ms. Spivey also writes for "The Groundlings" theater, in Hollywood, CA.

SHERI SIMON
Art professor, California State University, Chico

MEGUMI TANIGUCHI
Composition instructor, University of Hawaii.

LARRY THOMPSON
Graduate student, Engineering, California State University, Chico

LYNN TROYKA
Composition instructor, Queensbourough Community College, City University of New York. Past chair of both the Two-Year College English Association and the Conference on College Composition and Communication, Troyka is also author of several popular textbooks.

CHARLES TURNER
History professor, Butte College, Oroville, California

KEENA TURNER
Former professional football player for the San Francisco 49ers, former assistant coach at Stanford University, currently a television sports broadcaster.

JANET TURNER
Police officer in Chico, CA.

LEWIS ULMAN
Director of the computers-in-composition program at Ohio State University.

DR. VICTOR VILLANUEVA
Director of the Composition program at Washington State University, and past Chair of CCCC.

MARTY WALLACE
Graduate student, teaching assistant, Department of Chemistry, California State University, Chico.

BILL WALSH
Professor Emeritus from Stanford University, Walsh is the former coach and current general manager for the San Francisco 49ers. Author of the book *Finding the Winning Edge*, Walsh tutored many of today's NFL head coaches and is widely considered the most influential football strategist of our time.

JOESEPH WAMBAUGH
Former police officer and former English teacher, Wambaugh has written several best-selling novels, including *The Onion Field*.

DEBRA WILSON
Actress/sketch writer for the Fox television comedy show *Mad TV*, Wilson is also a respected motivational speaker.

Who's Who in the Telecourse

JOHN MORGAN WILSON
Known for his award-winning mystery/crime novels starring ex-newspaper reporter Benjamin Justice, Wilson is a former journalist, and has written and produced for television. He also conducts writing workshops for UCLA.

KIMBERLY WISE
Composition instructor, at Cypress College, CA.

BRUCE WOODS
Editor of *Alaska Magazine*, Woods is the former editor of both *Mother Earth News* and *Writer's Digest*.

GEORGE WRIGHT
Political Science professor, California State University, Chico.

ANNE WYSOCKI
Composition instructor, Computers-in-composition specialist, Michigan Technological University.

Students
A very special thank you to the many students who participated in this series, including those from the following schools who appear in live scenes of the telecourse programs:

Butte College (Oroville California)
California State University (Chico, California)
Middlesex County College (Edison, New Jersey)
Shasta College (Redding, California)
University of Hawaii

Student interviews
Gregory Andrus – Middlesex County College
Corie Kimino Cushnie – University of Hawaii
Mike Gratton – Butte College
Jeremy Marshall – Shasta College

Ethlyn Manning – Middlesex County College
Xavier Pino – Butte College
Amy Spencer – Shasta College
Mark Spencer – Shasta College
Jenny Stigle/Magellen – Shasta College
Robert Stansberry – Shasta College
Mark Zempel – California State University, Chico

Additional thanks to
 Janet Albright – librarian, Shasta College

"Being able to express yourself and interact with other people using the King's English is probably the most important thing, in an educational process. And, it's the most important thing in your future, in the workplace, in any career that you choose."

BILL WALSH, general manager, San Francisco 49ers, professor emeritus, Stanford University

Introduction to the Topic

Maybe you registered for this course because you love writing and can't wait to write a college research paper. Maybe you're a student who enjoys homework so much that the prospect of spending the weekend writing an expository essay (perhaps comparing and contrasting the angst of post-modern existential philosophers with the musings of deconstructionist, prepostmod-ern newtraditionalists) is much more allur-ing than the thought of going to a dance club or spending time with your friends.

Or maybe you're taking this course because all undergraduates at your college or university are required to.

Composition instructors know which rea-son is more likely. As we gaze at the sea of faces the first day of class, we often wonder how we'll connect with the students.

We could start this book with a sales pitch and, like a car advertisement on television, imply that success in this course will improve your romantic life, cure your cholesterol problem, add sparkle to your smile, and turn your wardrobe tastes into the latest fashion statement.

Unfortunately, the budget in most English departments is too small to finance such a public relations campaign. We will have to settle on this simple pledge:

Take the lessons of this course seriously, and you have a much better chance of suc-ceeding in all college courses that require writing and reading.

And, if you remember the lessons of the course beyond college, we'll guarantee a great job, a positive bank balance, a new home, and low, low monthly interest rates for the rest of your life.

OK – so, we can't do that.

But after you've viewed this first program, we hope you'll see that success in *any* career can be influenced by applying the writing skills you will learn in this class.

Some students assume that the years spent in college are kind of like treading water before they have to deal with the realities of the "real world." The authors of this book and creators of the telecourse believe you'll soon discover that there is no difference. The experiences you need to succeed in the real world start now.

Learning Objectives

This program and *Telecourse Study Guide* chapter will give you an overview of the thinking and writing strategies you will be studying in the programs on description, narrative writing, process analysis, comparison and contrast, definition, persuasion, and argument. The writing challenges ahead, in both academic and on-the-job settings, are built around strategies of thinking and writing called "genres" by some instructors and "rhetorical modes" by others. The formal study of critical thinking, research, writing under pressure, and composition with computers also introduce strategies for thinking as you write – and will apply to experiences beyond this course.

This video program works in harmony with the essential premises of Workshop 8, "Writing in the World: An Interview about Writing," from *A Community of Writers* by Peter Elbow and Pat Belanoff:

- It's interesting and helpful to investigate the remarkable variety of kinds of writing that people do for school, for work, and on their own.

- It's also interesting and helpful to interview people and investigate the different ways they go about writing. It is usually reassuring, whether we discover similarities ("Wow – she has the same experience I do"), or differences ("How interesting – she has a completely different way of going about it").

"Trying out Genres" (pp. 44–55) provides an overview and discussion of the genres discussed in this video program as well as some others.

Before Viewing

Before previewing the thinking and writing strategies you will study in this course, think about the skills you'll need for writing in the career that you hope to pursue. If you have not declared an academic major, imagine a career you would enjoy – and consider the writing challenges that might be required. Just for fun, list the things you expect an English composition course might cover.

While Viewing

Note the thinking/writing strategies introduced by the various characters in the television series. Though the topics are introduced only briefly, we will focus on each individual skill or technique later in the course. Become aware of the various genres (or rhetorical modes) and pay careful attention to how thinking/writing strategies such as description, narration, argumentation, persuasion, comparison, and definition are used in the various professions. Also note the similarities between the way you research, write under pressure, and use critical thinking in the classroom and the way these same skills are used by writers representing various occupations.

After Viewing

The "Main Assignment" on page 214 of *A Community of Writers* is an excellent practical use of the strategies discussed in this video program.

Make an inventory of the thinking/writing strategies you feel confident about in your own writing. Create a separate list of techniques that you know you need to work on. Consider contacting people who are successful in a career similar to the one you are interested in pursuing (graduate students, professors, and people in the working world), and find out what the writing and reading challenges are like in that field.

Review the list of things you expected English composition to cover that you made before watching this program and make two new lists. Make a new list of things you will learn in this course that you did not expect to study. Make another list of things you expected to study that this course will *not* cover.

Viewing Guide

It is important to establish a link between the lessons learned in a composition course and the writing you will produce in the world beyond school, since you will apply many of the strategies you learn in college composition courses to the working world.

The producers of this telecourse and book have surveyed a diverse group of people who write on the job. You'll meet many of them in this first telecourse program and will encounter them in subsequent programs. Their views on writing are combined with advice from composition instructors and students.

The introductory program also provides an overview of the thinking/writing strategies covered in the several programs of the telecourse and the related chapters of this *Telecourse Study Guide*.

Rhetorical modes

For decades, instructors have assigned expository essays that required students to describe, to narrate a story, to compare and contrast, to define a term, to argue, and to persuade. These categories, or genres, of writing are useful, because many assignments in courses across the campus ask students to compare and contrast two items, argue a point, and so forth.

Elbow and Belanoff discuss the expository essay form on page 48. The analysis of the difference between starting with form and starting with content is in the section "Are Genres Form Or Content?" (pp. 53–55). Elbow and Belanoff point out that a genre is not just a mold to pour unformed raw writing into; instead, it can serve as a way to *generate* or invent content.

Your instructor's approach to assignments in this course might surprise you. Instead of simply asking you to write an essay in a particular genre ("This week, class, I want you all to write a comparison/contrast essay"), the instructor will usually expect you to know *why* you are using one of these genres to address a certain writing challenge.

Thinking and writing strategies in the "real world"

It's not hard to find practical applications of these strategies in school, in the workplace, or in the upper-division classroom. That's because rhetorical modes reflect the way most people reason things out. For that reason, many instructors try to give assignments within a context. In other words, they show *why* comparison might be used by a scientist or *why* persuasion might be used in a politician's speech.

Kathleen Bell, an English instructor from the University of Central Florida, puts it this way: "My approach to using definition, or process or argument or any of what we call 'modes,' is contextual because those are *thinking* strategies. And it's because they're thinking strategies that they become *writing* strategies. It is not because they're writing strategies that become thinking strategies."

Mike Rose, an expert in composition from UCLA, explains a research project that he and several colleagues conducted to study the application of writing skills used in college classrooms beyond the first-year writing course. After studying hundreds of sample assignments from typical freshman, sophomore, junior, and senior courses, Rose and his team found evidence that these rhetorical modes, or genres, represent essential skills.

"What we saw was that if there were certain strategies (we call them 'thinking/writing strategies') that … if students had the strategies under their belts, they would actually be able to go a long way toward doing well in a wide range of courses," Rose says.

"These strategies are not going to come as any surprise. Comparing: comparing one poem with another poem; comparing one theory in political science with another theory in political science; comparing one organism in a biology class with another organism in biology class. Or defining: That includes giving back definitions that have been given to you in textbooks or lectures but also creating definitions – creating definitions of physical processes, of literary devices, of social phenomena."

Rose and his colleagues also discovered that process analysis (the art of explaining how to do something), a sense of narration (or good storytelling), and description were all essential thinking/writing strategies for successful writing in all undergraduate classes.

The telecourse program goes one step further, introducing individuals who use the same writing strategies on the *job*. Since individual chapters in this *Telecourse Study Guide* (combined with programs in the telecourse) will study *each* individual thinking and writing strategy in depth, we'll merely introduce them at this point.

Narrative writing (storytelling)

A quick sampling of careers shows that almost every occupation uses some variation of narrative writing or storytelling.

Advertising executive Jeff Goodby (known for his "Got Milk?" ad campaign) uses the narrative genre as the basis for the thirty-second skits that become his television commercials.

"Advertising's all about storytelling," Goodby explains. "I think the most persuasive thing in the world – going way back to primitive times – is a story well told; and advertising makes use of that all the time."

We also learn from our survey of careers that police officers use a form of narrative to relate events in their arrest reports. Journalists and film producers use storytelling to relate both real-life and fictional events. And many people use a form of narrative just to keep track of what is going on in their lives or on their jobs.

Musician Joe Satriani, for example, uses a form of narrative writing as a way to capture his thoughts during the recording of his instrumental jazz/rock tunes.

"My manuscript papers look pretty funny because there will be little illustrations and there will be stories," Satriani explains. "I put the time and the date and a place and what it was about and what led up to the beginning of the inspiration. I put what I played it on – I'd even get detailed: black guitar with a drop D tuning and with this particular effect. I guess I try to get that piece of paper to capture the mood as well as the nuts and bolts about the chords and the melody and the rhythm."

Description

San Francisco 49ers coach and general manager Bill Walsh explains that in professional sports, certain types of descriptive writing will often decide who wins or loses a game. Detailed scouting reports and an in-depth game plan make extensive use of description. And though it might be difficult to conjure up the image of a three hundred-pound lineman reading scouting reports and game plans in his hotel room the night before a big game, that is exactly what many of them do.

"There'll be a test at the end of the week, on that week's plan," Walsh says. "And that's a *written* test. And basically questions are asked, and players are expected to answer. And this is where their writing skills become important."

Description is important in every career that requires technical, creative, or interpersonal writing. In the telecourse, you will meet police officers, scientists, nurses, and engineers who all depend on accurate description. You'll also meet novelists, sculptors, and musicians who use description with a more artistic flair.

Comparison and contrast

The technique of comparing and contrasting is so common that many professional writers use it automatically, without deliberately thinking, "Now I need to compare and contrast."

Emily Spivey, a staff writer for the Fox television show *Mad TV*, explains that, in her occupation, "You definitely use contrast and comparison to make points in comedy." The humor, Spivey explains, often comes from the contrast between what the audience *expects* to see and the unexpected plot twist thrown in to create a laugh.

She illustrates with a skit that you'll see actors and writers working on later in the telecourse. The joke is built around a spoof of an advertisement for a "Home Theatre System." The audience expects a normal commercial featuring a normal family enjoying a high-tech entertainment system – the type that emulates the movie theater experience in the home.

The laughs come from the unexpected: A fictional company, the Spishak Corporation, which sells the systems, delivers everything that is *annoying* about a movie theater experience.

"If it were a real great home entertainment system, you would have the giant screen," Spivey says. "In contrast, Spishak gives you like a little twelve-inch monitor and the broken seats. The sound system is actually a speaker in the other room blasting a different movie."

You will find, throughout this telecourse, that the thinking/writing strategy of comparison and contrast is routinely used in a variety of professions, including law enforcement, engineering, and marine biology.

Definition

Our survey of occupations shows that many require the skills of definition writing. Police officer Janet Turner explains that this thinking/writing strategy is used on a daily basis in law enforcement, though the officers see the genre quite differently than English instructors.

"Definition is very important," Turner says. "Not only in identifying the crime – because you want to make sure all the elements, all their acts, constitute or define the crime – but also the words you use in your report. You have to be careful with the words you choose, because defense attorneys will play with that in court."

We learn in the telecourse that a definition can have an agenda. In other words, the author might be using the definition to make a point. This type of definition writing is an effective device in argument and persuasion – especially if the writer is creating his or her own definition of a concept or idea. This type of definition might be used in a political science debate or as part of a formal academic argument

In the telecourse, you will see that a slightly more technical application of definition writing is also relevant for nurses, farmers, attorneys, and scientists.

Process analysis

Process analysis – the art of telling somebody how to do something – may not be a writing skill required in every job. However, it would be nearly impossible to name an occupation where you didn't have to read process analysis or "how-to" writing to succeed.

This kind of writing is used in everything from owner's manuals to recipe books. Some process analysis is dense and poorly written. However, well-written process analysis can be pure fun to read if the author composed it with some flair.

David Ellefson, bass player for the rock band Megadeth, is the author of a book called *Making Music Your Business*. Though Ellefson's intent is "not to write a formula for how to become a rock star," the entire book is a practical process analysis of how to deal with the quirks, sharks, and perks of the music industry.

"I did not want this to be 'how to make a million bucks and get rich quick in the music business overnight' and try to pump up and motivate and get people going and stuff like that," he says. "I was writing specifically to musicians – probably a lot of young musicians. So it gave me an opportunity to rewind my life, go back to when I was 13, 14, 15, 16 years old."

Ellefson's writing is aimed exactly at that target audience: young musicians who play at various levels, from purely recreational to semiprofessional, and who read the music trade magazines often enough to know some of the jargon of the business.

You will learn in the telecourse that the technical writing used by engineers, mechanics, woodworkers, or scientists is often in the form of a process analysis.

Writing for the discourse community

Each of the writers in the telecourse is representative of his or her "discourse community" – that is, a group with the same academic, career, or recreational interests. Ellefson is used to the style of writing common in music magazines; Spivey is comfortable using comparison/contrast within the discourse style of Hollywood scriptwriters. Walsh is used to the way football coaches use description; Goodby is successful with storytelling that uses the language of the advertising industry. Turner knows the importance of using definition correctly within the criminal justice system and shapes her writing to communicate directly to judges and attorneys.

When you choose a career, you will write and read materials composed of the language, jargon, attitude, and style appropriate for that profession. You will also apply thinking/writing strategies in a manner similar to the way others in your discourse community use them.

Keep this in mind when you write "expository essays" in an English class. Though the practice is important, you probably won't be asked to write an "essay" at your job. However, you will certainly need to know how to define, narrate, compare, and describe.

Nowhere is that need more evident than in the way the various professions approach intellectual discussion and debate (or formal "argument") on the critical issues of their discourse communities.

Argument and persuasion

The most common style of writing in your upper-division college courses will likely be a variation of a style sometimes called a "formal academic argument."

The formal argument is a nonadversarial style of writing that is somewhat persuasive but has a higher goal of demonstrating reasoning and logic. Since there are so many other forms of persuasive and argument writing, this course separates the study into two separate units and continues the discussion of persuasion and argument into units about critical thinking and research.

PERSUASION

In Workshop 10, "Persuasion," in *A Community of Writers*, Elbow and Belanoff point out that most forms of persuasion rely less on formal rational argument than on reaching out to audience members and getting their interest by appealing to experience and emotion.

Advocacy journalists use informal persuasion in their style of newspaper to make political points – entertaining the readers and perhaps inspiring them to action. This is *not* the journalism of the mainstream press, which (at least on the surface) strives to be objective. The primary mission of the advocacy journalist is to publish opinions and influence readers. This style of persuasive writing is an American tradition so important that the First Amendment to the Constitution protects the freedom of the press to publish such opinions. (Several of the architects of the Constitution published their own advocacy newspapers.)

In the telecourse, you will encounter Tim Bousquet, who writes and publishes a weekly newspaper that advocates progressive political views.

Political magazines like his are aimed at an audience that has similar beliefs – although his writing will at least try to provoke those who disagree with him to consider alternative views.

"What I'm trying to do is give ammunition to my political associates – to give them a rhetorical inventory of how to fight these absurd political ideas," Bousquet says. To be persuasive, Bousquet makes sure to keep up with the views of his opposition.

"I read the right-wing press every day," he says. "There are actually some right-wing authors who are very, very good at what they do; most of them are just nonsense and just kind of like ugly people spewing out stuff. But some of them are real intellectuals – and those are the folks who have to be dealt with on a serious level. Mainly, I try to show how the arguments are false; they're not internally consistent. I'm not writing *to* them; I'm writing to people who read my paper who are, by and large, folks who agree with my politics."

Argument

In Workshop 11, "Argument," page 277, Elbow and Belanoff take care to separate argument from persuasion. The nature of argument, they point out, differs from field to field, or from discourse community to discourse community. Although there is no one magic formula for writing an argument, this type of writing is generally more logical and more carefully reasoned than a piece of informal persuasion.

John Merz, an environmentalist who works in the same Northern California community where Bousquet publishes his advocacy journalism, uses a form of formal argument to communicate with government officials about the local ecology.

Merz must also be persuasive, because his goal is to protect California's wildlife and natural resources. However, his arguments must be more tightly *reasoned* than persuasive in order to communicate effectively within the discourse community of lawyers, politicians, and judges.

"If you get involved in a legal argument, quite frankly, it is confrontational," Merz explains. While Bousquet might use highly charged, emotional phrases to write about the same issues for his newspaper audience, Merz must use the toned-down language of the formal argument, even if his feelings are just as passionate.

"If you have a position and you believe it is correct, and you believe their position is incorrect, you're trying to *show* them," Merz explains. "But you're also using your interpretation of the law to demonstrate what leads you to this conclusion. There's a dialogue, but it's at a different level."

Research

John Merz talks about the discourse of environmentalists and politicians as a "dialogue," even though much of it is written on paper. Academics also refer to a written body of work as a "conversation." To join that conversation (and add something of value) a student is expected to be aware of what everybody else is saying.

This is where research comes in. Certainly, Merz cannot engage in a dialogue with a judge who is making a decision about the rivers Merz is trying to protect, unless he arrives in the courtroom armed with stacks of statistics, environmental impact reports, and findings from scientists who have studied the environment. When Merz wins such a battle, it's likely an opponent will remark, "That guy did *his* homework."

Most writers are introduced to the process of research in the classroom. However, research is a necessary survival skill for many occupations, from working as a scientist to excelling as a comedy writer or political analyst.

In the telecourse, political opponents Al Franken and Rush Limbaugh both explain that, though their views are diametrically opposed, they use essentially the same techniques to wage their war of words: Both dig up data through the Internet; both read stacks of newspapers; both hire research assistants to scour the libraries and wade through government archives.

"It's hard to make an *original* argument, certainly, based on no research," Franken says. In fact, Franken claims that his best-selling book *Rush Limbaugh Is a Big Fat Idiot* "was *about* the research." The satire and political jabs would be useless, he says, if he could not back the barbs with facts.

Limbaugh also credits his success as a conservative radio talk-show host to deep research. "If you have a thirst to learn, you *have* to do research," he says. "That's what education is and what learning is. There's no such thing as acquiring additional knowledge (above and beyond what you are) without doing research. And the key ingredient is *wanting* to do it. The key ingredient is being jazzed when you succeed at finding what you're looking for."

Scientists interviewed for the series were even more passionate about research. According to veterinarian Jim Esh, "All of science is research. Science is truth; science is what you actually know to be true and then communicating that. You may learn the most profound truth in the universe, but unless you can put it down in an objective way that can be repeated and understood by other people, it's not science yet."

Journalist Chip Bayers, of *Wired* magazine, says that the research skills he learned in college helped him succeed in his profession.

"I think there's very little difference between what I did in school in terms of having to structure a term paper or structure an essay and what I have to do here as a magazine writer," Bayers explains. "It all comes back to fundamentals. I have to go out, I have to do my reporting. Or in the case of the student days, I had to go out and do my research. I have to have multiple sources – or multiple documents supporting a point. I've got to argue that point effectively, and I've got to link all of those ideas together in a kind of flow that makes a clear and convincing argument to a reader."

Critical thinking

Underlying all research, argument, and persuasion is a notion college instructors call *critical thinking*. Though all participants in a debate or academic discussion like to think of themselves as critical thinkers, it is difficult to define the term.

In fact, an entire unit of this telecourse explores the way instructors, students, and writers define and apply their understanding of critical thinking in the classroom and in the world beyond school.

Novelist and English composition instructor Chitra Divakaruni offers this example from academia: "Critical thinking is when you look at the information available to you – and you can see past a group of disconnected events (or a group of disconnected facts) – and you see the connections. You begin to see how things fit together, and you begin to see inner meanings."

This approach makes sense when you are trying to organize a pile of research notes to write a term paper. Before you embark on such a demanding project, it might be good to see examples of critical thinking in real-life applications.

For example, U.S. District Judge Helen Gillmor says, "When my law clerks are given the briefs in a particular case, they'll be given a pile a few inches thick of things to read."

The reading material Gillmor gives her clerks is much like the information a student will find in a library, only instead of books and journals, the clerks must read and evaluate evidence and arguments filed by the attorneys on either side of the case.

"I also want the clerks to do independent research," Gillmor says. "Otherwise, the level of our work is going to be governed by whatever the level the lawyer has. We take what has been provided by the lawyers as a starting point, and then we'd go to the case law and the statutes, and we use our own independent *critical skills* to decide."

In other words, Gillmor explains, her court does not depend on the skills of the lawyers on either side of the case. She prefers to do her own critical thinking to determine justice.

Computers in composition

Computers have changed the way we compose essays, term papers, and other academic assignments. Computers have ruled the world of commerce and business for decades; the academic community is just now catching on to the significance of this revolution.

English instructors are aware of this phenomenon; today's composition courses often include a good hard look at how word-processing programs affect the process of writing.

As instructor Michael Bertsch notes, "Many students don't realize how much writing has to be done in the world of work. And that's one of the reasons I argue very strongly to teach on computers. To have the people always *immersed* in the text."

The courtroom is an excellent example of how computers have affected the way we write. On the video, we see Judge Gillmor and her clerks working in a room lined with law books. The books in many law offices are primarily for show, however. Most legal research is conducted through electronic databases these days.

Computers have also affected the very way many of us *compose* our thoughts. Science fiction writer Kim Stanley Robinson echoes the view of most of the professional writers surveyed for the telecourse. "I would say that most of my published worked has gone through probably a dozen serious revisions. This is partly the result of working on the computer where you can do the revising without retyping in all this stuff that you *aren't* revising."

Dave Barry, a novelist and Pulitzer Prize-winning humor columnist for the *Miami Herald*, says that computers are "the most wonderful thing that ever happened to both professional and amateur writers – on many levels."

In addition to writing his columns with a word processor, Barry uses the computer to keep in touch with his readers, to conduct research for his columns, *and* to sharpen his vocabulary when the need arises.

"It's so much easier to look things up and get them right," Barry says. "You are much more likely to look up the definition of a word, if it's just [a matter of] hitting a keystroke on your computer – and you can easily find out what that word means: all ten definitions."

Barry suggests that the computerized dictionary increases vocabulary, because students previously "refused to haul out their clunky old dictionaries every time they needed a new definition."

Barry also believes that online communications have increased literacy to some degree, just by requiring people to write and read – much like they used to, before television and radio. "One of the benefits of computers is they're *forcing* people to write again," he says. "People used to pick up the phone; now they e-mail. E-mail is not great literature, but it's still putting words down. People are back to writing and reading."

Writing under pressure

The more you observe writing situations on the job, the more you discover that the skills needed to excel in the "assignments" for writing in the "real world" mirror those learned in a well-designed English composition course. Chapter 9 of this *Telecourse Study Guide* and the related telecourse program, for example, examine the challenges of "Writing Under Pressure," with a focus on writing well on essay exams and in other similar academic situations.

The main premise of this telecourse program is that the process of writing can apply to high-stakes writing situations, if the writer is well practiced and confident.

Certainly, you would expect that doctors, lawyers, and journalists have to write under pressure. You might be surprised to find that high-stakes writing is also required in less obvious places, such as the office of a repair shop for big-rig trucks.

Robert Stansberry, an engineering major and diesel mechanic, explains that the lessons learned in this unit apply directly to a job like his.

"You have to write under pressure, because a truck comes in, he's a cash job, and he has to go that same day," Stansberry explains.

The documents justify repair bills of several thousand dollars and could even be used in a court of law, if the repairs were implicated in an accident.

The mechanic must know computers and apply the lessons of drafting, revising, and editing to turn out a clear and accurate statement. Though he isn't taking an essay exam in a college course, the stakes are still pretty high.

Summary

The goal of this first chapter and telecourse program is to show that the skills studied in English composition are used beyond college and will apply directly to the writing challenges you will have on the job.

Each of the concepts introduced in this first program will be the focus of an entire telecourse program along the way to the program "Writing Across the Disciplines," which is designed to summarize the series.

As you watch the other programs in the telecourse, read the other chapters in your textbook and the *Telecourse Study Guide*, and work on the homework assignments for this class, keep your own career goals in mind. Though some of the very best English instructors and writers in the country will be giving you advice that is traditional in a first-year writing course, most of the lessons you learn will be reinforced by everyday folks who use those skills every day of their lives – in the world beyond the classroom.

Integrating the Text

The discussion of writing genres in Workshop 8, "Writing in the World" (pp. 213–231) and Workshop 2, "Trying Out Genres" (pp. 44–55) parallels the points made in this program. As Elbow and Belanoff suggest, concentrating on content first and form later turns out a different type of writing than concentrating on form first, and then worrying about content.

Many composition classes tend to emphasize the second approach, assigning a description essay one week, a comparison essay the second week, and an argument essay the following week. In the writing that we do beyond school, content is usually emphasized first, and the writer eventually finds a genre – a "thinking/writing strategy" – or a form that works.

Elbow and Belanoff point out that, "Because language is inherently both form and content, we can never really have pure content or pure form. If we use process writing to study our tendencies of mind when we write, we will gradually learn when it's helpful to put more attention on form as we write, and when it's helpful to put more attention on content."

Workshop 8, "Writing in the World: An Interview about Writing" (pp. 213–231), emphasizes investigating the different kinds of writing that people do for school and for work. The workshop gives guidelines for learning the connection between the academic essay and writing in the world of work – one of the main themes in this telecourse program.

Workshop 8 is essentially an extended exercise that will help you learn from interviewing someone about how he or she writes. We recommend you use this assignment to interview someone who works in a career similar to the one you hope to follow. The list of questions on page 219 are particularly helpful for such an interview, and several sample interviews are included at the end of the workshop, as models for you to consider.

No doubt, you will discover in the interview that many of the writing techniques and tasks introduced in the first two programs of the telecourse (and covered in depth in the next 25 videos) are used extensively by your interviewee.

Although the telecourse goes to great lengths to show how writing is used in a wide variety of different careers, it is possible that only a few of those interviewed will work in field you are considering. There's nothing like in-person contact with someone who is successful in your field to cement the lesson: the skills learned in composition will be used, one way or another, by everyone who is successful in the world of work.

Exercises

Check with your instructor for your formal assignments. You will be asked to do exercises from the *Telecourse Study Guide*.

Exploring school writing/real world further
EXERCISE I
Depending on what is applicable to you and your current employment situation, list the writing challenges in

- Your current job
- A parent or older sibling's job
- Your ideal career choice

EXERCISE 2

Take a look at the "Letters to the Editor" in the local, campus, or regional newspaper at your college's library. Notice the arguments used and writing abilities that are evident in these letters. What sort of criteria do you think that these newspapers use to choose which letters get published? While reading the letters, make a list of anything you find them to have in common: these are likely to be close to the criteria used in their selection. Keep this list in your notes. You will refer to it later in the semester when you write your own letter to the editor. It will also be a good source of topics for open-ended assignments.

EXERCISE 3

List different types of writing assignments (including exam questions, lab reports, and papers) where you have had to apply (or anticipate you may need) thinking and writing strategies similar to those introduced in this program. (Examples: definition, argument, comparison, process analysis, description, narration, persuasion.) For a more focused version of this exercise, take one course, or one academic discipline, and try to list situations that will require use of these strategies.

Here's an example in biology:

- Explain the process of the Krebs cycle.
- Define *mitosis*.
- Compare and contrast an enzyme and a catalyst.
- Describe rigor mortis.
- Tell the story of how plant life turns sunlight into carbon-chain chemicals that are the basis for all life forms.
- Argue for or against mandatory government regulation of the amounts of sugar, fat, and salt in public school cafeteria meals.

EXERCISE 4

1. For this exercise you will be asked to consider people to interview about the writing they do outside school in their everyday life. Possible interview subjects could include

   - A professional (lawyer, doctor, engineer, etc.) working in a field in which you are interested
   - Someone who writes fiction, poetry, or newspaper articles either professionally or for pleasure

2. To prepare your questions for the interview, take a look at the short description of each of the *Telecourse Study Guide* chapters. Design questions that address the subjects of each of these chapters in a way that is appropriate to the kind of writing performed by your subject.

3. During the interview, take careful notes or (with your subject's permission) record the interview so that you have an accurate record of the various topics that you and your subject discuss.

4. After the interview, review your notes or recording, and create an outline, tree, or bubble diagram to organize your subject's responses according to which topic/question they belong. We hope that you will also find that you have gathered remarks about pertinent issues that go beyond your original set of questions and shed light on the individual perspective your subject has about writing.

5. Use your organized interview information to write a rough draft of a short essay that reports what you have discovered about your subject's experience with writing in the real world.

Exercise just for fun

Go to your campus career center and inquire about jobs that you might see yourself doing with the degree you are working toward. If your campus doesn't offer this type of service, you can find generic applications at any office supply store. Ask for any applications that you can take with you to fill out, making sure to get two copies of each. You are going to fill out the first copy with the intent of sharing it with and amusing your classmates. Use the second form to write a formal job application as an assignment for your instructor.

Revision exercise

In this exercise, you will use the rough draft created in Exercise 4 as a starting point for revision. The goal of this revision will be to incorporate the major topics of writing instruction presented in this class (as represented by each chapter in the workbook) and to show how they relate to the writing experiences of your interview subject in the real world. Understandably, not every instructional topic will be represented in the results of your interview, but try to make as many connections as possible.

Quick writing exercise

Your instructor may ask you to do a quick focused freewrite about the difference between the writing you do in school and the writing you do in the world beyond school. Those of you who are taking the course through a distance-learning system may be encouraged to share your thoughts in a discussion thread or to post your ideas on an Internet bulletin board. If you are writing your thoughts out by hand in a process journal, you might use these questions to stimulate ideas. This is a freewriting exercise that will not be graded. You can use any of the following questions and statements to kick-start your thoughts about the connection between school writing and the real world:

Are you taking this class because you are required to? Your instructor will harbor no grudges if your honest response indicates a reluctance to take English composition. It is not necessary to pretend you have a great love of writing if, on registration day, this class sounded about as appealing as an appendectomy without painkillers. All of that aside, do you imagine there will be any links from the assignments in this class to the writing in the real world? Or do you feel that English composition will have very little connection to the rest of your life? If you do see a connection, what do you imagine you can bring from a writing class that will help with tasks in the working world? If you do enjoy writing, and you are looking forward to this class, can you imagine how your comfort with writing can help in your career?

Exercise related to *A Community of Writers*
Since this is the first week of the course, we'll foreshadow a technique you will use and a series of exercises that you will participate in throughout the course.

The technique is known by various names, including freewriting and generative writing. One the early telecourse programs will focus entirely on how this type of writing is practiced. The basic idea is quite simple: write quickly and spontaneously, without worrying about correctness or audience.

The series of exercises are designed to get you to think about the writing process. Each week, your teacher might assign a question or topic, and ask you to write freely for a time period. You may be asked to write a half hour or for only 10 minutes. In a traditional classroom setting, your instructor may ask all students to scribble in their writer's notebooks. In a distance learning environment, the teacher might ask all students to post a quick "freewrite" on a bulletin board. When the responses are collected together, this often results in an interesting discussion thread.

For example, the teacher might ask a class of 25 students to each write for 15 minutes about how they organize their papers. The resulting discussion thread will show 25 different approaches. Some of the responses will start: "I always use an outline first." Others will start: "I never organize my papers, and they often read like my dorm room looks."

Some of the topics for the writing exercises will be ideas generated by your instructor. Other exercises will be built around questions posed in this Study Guide. Finally, many of the exercises will be built around the "Process Journal" questions in each workshop of *A Community of Writers*.

This week, read the section "Process Journal" on pages 14 and 15 of

Workshop 1. This passage will give you an overview of how Elbow and Belanoff view this series of exercises.

There are short-term goals and long-term goals for this series of quick writing exercises. One short-term goal is to create a discussion forum and opportunity for individual students to think critically about each aspect of writing we are studying. One long-term goal is to help you learn how to write a very long paper as painlessly as possible. Another goal is to help you assemble a paper that resembles the "Autobiography of Myself as a Writer," described by Elbow and Belanoff in Workshop 16, "Autobiography and Portfolio" (pages 417 to 442), in *A Community of Writers*. (Some of these essays are also called "Case Study of Myself as a Writer.") It is likely that your instructor will assign this workshop near the end of the course.

In the workshop, student essays are published as examples of how you might put together an "Autobiography of Myself As A Writer" or "Case Study of Myself as a Writer." These are essays where the students examine their own growth as writers and analyze their own writing processes. Though this is near the end of the textbook, it's not a bad idea for you to look ahead to see one of the long-term goals of the course.

It is common for a student to be intimidated by the sheer size of a ten-page assignment. However, students who follow the Elbow and Belanoff "Process Journal" plan and generate a half-page (or more) in each of the 26 instructional units are often astounded at the end of the semester, when they copy and paste all of the quick writing and process journal responses into one long document, and find that they have accumulated 10, 20 or even 30 pages of thoughts about the writing process.

It is not a coincidence that teachers often ask students to combine and mull over this collection of quick writing and process journal responses near the end of the semester, when the focus of study shifts from generating and drafting to revising and editing. And, it is not a difficult exercise to put a very nice essay together by following these simple directions: Copy and paste the various passages into one long document. Look at the raw information and create a rough outline that will organize the thoughts into a logical sequence of ideas. Craft a few transition sentences to make one passage flow smoothly to the next. Edit the sentences to create a very elegant essay that traces your development as a writer throughout the semester.

This is a big chunk of thoughts to consider in the fist week of the semester. We don't expect you to understand this entire exercise yet, because the course has just started. The short term value of the quick writing exercises and process journal entries will emerge, as you do the exercises in each unit. The goal of the long-term exercise will be addressed again, in the Process Analysis and Critical Thinking units.

Quick Review

1. Writing styles such as description, argument, and comparison
   a. should never be mixed together, because the styles will clash and make the essay ineffective
   b. are called "thinking/writing strategies," "rhetorical modes," or "genres" by various instructors
   c. are of little use in the real world beyond the English composition classroom.
   d. all of the above
   e. none of the above

2. The techniques for writing under pressure that are studied in this course
   a. can help in many on-the-job writing situations
   b. can help in many essay exam situations
   c. can help in many take-home assignments with a quick turnaround
   d. all of the above
   e. none of the above

3. Research, as studied in English composition,
   a. is almost never used on the job
   b. is almost never used in upper-division undergraduate courses
   c. is almost never used in graduate school
   d. all of the above
   e. none of the above

4. Computers can help with composition in
   a. the research stage
   b. the composing or drafting stage
   c. the revision stage
   d. all of the above
   e. none of the above

5. A "discourse community" could be
   a. a group of people who have the same academic interests and who read and write in a similar way
   b. a group of people who work in the same career and who read and write in a similar way
   c. a group of people who have the same hobby and who read and write in a similar way
   d. all of the above
   e. none of the above

"Writing is a very organic thing. Writing is something that grows on its own. People can use outlines. People do write down the purposes for their writing. And they write down their preliminary thesis statements and all that; but, essentially, when you go through the process of writing, you are going through a process of *discovery*. I tell my students that they'll really not know what they're writing about and what they want to say until they've actually written the first draft of that paper. That first draft I think of as a voyage of discovery for them. Normally, what happens is – the student will come to the end of that first draft and realize what he or she is trying to *get* at. And then the process of revision comes about. And that's the most important part of the writing process – revise, revise, revise."

SANTI BUSCEMI, Middlesex County College

Introduction to the Topic

Often, in composition courses (and in other courses), your instructor will ask everybody to write an essay or a research paper about a topic you are all studying together. Usually, the instructor is trying to make a point by connecting ideas; your job is to try to find those connections and add some original thoughts to the class discussion. You are to do this even if you have only a marginal interest in the topic the professor finds absolutely fascinating.

Finding something original to say about an assigned topic is tough enough. It's some-times even more difficult for a student to find something to say if the assignment allows him the choice to write about *anything*.

Facing such a writing challenge, you have to use your brain in a completely different way. You have the luxury of writing about something that is personally intriguing. However, the immense number of possibilities may make focusing on any one topic seem like a disconcerting and potentially hazardous venture. After all, the teacher may judge you on the very nature of your choice.

Trying to find something to say is not a challenge unique to students.

When you use writing on the job, you'll encounter similar situations. If the boss asks you to write a report, you'll have no choice but to oblige – even if the work assignment proves the boss has the imagination of the slowest camel in the herd.

Sometimes there is room for creativity – as when you're given the task of coming up with new ideas for the office Christmas party. That's a challenge of another stripe, especially if the combination country rodeo-alien abduction holiday theme party was less than a success last year.

Professional writers also devise strategies to find something to write about, since their deadline schedules – and paychecks – depend on their coming up with original and compelling topics. You'll discover in this program that the techniques to develop strategies for both open-ended and narrowly defined writing assignments work for other writers, as well.

This program will also illustrate several important aspects of the writing process that you will study in more detail throughout the course.

As it turns out, the process of finding something to say does not stop at the brainstorming and prewriting stage. Every step of the way, the individual tasks of reading, drafting, organizing, listening to feedback, and revising all add up to a *process* that reveals ideas. In other words, writing is an act of discovery; it is not just putting words on a page.

Learning Objectives

After viewing the television program and reading this *Telecourse Study Guide* chapter, you will have an overview of the various stages of the writing process that will be studied throughout this course. This overview emphasizes that writing is a way to reveal ideas. You will learn that the act of "finding something to say" does not stop at the early brainstorming stages, when you have decided on a topic. You'll learn that, at *every* step of the process – from prewriting to editing – you are still discovering what you want to say.

These learning objectives work in harmony with the essential premises of Workshop 2, "From Private Writing to Public Writing," in *A Community of Writers* (pp. 31–65):

- Many people don't feel safe as they write. Lack of safety usually makes it harder to write

- Private writing is one important way to achieve safety in writing. It is usually easier to express our feelings and thinking and to find words if we write words that are not for the eyes of others. *After* we write privately, we can look back over what we've written and use parts of it for pieces meant for the eyes of others.

- About flexibility of genre: It's not hard to take some writing we've produced in one or two sessions, particularly if it's fairly messy or unformed writing, and use it as the germ for different pieces in different genres. For example, we can easily use the same raw ingredients for making a story or an essay – or for making an analytic essay or a persuasive essay.

Read Workshop 2 "From Private Writing to Public Writing," in *A Community of Writers* (pp. 31–65).

Before Viewing

Before you formally study the variety of writing tasks that make up the "process" of writing, think about how you usually approach writing something important – whether it is a document for work, a letter, or a school assignment. Consider the following questions about your own writing: How do you come up with ideas? How do you expand on rough ideas? Do you show your work to others? Do you usually turn in a first draft, or do you add new ideas as you build a document?

While Viewing

Compare your own approach to "finding something to say" for a college assignment to the suggestions given by the instructors, writers, and students featured in the program. Notice how various writers use the expected techniques of reading, research, and brainstorming to come up with ideas. Observe how the guests in the program talk about important aspects of the writing process, including drafting, revising, editing, and peer feedback. Pay careful attention to how *every* stage of composing a document provides opportunities to discover new ideas through the writing. Consider how you might incorporate some of these writing process techniques into your own writing. (Remember: This is an introductory unit. We will study each aspect of the writing process individually throughout the course.)

Compare the various writing tasks introduced in this program with those introduced in *A Community of Writers*. Pay careful attention to the techniques such as freewriting and summing up.

After Viewing

Make an inventory of the writing process techniques with which you already feel confident with in your own writing. Create a separate list of techniques that you have never tried or that you know you need to work on, understanding that we will study each technique in separate telecourse programs and *Telecourse Study Guide* chapters. Consider: Do you know students who stop thinking after the original brainstorming and drafting stage? Does your own approach to the writing process allow you to add new ideas to your work as the paper evolves?

Viewing Guide

Here's a common scenario: You've been asked to write an argument/persuasion essay or some other typical college course assignment. The instructor could have a predetermined topic or the subject could be of your own choosing.

You sit down at the computer, hover your fingers over the keyboard, pause – pause again – and then get up to wash the dishes.

When the dishes are finished, you sharpen a pencil, pull out a fresh pad of yellow paper, stare at the blank page – and then decide to sweep and mop the floor.

Your living space is looking good, but that course assignment isn't any closer to getting finished. One reason you might have trouble starting an assignment is that the very *act* of writing is a process of discovering what you want to say in the first place.

In other words, you should not expect to know everything you want to say as you start to write a paper. It is *normal* to create more than you need and then toss out huge hunks of what you write, keeping only the best parts. And it is quite possible that you won't know exactly what you want to say until you get to the end of the process.

Adopting this attitude toward writing can be a comfort to students who freeze up at the beginning of a writing process. It is liberating to know that everything you write does *not* have to be in the final draft.

The same philosophical shift toward writing can also be a shock to those who peck out the absolute minimum: writing (and turning in) only one draft of *exactly* three pages for every three-page assignment.

To get an idea of how limiting such a bare minimum approach could be, let's consider the approaches of several successful professional writers.

Charles Johnson, an award-winning novelist and English instructor from the University of Washington, explains, "What's interesting to me about the process of creation is that it is a process of *discovery*. An idea will occur – and you pursue it – but what happens is, it's a dead-end. And you say, 'Ah, that doesn't really fit' – it may have gorgeous writing, it may be beautiful, but you're going to have to take it out."

For his novels, Johnson may generate as many as three thousand pages in order to discover the ideas that make up the three hundred pages he wants to keep.

Novelist Tom Robbins also sees writing as a process of discovering ideas. When Robbins sits down with a yellow pad of paper and a pen to write his books, he does not know where the quest will take him. It is the state of *not* knowing what will happen next that keeps him interested in writing.

"I look upon writing as an adventure – and if I can't surround the act of writing with a feeling of adventure and surprise and even a little bit of terror, then I would have to force myself to go to work every morning," Robbins says. " If I can't delight myself with discovery, how am I going to delight the reader with discovery?"

One entire strand of telecourse programs and *Telecourse Study Guide* chapters focuses on individual aspects of the writing process and *shows* you how to conjure up ideas at every step of the way.

Most composition instructors believe it is just as important for a first-year writing student to learn this aspect of writing as it is for a professional writer. Thomas Fox, of California State University, Chico, explains: "Finding something to say is sort of a long and important (and sometimes often overlooked) part of the writing process. Teachers sometimes just give an assignment and expect students to write. But they can't do that without a lot of information first."

Fox speaks for many other instructors when he says students need to "fill up their brains" at various stages of composition by participating in prewriting activities, taking notes, going to the library, talking in groups, and generally gathering as many ideas as possible. Often, the process of filling up your brain with ideas starts with reading.

Reading as a writer and reading as a thinker

Although this is primarily a writing course, the *Telecourse Study Guide* has two chapters about the process of reading. In those units, you'll confirm what you probably already know: It is quite difficult to become a good writer without spending quality time as a reader.

Most composition courses reintroduce the academic study of *how* to read – a process some of us have not explored formally since early grade school. College reading can be challenging, and this course will examine a variety of strategies to improve your ability to conquer difficult text. It is a process that carries in which almost every occupation you must learn to read and think to succeed.

For example, the field of law enforcement depends heavily on the ability to be a critical reader. As police office Janet Turner observes, "There's a surplus of reading in this job. I just wish I had more time just for going through all the code books ... there's so many things that you don't know – not only that, there is the new case law, the things that are constantly coming out from court decisions. There are all sorts of things that you can get subscriptions to – police magazines for your tactics, for guns, and all that. There's just a plethora of stuff that you could be reading twenty-four hours a day."

Turner learns to read as a thinker, critically evaluating the issues of her profession. As she reads, she is also absorbing the conventions of various writing styles within the law enforcement community.

This is an important aspect of reading: The telecourse also studies how to read as a *writer*. Frequently, teachers make reading assignments so that all the students in a class will have a common experience to respond to in the writing. You can quote the author you are reading and bring her words into your own document – or the reading may inspire you to think in completely new directions.

There's another important reason to assign the work of good writers: A writer-in-training feels the way the words are used – the rhythm, the style, and the tone. In fact, many instructors agree that students learn much from emulating their favorite writers.

David Guterson, author of the novel *Snow Falling on Cedars* and a former English teacher, explains that fiction writers also use a modeling technique to develop their individual styles. "I think that it's quite natural and necessary for a writer to be highly imitative and derivative for a fairly extended period of time early on," Guterson explains.

"This could go on for ten years, as you try out different voices. But as you mature as a person, as you grow as a human being, you grow into your own voice – into your own identity. As you discard possible identities as a human being, you discard possible identities as a writer, and you become more clear not only about who you are as a human being but who you are as a writer. And that's when your voice emerges. But it can't happen unless you've gone through this process of experimenting with being derivative."

Voice

Many teachers and writers interviewed for the telecourse feel that developing a confident, individual voice is one of the most important aspects of the writing process.

Journalist John Morgan Wilson points out that developing a writing voice is like learning to speak. A child practices for many years, developing a "voice" that matures and changes over time.

"If we never used our vocal chords, we would have a very weak voice and it would be erratic and it would be in fits and starts," Wilson says. "When we start out as writers, most of us have weak, erratic voices. They're uneven, unsure of themselves and inconsistent. But the more you write, the stronger that voice becomes."

Betsy Klimasmith, an English instructor from the University of Washington, adds that finding the right tone and voice for a college writing assignment can certainly affect the outcome – and can even contribute to helping you find what you want to say.

"The issue I see most often is that you'll have a tone or voice that's very natural to you – a kind of voice or tone that you would choose if you were writing in a situation where you weren't being graded or being evaluated or being judged on the work you were doing," Klimasmith says. The trick is to find a way of blending that personal voice with the academic voice needed for the college assignment.

Freewriting and generating

In the textbook *A Community of Writers*, Elbow and Belanoff pose the question, "Why should freewriting be so helpful if it is so easy and invites carelessness in writing and thinking?"

The answer, they say, is that the same invitation inspires our *best* writing and our *best* thinking. In fact, Elbow and Belanoff strongly advocate the practice of freewriting to generate ideas and discuss why it works in the section "Exploring theory: Freewriting and Process Writing – Why We Think Freewriting is Important" (p. 15).

One of the best ways to discover that personal voice is to simply forget about who will read or criticize your work and just *write*.

Many students have written *only* to please an instructor; they have never written just for themselves. This unit is designed to move you away from that mind-set.

If you can learn simply to *think* as you scribble or type on a keyboard, you can generate tons of ideas. The act of thinking *while* you create text is called *generative writing*, or *freewriting*.

In freewriting, the words can be spelled incorrectly and the sentences can be mangled – and nobody will care. Freewriting shouldn't matter any more than the silly stuff you were saying *way* after midnight at a party last Saturday night or the goofy e-mails you send out to your best friends. This is writing that is not meant to be taken seriously or even read by anybody but you.

Scott King, a staff writer for *Mad TV*, explains how he uses this style of writing to generate ideas for his television show. *Never* censor yourself, King says. "Write down every single idea. I think that's totally key. If you get into deciding 'this is not funny' before you've even gotten the idea down on paper, well, then, you're stopping the good idea from coming."

Freewriting might spin out pages of good ideas, but they are mixed in with garbage – much like a dream might be a random scanning of ideas in your subconscious. Your challenge is to learn how to extract the best ideas from the silly musings. Once you have identified the best thoughts, most instructors want those ideas arranged in a coherent, scholarly presentation. That leads us to the next step in the writing process.

Organizing devices

The "Organizing Devices" video in this telecourse surveys a variety of organizing devices that range from the traditional outlines to more artistic, free-form approaches such as clustering and list making.

The main premise of the telecourse unit on organizing devices is that each writer seems to find his or her own best approach to the task of ordering random ideas.

Beverly Moss, a writing instructor at Ohio State University, explains that she (like many other instructors) has changed the emphasis in teaching the process of organization.

"I used to teach *outlining* as the way to do it," she says. "Now I would train new teachers to present a *variety* of methods for planning. Some people may outline. As a writer, most of the time I have to outline. But I know other people who don't need to do it that way; they can do the clustering or just *lists*. So I think we need to introduce to students the *variety* of approaches and ask students to think about what works *best* for them. That helps them move from the planning to the drafting."

Elbow and Belanoff also discuss organization on two pages of the "Sharing and Responding" section about peer feedback (pp. 514–544). Their approach might seem unusual at first. Elbow and Belanoff turn the process around, suggesting you use either a skeleton outline or a descriptive outline to evaluate what another writer has written. Then, as a reader, you can better tell the author what is actually being communicated by the early draft of the piece.

When receiving similar feedback as a writer, you will learn quite a bit by seeing how your readers might impose their own organizational schemes on a draft you have already written. These peer feedback outlines can serve as a bridge between an early draft and a final revision.

This brings up one of the hardest points to make for any reasonably talented college-level writer. Though it is tempting to get the assignment over with, your early drafts should *just be the start* of coming up with ideas.

A first draft may be good enough to pass the class – or even to earn a decent grade. In fact, if you are skilled enough with writing basics to get commendable grades by jamming out a first draft, you might experience a disadvantage when it comes to pure learning. The true *insight* comes when you are willing to revise and polish the work until you are deeply satisfied.

We hope that, when you start to organize and revise your early ideas, you are still *actively* engaged in the process of finding something to say.

Revision

Many writers and instructors suggest that the final revision is when the really important ideas emerge.

"One thing that I'm really finding is that students have no idea what revision is," says Maria Madruga, Writing Center director at Shasta College. "They really don't realize that revision is *rethinking*. I tell them, 'That is a perfect first draft.' But they're handing in first drafts. That's why writing centers are so great. Because the writing center basically pushes a student to rewrite, rethink – and *that*'s revision."

The textbook *A Community of Writers* examines the process of revision in two sections, Workshop 6 "Drafting and Revising" (pp.149–188), and Workshop 7, "Revision through Purpose and Audience: Writing as Doing Things to People (pp.189–212).

Elbow and Belanoff see writing not just as a recording of what you've already thought, but as a way of building or creating new ideas on the basis of old ideas; often, these ideas only come to you as a *result* of your writing and revising. They also point out that revision requires becoming consciously aware of your own purposes and ideas – but revision also helps you become aware of the effects your language is having on others.

Nowhere is the effect of writing measured more directly than in the response to advertising. Jeff Goodby, an award-winning producer of television advertisements, points out that the writer knows immediately in his business if the audience "buys" the writing. For that reason, a great deal of work is put into the revision of each thirty- or sixty-second television spot that he creates.

"I think one of the hardest things about writing in general, no matter what form you're working in, is that when you *start* doing it, you're afraid to revise," Goodby says. "But if you're afraid to revise, you're afraid to write. In commercial writing, you're revising all the way to the very end of the process. One of the things that really happens here (and it happens in all kinds of writing) is – you discover things don't work. You have to be open all the time to going back and fixing it."

Quotes and citations

In an academic setting (and in the world beyond school), the writer uses research and reading to develop new ideas. An important part of finding something to say is learning how to blend or synthesize ideas gained from reading through books, magazines, journals, and Web sites with your *own* ideas – until you create something original in your own voice.

An essential part of that process is giving credit to those whose words and ideas you borrow. This required task is explained in more detail in the telecourse program on "Quotes and Citations." It is quite acceptable to use the words of another person in your writing; in fact, you are usually *encouraged* to use authoritative quotes as strong evidence to back your claims and ideas in a good academic paper.

However, if you do not cite your sources properly, you could be accused of plagiarism – or theft of the ideas and words originated by another writer.

As Middlesex County College English instructor Santi Buscemi explains, using somebody else's ideas or actual words without giving him credit is considered plagiarism – even if the mistake is unintentional. "When you use someone's exact words, you've got to put it in quotation marks," Buscemi explains. "But even a paraphrase or a summary, which uses somebody else's ideas, must be cited."

Elbow and Belanoff explain the technical aspects of learning how to properly acknowledge a source with internal text citations and a "Works Cited" page in Workshop 12, "Research," in *A Community of Writers* (pp. 314–322).

Peer feedback and collaboration

Sometimes, in both the classroom and the world beyond school, the best way to come up with something to say is to work with another writer or a team of writers. As we've said, peer feedback is an excellent way to start the revision of a paper – and it is often in the revision stage that *real* insight is added to an early draft.

A team of writers can also collaborate through the entire writing process, starting at the brainstorming stages and finishing with the final editing and polishing.

Elbow and Belanoff emphasize the collaborative learning and peer feedback processes throughout almost every workshop in *A Community of Writers*, with exercises in each workshop that encourage students to work on their essays in small groups. Workshop 3, "Collaborative writing: Dialogue, Loop Writing and The Collage" (pp. 67–98) and the entire "Sharing and Responding" section at the back of the book (pp. 507–58) explore these topics in depth.

To some students, classroom exercises that require them to write and learn with a team can seem like busywork – tedious assignments that the instructor whipped up to pass the time in class. However, these are more than academic exercises. Collaborative writing in the business world is the norm rather than the exception; instructors who introduce these skills early in your academic career are trying to prepare you for life beyond school.

The television newsroom is a prime example of how lessons of collaborative learning are applied on the job. In the telecourse program, reporter Greg Liggins of KTVU in Oakland, California, D.C., explains, "When we walk into the news meeting in the afternoon, it's a collaborative effort to come up with the evening [stories] ... we have a group of people who live in different parts of the Bay Area who see and hear different things, and we use the news meeting to not only talk about the preplanned, must-cover events but also to consider some of the things that we're seeing and hearing."

Editing

The editing stage is where most writers proofread their documents and fix surface errors. This is a meticulous, time-consuming responsibility and it is absolutely necessary for clear communication.

News anchor Dennis Richmond of KTVU in Oakland, California, says that once the collaborative group decides on the story topics, peer editing is an essential part of the process to turn out the final result. "Everybody makes mistakes – all of us. And there's a chain in which they should be caught. I'm the last link in that chain. If I don't catch it, it's going to go out on the air. So if I get a chance to read a script before we come out here, and there's something in there that just doesn't fit, I say, 'Well, wait a minute.... If I don't understand that, they (the viewers) aren't going to understand it."

Three programs in this telecourse are dedicated to helping you learn how to detect and correct errors in sentence structure, word choice, and mechanics.

A Community of Writers also offers a section of mini-workshops in Part II, "Editing" (pp. 479–506). These workshops are excellent companions to the three telecourse programs and Student Study Guide chapters about editing.

Summary

It should be remembered that even in the editing stage, it is never too late to focus on finding something to say. Though your draft may be only a few spelling corrections away from being ready to send to the instructor (or to an editor for publication), the possibility always exists that one more brilliant idea will pop into your head.

Mike Rose of UCLA summarizes the process of finding something to say: "Any good piece of writing has to emerge from some kind of understanding of what you're talking about. The understanding comes as you *do* the writing – writing rough drafts, sloppy first takes at something, scribbling things on the backs of napkins and brown bags and what-not. That writing helps you understand in a way that then enables you to maybe write more clearly ... so that what happens is there's kind of this reciprocal relation between writing and understanding. Writing and understanding. Writing and understanding – and then getting to the place where you hopefully understand something enough to be able to write about it in a way that's coherent and that connects to some other reader."

Integrating the Text

Read Workshop 2, "From Private Writing to Public Writing," in *A Community of Writers* (pp. 31–55).

Our main goal in this video is to introduce all of the programs in the course that focus on the process of writing. We also want to emphasize the notion that writers can find new ideas at every step of the writing process, not just when they first sit down to start the essay. This idea is supported throughout the Elbow and Belanoff textbook. For example, in Workshop 6, "Drafting and Revising," the authors write, "The process of writing and rereading *changes you*. At its most extreme, this level of revising may mean that you crumple up what you've written and aim it toward the trash basket." Of course, it is probably more common to keep huge chunks as you discover new ideas to add and trim out the weaker sections.

The most obvious aspects of the writing process that help you find something to say (freewriting, generative writing, using peer feedback, and reading) are introduced in this telecourse program. The type of freewriting or generative writing that is intended to help create ideas for a piece of public writing is explored in Workshop 2.

Exercises

Check with your instructor for your formal assignments. You will be asked to do exercises from the *Telecourse Study Guide*.

Finding something to further say
EXERCISE I
Generate the following lists:

- List some things to describe. Include some things you might *have* to describe – including descriptions needed in assignments for other classes or descriptions needed in your work. Include some things you might like to describe just for fun. (Describe a favorite food or a friend or a favorite place.)

- List some things you could explain how to do: Include a favorite dish you like to cook, a skill you have mastered, or an obstacle you have overcome. Include something you would like explained to you better (example: how to install a software program on your computer). Include something at work or in another class that you *know* how to do well – or something you *need* explained better to you.

- List some favorite stories that you always tell friends. We all have stories like this that we tell in the middle of a long road trip, when there is nothing else to do. Include moments that changed your life, moments that made you laugh or cry, or moments that were so unusual that you can rarely convince friends that they really happened.

- List some things to define. Include some things you might *have* to define – including definitions needed in assignments for other classes or definitions needed on the job. Include some things you might like to define just for fun. (Define your role in society. Define an emotion. Define a key aspect of a hobby, sport, or other activity you are passionate about.)

- List some things you would like to persuade others to think about or believe. Perhaps there are issues you want to debate, discuss, or dispute with others. Consider a purpose: for example, to get someone to spend money on something or to get someone to participate in a political cause. Think about whether you wish you could change someone's attitude concerning a topic you feel strongly about.

- List things you find yourself often comparing and contrasting: men and women, football and basketball, television and movies, and so on. List things you find yourself dividing and classifying. For example: music, vegetables, dogs, and such.

EXERCISE 2

Do you dread writing an essay about a subject of your own choosing? Do you find yourself wishing you could remember that interesting point you made during yesterday's philosophical lunch table debate about the relative merits of pizza as a dietary staple? If so, consider starting a writer's journal. This can be as elaborate or casual as you wish; the important thing is to devise a way that will work for you to document and store any ideas that come to you at any given time throughout your day. Some people prefer to achieve this with a daily scheduled session during which they write down their ideas of the day; others need to get things down on paper at the instant, inspiration hits in order not to forget. In the same way that each person must discover that his or her own optimal organizational system, your unique method for keeping track of ideas will no doubt combine elements of several strategies. However you maintain your writer's journal, you will be glad to have it as a reference when you need to quickly come up with a writing topic of interest to you.

EXERCISE 3

Another way to find something to write about is to perform a "freewrite" to try to flesh out any interesting topics that might be floating around in your subconscious. This form of "brainstorming on paper" often proves a useful technique for helping writers who cannot get started. The purpose of freewriting is simply generating words. Correct grammar or organization should not be an issue. There is no "correct" way to do this, so experiment with your own variations of these suggested steps:

- Depending on your personal preferences, begin with either a blank computer screen or writing pad and a watch or clock.

- Set a time of one to ten minutes for the freewrite.

- Write or type about *anything that comes into your head*. Don't stop until the time is up.

Afterward, as you review what you have written, transpose (or cut and paste) any interesting ideas or phrases to a new blank file or sheet of paper and organize them. Do this until you've discovered anything that might serve as interesting subject matter for the assignment you are trying to start. Write a rough draft of a paragraph using these sentences.

Exercise just for fun

Take a good solid look at your writing, and freewrite a response to one or more of these questions:

- How do you personally react when an instructor tells you what to write about?

- How do you personally react when an instructor tells you may write about any topic?

- Do you already have the writing skills that allow you to narrow down a wide topic to one clearly identifiable sentence related to the topic?

- Consider the way you react to an inflexible writing assignment. How does your way of reacting to this type of assignment compare to the advice given by the instructors, writers, and students featured in the program?

Revision exercise

In this exercise, you will create a new draft of an essay by revising and building on the paragraph you created in Exercise 3. Begin by reexamining your freewrite, the interesting ideas and phrases you pulled from it, and your organization of those ideas and phrases.

- Identify and expand any ideas that need further explanation.

- No matter how intuitively correct something might seem to you, make sure to add sentences that make adequate transitions between thoughts and provide your reader with clear and understandable connections between related concepts.

- Next, identify or compose and insert a controlling sentence for your paragraph. This should be a sentence that summarizes the main point.

Find any sentences that do not fit within the controlling idea of the paragraph and remove them. These sentences might be the starting points for the rest of the paragraphs in your essay.

Quick writing exercise

Your teacher may ask you to do a quick focused freewrite about finding something to say. Those of you who are taking the course through a distance-learning system may be encouraged to share your thoughts in a discussion thread or to post your ideas on an Internet bulletin board. If you are writing your thoughts out by hand in a process journal, you might also use these questions to come up with ideas. This is a freewriting exercise that will not be graded. You can use any of the following questions to stimulate your thoughts about the various aspects of the writing process. This may be the easiest course assignment you have during your entire undergraduate career. It could also be one of the most important exercises of the semester:

Make lists.

That's it. Would you like more than a two-word assignment? OK. Make lists of things that make you happy. List hobbies. List things that make you angry. Make lists of things you would like to debate. Make lists of things you would like to change. Make lists of things that make you laugh. Make lists of things that you are very interested in. Make lists of things that surprise you.

It is a good idea to make lists of ideas in the first week of class. You'll notice that other exercises in this unit also involve making lists. Keep these lists somewhere. Then, later in the semester, refer to these lists every time an instructor makes an assignment where *you* get to pick the topic and you are tempted to say, "But I have no idea what to write about." You have started the process of brainstorming, just by making a few lists.

A secondary goal of this telecourse is to preview the writing processes you will study throughout this class. You will notice that you can work at "finding something to say" at every step of writing. Workshop 2 "From Private Writing to Public Writing," discusses open-ended writing processes from Elbow and Belanoff's perspective. You may use the questions in the "Process Journal" of this workshop (pp. 56–65) as an additional source of inspiration for this quick writing exercise.

Exercises related to *A Community of Writers*
Exercise 1
Read the section "Private Writing" in *A Community of Writers* (pp. 32–37). Compare these writing tasks to those introduced by the video program, "Finding Something to Say."

Exercise 2
Though you are probably watching this program the first week of the term, it is not too early to start thinking about the topic of your research paper. The sections "Deciding on a Topic" and "Designing a Research Plan" (pp. 304–305) complement the points made in this telecourse program about using research to come up with ideas. Read this section, and start to brainstorm some good potential topics for a research paper.

Quick Review

1. A writer discovers new ideas during
    a. the freewriting stage of composition
    b. the outlining/organizing stage of composition
    c. the peer feedback stage of composition
    d. the revision stage of composition
    e. all of the above.

2. The following is not considered a good practice in composition of college-level work:
    a. seeing and using peer feedback to revise
    b. plagiarizing quotes
    c. using paraphrased and summarized quotes
    d. all of the above
    e. none of the above

3. When composing a formal paper
    a. A student should never resort to freewriting, because it invites a chaos of ideas.
    b. A student should always use a traditional outline, because it has been proved to be effective.
    c. A student should select the organizing device that is most suited for her style.
    d. All of the above.
    e. None of the above.

4. Writers in college
    a. often use reading of assigned materials and research in the library or on the Internet as a way to develop ideas for papers
    b. should never imitate or emulate the writing style of a successful author, because that would be considered imitation or thievery
    c. should work hard to shed their informal, personal "writer's voice" and always strive to create a formal, impersonal, objective academic voice
    d. all of the above
    e. none of the above

5. In the world beyond the college classroom,
   a. You will never have to write on an assigned topic like you do when an instructor tells you what to write about.
   b. You will never have to suffer through a collaborative writing experience similar to the silly team-writing exercises you are forced to try in a classroom.
   c. You will almost never have to read and interpret difficult materials like you are required to in a college class.
   d. All of the above.
   e. None of the above.

"When you're trying to describe something and you want the essence of that thing you're describing to reach the reader on a deeper level, metaphor and simile are how to do it. I don't reel these things off the top of my head. Sometimes they pop out, but usually if I want to describe something – an object or place – I'll pause and close my eyes and imagine that object or that place in my head and try to find the words that will convey its essence in as fresh a way as possible. And that's fun."

TOM ROBBINS, novelist

Introduction to the Topic

Most people strive to describe well. Without good description, even a casual conversation will be flat and boring. If part of a dialogue is relating an experience to friends, you might illustrate and elaborate. You fill in details, trying to make the tale come alive. You describe.

In college, you describe in classroom discussions. And you soon encounter writing situations that are much more important than a "description essay" that you might knock out just to get a grade in an English composition class. You bring the skills learned in an English course forward to your upper-division classes. You describe in lab reports; you describe in term papers; and you describe on exams.

Beyond school, you realize that the *content* of your writing is more important than the *form*. Again, you're not just writing a description essay for an instructor. Nurses write to describe patients' condition; engineers write to describe their design projects; chemists write to describe results of experiments; journalists write to describe events.

You'll practice the art of description in this unit, but you won't stop here. Clever students will build on this lesson and apply the skills of description to narrative writing and storytelling. Narration and description will eventually become part of a good argument paper – until, by the end of the term, you'll be combining *all* the skills you learn to write longer, more sophisticated academic research papers.

But for now, your goal will be to learn how to depict something so well – with mere words – that your readers will experience what you are describing almost as if they were with you.

Learning Objectives

After viewing the television program and finishing the writing assignments, you will know when description is needed – in everything from the personal and aesthetic descriptions of storytelling to the more technical descriptions used in careers such as engineering, medicine, journalism, and police work. You will also practice the skills of description, with capable guidance from some of the best writers and instructors in the country.

These learning objectives work in harmony with two chapters in *A Community of Writers*. One of the essential premises of Workshop 4, "Getting Experience into Words: Image and Story," is: The best way to make your own words powerful is to make sure readers actually see, hear, and feel what you are experiencing. The video on description also works well with Chapter 14, "Text Analysis through Examining Figurative Language," in which one of the essential premises is: "Metaphors and other kinds of figurative language represent language at its most creative or generative."

Before Viewing

Before you formally study this topic, consider the techniques you have already developed for description. Experiment by informally describing something to friends, without actually telling them what it is you are depicting. Try to determine what works and what doesn't work in your portrayal. Then, think of situations in which you have had to use similar descriptions – situations such as coursework assignments or writing on the job.

Read Elbow and Belanoff's Workshop 4 "Getting Experience into Words: Image and Story" (pp. 99–119) Also, read Workshop 14, "Text Analysis through Examining Figurative Language" (pp. 363–83).

While Viewing

Compare the descriptive skills you already have with the methods recommended by the instructors, students, and professional writers in the telecourse program. Note the techniques that you haven't already mastered, with the intention of trying these ideas in the next descriptive passage in your own writing. Become aware of the various styles of description used in different occupations. Notice how Larry Thompson (an engineering student) uses many of the recommended techniques in his technical description, and how Miles Jordan (music critic for *Jazz Times* magazine) uses similar methods to describe the rhythm-and-blues band Little Charlie and the Nightcats.

Reconsider the section "Exploring Theory: Figurative Language as a Window on the Mind" (pp. 371–373), in which Elbow and Belanoff discuss why metaphor and simile are powerful in any kind of writing. The entire chapter "Getting Experience into Words: Image and Story" explains the kind of thinking that led both the telecourse producers and the textbook authors to offer back-to-back studies of description and narrative writing.

After Viewing

Using the exercises at the end of this *Telecourse Study Guide* chapter, practice the art of description. Also, look for *good* examples of description in the reading you encounter in everyday life, including your recreational reading and the reading you do for other college courses. Be on the lookout for examples of poor descriptive writing, and consider how the writers could have done a better job; try to determine what is lacking in the *bad* examples. Look for examples of descriptive writing in your chosen profession or academic major. Determine what is considered appropriate (and inappropriate) description within that discourse community, and develop strategies for applying the lessons learned in this course to writing within that community.

Viewing Guide

In the first few segments of the television program, you will see that description is part of many real-life experiences. Description is not a magical skill that is somehow monopolized by best-selling fiction writers. It is a skill that can easily be mastered by any writer-in-training willing to study the techniques.

Many novelists are talented at description, of course – so you can certainly learn by reading descriptive passages in a novel by Sue Grafton, Chitra Divakaruni, Frank McCourt, or Tom Robbins. But you can also learn about description from a football scouting report or books by legendary coach Bill Walsh. In the video, we learn in quick succession that the writing of a woodworker, an agricultural scientist, and a police officer all depends on accurate – and, sometimes, vivid – description.

The basic strategies of description remain the same, but subtle differences in style will emerge as the needs of each writer change. Often, these needs are determined by the purpose and the audience.

To illustrate this point, Dr. Elaine Maimon of Arizona State University gives two examples of how a snake might be described. The writing in a scientific field guide is much different from the description of a snake in a poem, because the *purpose* is different. The audience is also quite different.

In the video, police officer Janet Turner explains how she uses description in her accident reports and arrest reports. Her purpose isn't to entertain – it's to make sure that her observations are perceived accurately and justly by the court system. She is not writing for readers of fiction; her audience will be prosecuting attorneys, defense attorneys, and judges.

According to Turner, "If you don't write a good report, they're going to fight the case, because there will be a lot of loopholes. You need to use a lot of description. You want to know how hot it was, how cold it was, what the lighting looked like, how many people were around, what the suspect did – every action. From the minute you go to that call to the minute you leave the call, you're recording every minute detail in your mind."

Using all five senses

Though the intent of their descriptions is very different, both police officers and fiction writers have a similar goal in mind – to paint a picture with words. Edna Buchanan, who writes about crime as a novelist and journalist, explains that she developed the skill of "seeing as a writer" while she was employed at a newspaper in an entry-level position. Like many reporters on small papers, she was required to take her own photographs as well as write up the news. "I learned visual imagery was important," Buchanan says. "I wanted to know every little detail at the crime scene: What sort of flowers were blooming along the walkway? Were people watching television when the bullets came through the window? What color was the cat? I think it was because I was a photographer first – I always thought very much in visual terms, and I guess I do that in my fiction as well."

Buchanan has earned major awards (including the Pulitzer Prize) for her writing, because she has an uncanny ability to make the readers see the scenes she is describing. Many young writers tend to forget, however, that we have more senses than sight. The best writers learn how to appeal to *all* the senses.

In the video, Frank McCourt explains how even the tastes of cafeteria food can provide an interesting study in description. Novelist and educator Duff Brenna suggests that smell, more than any other sense, triggers memory. He uses his grandfather's cigars and his grandmother's pasta sauce as examples.

Novelist Charles Johnson observes, "Everything is biased toward this particular organ, the eye, ... but, if I can get them all working together, particularly smell and taste and the tactile feel of things ... I feel, then, that a descriptive passage is full. It has realized its experiential potential."

From personal to academic description

Interestingly, many of the previous examples of good description given by the novelists in this program are about very personal experiences. For example, Frank McCourt revels in describing the sense of taste, in large part because of a childhood of abject poverty in Ireland, where a decent meal was considered luxurious. Chitra Divakaruni writes about moving to America from India, and she shares her experiences through rich, sensory images.

In the video, instructor Megumi Taniguchi suggests that personal descriptive writing is where most writers-in-training have their first positive experiences of communicating on the silent page. Early assignments in description can also provide an opportunity to make a transition from enjoyable, introspective writing assignments to the more demanding types of description used in upper-division college courses.

Description is, Taniguchi says, "the bridge between the personal writing and the academic writing."

Favoring details over generalities

In the video, we see Santi Buscemi compliment Gregory Andrus, a student at Middlesex County College, for his moving and very personal essay about his mother's piano playing. The piece is emotional and packed with details.

Later in the program, Buscemi explains to students in his class that the essay was effective because Andrus revealed descriptive details with careful word choice, using strong active verbs and concrete nouns.

Most writers and teachers chant a similar mantra: It is important to avoid generalities and use specific details in good description. Mystery novelist Sue Grafton puts it this way: "With description, the question is always one of specificity. It isn't sufficient to say, 'The marketplace was filled with colorful costumes and a cacophony of sound.' What color were the costumes? What cacophony? We're taught these sort of all-purpose words and we think we've described something. If you can, be specific. I choose, sometimes, two or three small details and let that carry the larger sense of the matter."

Care with adjectives and adverbs

Many beginning students overseason a description with peppery adjectives and adverbs. While a pinch of modifiers can add flavor to a description, too much can smother the meat of the sentence – the nouns and the verbs.

Buscemi advises, "Use adjectives, but don't use them loosely, and don't use them promiscuously. If you use an adjective, make sure it adds something. A lot of beginning writers will go ahead and pile adjective upon adjective upon adjective, but they will be the same adjective. 'He wore a dirty filthy shirt.' Well, filthy shirt will do it, thank you very much."

Pulitzer Prize-winning editorial writer Richard Aregood expresses a view popular with newspaper reporters and many other writers skilled in description: "Journalists instinctively flee from adjectives, because it's almost a disease. The best description you can possibly do is ... stark verbs. Verbs are the life of things. You get too many adjectives all clumped together, they start fighting with each other. They don't carry you forward the way a verb does. It's lazy too. It is a very lazy way of writing to try and set a scene by just modifying the crap out of everything. You sound like a thesaurus ... simple nouns and verbs. They still work."

Concrete nouns and active verbs

Novelist and English instructor Duff Brenna uses a clever metaphor – "Fifi" – to illustrate how the choice of concrete nouns over abstract nouns can clarify a description.

Brenna starts with the general word *animal*. He then shows how a succession of word choices can sharpen the image, moving from *animal* to *dog* and then from *dog* to *poodle*.

"What would be more specific than *poodle*?" Brenna asks. "If you say *Fifi*, you see some little curly-haired white mutt that yaps at you all the time." In a good description, Brenna says, if every noun can be as specific as *Fifi*, the writer will be painting a more accurate picture.

Good writers prefer to use the active voice instead of the passive voice. Experienced writers also look for verbs that show more action. Note, however, that though the words *action* and *active* sound similar, the concepts are slightly different.

Passive voice constructions usually use variations of the verb to be (*is, was, be, been, am, are*, etc.). The passive voice also contains subjects that are acted upon; in active voice, the subject is doing the acting.

In this example, the sentence is written in passive voice:

The ball was thrown by the pitcher to first base in between every pitch.

The active voice is better, because the "star" of the sentence is doing the acting:

The pitcher was throwing the ball to first base in between every pitch.

The sentence can still be improved. With just a little effort, the writer can make the description more vivid – with fewer words – by replacing the flat, nondescriptive verb construction "was throwing" with a more specific verb that shows some action. Notice how different, and how specific, each sentence is – simply because the writer selected a precise verb:

The pitcher lobbed the ball to first base in between every pitch

The pitcher fired the ball to first base in between every pitch.

Use original figurative images and avoid clichés

Most writers emphasize original figurative images (metaphors, similes, or analogies) in good description. Beginning writers often instinctively feel the need for this type of writing, but many (because of either laziness or lack of knowledge) resort to stale images that have been around for decades – or even centuries. Joseph Wambaugh, a former English instructor and police officer (and now a very successful novelist), notes, "Good metaphors don't just pop into my head. I work at it. I'm obsessive in using hyperbole and fig-urative language.... But when I taught freshman composition, I was con-stantly writing, 'Cliché, cliché, cliché, cliché!' across every essay that I read. Sometimes, it's just a matter of just veering off two degrees in a piece of figurative speech, and you're not uttering a cliché anymore. You turn around a cliché, and you've said something original."

The following is a random sampling of clichés, and an estimation of their earliest recorded use in written history, just to show how old and stale they are. (Source: *The Dictionary of Clichés* by James Rogers, Wings Books, 1985.) If you catch yourself writing an overused image like one of these, it probably means you feel the need for a metaphor or simile. Instead of using an old, hackneyed phrase, come up with your own origi-nal figurative image. It takes a little more work, but you will become a bet-ter writer.

- Not worth a hill of beans – Robert of Gloucester, 1297
- Out of the frying pan, into the fire – Sir Thomas Moore, 1528
- Cry over spilled milk – James Howell, 1659
- Like a fish out of water – St. Athanasius, A.D. 373
- Pull yourself up by the bootstraps – James Joyce, 1922
- Raining cats and dogs – Jonathan Swift, 1783

With a little more work, a writer who uses dusty old phrases like these can come up with an original image. Try it yourself. (See the revision exer-cise later in this chapter.)

Integrating the Text

Workshop 4   "Getting Experience into Words: Image and Story"
              (pp. 99–120)
Workshop 14   "Text Analysis through Examining Figurative Language"
              (pp. 363–384)

Workshop 4 follows the thread of Workshop 2, emphasizing the natural transition from personal writing to academic writing. Elbow and Belanoff agree that description leads gracefully to the first stage of narrative writing; they combine the study of both in this chapter.

Many of the teachers and writers in the television program have sug-gested that the writer must strive to make the reader experience or "see" what is being described. For advice on how to achieve this necessary "vision," consider the first three "Workshop Activities for Developing Images" on pages 100 to 103.

In *A Community of Writers*, Elbow and Belanoff write, "If you want to get your reader to experience something, *you* must experience it. If you want your reader to see something, then put all your effort into seeing it. For your reader to hear or smell something, you must hear or smell it. Put all your effort into it, as if you were having a vision."

This is an excellent connection with the well-known writers in the video program who coach students to use *all the senses* to describe.

Though the key of description is to make the reader "see" something – though the writer uses nothing more than spots of ink on paper – many writers suggest that peripheral vision is just as important as looking directly at an object. They therefore endorse use of figurative images.

In Workshop 14, Elbow and Belanoff provide an excellent explanation of why figurative language works, noting, "Figurative language appeals to the mind at a deep level … it's in the nature of the mind to see things as *like* other things or standing for other things." To learn more, read the section on "Exploring Theory: Figurative Language as a Window on the Mind" (pp. 371–373) carefully.

This workshop also has an excellent explanation of the difference between a metaphor, a simile, an image, and a symbol (pp. 364–367).

Finally, don't forget to read the passages from the "Readings" section (pp. 110–119). The two essays by student Mitchell Shack illustrate how a simple description can grow in to a complete narrative. The essays "Reverie" by Jane Tompkins and "The Perfect Swing," by Joel Southall use all the techniques recommended in this unit. Eudora Welty's "A Worn Path" combines descriptive skills with storytelling – a subject you will study in the next few units.

Exercises

Check with your instructor for your official assignments. You will be asked to do exercises from the *Telecourse Study Guide*.

Exploring description further

EXERCISE 1

Knowing that your instructor might eventually ask you to write a story for the unit on narrative writing, describe a scene, place, character, or sensation that could launch the story. Use the techniques emphasized in the television program.

EXERCISE 2

Write two brief reviews of a recent dining experience. This can be an expensive dinner at a restaurant, a hurried lunch at the school cafeteria, or a traditional evening supper at home with the family. Make sure you have described the entire event, appealing to all five senses. The first review should be in your own voice. The second review should be through the eyes of someone who comes from a country where such meals are scarce. Make the reader taste, smell, see, hear, and feel the entire experience. (Thanks to Frank McCourt for this one.)

Exercise just for fun

Practice writing a descriptive passage about an event you attended. In the telecourse program, music critic Miles Jordan provides a model as he paints a picture of the rhythm-and-blues band Little Charlie and the Nightcats. List the techniques that Jordan uses, including his brief ad-libbed narrative about the band. Your practice description could be a similar review of a performance in music, theater, sports, and the like. (Actually being present always provides more sensory input; but if you are desperate, you could describe a televised performance.) Try to relive the event by making your audience hear, feel, and see the show – perhaps even taste hot dogs and smell popcorn.

ALTERNATIVE EXERCISE

Describe Little Charlie and the Nightcats from your own point of view, based on what you could see and hear on the video.

1. Invent a metaphor or simile to describe Little Charlie and the Nightcats (or another performer).

2. Design a comparison to describe Little Charlie and the Nightcats (or another performer).

3. Relate one specific detail you noticed to describe Little Charlie and the Nightcats (or another performer).

4. Use one of the five senses to describe Little Charlie and the Nightcats (or another performer).

5. Select one noun, verb, or adjective that helps describe Little Charlie and the Nightcats (or another performer).

Exercises related to *A Community of Writers*

Several exercises in *A Community of Writers* are appropriate for this unit on description, though they may overlap with other units of the telecourse. In Workshop 4, "Getting Experience into Words: Image and Story," Elbow and Belanoff present several exercises that help students write descriptively. The first three exercises in "Workshop Activities for Developing Images (pp. 100–103) apply specifically to this unit. The ultimate goal of these exercises is to develop a good description into a story, so the second half of this assignment will carry over to the telecourse unit "Narrative Writing."

The exercises in Workshop 14, "Text Analysis through Examining Figurative Language" are about analyzing text, and will more than likely be assigned by your teacher for the telecourse units "Reading as a Writer" and

"Reading as a Thinker." However, the sections on understanding the difference between metaphors, similes, and other kinds of figurative language are perfect for a discussion of how such images work in descriptive writing – and an excellent companion for the exercise on revising clichés in this unit.

Revision exercise

Identify a cliché in your own work. (Don't be embarrassed – even great writers catch themselves unintentionally using hackneyed phrases in early drafts.) If you find a trite phrase in your own work, assume you used the banality as a "marker" to show that you needed to put an original figurative image in this passage. Create your own metaphor or simile to take the place of the cliché. To practice, start with the list below. Substitute an original image for each cliché:

Not worth a hill of beans

Your own image for something worthless:

Out of the frying pan, into the fire

Your own image for leaving a bad situation for one that is worse:

Like a fish out of water

Your own image for feeling out of place:

Raining cats and dogs

Your own image for hard rain :

Quick writing exercise

Your teacher may ask you to do a quick focused freewrite about the topic you are studying in this unit. Those of you who are taking the course through a distance-learning system may be encouraged to share your thoughts in a discussion thread or to post your ideas on an Internet bulletin board. If you are writing your thoughts out by hand in a process journal, you might use these questions to stimulate ideas. This is a freewriting exercise that will not be graded. You can use any of the following questions to help you think about descriptive writing:

What did you know about description before watching this telecourse program? What new ideas did you come away with? What is the difference between the types of description used by fiction writers and the description you might use in your academic major? What are the similarities? How can you describe better, now that you have studied the process?

You may use the questions in the "Process Journal" section of Workshop 4, "Getting Experience into Words: Image and Story" (p. 286) in

A Community of Writers as an additional source of inspiration for this quick writing exercise.

Additional reading

In this program on description, two students (Ethlyn Manning and Gregory Andrus) read excerpts from their work. Both complete essays are included in the appendix of this *Telecourse Study Guide*. Throughout the semester, your instructor may assign various exercises regarding these essays. In this instructional unit, your teacher may also ask you to study and comment on the techniques of description used in these essays – or in essays published in *A Community of Writers*.

In the telecourse program, author Chitra Divakaruni reads the following passage from her short story "Clothes" to illustrate the use of figurative images in description:

> It is hard for me to think of myself as a married woman. I whisper my new name to myself, Mrs. Sumita Sen, but the syllables rustle uneasily in my mouth like a stiff satin that's never been worn.

A substantial excerpt of Divakaruni's story is published in the appendix. Show how Divakaruni continues to use figurative images to describe in the story. What other techniques of description does she use in this piece?

Critical reading

Excerpts from the essay "My Mother's Soul" are read by student Gregory Andrus in the video about description and the video about narrative writing. The essay is reproduced exactly as submitted by Andrus to his instructor and can be found in the appendix. (You may be assigned to find editing errors in the essay in future units about revision and proofreading for language problems.) As you read, identify the strengths and weaknesses in this essay. For this unit of instruction, pay special attention to the techniques Andrus uses for description.

Quick Review

1. In writing a description, which sense should the writer attempt to stimulate?
   a. smell
   b. sight
   c. sound
   d. touch
   e. all of the above

2. Which statement accurately reflects points and attitudes expressed in the video?
   a. Accurate description is an important aspect of a police officer's job.
   b. Inexperienced writers favor visual description but sometimes forget the other four senses.
   c. A cliché is usually a tired metaphor, and it should be replaced by an original figurative image.
   d. None of the above.
   e. All of the above.

3. Writers and teachers make the following recommendations regarding good description:
   a. Use as many colorful adjectives and adverbs as possible.
   b. Use passive verbs.
   c. Use concrete nouns.
   d. None of the above.
   e. All of the above.

4. Which is *not* a true statement about using figurative language to describe?
   a. Metaphors and similes are only useful in poetry and literary novels.
   b. Good description favors specifics over generalities.
   c. Good writing can make the reader experience, or literally "see" what you are describing.
   d. Straightforward comparisons also help with description.
   e. Descriptive writing is an effective bridge between informal personal writing and more demanding types of writing in upper division college courses.

5. Which statement is supported by the telecourse program and *Telecourse Study Guide* chapter?
   a. The skills of description have little value in academic or technical writing.
   b. Skills of description are more important for fiction writers than they are for other types of writers.
   c. Those who use descriptive writing on the job can learn from the techniques of description used by good fiction writers.
   d. None of the above.
   e. Each of the above.

6. Which statement reflects a main premise of Elbow and Belanoff's Workshop "Text Analysis through Examining Figurative Language"?

    a. The skills of description have little value in academic or technical writing.

    b. To avoid confusion, writers should forget about description when studying narrative writing.

    c. A good way to write a story is to let it grow out of a strongly experienced image.

    d. None of the above

    e. Each of the above.

"It's authors who teach students to read; it's authors who teach students to write. Teachers just help them. Teachers go, 'Look over there, there's something neat to read and there's something neat to write about.' So we don't do the teaching, really. They learn to read by reading, and they learn to write by reading well-made text."

MICHAEL BERTSCH, Butte College

Introduction to the Topic

Why would a telecourse about *writing* have two entire programs on *reading*?

The answer is simple. Consider these truisms:

You can't learn to play guitar without *listening* to a lot of music.

You can't learn to play basketball without *enjoying* the game as a spectator.

It just makes sense. If you don't ever learn to read well, or to appreciate well-made text, how can you ever learn to write?

Part of the process of becoming an effective writer is to let the words of other successful writers flow through your eyes and bump around in your brain. Eventually, you will get a feeling for the way words work best on a printed page (or on a computer screen).

Of course, just as the beginning guitarist spends many hours playing scales and the fledgling basketball star plays for hours in the gymnasium, the inexperienced writer must *play* with words.

Notice we emphasize the fun aspect of this practice. There's an element of joy in playing basketball or playing a guitar. If you can learn to *play* with words, the process of reading and writing will become easier.

Consider: Most of the writing you do is for an instructor. In fact, most of the reading you do is for an instructor. Imagine how much trouble you would have keeping up a conversation, if the only time you talked was when you were assigned a speech to recite in communications class – and if the only time you *listened* to human speech was when you were required to, in school.

You don't learn to write *solely* by listening, watching, or reading – but all *can* help.

With that in mind, any reading will be good practice for writing – just like any idle conversation can help you speak more fluently. So the idea of this unit is to immerse yourself in text. Read e-mail, cereal boxes, discarded newspapers, textbooks, and anything else. The next time you are in a long line at the grocery store, pick up a tabloid and read about the three-eyed Elvis aliens. And remember: Any time spent absorbing the printed word will help you become a better writer. If someone in the checkout line makes fun of you, just tell the shopper you're doing your coursework.

Learning Objectives

After viewing the television program and finishing the assignments, you will have a few insights into the way you read. For instance, you will learn that you read in several different ways: for pure enjoyment, for study, to emulate a style, to "make meaning," or to gain new knowledge. You will become aware of the ways others read and how that affects everything from the grades they get to the way they write to the way they view the world around them. From hearing the opinions of others about reading, you will develop strategies for using your own reading to mature as a writer.

Mini-Workshop B, "Double-Entry or Dialectical Notebooks" (pp. 450–453), introduces active-reading techniques recommended in these telecourse programs. Workshop 13, "Interpretation as Response: Readings as the Creation of Meaning," includes a section (pp. 346–348) that emphasizes a key pointing this program: emulating writing you admire can improve your own compositional style.

Before Viewing

Before formally studying the subject of reading as a writer, reflect for a moment on the types of things you *already* read. If you have time before watching the telecourse program, informally survey your reading habits for a few days – or even a week. Include recreational reading, reading at work, reading for school, reading of billboards, reading of food labels, reading on the Internet – all of it. Determine how your reading changes in different situations. Think about whether you consciously or unconsciously emulate any of the writing styles that you encounter along the way.

In Elbow and Belanoff, read Mini-Workshop B, "Double-Entry or

Dialectical Notebooks," paying close attention to the section "Exploring Theory" (p. 452).

While Viewing

Take note of the strategies for reading advocated by the writers, instructors, and students in the television program. Determine if any of those strategies reinforce skills you have already developed for reading as a writer. List any new strategies for reading that you have not encountered before, and try them out the next time you read. Notice the similarities (and differences) in attitudes about reading as a writer that are expressed by various guest in the telecourse program.

After Viewing

Using the exercises (in the *Telecourse Study Guide*) and the advice you gather from the telecourse program, consider how the materials you read affect your ability as a writer. (The exercises on emulation in this *Telecourse Study Guide* will help you actively blend your reading and writing activities.) Reflect on the differences in language, style, tone, and diction of the representative styles of writing in your various college classes. Think about what makes good and bad writing within each discourse community, including the writing you might compose for different classes, for work, or for your own personal use. Imagine how reading the writing in the style of each of those communities will affect the way you write in each situation.

Viewing Guide

You can't learn to write without reading.

Consider the words of Peter Farrelly, scriptwriter for such cerebral masterpieces as the films *Dumb and Dumber* and *There's Something About Mary* and the author of several successful novels such as *Outside Providence* and *The Comedy Writer*. Farrelly explains his relationship with reading this way: "Your brain does become accustomed to the written word. It's almost like when you play a video game. At first it's a little difficult. And then, all of a sudden, as you get it down, you start getting hooked on it. That's what reading is like for me. Once I started reading, my brain became accustomed to the written word."

Here's journalist, novelist, and instructor John Morgan Wilson on the same subject: "All the answers that a beginning writer needs to learn to write well are in what's already being written and being published." You have to learn to read differently – not to read as a reader anymore but to *read as a writer*. How does someone open an article? How do they write their lead sentences? What's the structure of the piece? How do they use quotes? How do they paraphrase? How do they write descriptive passages? All the answers a writer needs to know are in the writing. That's why reading is so important."

Reading more than once

Experienced writers read several different ways. They read for pleasure. They read to study the way other writers put words on the page. They even learn to read their *own* work as a member of the audience, rather than as the creator of the work. Literary novelist Ernest Gaines (author of the National Book Critics' Award-winning novel *A Lesson Before Dying*) says, "Usually, my first reading of any book is just as any reader would read it. I don't try to break it down; I just read for the pleasure of it. Later, if the book interests me, then I would go back and see exactly what the writer was doing. Because I always learn. I am constantly learning from reading a good writer."

Best-selling mystery novelist Sue Grafton uses a similar approach. Though every book Grafton writes hits the best-seller charts, she claims to learn something new every time she reads another author.

"If you're trying to learn to write, find a piece of fiction that you love," Grafton advises. "Find a piece of fiction that makes you laugh or cry or something that scares you. Read it for pleasure and then go back and break it down and figure out how the writer did it. I read a book for pleasure. Then I get to the end and go, 'Why did I cry? What was it that made me laugh aloud?'"

Almost every writer surveyed for the telecourse stated a variation on this theme. Though many emphasized that there is much to learn from reading the literary classics in the standard English curriculum, they also believe students can learn from reading for pure pleasure.

"I think writers-in-training can learn from their favorites," says Grafton. "You don't have to study Dostoyevski or even Shakespeare. If you're entertained by Danielle Steele, go read a Danielle Steele book and figure out how she makes your heart go pitty-pat. Same thing.

"I go back and I look at a book or a piece of fiction very analytically. I'll break it down; I'll start analyzing how a writer has created that effect. How does Stephen King create suspense? Why is it that he can describe a dead cat coming back from over the pile of sticks and give you the creeps when this stinky cat walks through the room? He does it with language. He's using the same words the rest of us use. But he's using them a little more artfully than some, and so he can create an effect."

Removing the passive aspect of reading

In *A Community of Writers* Elbow and Belanoff note, "reading my *look* passive; we sit quietly and let the image of the words print itself on our retina and thus pass inwards to our brain. But reading – indeed, all meaning-making – is a deeply *active* process."

This active process is an extension of how we deal with the world around us. When we read, we don't so much *find* meaning as we build and create meaning.

Making meaning

In the telecourse program, Cindy Selfe of Michigan Technical University suggests that this "making-meaning" process starts with learning how to "read" the "text" of the world around us. The process continues with learning to make meaning from words on a page. Selfe uses her experience of walking through the Chinatown district of San Francisco, trying to make meaning of what she sees, as an example.

"You see text everywhere we go," Selfe says. "When you go into Chinatown, for example, you would read the text of the people passing by, the cultures that they come from, the nature of their business, the bustle of the streets, the signs in the stores, the goods that people are selling in stores.

"Language is the basis for our recapturing experience. We use language to take experience from one level to another level – to take it from the level of observation, vision, sight and bring it to the level of reflection. It's a way of re-presenting vision for other people to read."

Redefining the word *reading*

According to Selfe, "We read the clothes people wear; we read the jewelry that they have on; we read the length of their hair; we read the makeup they have on. All of these things are text, and most of the time we interpret those texts in ways that are very subtle."

Selfe's definition of *reading* might be quite different from the one you brought to the course. Most students think of reading as an extension of high school homework assignments – interpreting "classic" novels, such as *Moby Dick* and *The Great Gatsby* and writing essays about hidden meanings and themes and symbolism to please the teacher and get a good grade.

College instructors often expand that definition to include "reading" a situation or interpreting life.

Min-Zhan Lu of Drake University also expands the meaning of *text* – along with expanded understanding of the word *reading*. "You cannot teach writing without teaching reading," she says. "And I would always start with a text. What I mean by text: It doesn't have to be a *written* text. It could be a movie; it could be a novel; it could be a scientific presentation of an issue."

Young writers take in information by learning to decode various types of "text" and, as writers of text, learn how to encode information for communication.

This process of "making meaning" is the essence of reading as a writer.

Elbow and Belanoff observe, "When we have trouble reading, it's often because we've been mistakenly trying to be passive – trying to make ourselves like good cameras."

The human brain does not work that way, they say. Instead, our minds use several stages to make meaning, and it takes a conscious effort of the reader to interact with the text.

This process is the same process we use to "read" a situation or read a textbook. Each reader may have slightly different interpretations of what the book or situation means. And, that is the way it is *supposed* to be.

Active participation in reading

No matter how you define *reading*, the advice is still the same: Don't just sit there and absorb the data. In the telecourse program, several instructors and writers recommend reading techniques that include actively marking the textbook (or writing in a double-entry notebook) while you read.

Ariel Gonzalez of Miami Dade Community College recommends: "Read with a pen, underline, make marginal comments, so that as you are reading, you are *physically* having to underline. You are physically having to make notes; thereby, that's stimulating your thought process. You are having to think about the text as opposed to just going through it fast and just swallowing up the huge portions that might help you on a quiz."

However, Tom Fox of California State University, Chico, warns that engagement with the mind is even more important than physically interacting with the book. "The most discouraging thing is when you see something like, the student has underlined every single thing," Fox says.

Students who underline almost everything in a book, he says, are not really sifting through the information, actively selecting what is important or not important. The ability to discriminate between different kinds of information is a key part of *actively* reading.

Learning how to actively read your own work – especially after an early draft – is another essential part of the process of becoming a good writer.

"Students should be also able to discriminate, in the process of writing, between what is significant and what is not significant in their own writing and their classmates' writing," Fox says. "So I don't discriminate between the text that I assign for them to read and their own text."

Emulation – modeling

One of the best ways to learn how to write well is to read the writers you admire and then model your writing after their styles.

Many writing instructors suggest that students can learn important lessons about tone, style, diction, and voice by simply emulating their favorite writers. It is not exactly thievery, as long as the student is just "borrowing" the style.

The late Charles Kuralt, a journalist famed for his books and for his television feature writing, offers this commentary: "I know that when I sit down to write, I can hear the rhythms of good writers in my head. Sometimes I can even tell you which writers' rhythms I am listening to as I write a piece. To train oneself as a writer, do an awful lot of reading."

Novelist and instructor Himilce Novas has similar advice. "I think writers are pantomime artists in our beginning stages," she says. "Later, when you have your own voice, you're still a pantomime artist because you're always trying to capture the voice and thought and the way people speak. There isn't any writer who has not … started by imitating some writers. Then you move on; you trash everything you've ever copied. You throw all that derivative stuff out and somehow your own voice emerges."

Reading in your discourse community

A similar modeling process will work in your upper-division and graduate school writing – and, after you graduate, in the working world. You will read the good (and bad) writing of those in your discourse community, and you will strive to communicate in a manner similar to those you admire.

In the telecourse, the concept of writing within a *discourse community* is introduced by Butte College composition instructor Michael Bertsch, who observes, "We speak the way our speaking community speaks; we write the way our writing community writes. If I can immerse students in correct and rich language, it becomes natural. It's like a musician playing scales."

Chris Lowe, a marine biologist, is an excellent example of how a scientist learns to write for his own community by reading the work of others in the same social and professional circles.

Lowe explains that he learned to write by reading the good (and bad) work of others in his discourse community of scientists and scholars. "I was a horrendous writer. And it wasn't until I got to graduate school that I really learned how to write. One of the things that helped me improve my writing was reading other people's writing. When I had to teach classes and grade papers, I would read papers and I would think, 'I have no idea what this person's saying.' And although I understood the concept (because I taught them the concept), their ability to relay that information back to me was horrible. If I look back at papers that I had written in high school, I see the same sort of bad writing style."

Summary

Lowe's comments echo many of the most important concepts of this telecourse program. It is good to read and emulate the work of those you admire. To write well in your discourse community, you should read the work of those in your profession. To be a good writer, your reading should be active and not passive. To learn how write well, you have to look at your early drafts as if you were part of the audience.

In learning how to read as a writer, it is very important to step back and look at *your own* work. According to Elaine Maimon of Arizona State University, "One of the most basic skills that a writer needs is to be able to sit down and read what you've written at first and make some critical decisions about it. Sometimes you'll read it and you'll say to yourself, 'This helps. This has clarified a problem that I've been working on. I will put this piece of writing aside and be very, very happy that a freshman composition teacher showed me the power of writing for self-exploration.'

"Sometimes you'll read the same piece a couple years later. That's the beauty of writing. It's still there. And you'll say, 'That helped me at the time with a problem I was working on, but there's a metaphor in this piece that is really powerful and that I can use. And I learned that in freshman composition: how to read my *own* writing.'"

Mini-Workshop B, "Double-Entry or Dialectical Notebooks," covers active note-taking techniques recommended in these telecourse programs (p. 450).

In the section "Exploring Theory: Dialectical Notebooks and the Parallel between Reading and Writing" (p. 452), Elbow and Belanoff point out that the central activity in both reading and writing is "the making of meaning."

Words cannot transport a writer's meaning into our heads," Elbow and Belanoff state. They can only give us a set of directions for creating our own meanings in our own heads – meanings which, if all goes well, will resemble what the writer had in mind.

The effectiveness of *your* writing can be improved if you actively take notes about the writing style while you read.

The authors address several of the other topics covered in this telecourse program in Workshop 13, "Interpretation as Response: Reading as the Creation of Meaning" (pp. 337–361), which we will work more closely with in Chapter 18. One useful suggestion from Workshop 13 is to find a writer you admire and try to emulate his or her style – almost as if you were trying on another writer's coat, to see if it fits your own personality.

Of course, it is not your intent to keep the coat (or writing style) you are borrowing; you just want to see if the style is comfortable so you can make your own decisions about how to express yourself.

This notion of emulating (or flat out imitating) another writer's style – with a goal of learning to develop your own style – is addressed in both the video program and in *A Community of Writers*. A variation of this activity is included in this Study Guide chapter.

Exercises

Check with your instructor for your formal assignments. You will be asked to do exercises from the *Telecourse Study Guide*.

Exploring reading as a writer further

EXERCISE 1

Read a passage of fiction, nonfiction, or political persuasion. Or read something humorous by a writer you admire. Make sure your choice is something you *enjoy* reading. After you read the passage, identify and list the things that make the writer's work unique and enjoyable.

EXERCISE 2

Using the writing in your own discourse community – or an essay from the textbook – write a couple of paragraphs just for fun, trying to imitate the author's style.

Here's one approach:

1. Type the paragraphs into your computer. This will give you a strong feeling for the rhythms, vocabulary choice, and sentence structure.

2. Next, copy the paragraphs. Paste them in a different window. Now, pick a similar subject and mimic the author's style by substituting key nouns, verbs, and adjectives – but keeping the sentences as close to the original version as possible.

3. Next, close all the windows, and open up a clean document. Pay homage to the author you admire by writing something in a similar style. Try to remember the texture of the writer's work, as you emulate the style.

4. Finally – and most important – forget everything you have just tried. Work hard to develop your *own* style.

EXAMPLE

Just for fun, the author of this *Telecourse Study Guide* will emulate a passage from America's top-selling mystery novelist Sue Grafton – a writer who has a very recognizable style. This is from *M Is for Malice*:

> I began to descend, one hand on the railing, the other clutching the file. I pivoted, reluctant to turn my back on the darkness behind me. For a moment, I scrutinized the stretch of corridor I could see. Something hovered in my peripheral vision. I turned my head slowly, nearly moaning in fear. I could see sparkles of light, almost like dust motes materializing in the stillness. I felt a sudden rush of heat and I could hear ringing in my ears, a sound I associated with childhood fainting spells. My phobia about needles had often inspired such episodes. When I was young, I was often subjected to a typhoid inoculation, a tine test for tuberculosis, or a periodic tetanus injection. While the

nurse took the time to pooh-pooh my fears, assuring me "big girls" didn't put up the fuss I did, the ringing would begin, building to a high pitch and then silence. My vision would shrink, the light spiraling inward to a tiny point. The cold would rush up and the next thing I'd know, there'd be anxious faces bending over me and the sharp scent of smelling salts held under my nose.

I leaned back against the wall. My mouth flooded with something that tasted like blood. I closed my eyes tightly, conscious of the thudding of my heart and the clamminess in my palms. While Guy Malek slept, someone had crept along this hallway in the darkness last night, toting a blunt object of sufficient brute matter to extinguish his life. Less than a day ago. Less than a night. Perhaps it had taken one blow, perhaps several. What troubled me was the notion of that first bone-crushing crack as his skull shattered and collapsed. Poor Guy. I hoped he hadn't wakened before the first blow fell. Better he slept on, before the last sleep became final.

The ringing in my ears kept on ...

The emulation by Peter Berkow, television producer, and composition instructor at Shasta College:

I stumbled out of the waterbed, one hand scratching my belly, the other hand groping in the darkness for the light switch on the way to the bathroom. I stubbed my toe on a chair in the living room, reluctant to step on the sleeping house cat. For a moment, I adjusted my eyes to night blindness. Something hummed in my computer office. I turned my head, moaning at the thought of more online papers to grade. I could see the bluish glow of the computer monitor, although it was supposed to be in slumber mode. My ears filled with the shrill sound of missing a deadline, a clamor associated with my journalism days. As a cub reporter, I was often burdened with a feature on the city council, a music review, an exposé of welfare fraud – all due before I was finished revising. While the editor urged me to finish, assuring me "we don't need a Pulitzer with this one," the cacophony of police scanners, printing presses, and frantic typing of other reporters would build to a crescendo and then silence, once the deadline had been met. My body would slump, relaxing in the worn reporter's chair. The next thing I'd know, I would be the only soul in the newsroom, vacantly gazing at the empty glow of my computer.

I leaned against the hallway door, my mouth filled with the taste of last night's pizza. While my wife and I slept, some mysterious student had entered the English 1-A forum and accidentally had booted up my slumbering computer. A poorly written term paper was developing on the screen, word by misspelled word. An undeveloped thesis. A comma splice. Undocumented quotes. Less than five hours ago, I thought I had graded the very last of the pile. What troubled me was, this was the student who had procrastinated all semester. Poor kid. I hoped he didn't really need to pass. Better he take the class again, turning in sections of the term paper throughout the semester, as I had suggested, instead of waiting for the night of the semester's final.

I printed out the finished term paper, grabbing my red pen ...

Exercise just for fun

Look in your school's class catalogue and carefully read the description your instructor wrote for your English composition course. While preserving the style of the piece as best you can, write a parody describing the learning objectives and grading policies of a course that teaches something absurd (like underwater basket weaving).

Revision exercise

In this exercise, you will create a new draft of an essay by revising and building on the paragraph you created in your Quick Writing exercise for Chapter 3 of the Telecourse Study Guide. Begin by reexamining your freewrite, the interesting ideas and phrases you pulled from it, and your organization of those ideas and phrases.

- Identify and expand any ideas that need further explanation.

- No matter how intuitively correct something might seem to you, make sure to add sentences that make adequate transitions between thoughts and provide your reader with clear and understandable connections between related concepts.

- Next, compose and insert a topic sentence for your paragraph.

- Find any sentences that do not fit within the controlling idea of the paragraph and remove them. These sentences will be the starting points for the rest of the paragraphs in your essay.

Quick writing exercise

Your teacher may ask you to do a quick focused freewrite about the topic you are studying in this unit. Those of you who are taking the course through a distance-learning system may be encouraged to share your thoughts in a discussion thread or to post your ideas on an Internet bulletin board. If you are writing your thoughts out by hand in a process journal, you might use these questions to stimulate ideas. This is a freewriting exercise that will not be graded. You can use any of the following questions to provoke thoughts about reading as a writer:

What do you read for fun? What do you think your teachers would think of the material that you read for fun? If you don't read anything for fun, when did you stop having fun reading? Most children love reading; can you trace a time when you lost that feeling? What have you learned from writers you enjoy reading? What is the writing (and reading) like in the discourse community of your chosen profession? Is there a writer in your discourse community whom you admire? If so, why do you admire this writer's work?

The questions in the "Process Journal" section of Workshop 13, "Interpretation as Response: Reading as the Creation of Meaning" (p. 349), in *A Community of Writers* may be an additional source of inspiration for this quick writing exersise.

Exercises related to *A Community of Writers*

EXERCISE 1

Mini-Workshop B, "Double-Entry or Dialectical Notebooks," covers active note-taking techniques recommended in the video programs (p. 450). In the section "Exploring Theory: Dialectical Notebooks and the Parallel between Reading and Writing" (p. 452), Elbow and Belanoff point out that the central activity in both reading and writing is "the making of meaning."

You'll work more carefully with this workshop in another unit of the telecourse. For now, your exercise is to browse through the information and devise a similar technique for active note-taking while you watch the video programs. You should not be watching the programs passively; think of yourself as "reading," or making meaning from the programs. As you do, devise a notebook system that will allow you to read the programs as a writer.

EXERCISE 2

The third activity of Workshop 13 is titled "Responding as a Writer: Responding in Kind" (pp. 346–348). In this exercise, Elbow and Belanoff ask you to emulate another writer's style. Though this "reading as a writer" exercise is built around a poem in the textbook, you can easily adapt a similar exercise to learn how to write in your discourse community.

First, see how Elbow and Belanoff suggest you emulate the poem. Then, pick the writing of someone who you admire in the academic major you intend to pursue. It can be a piece of writing borrowed from a student a few years ahead of you, an article in a journal, or a passage from a book. Elbow and Belanoff recommend that you borrow the texture, the structural features, and some of the prominent elements of the writing you are emulating. You can try an experimental draft, writing in this style, but making big enough changes so that "no one would ever see the relationship" to the original piece.

The first goal of this exercise is to learn how writers in the discourse community "speak" on the page, but the ultimate goal is to develop your own variation of the writing style you are emulating.

Additional reading

At this point in the semester, it would be a good idea to browse through the writing samples in the appendix. As you look through the writing samples, try to find writers whom you might want to emulate. Take one sample, and read it as a writer – looking for techniques you might be able to adapt to your own writing style.

For example, as you are writing a narrative or descriptive piece, read the excerpt from Chitra Divakaruni's short story "Clothes" or the excerpt from Frank McCourt's novel *Angela's Ashes*. Both of these instructors and authors make an impact in the first few programs of the telecourse.

As you read these two brief excerpts, what techniques can you borrow from these two writers that can help improve your own work?

Quick Review

1. Instructors and other guests in the program suggested that
   a. Any kind of recreational reading is good for a student who is interested in writing.
   b. Students should read the work of only respected writers of classic prose.
   c. Students gain very little from reading the work of other students.
   d. All of the above.
   e. None of the above.

2. Instructors and other guests in the program suggested that
   a. It is completely unethical to ever copy another writer's style.
   b. A beginning writer can learn quite a bit by emulating another writer.
   c. It is impossible for a beginning writer to develop an original voice.
   d. All of the above.
   e. None of the above.

3. The *Telecourse Study Guide* and telecourse program suggest that
   a. A good writer reads things more than once.
   b. Reading for entertainment and for analysis require different mind-sets.
   c. Active reading is better than passive reading.
   d. All of the above.
   e. None of the above.

4. According to guests in the telecourse,
   a. We speak the way our speaking community speaks; we write the way our writing community writes.
   b. It is good to write in the book as you read, to get more active in the process.
   c. Even award-winning, best-selling writers try to learn about writing by reading the work of others.
   d. All of the above.
   e. None of the above.

5. To avoid reading passively, instructors in the telecourse recommend:
   a. Students should underline or highlight as much as possible as they read.
   b. Students should never desecrate a book by marking directly on the pages.
   c. Students should learn to discriminate between what is important and unimportant as they interact with the text they are reading.
   d. All of the above.
   e. None of the above.

"In college I was introduced to a very formal approach
to story writing: the old structure of conflict, rising
action, climax, dénouement – and some very formal
notions about what constitutes narrative. This was
not in an environment which suggested that somehow
this should restrict you; rather, it was in an
environment that suggested that this is an important
starting place. You should be able to do this well; this
is important; ignore it at your peril. And once you feel
sufficiently comfortable in that structure, *then* feel
free to move on."

DAVID GUTERSON, novelist and former English teacher

Introduction to the Topic

What is narrative writing? According to most authors and instructors, it's a mode of composition that relates a series of events using the same strategies of storytelling with which humans have spun tales for thousands of years.

When you are asked to produce a short story in a composition course, it might seem at first like an assignment that has little connection to the writing you will be doing beyond your English class.

Of course, English majors who plan to study creative writing will enjoy the coursework. But why should an engineering student, a biology student, or a criminal justice student study this style? The answer is that, though this thinking/writing strategy is the heart of any good short story, novel, or movie script, the skills of narrative writing are not just limited to drama.

Science fiction writer Kim Stanley Robinson expresses the view of most writing instructors when he says, "I think that *all* writing is narrative. There is no such thing as non-narrative writing. If you examine the driest editorial, or even the pure scientific article, what you'll find is, it tells a story." The video introduces several writers who use narrative writing on the job, confirming Robinson's view.

There's another reason most first-year writing students practice storytelling and narrative writing, even if their upper-division courses mostly require formal arguments or technical writing.

We all tell stories in our day-to-day conversations. For many, it is fairly painless to make the next step: committing those stories to paper. Instructors traditionally have seen personal narrative writing (or story-telling) as an effective tool to move students from fun, contemplative writing about the self to the more difficult, objective, scholarly writing. For example, at New York University, the freshman composition curriculum designed by Dr. Pat Hoy heavily emphasizes a style he calls the "familiar essay" – a variation on personal narrative writing and writing stories about your own life.

"The academic essay is a more formal defense of something," Hoy explains. "You are doing all the thinking off of the page in the academic essay. The outline is constructed, the evidence is marshaled in, and you say, 'I'm going to prove some thesis.' The familiar essay does not have that kind of insistence, so it encourages the kind of personal thoughts that are exploratory."

Hoy starts students at NYU with a heavy emphasis on familiar essays and personal storytelling. Much like the structure of this telecourse, the composition course at NYU gradually moves students to assignments that require more challenges in critical thinking, analysis, and classic argument.

Composition courses are often shaped this way. The assumption is that students will retain the skills gained in the personal storytelling exercises at the beginning of the semester. When the writing challenges of the upper-division courses in their academic majors inevitably demand writing with a strong underlying narrative, the students will be acquainted with the required skills.

Learning Objectives

After viewing the telecourse program and finishing the writing assignments, you will have a sense of when narrative writing is needed – in all styles of writing. That includes narrative passages in fact-based writing (reports filed by journalists or police officers, papers created through scientific research, etc.) and academic writing (including exams, term papers, dissertations, etc.), as well as the narrative styles of the "familiar essay" or storytelling in fiction. You will also practice the techniques used by accomplished writers to create effective narrative writing and storytelling.

These learning objectives work in harmony with the essential premises of Workshop 4, "Getting Experience Into Words: Image and Story" in *A Community of Writers* (pp. 99–119).

- The best way to make your words powerful – to make readers *experience* the meanings in your words – is to make sure that *you* actually experience what your words are about. Finding nice words is all very well, but actually experiencing your meanings – seeing, hearing, and feeling what you are writing about – is another thing. It takes extra energy and concentration.

- A good way to write a story is to let it grow out of a strongly experienced image.

Before Viewing

Before you formally study this topic, think of the techniques of storytelling you already know instinctively. Experiment with the style by telling one of your favorite stories to a friend, or bunch of friends, in an informal setting such as the campus cafeteria, a local weekend hangout, or a campfire. Then, practice telling the same story on paper (or in an e-mail), with a quick first-draft sketch. Also, evaluate the skills in storytelling you already have and imagine how they might apply to the narrative of a more academic style of writing, such as a research paper.

Read Elbow and Belanoff's Workshop 4, "Getting Experience Into Words: Image and Story" (pp. 99–119).

While Viewing

Compare the skills you already have in narrative writing and storytelling with the techniques recommended by the instructors, students, and professional writers in the telecourse. Note the skills that you haven't already mastered, and plan to try these skills in a passage of your own narrative writing. Become aware of the various applications of narrative writing used in different occupations. Notice how reporter Debbie Cobb of KHSL television and student Gregory Andrus of Middlesex County College use narrative writing in the examples in the telecourse.

After Viewing

Using the examples in this *Telecourse Study Guide* and in your textbook, practice the art of narrative writing and storytelling. Be on the lookout for good and bad examples of narrative writing you encounter in everyday life, including textbook assignments from other classes, recreational reading, and reading you do on the job. Try to determine if the methods recommended in this telecourse program are evident in the good examples; pinpoint what is lacking in the poorly written examples. Watch for what is considered appropriate (and inappropriate) narrative writing within the discourse community of your academic major or chosen profession.

In *A Community of Writers*, compare the use of narrative writing in the short story "A Worn Path," by Eudora Welty (pp. 115–119) with the use of narrative in the scientific writing of Anne Fausto-Sterling (pp. 400–406) in her piece "A Plethora of Theories: Biological Storytelling."

Viewing Guide

Everyone has a good story to tell, but narrating the tale isn't always easy.

So, once upon a time, some genius invented the basic story structure. And, realizing this was a good form, the genius shared the idea with others. The story structure had a satisfying shape and an effective way of delivering a message; it was a big success. After this perfect yet basic story form hit the top of the best-seller charts, the manager of the genius absconded with the profits and ran away to Athens. But the genius learned many lessons from the experience and became a better person. The end.

Most of us know this basic story structure subconsciously. We know it, of course, from the study of classic novels and the works of Shakespeare – but variations of the same form appear in fairy tales, cartoons, and almost every movie or television episode ever produced.

The narrative shape

Science fiction novelist Kim Stanley Robinson offers this synopsis of the basic narrative shape: "There is a classic structure that I believe was described by Aristotle: the introduction of the *problem*, the *complications*, the *climax*, and the *dénouement*."

Writers and teachers use the term dénouement to indicate a final unraveling and winding down of the plot.

Robinson continues, saying that the good storyteller uses that basic Aristotelian structure of a story in the same way a jazz musician improvise around a simple melody. In other words, if writers followed the formula too closely, the stories would all start sounding the same. A good writer learns to bend the rules of the formula.

Many authors explain the classic structure of a short story as a narrative arc. Longer stories (novels, plays, or movies) have a series of narrative arcs within the bigger arc of the story. Novelist Lisa See explains it this way: "I try, in every scene, to have some kind of a narrative arc building up to something bigger. Within those little scallops, there's this big arc."

According to See, every story and every scene can be summarized in a few words to indicate a stage of the story. "So with the *Wizard of Oz*, you can reduce that story to three words: *Kansas. Oz. Home*," she says. "And there it is: it's the beginning, middle, and end. I try to use that idea, even if

I'm just writing a two-page scene, because each scene should be able to stand on its own."

A variation of this shape is used in most academic writing, even if the underlying narrative is not used to tell a story. For example, the formal argument of a research paper usually uses the introduction of the thesis, the development of evidence, and the summarization of the argument in a conclusion in much the same way.

Character development

In the video, mystery novelist Sue Grafton suggests that the way to avoid a hackneyed repetition of the same old story structure is to focus on the personalities driving the story.

"Much of the structure of storytelling sounds formulaic or artificial at first; you have to have a conflict; somebody has to want something; you have to have a beginning, middle, and end. That sounds so dumb, but it's completely true," Grafton says.

In Grafton's view, it is the development of a character that makes each story unique. She points out that many characters are on a quest to fill a need or a want.

Novelist and literary agent Peter Rubie agrees, noting: "If you're not giving your character interesting problems to solve, then it's not going to be an interesting story."

Writer and English instructor Geoffrey Philp puts character development within the context of classic narrative shapes we are all familiar with. Philp explains that the well-written plot gracefully reveals the moments along the way that lead the main character to the confrontation or decision.

"In the [cowboy] westerns, it would be the obligatory sundown scene. It's that point where the character can either go this way or that way. It's a moment of *choice*. And then you have the dénouement – the whole catharsis. In Shakespeare, it ends in marriage if it's a comedy; if it's a tragedy, everybody dies."

Actress Mo Collins shares some of her techniques for building a fictional personality based on real-life characters, using her character "Lorraine" from the sketch comedy show *Mad TV* as an example.

"Use lots of observation," Collins says. "Everywhere you go, there's slices of people who are outputting information for you. And you can take a potpourri of ideas and put them into one character like Lorraine from the television show. Lorraine is a culmination of many Minnesota women that I grew up with. As cartoon-y as she is, she is also very based in reality.

"I do that with characters, I like to make lists about my characters – things I like about them, things that I *don't* like about them – how they make other people feel. I like to make collages on my characters. It's great to go through magazines and cut out ideas about a character; if you look at the piece of art, then it forms a personality."

The approach Collins uses is very much like a technique novelists and short story writers use to create an imaginary character who blends the traits of several real-life people. Law enforcement agencies also use a similar technique in criminal investigations, building a "composite character" from clues that lead to the real perpetrator of the crime.

In a short story, the writer does not have much room to let the reader know the character thoroughly; there are usually just enough pages to give some insight into one key aspect of the character's personality that changes through the course of events.

However, the lessons *learned* by the main character can be very important in narrative writing, whether you are writing about yourself, a friend, or a fictional character. The ending of the story often reveals a change in the character that allows the author to make a point or offer a moral to the story.

Theme – thesis – main point

The theme is an important aspect of most stories. Without a clear central point, the reader will often feel that the narrator is simply relating a random series of events that lead nowhere. Unlike the thesis in a formal argument, which is usually a central claim offered as a declarative sentence early in the paper (and defended throughout the essay), the moral is often saved for the resolution of the narrative. In many instances, the main point is never even fully stated; it can be *implied* through the narrative in a way that lets the reader imagine the ramifications of the events in the story, long after reading.

No matter how artfully the main point is disguised, it is always there – unless the story is written in an experimental style designed to challenge conventions.

Charles Johnson, a National Book Award winner and writing instructor, feels that every good story should have a theme or main point to give meaning to the events being related by the narrator.

"A theme is basically the central idea, and it usually is interwoven with the conflict of the story," Johnson explains. "What kind of dilemma does the character face? If you don't have that, then you don't have an organizing principle for a short story. Without that, at the end of the story, you couldn't say, 'What is the moral of this story? What do I walk away with?' Every story is about something, just the way an essay is about something."

Unlike an academic argument, where the writer usually has a thesis and an outline before the final draft, the writer of creative fiction sometimes doesn't know the point of the story until the process is almost finished.

"Sometimes the theme is not clear to the writer until he or she gets to the end of the story," Johnson explains. "That's a case where the writer may have to do another draft, so that the ending is foreshadowed – and we're aware earlier on of what's at stake in this story. Just as we would be with a newspaper article [which is] basically telling the reader what it's *about* in the first paragraph. It has to be there pretty early to catch our interest."

Pace and tone

The effective storyteller learns how to control pace and tone through clever use of language. These skills translate to *any* kind of writing.

Journalist, novelist, and writing instructor John Morgan Wilson observes, "When you talk about pace in writing, it can apply to both non-fiction and to fiction. The pace is simply how fast the story moves. Ideally, pace will be varied; if you've got page after page of quotations – long blocks of text, lots of figures and data – the pace is going to be very slow. So you look for ways to speed up that pace. You inject a short, bright quote here if you've got one – and a long block of text there – and you break up your sentences."

Johnson explains how he purposely affected pace in a passage in one of his books. "If I'm doing a very intense scene, with lots of action and emotion – take, for example, the novel *Dreamer*, where Martin Luther King is almost overwhelmed by an angry mob – it was not an appropriate place to write very long periodic sentences. It was a place for short, simple, blunt sentences that clipped right along."

In other words, Johnson says, pacing often comes down to the simple matter of the author's deliberately selecting sentence length and sentence structure to create an effect.

In a more reflective passage of the book, Johnson purposely selects more complex sentence structures "that will lift you up and hold you in the air for just a moment and then bring you down."

Former English teacher and novelist David Guterson takes extra care to create the correct tone for his stories.

"Of all the components of the writing craft, tone is an essential one," Guterson says. "Tone is something that you have to *control.*"

A large part of that control, Guterson says, is word choice. It is easy to select a word based only the dictionary definition. But, he says, if you don't consider the hidden meanings, the implied attitude behind the word choice, and "if you *don't* worry about other aspects of the word: its *tone*, its *connotation*, the way in which it impacts the plot – then you're not doing your job."

Plot

"Out of all the components of craft, narrative action is probably the most challenging for writers," Guterson observes. "The sense of theme and characterization mean nothing unless they're in the context of a drama – of the story that's moving forward."

Often, the narrative essays written by students lack this sense of *story* that many writers talk about; instead, they simply relate a series of seemingly random events.

The solution, according to Guterson, is to relate the events in *a cause-and-effect* fashion. For example: *first* you read this *Telecourse Study Guide* chapter. *Then,* because you were prepared, you understood the presentation on the video. *Because* at least one writer on the video inspired you, a story idea popped into your head. *In spite of* the instructor's assignment to write a short story, you sat down and wrote a novel. *Since* the novel was a best-seller, you were able to purchase an island and buy your English instructor a vintage 1965 Les Paul guitar as a thank you gift.

A simple use of transitions can give a sense that one event in the story is leading to (or causing) the next event. Learning how to create such transitions is an important basic skill of storytelling – and of any other kind of narrative writing. Which brings us back to other uses of this type of writing.

Narrative writing on the job

Though you have been considering how fiction writers compose a short story, you should remember that narrative and storytelling skills are frequently needed in on-the-job writing.

When journalists describe a newsmaker or when police officers describe a lawbreaker, they are also developing a character. Though these writers are not inventing works of fiction, they are relating a real-life story with a classic narrative arc.

In the telecourse, we see reporter Debbie Cobb unconsciously touching the face of a newsmaker on the video screen in her editing room. Cobb is sharing her feelings about the main character in the story: Jackie Ferris-Rees, a mother and public figure who is an inspiration to others who are also battling cancer.

With this affectionate gesture, Cobb adds, "This person is so incredible – to have to go through that kind of experience publicly would be so difficult. Yet she continues to smile, she continues to have an awesome sense of humor. This is somebody that I want people to know in our community."

Cobb's feature news story is an excellent example of storytelling, with extraordinary character development and a classic narrative arc. Since Cobb has such strong feelings about the story, it is difficult for the viewer not to care about the real-life character she so skillfully reveals.

Police officer Janet Turner's job involves equally vivid character development as she describes characters in her police report many of us would rather *never* meet. Her reports also have a narrative shape, though the telling of the "beginning, middle, and end" of the events is not meant for entertainment. The "story" of an arrest is narrated objectively and chronologically for later reference in a court of law.

A similar narrative "shape" will be expected in almost every formal academic argument and research paper that you will be asked to compose in upper-division classes. Keep that in mind as you practice the narrative style in this unit.

Blending rhetorical modes

As we study narrative writing, it is important to note that all good story-telling contains a blend of other thinking/writing strategies we study in this course, including description, definition, argument, comparison, and process analysis. The more we study these thinking/writing strategies (sometimes also called "genres," or "the rhetorical modes"), the more we find that good writers mix and match them. In other words, the content is more important than the form.

Often, students are confused and ask questions like, "Am I doing something wrong? I'm getting mixed up, because my narrative paper seems like a description paper, and my process analysis paper seems to tell a story, and my comparison/contrast paper seems to argue a point."

This is the way good writing is supposed to work.

Workshop 4, "Getting Experience Into Words: Image and Story," starts on page 99 of *A Community of Writers* – but the authors ask students to resist getting into story telling until page 103. Elbow and Belanoff introduce description first; then they use the description as a jumping-off point to build a story. They are purposefully asking students to blur the distinction between the two genres.

Summary

Novelist and English composition instructor Chitra Divakaruni shares her own relationship with these rhetorical modes by explaining that she thinks about the purpose, thesis, audience, and tone of a piece of communication *first*. Then she considers the genre or thinking/writing strategy.

Divakaruni then explains, "Once I've figured those three things out, then I begin to think, 'Well, perhaps this rhetorical mode would bring all of these things out adequately.' I think particular rhetorical modes are conducive to certain atmospheres. The first thing I would want to teach someone about narration – for example, a police officer – would be, look at narration as a way of organizing random detail. When you're going to write, you're going to be using a number of modes together, so your report might start off as narration. First this happened; then I saw this. And so we move from one skill [and one mode] to another."

Divakaruni returns to a very important concept: Content determines the form, or genre. This instructional point will be reinforced in several units of this course.

In the real world, you won't be asked to write a short story, do a comparison paper for a course, or argue a point on an essay exam. You will encounter writing tasks, however, that will require skills of narration, comparison, and argumentation.

Keep that in mind as you study the concepts presented in this video program.

Integrating the Text

WORKSHOP 4 "Getting Experience Into Words: Image and Story"
(pp. 99–120)

A Community of Writers introduces this topic in the passage "Narrative or Story," on page 45 of Workshop 2, "From Private Writing to Public Writing." In this discussion of various genres, Elbow and Belanoff talk about the structure of a story. They recommend looking for and enhancing "crucial events, moments and turning points" of the narrative.

This is excellent advice and standard storytelling technique. The best stories, as we learned in the video program, have a definite shape that features these key points.

As most instructors will tell you, there can be a direct link between private writing and storytelling. Often, you will find that your journal entries, freewriting exercises, and diaries have passages that come very close to narrating events in a classic "narrative arc."

Workshop 4 traces the natural progression from describing the details of a scene to suing that scene as part of a story. Activity Four on page 103 is designed to move the student from describing toward telling a story. Elbow and Belanoff suggest starting with asking the question, "What happens next?" and letting the story grow out of enriching an image. Activities Five (p. 104) and Six (p. 105) are designed to extend the story idea. These techniques, combined with advice in the telecourse, will offer you several approaches toward developing your own stories or narrative essays.

Exercises

Check with your instructor for your formal assignments. You will be asked to do exercises from the *Telecourse Study Guide*.

Exploring narrative writing further
EXERCISE 1
Remember an event in your life with which you associate strong emotion. Then, beginning just before you experienced that emotion, write the scene in moment-by-moment detail so that the reader can follow the experience exactly as you felt it.

EXERCISE 2
Recall the most memorable event you can dredge up from your experiences in elementary school. Write a paragraph (or more) telling an old schoolmate about the special event. Before you start writing, think about one special event. Remember how the event started and where it happened. Next,

think about what happened during the event and who was involved. Finally, write down the outcome of this special event. Now write a paragraph (or more) telling your old schoolmate about this special event.

EXERCISE 3

Do some quick private freewriting about the weirdest or funniest moment in your life. If you've told this story to friends a few times, it should not be difficult to stretch the freewriting into a full-length narrative essay. This is usually something that is fun to write about – so take care to bring out the humor. A hint about timing and a punch line: Humor often works best when it is least expected. Don't broadcast your punch lines. Example: I want to tell you about the funny moment when I slipped on a banana peel and broke my arm. Instead, just let the moment unfold naturally. The readers will see the irony or slapstick of the moment without your having to tell them to laugh.

Example: The night of my prom, my gown was perfect and the whole family was excited – even my three-year old brother, who was showing off for my date by mashing a banana into his face. I had a hard enough time walking in pumps, but when the high heels met the banana peels ... (add punch line here).

Exercise just for fun

In this chapter, actress Mo Collins talks about how she develops her sketch comedy characters for *Mad TV*. Collins recommends making lists, creating a collage, and jotting things down in a small notebook, as you observe odd characters in your own life.

AS AN EXERCISE:

1. Using the techniques described by Collins, create a fictional "composite character" based on people you know. Include friends, classmates, professors, and people you run into on campus or in your day-to-day life.

2. Using the techniques described by Collins, create a fictional character who is much like you – but different by just a few degrees in important aspects of behavior or personality.

Revision exercise

If you develop any of the exercises above into a formal essay for an audience, consider the following questions before you revise: Did you bring the lessons from description into this exercise? What lessons can you take from the tele-course narrative-writing program to make this story stronger? Can you develop the main character (in this case, yourself) by showing the changes in personality caused by the events? Does the story have crucial events, moments, and turning points that you can bring out? Can you control the tone and pace of the story through language choice and sentence structure?

Does the essay have a narrative arc, with a clear beginning, middle, and end? Is the ending a satisfying dénouement, or resolution, to the plot? Is there a way you can work some foreshadowing into the early part of the essay, without giving away the ending? Do you include enough challenges for the main character or complications to the plot to keep the story interesting to the reader?

Quick writing exercise

Your instructor may ask you to do a quick focused freewrite about the topic you are studying in this unit. Those of you who are taking the course through a distance-learning system may be encouraged to share your thoughts in a discussion thread or to post your ideas on an Internet bulletin board. If you are writing your thoughts out by hand in a process journal, you might use these questions to stimulate ideas. This is a freewriting exercise that will not be graded. You can use any of the following questions to help start the freewriting about narrative writing and storytelling:

What is your favorite story of all time? What makes it a good story? Do you have a story you eventually tell all new friends about a moment in your life, or something strange that happened to you, or something funny, frightening, or life changing that happened to you? How different would that story be, told on paper, than in person?

What does storytelling have to do with other styles of writing that you will be studying in school?

You may use the questions in the "Process Journal" section of Workshop 4 "Getting Experience Into Words: Image and Story" (p. 286) in *A Community of Writers* as an additional source of inspiration for this quick writing exercise.

Exercises related to *A Community of Writers*

EXERCISE 1

Read Eudora Welty's story, "A Worn Path" (pp. 115–119). Write down your thoughts about this essay. This is an open ended assignment. You might write down your personal reaction to the essay; you might analyze the techniques in the essay, thinking of lessons learned in the telecourse programs "Description" and "Narrative Writing."

EXERCISE 2

Read "Is Phoenix Jackson's Grandson Really Dead," by Eudora Welty (pp. 207–211). Compare your reaction to Welty's musings about her own work.

EXERCISE 3

Part I: Several excellent essays are published in Workshop 4. These include

"Image of an Ice-Cream Man," by Mitchell Shack (pp. 110–112), "Reverie," by Jane Tompkins (pp. 112–113), "The Perfect Swing," by Joel Southall (p. 114), and "A Worn Path," by Eudora Welty (pp. 115–119).

Though Eudora Welty's essay comes closes to the classic short story form, as explained in this telecourse program, all four essays use techniques of narrative writing as described in this instructional unit.

Considering the lessons you've learned about shape, theme, character development, pace, tone, plot and blending rhetorical modes (or thinking/writing strategies), analyze the effectiveness of one of these essays. (Your instructor may assign a specific essay for this exercise. Be sure to check for his or her expectations.)

Part II: When you read these essays, identify where an how narrative writing skills are applied.

Additional reading

The essay that student Gregory Andrus reads in the telecourse, "My Mother's Soul," is included in the appendix. Analyze the ways Andrus applies the lessons of this unit in his story. Is there a dénouement? Does character development help drive the plot of the story? What do you learn about the characters? What is the theme or main point of the essay? Can you see the shape of a narrative arc in this story? How does this piece compare to the narrative "Country Life" (also in the appendix) by Ethlyn Manning?

In the program about process analysis, several writers suggest that "telling the story of how to do something" is the best way to give directions. How does Steve Shanesy, editor of *Popular Woodworking*, use narrative writing and storytelling to make his writing effective? (Shanesy's piece is featured in the appendix.) How is Shanesy's use of storytelling different from the excerpt in the appendix from David Ellefson's book, *Making Music Your Business*?

Is there a narrative structure to the piece by sports reporter Mark Ibanez, "Cacti, Catchers, and Cucumbers," featured in the appendix? How is this piece similar to, and different from, the story by Gregory Andrus?

In the Viewing Guide, author Lisa See explains how a long story has an overall narrative arc and that each individual scene has a similar shape. How is the scene, in the excerpt from Frank McCourt's *Angela's Ashes,* shaped much like a short story?

Read Dave Barry's piece in the appendix, "Business Memos." How does Barry use the basic narrative structure to make his points?

In the excerpt of Chitra Divakaruni's story "Clothes" that appears in the appendix, what do you learn about the two characters in the narrative? How does Divakaruni's development of character drive the plot of the story?

Quick Review

1. Narrative writing and storytelling techniques
   a. are primarily used by English majors interested in fiction
   b. are useful, even in technical writing and writing for the sciences
   c. are never used in term papers
   d. all of the above
   e. none of the above

2. The word *dénouement* is a term used to indicate
   a. an introduction to the story
   b. a sweet coffee drink, originated in France
   c. the resolution to the plot
   d. all of the above
   e. none of the above

3. The *narrative arc*
   a. is a term used to describe the typical shape of a story
   b. includes the beginning, middle, and end of a story
   c. is a concept that dates back centuries, to the time of Aristotle
   d. all of the above
   e. none of the above

4. The effective narrative writer uses language techniques to control
   a. pace
   b. tone
   c. character development
   d. all of the above
   e. none of the above

5. A good narrative or story
   a. never develops a thesis or main point, like an academic argument
   b. is always structured around a clear, linear outline
   c. often has a central theme, or "moral to the story," similar to the thesis in an argument
   d. all of the above
   e. none of the above

"In a school situation, one of the biggest issues is that writing is supposed to be 'correct' – one of the words people use is *formal* ... for students, this often means 'write nice.' Write with your pinky held out when you hold the teacup. Don't use your own voice; use some put-on, careful voice – that doesn't just lead to stiff, formal, doily writing with your pinky stuck out – it leads to very restricted thinking."

PETER ELBOW, University of Massachusets

Introduction to the Topic

Even if it is a prank call from a so-called anonymous caller, most of us can recognize the voice of a mischievous friend on the telephone. The recognition is not just in the tonal quality, which is obscured by the poor fidelity. The rhythm of the sentences, the vocabulary choice, and the attitude usually reveal the identity of the jokester on the other end of the phone.

Is it also possible that, on a printed page, we each have our own recognizable voice? You'll discover through this lesson that there *is* a relationship between the spoken voice you've been developing since you were a toddler and the writing voice that you only *started* to develop in school.

Most instructors believe that good writers develop *several* voices – each appropriate for a different situation. Whether you realize it or not, you probably already have adopted more than one writing voice, including voices that work in letters (or e-mail messages) to various friends and a completely different writing voice for each of your instructors. This video program accompanies Workshop Five in *A Community of Writers* by Peter Elbow and Pat Belanoff (pp. 121–147). Together, the television program, textbook, and *Telecourse Study Guide* chapter will help you identify and refine the different voices you use with text.

Learning Objectives

After viewing the television program and finishing the writing assignments, you will be able to develop several distinct writing voices to help you communicate effectively in many situations, including the voice that works best in the discourse community of your academic major or your chosen career. You will achieve this goal by identifying voices you already have and by practicing techniques of composition that specifically affect the writer's voice. This will include developing an awareness of tense, point of view, and pronoun choice and learning the connection between attitude, tone, and language.

These learning objectives work in harmony with three essential premises of Workshop 5, "Voice," in *A Community of Writers*.

- Written language can make you hear a voice from the silent page and thereby capture the subtleties of the actual human voice.
- By sharpening your "reading" ear, you can learn to hear the voice (or lack of voice) that exists in most pieces of writing.
- You can also learn how to gain control over what kind of writer's voice (or tone, or feeling) comes across.

Before Viewing

Think about the writing voices you have already encountered, including those of your favorite fiction writers or authors in your academic or work-related discourse community. (Include writing that you enjoy and writing that you *don't* enjoy.) Mull over what you already know about voice by informally analyzing your impressions of these various writers. Also consider several samples of your *own* writing, including old letters to friends, old coursework assignments, job application forms, and so on. Think of the variations of your own voice, adopted consciously or subconsciously as you were writing these documents. Read Workshop 5, pages 121 to 147. Compare the voices of the writers in the brief essays (pp. 137–147) with your own writing voice.

While Viewing

Take notes on how each writer, instructor, and student defines the concept of voice and how each *controls* his or her own voice. Note that many of the guests on the program have their own views about what voice actually is – and that not all of them agree. Try to form your own definition of voice in writing. Pay close attention to the mechanical and technical language skills necessary to portray a confident and consistent voice. Carefully observe the attitude (or tone) reflected in the comments made by the Pulitzer Prize–winning editorial writer Richard Aregood, the satirist and liberal political activist Al Franken, and the conservative talk-show host Rush Limbaugh when they discuss emotional aspects of their own voices.

Reconsider the section "Exploring Theory: About the Human Voice" (pp. 134–136), in which Elbow and Belanoff discuss the similarities and differences between a spoken voice and a writer's voice. Pay attention to the following key points: Though each person's spoken (and, eventually, written) voice is like a fingerprint, we can adopt several different personas. When we write for different audiences, we use the appropriate "tone" of voice. And, in spite of the advantages of oral communication, people can become just as comfortable in writing as they are in speaking, or even more comfortable. Guests in the video support many of Elbow and Belanoff's key points. As you watch the program, look for those moments (especially in comments made by Dave Barry, Frank McCourt, Sue Grafton, and David Gutterson). Ask yourself: "On the basis of personal experience, do I agree or disagree with each of these ideas?"

After Viewing

Using the exercises at the end of this *Telecourse Study Guide* chapter and in your textbook, practice adopting and analyzing different writing voices. Become aware of your voice in future course assignments – and consider how you might carry those lessons forward to writing challenges beyond the classroom.

Viewing Guide

The idea of a writer's "voice" may seem unusual at first, if you usually think of a voice as sounds made by vibrating vocal cords. However, when you "speak" to others through printed words, you also have a voice. Each writer and teacher in the telecourse has a slightly different take on what actually *makes* a writer's voice. Some speak of voice as an extension of the writer's identity. In *A Community of Writers*, Elbow and Belanoff note, "People have demonstrably unique [speaking] voices: Voice prints are as certain as fingerprints for identification."

In the video, the humorist Dave Barry suggests that a voice in print is also unique. "I won't say 'conduit into the person's soul,' exactly," Barry says. "But it's like a *fingerprint* of that person's personality; it's the *writer's* voice. Good writers have very clear distinct voices. When you read them, it's not because you're fascinated in the topic. It's because you want to hear what that voice says about that topic."

More than one voice

As the writer and former English teacher David Guterson suggests, we all have more than one persona; each is genuine. In the video program, English instructor Geoffrey Philp of Miami-Dade Community College describes several of his own identities and the writing or speaking voice he adopts for each. In his college environment, he sees himself as Professor Philp; when visiting his parents' home, he adopts the voice of his mother's son, Geoffrey; when Philp plays dominoes with his friends, he uses the familiar Jamaican slang and speech patterns. Philp sees all his voices as natural extensions of his personality. Elbow and Belanoff add, "Of course, you are *not* necessarily trying to decide on *one* right voice for you. There probably is no such thing. You need different voices for different situations."

Voice in college environments

We all write for different reasons and audiences. In a college or university, the audience becomes instructors and other students in your discourse community. You may consciously develop several writing voices to make your ideas known in different situations.

In the video, Beverly Moss, director of the Writing Center at Ohio State University, encourages students to "think about appropriate language, diction, and style for the particular audience and the particular discipline that they have to be writing." In other words, Moss says, the voice you use for your sociology instructor is not the same voice you will use for your physics instructor.

According to Elbow and Belanoff, "Certain kinds of voice are frowned on in certain kinds of writing. In highly formal kinds of writing such as we find in business reports and scholarly journals, readers and writers seem to want formal voices: quiet, dressed-up, well-behaved, and impersonal voices.

Voice on the job

At work you will have to write for your bosses, your employees, your coworkers, and your customers. You may write to get funding or to document events for reports. Flexibility of voice is necessary for survival and success. In the video, Dr. Jim Esh explains at least three personas he must adopt when he is writing for his work as a veterinarian. They include a formal, objective voice when he is writing for a medical journal and an entertaining yet opinionated voice when he is writing a newsletter for pet owners. Esh also identifies a third voice, which he uses when writing to colleagues. This third voice is a cross between the two other voices – it is conversational yet professional. The need for multiple voices exists in almost any occupation.

Developing and controlling your writing voices

Many students and professional writers say that discovering a voice is what makes writing fun. John Morgan Wilson, who is a journalist and a writing instructor at UCLA, puts it this way: "Voice is like a muscle. You have to work it.... The less you write, the longer it takes you to find your voice. If we never used our vocal cords, we would have a very weak voice. When we start out as writers, most of us have weak, erratic voices. But the more you write, the stronger that voice becomes."

According to Elbow and Belanoff, "Papers often start off in one voice – sometimes a somewhat stiff or neutral or careful voice. Then they may change voice as the writer gets warmed up. Sometimes writers slide into yet other voices when they provide examples, relate anecdotes, and make asides or digressions." An intentional change in voice can be used to the writer's advantage – if the shift in voice is the desired effect, and if the writer is in control of the shift. But the effect can also be disconcerting to the reader. Elbow and Belanoff observe that while some teachers are open to *either* an informal, casual voice *or* a formal, impersonal voice, they may not like "a *mixing* of voices: hearing the *collision* of a casual spoken voice with a formal academic one. Your paper has a conflict of voices when the writing unintentionally shifts from a formal, third-person point of view to an informal, first-person point of view, or when it wanders back and forth from past to present tense."

Technical and mechanical aspects of voice

TENSE

Experienced wordsmiths are quite aware of specific techniques that help develop the writer's voice. Writers-in-training often receive corrections for "grammatical" errors in their papers – when, in fact, these students have adopted unsure or inconsistent voices.

For example, if has marked your paper several times with a big red "TENSE SHIFT," it could be that you simply never decided whether your voice should come from the perspective of present tense or past tense. This is a common problem for beginning writers who are composing narrative essays. Answer the following questions before you write a story: Do I want the reader to experience the story with me, *while* I am narrating? Or do I want to relate the story *after* it happened?

Once you have made a decision, it is an easy task to fix tense problems while revising. Simply read the story through one time, concentrating on *all* your verbs; revise your sentences to make the verbs *consistently* past tense or present tense.

POINT OF VIEW

Another important decision involves selection of pronouns to indicate first-person, second-person, or third-person point of view. Writers who are not in control of voice also find red marks on their papers for "shifting of point of view" or "shifting voice."

Some grammar instructors actually refer to pronoun choice as the *voice* (instead of the point of view) that you are using in an individual sentence. Point of view is so closely connected to your writer's voice that very stylized novelists such as Frank McCourt and Tom Robbins take extra care in choosing their point of view. According to Robbins, "The voice *is* really the POV – the point of view. Even if the narrator is clearly the author, there still is a voice that tells the story that has to be a reflection of something more than just the author. All these things have to be in harmony. So you have to find the right tense and the right pace … and the right color and tone and texture."

Before writing a paper, consider how pronoun choice and point of view affect your voice. Later, when you proofread, check to see if your point of view (and thus your voice) wanders or collides with other sections of the paper.

First person is from the eyes of the writer, using the pronouns *I, me, we, us,* or *our. I* am aware of how *we* determine the point of view of the writer, by: choice of pronouns.

In the video program, Frank McCourt (author of the Pulitzer Prize-winning memoir Angela's Ashes) explains how he felt most comfortable writing in the present tense and in the first person, using pronouns such as *I, we,* and *our.* That point of view works especially well in a fact-based memoir. However, it might not work well in other situations, such as scientific writing or formal research papers, where authors are expected to keep themselves out of the text as much as possible.

Second person addresses the reader directly, using the pronoun *you* – or, in very formal writing, the pronoun *one. You* should be aware of how *one* uses choice of pronouns to create a point of view.

In the video, Kathleen Bell, an English instructor at the University of Central Florida, explains that the second-person pronoun can produce a friendly or antagonistic tone, depending on the writer's attitude. "When I ask, 'When are you coming over?' it's pleasant and close. If you change your tone, the *you* becomes almost adversarial [for example: 'If *you* don't have all *your* ducks in a row …'] and people feel offended, because *you* is a very personal pronoun."

Third person is abstract, as if the author is observing the action from a distance, using the pronouns *he, she, it, them, they.* When many first-year students use third-person pronouns, *they* are barely aware of the choice. When Molly uses third-person pronouns, *she* knows exactly what *she* is doing.

Formal, academic writing favors the third-person point of view. Most instructors will make critical comments if you use the first-person or second-person pronouns in a research paper or a formal argument. This is what the history professor Charles Turner at Butte Community College means when he observes on the video, "My students, for example, when they're writing a historical analysis paper, will use the first person. It's a tough lesson in historical analysis and I'm tough with them. I say, 'Nobody cares about your opinion. What do the facts and evidence say?'"

TONE

As David Guterson observes, "There's a conscious exertion of will on the part of the [good] writer to modulate tone to make it serve the story. Of course, tone is a function of language, so you choose the sentence length, the variety of sentences, the sentence structure, the words themselves to evoke or elicit a particular mood." Guterson (author of *Snow Falling on Cedars*) is aware that in his own work he can swing from a nostalgic, sentimental tone to a dark, ironic tone simply by emphasizing different types of vocabulary.

Careful selection of words can personalize and shape the tone, or attitude, of your writing. Consider how different you would feel if someone described you with each of these words: *slim, skinny, slender, gaunt, lean, anorexic, svelte, bony, wiry*. Although these are all variations of *thin*, each word has its own suggestion, which goes beyond a dictionary definition. This implied meaning, or connotation, profoundly affects the tone of the statement.

All writing – from a fictional work of mystery to a legal brief in court – has a tone. A writer's tone can make you *feel* the writing's emotional overtones. The mystery writer and journalist John Morgan Wilson puts it this way: "Voice is that kind of invisible driving force that drives your narrative forward ... just as all of us have a conversational way of speaking. It might be *faltering*; it might be *stammering*; it might be *weak*; it might be *troubled*; it might be *angry*."

Summary

Developing a voice is a complex issue, and many instructors have very different views about it, even about what makes a voice.

Mike Rose, instructor in the writing program at UCLA, summarizes this video program's instructional objectives, noting that voice is a controversial issue among instructors. "Some writing folks talk about voice almost as one's identity," Rose says. "Others talk about voice in a little bit more of a technical way." Rose tends to favor the latter view. "A voice in writing comes out of a lot of hard work – getting sentences right, finding words that express things in certain ways, matching words to experience.

"The final thing to say is that writers don't have just one voice."

Integrating the Text

WORKSHOP 5   "Voice" (pp. 121–145)

Workshop 5 teaches that the infinite nuances of speech found in tone, volume, cadence, rhythm, pitch, diction, and so forth – in short, voice – exist in writing as well. You can sharpen you rear for voice, discover voice in your own writing, and tailor that voice to shape your discourse.

Elbow and Belanoff caution that whether you dress your writing up or dress it down, you always want the results to fit yourself, the writer!

Many authors and teachers have speculated about the nature of voice. Read what some have said on pages 137 to 138. Eudora Welty's excerpt from *one Writer's Beginnings* is particularly apt: "... there has never been a line read that I didn't hear." It is this connection between verbal and written expression that is the core of Workshop 5. Welty's comments link directly to John Morgan Wilson's setup to Frank McCourt in the video: "... the way to find out what the voice is, is to read different writers. Read them aloud and listen to the quality of the prose and power and the momentum that drives the narrative forward. That's the voice."

Listen to McCourt's "voice" as you read the sample from his book in this Student Study Guide – and as you do this, consider the comments by both Welty and Wilson.

The first step in mastering voice is to learn to recognize it in others' writing (pp. 123–127). What are the different ways a passage of writing could sound when read aloud? How could the voice be described? What does the voice reveal about the author?

Elbow and Belanoff ask you to cull passages from your own writing to examine your voice (pp. 131–133). There are many ways to do this. You could create a collage of voices in your own writing (with the aid of the collage exercises outlined in Workshop 3, (pp. 76–79), rewrite a passage solely for voice, or write an essay that comments on the voice in a passage. Many such exercises can also be done in collaboration (see suggestions on page 132) and are grist for a process journal (p. 133).

Finally, don't forget to read the passages from the "Readings" section (pp. 140–147). Some are by students, just like you, taking a first-year writing course. Others are by authors ho have made their living writing. A maxim has it that one learns to write by reading. We would add that reading is where most writers find their inspiration. In fact, reading the essays in this section (or work by your classmates) may be just the place to begin before delving into this unit on voice.

Exercises

Check with your instructor for your formal assignments. You will be asked to do exercises from the *Telecourse Study Guide*.

Exploring voice further
EXERCISE I
Take a brief passage (two to three paragraphs) from one of your own essays

and rewrite it from three different points of view: in first person, in second person, and finally in third person. This should take no more than ten to fifteen minutes; it is just an experiment to show how point of view can affect your voice. You should not have to change more than a few words per sentence. How does a change in point of view affect the passage?

Exercise 2
Rewrite the same passage in present tense (if it is in past tense) or in past tense (if it is in present tense). If you were consistent in the original draft, you should have to write only one new draft of this passage – but you will have to pay careful attention to each verb. How does change of tense affect the passage?

Exercise 3
Take the same two- to three-paragraph passage and slightly alter key words so that one version is written in a light, humorous tone. Create another version with a formal, serious, or angry tone. Look for words with strong connotations that affect tone. How does this exercise affect the passage?

Exercise 4
Consider the following excerpts from the telecourse.

Excerpt 1. Richard Aregood, a writer of fiery newspaper editorials, characterizes his tone and his writing voice this way:

> I believe in Sicilian-style anger in editorials. They should be served cold. It should be just laid out there in the coldest possible way. Ferocity drives people away. But a cold shield of anger is effective, because people will then sympathize with you rather than cringe in your face. You're not frightening them quite as much as you would be if you were yelling at them.

Excerpt 2. Conservative talk-radio commentator Rush Limbaugh characterizes his voice and tone this way:

> I strive not to be emotional. At least, I don't want to be predominantly emotional ... because I think that, when used by itself, it's [emotion is] phony. I think it's very disingenuous. I try not to use any at all. I am obsessed or, that's the wrong word, I guess. But I'm primarily focused on the logical. I love the analogy technique. I, of course, am the epitome of ethics.

Excerpt 3. Al Franken characterizes his own voice this way:

> I find that a lot of people live life to be indignant ... and I find that fairly unattractive. That's why I became a wiseass – because, to me, it's an easy way to make ethical points ... a more attractive way to make ethical points. Anger and humor go together a lot. I don't think of myself as an angry person, but I think it's appropriate to be angry at certain kinds of things.

Notice that each of these people in this telecourse program has an identifiable attitude. The tone (or attitude) shows through in their speaking voices and in their writing voices. Whether you identify with (or dislike) the various people featured in this telecourse, consider the tone they evoke as they describes their own voices. Do you agree with each writer's self-characterization? After evaluating the tone of each person in the program, consider your own voice. Does your spoken voice (and your writer's voice) ring with conviction? Does it come across as flat and academic? What other words might you use to describe your voice? Would most people characterize your attitude? How much does the tone of your spoken or writing voice change in various situations? Give two examples.

Exercises related to *A Community of Writers*

A Community of Writers emphasizes three exercises as the main assignment. The textbook asks you to:

1. Gather and analyze writing samples that illustrate different voices you have already developed.
2. Revise a sample of your writing with special attention to voice.
3. Write an essay that explores your various writing and speaking voices.

Read Workshop 5 (pp. 121–132) for a detailed explanation of these exercises.

Quick writing exercise

Your instructor may ask you to do a quick focused freewrite about the topic you are studying in this unit. Those of you who are taking the course through a distance-learning system may be encouraged to share your thoughts in a discussion thread or to post your ideas on an Internet bulletin board. If you are writing your thoughts out by hand in a process journal, you might use these questions to kick-start ideas. This is a freewriting exercise that will not be graded. You can use any of the following questions to stimulate your thoughts about discovering your writer's voice:

If you have a writer's voice, what words would you use to describe it? Are you sarcastic, angry, or funny? Are you serious and formal? What point of view do you prefer – first person, second person, or third person? Why? Is there a writer whose voice you can identify easily? What makes this writer stand out? What did you pick up most from the telecourse program on voice? Of those speaking in the program, whose voice made the most impact on you? Why? Do you think this telecourse guest will have a writer's voice similar to his or her speaking voice?

You may use the questions in the "Process Journal" section of Workshop 5, "Voice" (p. 133), in *A Community of Writers* as an additional source of inspiration for this quick writing exercise.

Exercise just for fun

Several exercises in *A Community of Writers* encourage students to emulate the voices of others – by writing like someone else or speaking a passage out loud, as if a different author had written it.

As a variation of these exercises, read any passage of your own work out loud while attempting to mimic the voice of Aregood, Franken, Limbaugh, or another writer featured in the program.

Just for fun, take a passage of your own writing and attempt to rewrite it in the imaginary voice of Aregood, Franken, Limbaugh, Dave Barry, Sue Grafton, or another writer prominent in the telecourse.

Revision exercise

This exercise is related to the exercise in *A Community of Writers* in which Elbow and Belanoff ask you to "Revise a sample of your own writing, with special attention to voice." Select an essay that needs revising. Determine tense, tone and point of view and the related verbs, pronouns, and adjectives that work best for your essay. Revise the entire piece, taking care to make tone, tense and point of view consistent throughout the entire essay in the final draft. This exercise works particularly well for any essay that has been criticized for "inconsistent tone," "shifting point of view," or "changing tense."

Here is an absurd example that manages to shift tone, point of view, and tense three times in one silly run-on sentence: *__I'm__ giddy to go shopping at the mall, but __you__ might have to be careful about prices aimed at shopoholics, because __this girl__ had to watch __her__ budget, and fight the price-gouging capitalist-pig store owners.*

While most people comfortably tolerate such shifting within informal conversations, it is not appropriate for most types of writing. This kind of shifting can be very distracting and confusing to the reader. For example, some students feel the need to slip into a brief passage of informal first-person voice ("I believe") or second-person asides ("You'll never know") in on otherwise formal academic essay written from a third-person point of view ("According to most experts"). Elbow and Belanoff would say that such papers have differing voices that "collide." You may recognize similar shifts in your own early drafts, though the shifts may not be as absurd as the exaggerated example above.

Additional reading

Read the passage from Frank McCourt's Pulitzer Prize-winning novel, *Angela's Ashes*, reprinted in the appendix to this *Telecourse Study Guide*. He reads this passage in the telecourse program to illustrate the "voice" he discovered. What techniques does McCourt use to achieve the effect he desires – the voice of a child? Notice the unorthodox punctuation – exactly as published in the book. Why would McCourt, an English teacher for twenty-seven years, punctuate his book this way? What rules, emphasized in this chapter of the *Telecourse Study Guide* does McCourt *break* in order to achieve this effect? How would you characterize McCourt's voice? How does McCourt use punctuation, point of view, tense, attitude, and connotative language to create a distinctive tone and voice?

Quick Review

1. Which is not a true statement about voice?
   a. Audience has a big effect on voice.
   b. We use different "tones" of voice at different times.
   c. Writing can produce some of the same subtleties of "voice" as spoken language.
   d. Every writer has only one true voice.
   e. People can become just as comfortable when writing as they are when speaking.

2. To affect a writing voice, which parts of a sentence should be selected with care?
   a. pronouns
   b. adjectives with strong connotative meanings
   c. verbs
   d. none of the above
   e. all of the above

3. College instructors are likely to caution you against
   a. use of a formal voice
   b. use of an informal voice
   c. collision, or mixing of informal and formal voices in the same work
   d. none of the above
   e. all of the above

4. Speakers in the telecourse characterize the "writer's voice" in which way?
   a. A unique aspect of personality, almost "like a fingerprint."
   b. "There's a very important sort of technical or skill side to the creation of what we end up calling voice."
   c. "Voice is like a muscle.... You have to work it."
   d. None of the above.
   e. All of the above.

5. Which statement reflects an idea expressed in the telecourse program and Study Guide chapter?

   a. We all have more than one persona; each is genuine.

   b. Think about the appropriate language, diction, and style for the particular audience you are writing for.

   c. The less you write, the longer it takes you to find your voice.

   d. None of the above.

   e. Each of the above.

"Students must take care, when watching this program, not to get caught up in just learning a formula for step-by-step explanation in this type of writing. The writer must truly understand the process before trying to explain it, or it's just a big waste of time."

MIN-ZHAN LU, Drake University

Introduction to the Topic

If you've ever wanted to rent a flame thrower to crispy fry a new computer and the accompanying owner's manual, you've been the victim of poor process analysis writing. You know the style:

Reinitialize your hard drive, by pressing and holding the delete/tab/bomb keys at the same time. Before you do, make sure to back up your files.

Of course, the confused computer user has just erased three years of work in the pause between the first and second sentence.

Process analysis, also called "how-to writing," is common in our society, but few of us know how to do it well. It is fun to laugh at (and burn) poorly written owner's manuals and other types of how-to writing – until the day you also have to write in this style.

It is essential to learn how to compose effective process analysis writing. As a student, you might be asked to describe the process of an enzyme reaction in a biology lab – or to explain how to build a certain type of structure on an exam in a civil engineering class – or to discuss how a cultural revolution evolved, step by step, in a country you are studying in history class.

As a wage earner, you will certainly be asked to produce this kind of writing. Your employers won't ask you to write a "process analysis" essay for homework – but they might ask you to write an analysis of an event or to prepare instructions for a new employee.

Much of this writing will be just like the name implies: You must analyze a process and then communicate each step to someone who does not understand the procedure. Through the writing, you must explain *how* to replicate the process.

As you study this style in your English class, remember: These are not merely academic exercises. In the telecourse program, you'll notice that editors of *Popular Woodworking*, the *Artist's Magazine,* and *Writer's Digest* publish how-to writing more than any other style. And proficiency in process analysis is required in many professions. In the program, you'll see marine biologists, football players, and engineers applying these skills.

Elbow and Belanoff note on page 49 of *A Community of Writers*, "In scientific or technical writing, a process essay explains how to do something (e.g., how to go about making water from hydrogen and oxygen). But process essays are not limited to these disciplines. You can write about the steps to go through, for example, to cook a particular meal or prepare a garden plot in the spring – or to do something less concrete such as convincing a parent or teacher of something."

In the closing of this telecourse program, Chitra Divakaruni of Foothill College suggests the reason how-to books are often found among the bestsellers is because people *want* to read this style. Divakaruni also predicts that, no matter what your academic major, you will be asked to compose a variation of process analysis writing at some point in your education.

Assuming that her prediction is true, your learning of the thinking/writing strategy starts here.

Learning Objectives

After viewing the telecourse program and finishing the writing assignments, you will know how process analysis writing (also called how-to writing) is used in various academic disciplines and occupations. You will study what works and what doesn't work in this type of writing. You will also practice the techniques of process analysis and how-to writing, using the examples provided in the telecourse program as models.

Before Viewing

Before you study process analysis writing, think of the best and worst instructions you have ever read. Consider what helped you in the good samples of this writing, and try to figure out what frustrated you in the worst examples. Remember situations where you were asked to write directions for how to do something, and assess your effectiveness.

While Viewing

You will encounter several types of people in this program who use process analysis writing, including a scientist, a professional athlete, an engineer, a musician, a woodworker, and an artist. Consider how different the purpose and audience are for each writer; imagine the challenges you would have writing for a similar audience. Listen for tips, techniques, and general advice that would help you compose an essay in this style.

If you have been keeping a "process journal," as recommended in *A Community of Writers* (pp. 14–15), consider how your musings might be considered a type of process analysis, as described in this telecourse.

After Viewing

Consider how this entire telecourse is a study in process analysis – or one extended how-to book about mastering the skills of composition. Apply the skills learned in this unit to an essay, if your instructor gives an assignment where process analysis writing is appropriate.

Viewing Guide

Process analysis writing and "how-to" essays are common in academic writing, personal writing, and professional writing. In the first few segments of this program, you'll see that many different types of writers practice this genre.

Frank McCourt starts the program with an example of how this type of communication is a part of the everyday experience. McCourt reminisces about how he introduced process analysis to his students in Brooklyn, asking them to pretend they were giving directions to an out-of-towner wanting to learn the subway system. The results, he says, were much like many first-draft process analysis essays – filled with gaps where the author made inappropriate assumptions about the reader's knowledge.

The editor of the *Artist's Magazine*, Sandra Carpenter, talks about the need for clear how-to writing in her profession. As she considers freelance submissions to the magazine, she picks up a paintbrush and awkwardly tries to follow directions, saying, "If I can't do it, then it's not going to get across to the reader."

It's clear that this thinking/writing strategy is important in many professions and in personal writing. It is also important in many academic disciplines.

Chitra Divakaruni explains that it is important for a student who is learning process analysis writing "to be able to differentiate between what is absolutely necessary and what are just the frills." In other words, she says, the essay should have a clear distinction between main points and subsidiary points.

Once the paper is organized, she says, lessons already learned about description and storytelling can be applied to the "how-to" essay.

Blending rhetorical modes

As Divakaruni points out, effective process analysis writing combines several of the thinking/writing strategies we have already studied. These writing genres (called "the rhetorical modes" by some teachers) include description, definition, narration, and comparison.

In the video, *Popular Woodworking* editor Steve Shanesy says accurate descriptive writing in his magazine's how-to pieces is difficult but necessary. The reader, Shanesy says, "has to create in his own mind a picture of what it is you're describing; if he doesn't have a picture in his mind, he's lost. He doesn't have a map; he doesn't know where the road goes."

Student Mike Gratton says that the study of process analysis in his English composition course applied directly to his computer science courses. Gratton adds that definition, combined with "how-to" writing is very important when he has to create instruction manuals for the users of new software programs.

Several writers in the program suggest that narrative writing is a good thinking/writing strategy to combine with process analysis writing; storytelling can add a personal touch to the dry step-by-step instructions.

Tom Clark, editor of *Writer's Digest*, says that writers can achieve this friendly tone by telling the story of how they personally learned to do something. But, he warns, it is important not to obscure the directions with the personal anecdotes.

"Many pieces go wrong because the writers spend far too much time talking about their own experiences – rather than explaining to the reader what is going on here." Process analysis, Clark says, "is storytelling – but a very specific, very concrete, very structured story. If I'm building a deck, I don't really care *too* much about the personal experience. I want to know how do I put this board down so it doesn't warp?"

Sequencing step by step

All how-to pieces involve methodically breaking down the individual parts of a process and then explaining them in a logical step-by-step sequence. This is why narrative writing is a parallel skill. Storytelling techniques – coherence, unity, transitions – can ease the reader through the instructions and result in something more than the rote following of numbered steps to a recipe or formula.

"A thorough, descriptive, how-to article is really writing a number of articles within the article – because each step is a little story in and of itself," Steve Shanesy says.

"It involves a great deal of critical thinking to put paragraphs together so that one idea flows into the next logically and that the reader can follow," explains instructor Santi Buscemi. "This is especially important in process analysis; the reader has to know step three completely and clearly before she goes to step four."

If the thought flows through the entire document, so there is no break in logic between various points, it has *coherence*. If all the details in the writing support the main point, the essay has *unity*.

And, as Buscemi says, to create flow, the writer must practice the use of transitional words, transitional phrases, and transitional sentences. The process analysis essay provides a good opportunity to practice transition writing; these are all techniques that are important in any kind of essay.

Knowing the "how to" of a how-to

When writers *know* a process thoroughly, they can effectively explain it. Readers always appreciate advice from someone with years of experience; the veteran expert always has a few secrets or shortcuts to share.

Without depth of experience, a writer must compensate by thoroughly researching the process. As journalist and writing instructor John Morgan Wilson puts it, "The more vague you are and the more you try to get away with not researching and not bringing that detail to your work – people know right away you're faking it. They don't want to read it; they don't believe it. But bring enough detail to your work, suddenly it comes alive; suddenly people want to turn the page."

Additional research is often necessary, even for those who are quite familiar with the process they are explaining.

In the video, musician David Ellefson explains that, even though he had an intense personal knowledge of the ins and outs of the music business (from his many years on the road with his rock band, Megadeth), additional research was still necessary to complete his book *Making Music Your Business*.

"It forced me to put my ego aside and to reach out and say, 'Hey! I know this, but how can I relate this information to an audience in a way that can be simply understood?' Sometimes that required me going back and doing more research – so I knew even more."

Audience and jargon

Ellefson's awareness of the target audience was essential for effective how-to writing, as it is for all writers who compose a process analysis piece. In Ellefson's case, the projected audience was primarily young musicians. The language was specifically designed to resonate with that crowd. If he had ignored his audience members, Ellefson says, they might have perceived the book as condescending.

English instructor Santi Buscemi believes that such respect for the audience is the single most important element in effective process analysis writing.

"The first thing you have to realize is that your audience will probably know much less about your subject than you do," Buscemi says. "Therefore, you're explaining it; you're the expert. You need to define terms, and you *may* have to eliminate jargon."

On the other hand, a high level of jargon (or technical language) will work, if the writing is aimed at members of a professional discourse community familiar with the words of the trade.

"I know a lot of people who love to use the term *jargon* as one of their bogey words – something really negative," says Thomas Hilgers of the Writing Program at the University of Hawaii. "But jargon for an insider is never jargon. It's called 'professional vocabulary.' Jargon is only jargon to an outsider."

Hilgers emphasizes that it is quite important to *teach* the jargon, or professional language, in each academic discipline to improve the student's chances for achieving success.

Examples in the video illustrate how process analysis (and the expected level of skilled language) work in several different professions.

Examples and purpose

First, legendary football coach Bill Walsh and one of his former players, defensive star Keena Turner, discuss how process analysis writing is used in professional sports.

Another football player would have no trouble understanding terms such as *linebacker, receiver, defensive back*, or *quarterback* – all words used by Turner as he describes the process of how a linebacker defends against a star receiver such as Jerry Rice. A different audience – readers who are not necessarily fans – would need even the most obvious terms, such as *defense* and *offense*, clarified.

Awareness of the audience influences the level of professional language. The level of technical language intensifies in the next example, as marine biologist Ku'ulei Rodgers uses technical words and phrases such as *larvae, spat collectors, sample distribution*, and *Pinctada margaritifera*. These are all common professional vocabulary terms for her audience – other marine biologists – and the usage of the jargon is appropriate.

The essay's purpose drives the language – and the writing. In both cases, the writing of the football coach and the scientist aim to explain how to *repeat* a series of steps.

The goal of a coach's writing is to show how star players successfully execute a physical maneuver, so new players can replicate the process; the goal of the scientific research is to analyze a process and show how to replicate scientific procedures to confirm results of an experiment.

Rodgers explains, "The main point of the methods-and-material section of my paper is – if scientists want to replicate your experiment, then they're able to do it precisely the way that you did it. It will eliminate a lot of experimental error."

Her research paper, she says, is "exactly like a how-to manual" – or a process analysis essay.

Summary

In the final example, engineering instructor Ray Rummel tells how to do a metal casting. In the process, you can review many of the key points in this chapter, including how to use description, storytelling, professional language, and step-by-step instructions in a good process analysis.

In the engineering lab, we see an age-stained sign with a list of the key steps a student needs to follow in this potentially dangerous activity. But the list alone won't explain the process without Rummel's storytelling and description.

He starts with a time-honored description technique, using an analogy – comparing metal casting to making ice cubes in a freezer tray – to describe and bring life to the process.

Rummel's professional language and jargon are appropriate for his target audience – engineering students – as he describes the steps with technical terms such as *ingot, crucible*, and *refractory vessel*.

His straightforward step-by-step instructions explain the stages of creating the mold, melting the metal, filling the mold, breaking the mold, and finishing the detail of the metal part in a machining process.

As all good process analysis communication should, Rummel's directions warn students about the most common mistakes. In this case, such a warning is extremely important, since a spill of molten metal could lead to a severe injury.

Finally, Rummel uses storytelling techniques as he recaps and summarizes the process.

"The Egyptians did it six thousand years ago, and we've refined it," he says. "Nothing flies, floats, or rolls without casting either directly in the product – or in the history of the production of the product."

By the time Rummel has finished, even the casual listener has learned something about metal casting.

"What makes a good how-to article is really simple," says Tom Clark of *Writer's Digest*. "That is, you start the piece not knowing how to do something, and you finish the piece and you know about it. You know how to build a deck, how to press flowers, how to clean out a closet, how to manage your money, how to do anything. How-to writing is the most prevalent form of writing today – especially in magazines. It also goes by the name 'service journalism.' It's writing that serves."

Integrating the Text

The brief section on "Expository Essays" (pp. 48–49), also explains why so many teachers assign process and analysis essays – as well as other genres such as comparison/contrast and definition essays. You may have already been assigned to read Workshop 2, "From Private Writing to Public Writing," the section of the textbook that these passages appear in. It is a good idea to look at these passages again, as you consider this telecourse program.

Several essays in the textbook are samples of process analysis writing, such as "What Keeps an Airplane Up?" by Gary Kolnicki (pp. 410–416). Notice that Kolnicki aims one version of the essay at an audience of general readers and the other at teachers and students who know a bit more about physics. These two examples reinforce the points in the telecourse program about knowing your audience, and selecting the appropriate level of professional language (or jargon) in the process analysis.

In addition, *A Community of Writers* contains a series of "how to" essays presented as assignments or exercises. One good example is the assignment about how to make a collage about yourself as a writer (pp. 12–13), where the authors give clear step-by-step directions on how to create such a collage. Notice how Elbow and Belanoff first give a four-paragraph analysis of the process (combining a little definition, narration and description along the way) and then create an easy to follow step-by-step explanation that directs the students how to do the process.

Exercises

Check with your instructor for your formal assignments. You will be asked to do exercises from the *Telecourse Study Guide*.

Exploring process analysis further
EXERCISE 1
Look in the help files of your word-processing program and find some instructions within. Examples of tasks for which you can find instructions might include changing fonts, transforming text to superscript, formatting the spaces between lines, and so forth. Transcribe the given instructions into a document and try to follow them. As you do, provide a written commentary for each step in the instructions. For each step, make sure to pay attention to factors such as the following:

- Is it clearly stated and understandable?

- If not, can you say why it is confusing ?

- What seems to be missing?

- Is it targeted at a beginning or experienced user?

If you are studying this course through a distance-learning software program, you may apply the same exercise to the help files that explain how to access the course.

EXERCISE 2

Take a moment to think of something that you do well. (Don't be modest; everyone has something.) Do a five- to ten-minute freewrite about the process you have decided to describe. Grammar and spelling are not important in this step. You should just try to get down on paper as many factors as you can think of that go into performing the given process.

Later, go through the document you've created and identify the important steps in your process. Transcribe (or cut and paste) the steps into another document, and then order them from first to last in an outline. Fill in the blanks if there are steps missing.

Next, look through the rest of the document and try to identify anything else you left out during the freewrite. These may include common mistakes you've made while performing the task, interesting anecdotes related to it, or warnings about special care needed at certain points. Put these into your outline where they are important for the process you are describing.

Finally, follow through and refine the steps and the related comments to make sure that everything is in the correct order.

EXERCISE 3

Use the outline created in Exercise 2 as a guide for a first draft of a process analysis essay. Begin with a thesis statement that identifies the process that you are describing. Make use of transition words such as *next* and *then* and transitional phrases such as "after you've finished" and "before you continue." This draft can be very rough; like any first draft, you will be using it as a starting point to be refined in later versions.

Exercise just for fun

Research how your favorite dessert is made, and write a process analysis essay version of the recipe and instructions. Make sure your essay is *not just* a recipe. Make sure to tell a story of how you create this dessert. Through the use of this narrative, explain to the reader how to duplicate the results. Be sure to include warnings of how to avoid common mistakes. For a fun conclusion, describe the steps in an exercise routine designed to work off the calories ingested by devouring a double serving of your masterpiece.

Revision exercise

In this exercise you will use the rough draft created in Exercise 3 as a starting point for two different revisions. These will be as follows:

1. Write a version of the essay for a target audience made up of friends who have the same interest in and experience with the process in question as you do.

2. Write a version of the essay geared toward a target audience that hasn't the faintest idea of the ins and outs of the tools and jargon involved.

Quick writing exercise

Over the first few weeks of this course, your teacher may have asked you to try a series of focused freewriting exercises about various aspects of writing that you have been studying. Some of you may have shared your thoughts in discussion threads or on Internet bulletin boards. You may also have kept your responses in a process journal.

As a midsemester exercise, consider the following questions: How are your responses to those exercise like the process analysis writing described in this telecourse program? Can you start to cobble together a process analysis piece about how to write an essay for this class, using the quick writing exercises you have completed by this point in the course? If you have been keeping a "process journal," as recommended in *A Community of Writers* (pp. 14–15), consider how your musings might be considered a type of process analysis, as described in this telecourse. How might this be similar to the "Case Study of Myself as a Writer" essays that Elbow and Belanoff feature in Workshop 16, "Autobiography and Portfolio" (pp. 428–442)?

Exercises related to *A Community of Writers*

EXERCISE 1

Using the information gleaned from the telecourse program, analyze the entire textbook *A Community of Writers* as a process analysis study.

EXERCISE 2

Read the two variations of the essay, What Keeps an Airline Up?" by Gary Kolnicki (pp. 410–416). Using the questions on page 241, analyze the two versions of the essay. How do these two essays work as a process analysis?

EXERCISE 3

Read the assignment on how to make a collage about yourself as a writer (pp. 12–13), Analyze this passage as an example of process analysis writing.

Additional reading

An article by Steve Shanesy, editor of *Popular Woodworking,* is featured in the appendix. As you read this writing sample, list the techniques you recognize from advice given in the program about process analysis writing. Compare this to the process analysis technique used by Ellefson in *Making Music Your Business.* (This is also in the appendix.)

Read Dave Barry's piece in the appendix, "Business Memos." How does

Barry use humor to make his points? How could you use a similar satirical approach to write a process analysis of how to write a successful paper in college?

Much of Bill Walsh's book, *Finding the Winning Edge*, is a process analysis for how to put together a good team. How does the excerpt in the appendix, "Establishing Evaluation Tools," apply lessons learned in this telecourse program about process analysis?

Quick Review

1. Which of the following thinking/writing strategies (or "rhetorical modes") could help in a process analysis essay?
   a. narration techniques (storytelling techniques)
   b. description techniques
   c. definition techniques
   d. all of the above
   e. none of the above

2. Writers in the television series said that a key to good "how-to writing" is
   a. having an inflexible, definitive thesis
   b. quoting reliable sources
   c. clear step-by-step instructions
   d. all of the above
   e. none of the above

3. Though not all careers use process analysis writing, the telecourse showed that it is a valuable skill in
   a. professional sports
   b. the sciences
   c. engineering
   d. all of the above
   e. none of the above

4. The good process analysis writer
   a. uses critical thinking to explain how to do something
   b. needs to learn how to create strong transitions
   c. should be aware of voice
   d. all of the above
   e. none of the above

5. A writer who is creating a "how-to" essay should
   a. always use jargon and professional language to impress the reader with his or her knowledge and mastery of the subject
   b. always use words that just about every reader can understand
   c. select the appropriate level of language and vocabulary for the target audience of the essay
   d. all of the above
   e. none of the above

"I don't believe any writing is going to be good if it's just done in first draft. I think first draft is something that we do, just to see if we have something that's worth going on with. If it is worthwhile, I think we do a second draft – in which case, we take the junk out that doesn't belong and we add things that we didn't get in the first draft. The second draft, at least for me, is similar. The third draft, we have an opportunity finally to polish. If we're lucky, and the muses are with us, maybe we don't have to go beyond third draft. But sometimes it might be twenty drafts before everything is functioning. That's what we're trying to achieve, when we do revisions."

CHARLES JOHNSON
Novelist and instructor, University of Washington

Introduction to the Topic

The revision process is a way to rethink an idea – and a way to learn new ideas. It is *not* simply editing and spellchecking. Part of the process involves cutting away words, sentences, paragraphs, or even entirely superfluous pages. Even if the revision does not require cutting, a radical reshaping of certain passages may be just as important.

This is often painful to the beginning writer, who has labored to produce a paper of the "minimum length" for an assignment.

However, revision is a normal, constructive part of the composition process. You can learn the joy of revising, in the same way a sculptor revels in cutting away excess clay, rock, or wood to reveal the piece of art underneath.

The best writers often rewrite or reshape an original premise in the revision process. In this program, we'll see how the writers and actors at *Mad TV* rethink and revise the main point (or thesis) of their comedy sketch. Experienced writers know that revision includes rethinking their paper's focus, coherence, and unity. Such work requires looking at the effect of the *entire* paper; this is a process many instructors refer to as "global" revision. Much as an ecologist analyzes the health of each stream, river, lake, and ocean of the global environment, revision requires serious consideration of the thesis, topic sentences, and paragraphs.

Good writers often devise ways to reorganize a paper *after* the first few drafts, instead of sticking to an outline written before the drafting stage. In fact, many learn that a good time to outline is actually after the first two or three drafts.

Many successful high school and junior high school students, thanks to their natural talent for writing, were able to pass their courses even when their completed homework assignments were quick first drafts. Most of their "revisions" consisted of a few cosmetic changes in spelling and punctuation. Such students never even considered rethinking the premise or rewriting the paper.

Were you one of those students?

Most of the students in this course will eventually realize that the *process* of writing involves drafting, *revision,* and editing. Successful writers embrace this process as a natural method for creating a better document.

Many of you probably already have a pretty decent document that you are ready to hand in to an instructor for an evaluation. It would be so easy just to say, "This paper is done." But you may discover that what you have is merely a better-than-average first draft.

Learning Objectives

When you finish this instructional unit, you should understand how heavily the best student writers and professionals depend on revision to create excellent work. You will have devised your own strategies to revise – with an understanding that writing is a recursive process, with overlapping stages of invention, drafting, revising, and editing.

If you are an excellent student, you will eventually discover that revision is a state of mind that includes a willingness to revise – from the moment the first word is composed.

These learning objectives work in harmony with the essential premises of Workshop 6, "Drafting and Revising," in *A Community of Writers:*

- Writing is not just a recording of what you've already thought, but a way of creating new ideas on the basis of old ideas.
- Most of what we see in print has been revised.
- Revising asks you to focus on what others can help you see and add.
- Revising is hard work.

Before Viewing

Before formally studying this subject, reconsider your own personal relationship with the revision process, by answering the following questions: Do you usually submit to an instructor work that is essentially a first draft? Are you reluctant to cut passages in your papers that don't work, simply because you invested time in creating them? Have your papers in the past included entire sections that wandered from the main point? How did your instructors react to your papers? Are you up for the challenges of significantly revising papers already drafted for this class? What do you consider a draft, and what do you consider a final paper – worthy of presenting to your instructor, your employer, or your peers?

Read the "Main Assignment Preview" of Workshop 6, "Drafting and Revising," in Elbow and Belanoff's *A Community of Writers* (pp. 149–150).

While Viewing

Observe various revision strategies recommended by instructors, professionals, and students in the telecourse. Notice the strategies that will work best for you. Learn the various stages of writing where revision can be applied to your composition process. Think about how this statement from comedy writer Scott King relates to your own understanding of writing: "Writing isn't about turning in that sheet of paper. You've got to love the process. And part of that process is rewriting and revising."

Connect that sentiment to the philosophy about drafting and revising, as explained by Elbow and Belanoff in Workshop 6, "Drafting and Revising" (pp. 149–188), in which they emphasize that the process of drafting and revising is a way of building or discovering new ideas – it is not just a way of recording what you already think.

After Viewing

Read through the main assignment of *A Community of Writers* (p. 154) and consider the three levels of revision and how to apply them to a particular piece of your own writing.

Look over the exercises in this chapter of the *Telecourse Study Guide*. These exercises are designed to help you experiment with a variety of approaches to revising an essay. Become aware of your own attitude and practices regarding revision – and consider how you might carry forward new lessons about drafting, revising, and editing to improve your work in writing challenges beyond this course.

Viewing Guide

Why thoroughly revise your papers?

A common tendency of most students is to simply get the assignment over with. But the most successful students and professional authors learn that *serious* revision (not merely surface-level fixing of misspelled words or awkward sentences) is an important aspect of good writing. Even the best students need to learn to revise.

It's a challenge for an instructor to convince students who did well in high school to revise in college; these students have been rewarded with decent grades for papers that would be considered early drafts in more rigorous environments. Still, as the stakes get higher in upper-division classes and in the workplace, even "natural" writers learn to incorporate revision into their writing process.

California State University English instructor Thomas Fox explains, "One of the most difficult things for any writing teacher to do is to help students do a major revision on a piece, once they've done a good job with their draft.

"Especially with the good students, it's hard to have them go back and rethink it, rewrite it, add complete new paragraphs, and do – from beginning to end – a new draft. Once you have that great first draft, students want to breathe a sigh of relief and say, 'Oh, I did a good job.' But actually, at that point is when you have the opportunity for the *most* learning."

Beginning writers might take some comfort in knowing that famous writers – even those whose work reads as if it were composed spontaneously – spend a great deal of time in the revision stage. A good example is humorist Dave Barry, who explains in the telecourse program that "my whole writing process is not writing at all. It's revising. I'm revising before I even finish the sentence."

This attitude toward revision is as important in academic writing as it is for novelists, journalists, and humor columnists. Marty Wallace, a graduate student in chemistry, says in the telecourse program, "From a chemist's point of view, it's all rewriting. It's rewriting and rewriting and rewriting. Technical papers, particularly, are submitted to a journal and then they're peer-reviewed. None of them are ever simply accepted. Somebody will say, 'I'd like you to elaborate on this a little bit more' or somebody may find a technical error. There will always be a rewrite."

Critical thinking and revision

Writers who embrace the revision process eventually realize that *rethinking* the paper is part of the learning – or critical thinking process. (For a more complete discussion of critical thinking, see Chapter 23.) The process of drafting and revising and *redrafting* is a way to discover flaws, new ideas, and new conclusions.

Scientists often use revision in their research work. They start with a hunch, perform experiments, analyze the results, and revise their original ideas to reflect their new discoveries. Through analysis of experimental results, the original theory (or hypothesis) may be modified several times, until it is clear that other scientists around the world can confirm the conclusions by repeating the experiment in similar conditions.

Student writers often participate in a similar process. They propose a thesis – and then research the topic in the library and on the Internet. A writer with an open mind will often modify the thesis, and reshape the essay through the revision process, as more data are collected.

Whitlow Au, marine biologist at the Institute of Marine Biology, Hawaii, explains how a scientist views revision. "Generally, you need to start off with a hypothesis, because it gives you direction in terms of how do you proceed with your experiments. But then you also have to be very flexible.... The data you're collecting or the observations you're making *may* indicate that the hypothesis is not accurate. And you have to be flexible enough to begin to revise your hypothesis and begin to observe further and try to refine the whole process – so that eventually you'll make the proper kind of observations that support an accurate hypothesis."

According to novelist Charles Johnson, the work of a fiction writer is not that different.

"I have an idea, like a scientist has an idea," Johnson explains. "It's a hypothesis. How do you test it? You go in the lab. The scientist has a Bunsen burner, has chemicals – he comes out after his experiment, and maybe his hypothesis is disproven. Maybe the experiment was taking a direction he didn't know it was going to take. But he's open to see, in that process of *discovery*, where the hypothesis is going to lead. The same thing is true in fiction. It really is a process of discovery and you may find your ideas transformed by the end. Just as a scientist's ideas are transformed by the end of a laboratory experiment."

Revision at the thesis level

For beginning writers and professionals alike, it takes courage to admit your original ideas may be wrong. That is why most instructors recommend starting off with a "working thesis" – knowing that the main premise may change. Though the idea of a working thesis might sound like a classroom exercise that you'll immediately forget once you graduate, it's part of the process all good writers use.

The actors and writers at *Mad TV* talk about the revision process when the main point of a comedy skit is not working. In the business of comedy, the main point is called "the joke" – but the basic premise is the same as a thesis: It is sentence or two that summarizes the whole point. Emily Spivey, a staff writer, explains, "It's all about, 'What's the joke?' You want to get that out as soon, as soon as you can – like, page one. The first couple of lines.

111

'What's the joke?' It's terrifying when you've written a whole sketch and somebody will say to you, 'What's the joke?' And you know you've gone very wrong."

Pat Kilbane, a cast member and writer for the sketch comedy team, explains the actor's view: "That's always a tough thing, when you look at a sketch, and it's not working. You have to decide, 'Do we *just* have a structure problem here?' Certainly, it's kind of a sad thing, when you have a real structure problem, something that's just profoundly wrong with the sketch, but people are trying to polish it up with little lines here and there. Maybe it helps, but the real issue [the main point or the joke] hasn't been addressed."

Kim Stanley Robinson, a science fiction writer who has won every major award his genre has to offer, relates a similar experience he had in writing an editorial for the *New York Times*:

"I'm not an editorial writer; I'm a short story writer and a novelist. As a fiction writer, writing an editorial, I had no idea what I was doing.

"I only had twenty-four hours to write this. The first twelve hours, I revised the first version of this essay fifty times and it was always bad. Finally, I said to myself, 'There's a problem here; it's not just a matter of tinkering with sentences. There's a fundamental problem with the original idea of how to introduce this whole topic.' I finally just threw it out and started over again."

In these examples, the writers used the critical thinking process to change the basic premise of a piece. It is much like the process a scientist uses to modify a hypothesis, if the evidence shows the original theory is not quite on target.

Writers who have the audacity (and courage) to modify their original ideas with knowledge gained through reading, research, and thought are involved in the process of using their *brains*. English instructor Santi Buscemi explains how the process often works, when his best students apply critical thinking to an original idea as part of the revision process.

"The students start with a preliminary thesis statement, or working thesis. Then they'll write a paper that won't fit the thesis statement. That's OK! The drafting is part of a process teachers call 'discovery.'"

The real work of the writing is in the thought process at this stage; it is not just in the typing out of original ideas. Students start to *learn* exactly they want to say, as they draft.

Revision at the outline level

In the telecourse Betsy Klimasmith, English instructor at the University of Washington, suggests revising by playing with an outline after you have finished an early draft.

If you've already written a draft of the paper, and you realize that your ideas aren't fitting into a natural outline, Klimasmith suggests this stage of revision is a good point to consider the following questions:

- Does the paper need to be completely reorganized?
- Are certain ideas so out of context that they need to be eliminated?
- Are some passages so underdeveloped that you need to do more research?
- Is more original thinking needed in a passage that is mostly dominated by quotes?

Rethinking the paper at the outline level is a good way to address all of these questions.

Peter Elbow of the University of Massachusetts also suggests that the thesis isn't the only thing that might change during a thorough revision.

"The macro-revising stage is where it's so helpful to make an outline," Elbow says. This is an idea that contradicts the typical writing strategy of making the outline before the first draft of the paper is written. Elbow's approach assumes that the writer will discover ideas while drafting.

According to Elbow, writers should not start by making an outline. Too often, he says, a writer tries to make an outline when only a few of the important points that support the thesis have been revealed.

Elbow says to consider outlines as a "wonderful way to revise" after the first draft has created a "big fat mess" of raw ideas that far exceeds the minimum length of the paper.

While this approach might not work for all beginning writers, the premise certainly makes sense. Revision works best if the writer has generated a lot of material – more than is needed for the final document. Elbow's approach to revision goes one step further than a traditional outline; such outlines are essentially an abstract sketch of the paper done with word headings and incomplete phrases. Elbow suggests a variation of the skeleton outline in chapter 12, "Organizing Devices."

"If you have an outline that *just* consists of words and phrases, it's not forcing you to examine your assertion," Elbow says. "But put those ideas into complete *sentences*, with verbs that *say* something ... then you have a list of assertions. Then you can make an outline; then you can decide what order they go in."

Revision and focusing sentences

Some writers find that it is not necessary to write out a detailed outline, complete with Roman numerals, capital letters, Arabic numerals, and so forth. Instead, they tinker with a skeleton outline that is made simply from focusing sentences that summarize each subsection of the paper. This approach can work as a way to organize before the first draft or as a method to revise between early drafts and the final draft.

Each approach differs. Some writers create a topic sentence to focus every paragraph. Others might create five key sentences in a ten-page paper, as if they had a thesis sentence to summarize each two-page section.

Those who use this technique to revise try to identify key focusing sentences (or topic sentences) that summarize each subpoint of the paper, just before the final draft. If they discover a section that has not been summarized, they inject an organizing sentence that helps focus the main point of that portion of the paper.

As Betsy Klimasmith points out in the telecourse program, "The paper needs ideas to keep it together. Throwing facts around doesn't really help support an argument; the evidence has to be organized to support a claim." That organization most often comes in the form of a topic sentence or focusing sentence that ties the evidence to the main thesis.

Of course, sometimes a student discovers the topic sentence he or she creates during the revision process does not support the thesis. That means it's time to cut a paragraph or an entire section.

The joy of cutting

"If you've got a topic sentence or idea that really doesn't fit, sometimes the hardest thing to do is to cut it – especially if you're worried about writing a five-page paper and you're only on page four and one-half," Klimasmith explains.

Students who try to disguise this type of problem are easily spotted by an instructor, Klimasmith jokes, when they attempt to turn in a paper of the minimum length by using large margins and 14-point type to make the document look longer.

"If you're in that predicament, you probably need to do some more writing," she says. However, that writing should *not* be generated around a topic sentence that clearly doesn't support the thesis – or main point – of the essay.

Many writers discover, after they have generated a surplus of material, that cutting unnecessary paragraphs is actually an enjoyable process. Scriptwriter and novelist Peter Farrelly is one. "I prefer revising to actually putting it down. To come to a blank computer screen ... every time I look at it I think, 'Oh, God ... I've got *nothing* here now; I have to create something.' Once I've written a few pages, I love going back and making it better. It will be too long; then I go back and chop and cut.... That's the fun part for me."

Revision and peer feedback

Peer feedback is one of the biggest helps in the revision process, because you can test how your writing works with an actual reader who must make sense of your essay.

Elbow explains several stages of the peer review/revision process, using this scenario: "If you tell me what you liked, I learn quite a lot about how readers react to a text. If you tell me what you heard me *almost* saying – in other words, some of the ideas hovering around the edges of my piece or some of the implications of my piece – I learn a lot, and it also gives me ideas to use when I revise my piece. You show me some ideas that I didn't quite have, but I almost had. But you haven't criticized me – yet. So then we get to the stage where you can actually tell me which parts *didn't* work so well for you, and you can try and explain why – and I do the same for you."

An honest assessment of audience reaction is a vital aspect of the revision process. Peer feedback is part of revision – both on a campus and in professional settings. In the telecourse program, we see revision taking place with the writers and actors at *Mad TV* and with the students at Shasta College. This is work in every phase of revision: thesis level, topic sentence and focus sentence level, and outline level. We even see revision during the editing phase.

Revision and editing

One key concept emphasized by both the textbook and the telecourse is that editing and revision are not the same thing. This is a concept that many students do not understand when they first enroll in an English composition course.

Kimberly Wise, an English instructor at Cypress College, tells how she talks to her students about the difference between editing and revision. "You can't procrastinate," Wise says. "You've got to have so many hours for the prewriting phase and so many hours for the writing phase. You let it get cold on you, and *then* come back and revise. Revise does *not* mean spellcheck." Revision also does not mean fixing a few sentences with grammar problems. This is a position that Elbow and Belanoff support. In *A Community of Writers* they state: "many students equate revision with 'correcting mechanics' or copyediting. Experienced writers never confuse the two" (p. 152).

Still, it's never too late to revise – even during the editing process. Writing is a cycle. The best writers draft, revise, and edit and then – once again – draft, revise, and edit. A writer might be thinking about the revising and editing while drafting or about *additional* drafting and revising while editing.

It should be noted that trimming away the excess is one form of "editing." It is hard to take this aspect of editing seriously, though, if your draft is only the minimum length required by the assignment.

"I think my best advice for revising (and editing) is do more generating," Peter Elbow says, with a laugh. "If you're trying to write a three-page essay, and all you have is three and a half pages, you can't throw too much away. If your essay has to be three pages long, generate fifteen pages."

But then, Elbow says, "It's helpful to make a distinction between revising and *copy editing*. Copy editing is the fixing of sentences and getting things correct. There's three activities and they don't always come in stages ... though, it helps to *emphasize* them in stages – generating, revising, and copy editing.

115

"If we talk about them as distinct stages, that makes some theorists uncomfortable," Elbow cautions. "Those theorists may say, 'Well, wait a minute – writing is recursive. You write a sentence, and then you revise its thought, and then sometimes you revise its grammar or spelling right there – and you go back and forth.' In other words, people don't write in this kind of rigid way, 'First I'm going to generate, then I'm going to revise. Then I'm going to copy edit.' Most people mix it up a little bit."

Two views – a teacher and a student

The producers of this telecourse caught several amusing – and important – moments on camera that contrasted the views that instructors and students have of the revision process.

Butte College student Xavier Pino expressed a common view:

"I don't revise very much. My first draft is pretty much my final draft, other than a few grammatical changes and a couple of semicolons and things like that. I'll try to make sure it sounds good, it flows well. But I feel like ... what initially comes out of my head, that's what comes out. And if I revise it too much, I feel like ... what I originally said gets kind of jumbled up and lost. So I like the original thing that comes out of my head."

Pino's history instructor, Charles Turner, talked later in the day about this student's work, without knowing what Xavier told our cameras.

"Xavier is the kind of student I love to have in a classroom. He has a lot of life experience. He's the kind of student I would call a raw student, and he comes in with all this excitement and enthusiasm ... but, not necessarily the writing skills that he needs to have at this level. We can work with a student like that; we have that creativity that's there and can help him refine it into having a clearly defined thesis and organized paragraphs. He's going to have to get a little away from the free-flow type writing and be a little more structured. He needs to understand what topic sentences are to his paragraphs – and needs all the topic sentences to relate to his thesis statement – those kinds of structural things. The revision skills are not quite there yet. But the ideas, the excitement, the enthusiasm are there. And that's the essence of a good creative writer."

Summary

In the telecourse, Scott King, staff writer for *Mad TV*, summarizes what most of the instructors, writers, and students in this program are trying to get at, when they talk about revision. He explains that a successful writer learns to enjoy the *cycle* of drafting, revision, editing, drafting, and revising again, in the same way an experienced traveler learns to enjoy the journey as much as the arriving at the destination.

"You've got to love the process of it," King says. "Writing isn't about turning in that sheet of paper; it's the actual act of writing. And part of that is rewriting and revising – taking a teacher's notes or a peer's notes – and loving that process. It's like [physical] exercise. It's not, 'Now I've got a body; now I'm done.' You're always exercising to stay healthy; I think it's the same thing with writing. And I think the best writers always are about just revising all the time."

Integrating the Text

Workshop 6, "Drafting and Revising" (pp. 149–187), teaches that most of what you read has been revised, that revision is hard work, and that revision is *not just editing* – it is *rethinking* what you have accomplished in your early drafts.

A Community of Writers encourages students to start with a "quick and dirty" draft that emphasizes content over correctness. This allows students to generate much more than they need for a final draft, so that the cutting phase of revision will not be as painful.

For example, Elbow and Belanoff caution against spending too much time on a first paragraph because, "It's pointless to waste time on introductions which you will have to discard" (p. 151).

The authors suggest that you will probably discover, while drafting, that you *really* want to say something other than the original idea that you started with.

This fits with the telecourse advice to learn how to develop a flexible "working thesis" that is destined to change.

On pages 153 to 154, Elbow and Belanoff use an analogy to divide the process of revising into three distinct categories: rethinking, or changing the bones; reworking, or changing the muscles; and copyediting, or changing the skin.

This approach is very similar to various aspects of revision emphasized in the telecourse program – especially the concept of revising with a "skeleton outline" of topic sentences explained by Betsy Klimasmith, of the University of Washington.

Elbow and Belanoff also address the relationship between revising and grammar (pp. 161–163), noting, "The real problem with errors in usage is that they force readers into giving attention to the words instead of the meaning."

Finally, don't forget to read the extraordinary examples of essays at various stages of revision in Elbow and Belanoff (pp. 164–187). These sample essays show, stage by stage, how several authors went through the process of brainstorming, drafting, revising – and revising again – to create a finished result. The draft documents (and resulting revisions) range from case-studies of student compositions to professional articles. They provide an inspiration to students who still believe that more experienced writers are somehow able to bang out their best work in the first draft.

Exercises

Check with your instructor for your formal assignments. You will be asked to do exercises from the *Telecourse Study Guide*.

Exploring revision further

EXERCISE 1

Take any essay you are about to hand in to any instructor in any class. (This does not just have to be for an English composition class.) Write down the most important point (or most important sentence) from each paragraph on a sheet of paper. Make sure to use complete sentences.

If your paper is well constructed, the results will be a skeleton outline, or sketch, of your essay – starting with a thesis sentence that is followed by the topic sentence of each paragraph. If the sentences are blended in paragraph form, instead of an outline or list form, the sentences should read like a brief abstract or summary of your paper.

If the skeleton outline (or abstract) does not read coherently, and seems to lurch from idea to idea, an additional revision might be required.

EXERCISE 2

Take a document that you are drafting, and look at each *paragraph* to see if it works as a unit separate from the rest of the document. Consider the strength of the topic sentence in each paragraph. Consider whether the other parts of each paragraph are *unified* in supporting the primary point of the paragraph – and the main claim of the paper. Cut out (or rewrite) any spare sentences that seem to waver from the main point of the paragraph. After looking at the individual paragraphs as separate units, see if they all work as a whole. Does each paragraph connect to the next, with a smooth transition? If not, take two troublesome paragraphs and practice writing the ending of the first and beginning of the next so that the transition is more natural. After revising at the paragraph level, look at the essay as a whole. Does the paper need to be reorganized at the outline level? Do the individual paragraphs support your original premise? Does your original premise (main point or thesis) need to be revised to fit what you have *learned* from writing the essay?

EXERCISE 3

This exercise will take a bit of critical thinking. Consider challenging the assumptions behind Exercise 1. Is it possible that your paper will read well without a topic sentence in each paragraph? For example, if the paper is a longer document, could two or three or even four paragraphs be tied together by a "controlling sentence" that creates an effect similar to a topic sentence? If this will work, how would this new approach affect your revision of the paper?

Exercise just for fun

One interesting moment in the telecourse program is when student Mike Gratton admits his best revision came when a computer crashed and forced him to completely rethink a paper. This might seem slightly amusing, until – as it inevitably will – the same thing happens to you!

Here's an exercise to accompany your next experience, when a disc with your nearly completed paper becomes damaged, when your hard drive dies, or when a virus wipes out a draft.

First, go outside and yell at the moon. (This usually happens at night, just before your paper is due. By the way, other methods of frustration release will also work: Chop some wood, use your computer monitor for a discus, run two miles, etc.) When you are finished, try to look at this disaster as an opportunity to force you to revise.

Second, when the frustration is out of your system, sit down with a pad of paper and recreate as much of your essay, term paper, or response to a take-home exam as you can remember. Your brain's memory will, no doubt, be more reliable than the computer's. However, your brain will also do something a computer data *recovery* program will never do: it will help you revise the document, as you reconstruct it. That might include a new ordering of topic sentences, an improved thesis, better flow from paragraph to paragraph, and a stronger conclusion.

Third, find a computer that *works*, and type the document back in. (If you use the suspect computer again, devise a strategy to save or back up as you build the essay.) As you type in the essay that you have reconstructed from your memory, continue to revise. In almost all cases, the resulting document will be better than the original. Often, this also takes less time than desperate efforts to salvage a damaged disc or rescue data from a dead hard drive.

Quick writing exercise

Your instructor may ask you to do a quick focused freewrite about the topic you are studying in this unit. Those of you who are taking the course through a distance-learning system may be encouraged to share your thoughts in a discussion thread or to post your ideas on an Internet bulletin board. If you are writing your thoughts out by hand in a process journal, you might use these questions to stimulate ideas. This is a freewriting exercise that will not be graded. You can use any of the following questions to help you think about the way you approach revision:

- Are you one of those college students who *usually* turns in a first draft?

- Do you think: "This is just a draft," when you begin a paper, or are you trying to create a final draft in the first pass, so you won't have to revise?

119

- Have you ever cut an entire paragraph (or page) from an essay? Have you ever changed the entire point of an essay, "re-visioning" the entire piece, starting with the main premise, or thesis?
- Did the telecourse program give you any new ideas about revision, or is this same old stuff you have been hearing from teachers for years?

You may use the questions with the "Process Journal" section of Workshop 6, "Drafting and Revising" (p. 161), in *A Community of Writers* as an additional source of inspiration fro this quick writing exercise.

Workshop 6, "Drafting and Revising" (pp. 149–187), teaches that the processes of drafting and revising should be intertwined. In other words, you should *assume* you will revise, even as you create the early drafts. At this point in the course, you have already been encouraged to draft and revise by your teachers, and some teachers may be encouraging you to draft and revise some *more*, on the same essays you started early in the semester. You can only become expert in this process with practice.

The main assignment in Workshop 6 encourages you to start with "quick and dirty" writing and then move through a three-step process to revise the early draft by rethinking, reshaping, and, finally proofreading the work. When you start your next essay, follow the guidelines and see how this approach compares to the way you usually compose a paper.

Additional reading

Several student essays are featured in the appendix. They reflect different levels of writing ability, and several of the papers could benefit from revision. If you were assigned to revise any of the samples, how would you work with Gregory Andrus, Corie Cushnie, Ethlyn Manning, and Francine Taylor to improve their papers?

Quick Review

1. A good writer considers revision at
   a. the thesis level
   b. the topic sentence level
   c. the outline level
   d. all of the above
   e. none of the above

2. Revision can happen
   a. during the drafting process
   b. during the editing process
   c. through peer feedback
   d. all of the above
   e. none of above

3. According to Elbow,
   a. Writing is not just a recording of what you've already thought but a way of creating new ideas on the basis of old ideas.
   b. Revising asks you to focus on what others can help you see and add.
   c. Most of what we see in print has been revised.
   d. Experienced writers never confuse "correcting mechanics" with revision.
   e. All of the above.

4. An excellent writer in a composition class
   a. always sticks to the thesis, starting with the first draft
   b. has little in common with writers in the sciences
   c. can start with a working thesis that is much like a scientist's hypothesis, or experimental hunch
   d. none of the above
   e. all of the above

5. As a student giving peer feedback, you can help
   a. by just telling the writer what you liked
   b. by telling the writers what you heard them *almost* saying
   c. by telling the writers what didn't work for you
   d. all of the above
   e. none of the above

"The writing that you have to do in these cases is much like the writing you have to do in any other case; you have to really speed it up. You can do the whole writing process, *except revision*, in the ten minutes or half an hour or ninety minutes that you use to write this essay. You brainstorm, you list what you know, you organize it briefly, you draft it, and you leave a teeny bit of time to go back and make sure you didn't make terrible editing mistakes."

THOMAS FOX, California State University, Chico

Introduction to the Topic

When students learn about writing strategies in English composition, they are usually given several weeks to invent, draft, and revise a paper. This leisurely pace is good for creativity and "thinking on paper." The extra time allows the instructor to nurture the learning experience.

Outside of your freshman composition course, however, your writing experiences might be quite different. A history instructor might slap down an exam and ask you to pound out a comparison-and-contrast essay on the difference between the Russian Revolution and the American Revolution in fifty minutes – *after* you have answered twenty-five multiple-choice questions.

Your instructor in a biology, philosophy, computer science, engineering (or plug in a course title related to your major) class might ask you to write a take-home position paper in two days.

The stakes for performing well with writing on the job could be even higher. Deliver, and you get a raise; fail, and you're back to running the fry machine at the Greaseburger.

These writing challenges may approximate the *form* of assignments you get in a composition course, but the writing pace and stressful environment hardly resemble the relatively nonthreatening confines of your English classroom. Can you apply any of the techniques learned in this course to these other tension-filled writing tasks?

Definitely.

The learning curve of any English composition course is much like the early days of learning how to play a guitar, shoot a basketball, or drive a car. The student learns each individual step at a relaxed pace.

When it comes time to rip off a few hot licks at a concert, shoot a basket with the game on the line, or negotiate a freeway in the family sedan, the lessons learned at leisure click together.

The same will happen with your writing. With practice, you'll be able to apply the lessons learned in this course at many times the speed you are using them now. With time and experience, the writing will even be better, even though you will produce text in a fraction of the time.

The first step toward that goal starts now.

Learning Objectives

Students who complete this unit should start building techniques, strategies, and habits that are, essentially, warp-speed applications of the advice given in this writing course. The goal is to invent, draft, revise, and edit quickly – under pressure, in high-stakes writing situations.

These objectives work in harmony with Mini-Workshop E, in *A Community of Writers*, where Elbow and Belanoff address similar goals for: (1) writing when you have sharply limited time, such as when you are taking an exam, and (2) writing when you are anxious or confused, and therefore can't think straight.

Before Viewing

Read Mini-Workshop E, "Midterms, Finals, and Other In-Class Writing" in *A Community of Writers* (pp. 463–468).

Dig up some of the exams you have had returned from other courses – especially the ones that required essay answers. Consider the strategies (or lack of strategies) you used to respond to the questions. Detaching yourself from the course content in the exams, try to think of the writing techniques that help a student in a timed writing situation.

While Viewing

Evaluate the pressure-writing strategies offered by the instructors, students, and professional writers featured in the telecourse. In a double-entry notebook, write down the new ideas you encounter and be sure to note the effective strategies that you *already* use.

Think about the skills you have already learned in this course, before studying how to write under pressure, and notice the ones that would still be useful in a timed writing situation. (You should also imagine the techniques that would be a detriment in a timed writing situation.)

After Viewing

Complete the exercise, "Practicing the Technique," on page 468 of *A Community of Writers*.

Practice some of the skills you have studied by using the exercises in this chapter of the *Telecourse Study Guide*, to learn how to do better while writing under pressure. And make sure to apply the lessons you have learned to the next high-stakes writing assignment you encounter – in the academic environment or in the world beyond school. Think of advice you could share with a younger brother, sister, or friend just entering college – specifically, for writing challenges encountered during final exam week. Would it be a variation on the advice given in this program, or is there something that the teachers, instructors, and writers featured in this unit have overlooked?

Viewing Guide

Though the emphasis in this course is on the kind of writing where a student has several days (or weeks) to draft, revise, edit, and redraft an essay, much of the high-stakes writing encountered in the workplace requires the author to produce coherent and accurate text quickly. The video provides a couple of quick examples at the top of the program, with a police officer and diesel mechanic talking about writing under pressure.

Students also must learn how to write under pressure, especially when they are responding to essay questions on an exam or composing responses to take-home writing assignments on a tight deadline.

Every skill you learn in freshman composition still applies. The main difference is that the student has to adapt all of the lessons learned about writing at a *much quicker pace*.

Elaine Maimon of Arizona State University recommends that college students devise strategies in the first weeks of the freshman year to help them prosper in pressure-writing situations. "We're not talking about a formula for the perfect essay exam question. What is really important for students is that they are able to think strategically about what they are writing in the time they have to achieve it. Those are skills that are transferable and we [in English composition] ought to be teaching students to transfer them."

This chapter will introduce a variety of tactics that writers use to write under pressure so you can develop your own approach.

Key word concepts
The various subcategories of writing studied in an English composition course often come in handy when a student is trying to beat the clock while answering exam questions. Many students who are successful in high-stakes writing situations learn to quickly identify the rhetorical

modes (also called thinking/writing strategies) that are most appropriate for the task. Often, the instructor who designed the exam or assignment questions has clearly requested a specific *type* of response with a key word or phrase.

Beverly Moss, a writing instructor at Ohio State University, gives this example: "I think what's really important – not only with essay exams but with helping students understand how to read writing assignments – is to teach them to look for *key word concepts*. If a teacher says, 'Describe the process,' then we need to talk to students about what that means. That *doesn't* mean, then, that you do an argumentative essay. That's not what the teacher's looking for. The assignment is asking you to go through the steps of how something happened. Now the assignment may say *describe the process* and then *analyze*. Those are two different things that that assignment's asking for.

"Sometimes I think people get caught not understanding the difference. So you get the descriptive essay, when someone's asking for an analysis."

Moss also points out that garbled answers aren't always the students' fault. "Sometimes I think we [teachers] aren't always clear about an assignment," she says. "If we want an analysis, we should ask for it. I think students are right sometimes when they say, 'Some teachers don't know what they want until they get it.' "

In *A Community of Writers*, Elbow and Belanoff emphasize that the student should "Read the question carefully. Slowly. Repeatedly. Ask yourself questions like these: What is the instructor really asking? Is there more than one question, or a question behind the question?"

English teacher Patricia Scully adds this advice: "I teach my students to annotate the prompt. Write on the prompt; underline the key words. If it says *discuss*, make sure you have circled *discuss*. You know what those words mean. Other key phrases are *compare and contrast*, *argue* – the prompt is always going to be your thesis statement. They have it for you. Don't do too much work; do exactly what you're told to do."

Quick organizing devices

Students who just put a pen to paper and respond to exam questions without doing any prewriting often produce disorganized results. Organizing devices such as quick-sketch outlines can actually *save* you time. Building the response around one clear sentence (also called a main point, a premise, or a thesis) will also save you time and help unify your response. In the telecourse, instructor Chitra Divakaruni explains how she teaches her students to deal with pressure-writing situations. "Tests are generally asking you for information; they want to see if you can process and problem-solve certain kinds of issues. Therefore, you have to be clear, you have to be organized, and you have to manage your time. One of the things I teach them is a brief three-minute outline that they will write before they write their essay … in which they've organized all their points, they've put maybe a couple of important examples under each point ... and then they go for it."

In *A Community of Writers*, Elbow and Belanoff suggest two variations on quick organizing devices. For students who are relatively confident about how they will answer an essay-exam question, they recommend a one-step outline (p. 464). This is a variation on the skeleton outline they discussed in Chapter 12 and which we will review in the telecourse program "Organizing Devices." Students who are not sure how they will answer are encouraged to write a two-step outline, using two stages to organize their thoughts. Elbow and Belanoff describe the first stage as a proto-outline – a 'grab-bag' nonoutline" designed to dredge up as much raw information as the student can remember about the topic. The second stage is more like a "real outline" that puts the points in a logical order.

Elaine Maimon emphasizes that these activities are designed to help save time for some cursory copy editing. "In an essay exam, you need to learn to use the time well," she says. "It's probably not going to be wise to do a full-scale early draft or outline."

Additional time can be saved, she suggests, by anticipating questions that might be asked and practicing a bit of prewriting the day before the exam.

Proofreading under pressure

No matter what strategies you use to draft your response, Maimon advocates planning for at least a few moments at the end of the test for a quick proofreading. "Give yourself at least three to five minutes at the end, so that you can read it over. I think one of the biggest mistakes that students make is that they turn in to an instructor (who is going to put a grade on the exam) something that *they haven't read at all themselves*."

Errors in grammar, syntax, and clarity detract from your response, even if the *content* of your answer shows complete understanding of the material. This is true whether you are writing an exam, a grant proposal for research funding, or a job application.

By now you should be able to diagnose your own tendencies. Look at the feedback that you have received on your first few papers; it is usually pretty easy to recognize patterns – places you have repeated the same type of grammar or sentence structure error consistently. Chapters 22, 24, and 26 of this *Telecourse Study Guide* have exercises that will help you create your own checklist of language tendencies and common surface errors.

If you know your tendencies for making mistakes, it is a good idea to read carefully, using a personal editing checklist.

Are you one of those students who regularly has problems with apostrophes, homonyms, or comma splices? If you know you are, learn to proofread for those specific problems.

These types of errors are easy to overlook in a hasty first draft – and also easy to spot with a quick scan. Remember: If your audience expects you to sound articulate, credible, and scholarly, you don't want to make a bad impression with a grammatical blunder.

In *A Community of Writers*, Elbow and Belanoff recommend that students learn how to "talk onto the page" rather than try to construct grammatical sentences. "This talking will lead to some informality in wording, but that's perfectly acceptable in most exams," they say. "Just make sure you save some time at the end to go back over what you've written and make a few corrections in mechanics."

Audience awareness in high-stakes writing

It is very important to consider your audience when writing under pressure. In composition courses, we would say, "Consider the appropriate voice of the discourse community you are writing for." What jargon or professional vocabulary does the teacher *expect* you to use? Should the language be formal or informal? Is a humorous or angry tone inappropriate, or is responding emotionally effective with your specific audience?

Awareness of these issues can increase your effectiveness.

English instructor Geoffrey Philp of Miami-Dade Community College gives this example: "Since it is at a college level, you have to use the language of the particular discipline that you're in. So, for example, let's say you're doing biology. I expect you, after the first week, *not* to be saying *kneecap* anymore. I expect you to say *patella* and to use the words that are within the discipline. Because once you've entered this course, you are a member of that community of scholars."

Indeed, the very point of some exams is to demonstrate that you know how to use the professional language that you have learned throughout the semester. It is imperative, in those circumstances, that you demonstrate mastery of those terms.

A different look at research

When you're under pressure, an element of research is important, even during exams or take-home writing assignments.

The main difference is that you've conducted the research ahead of time, by taking good lecture notes and carefully reading all course assignments. Pat Patterson, a psychologist from California State University, teaches study skills seminars. According to Patterson, the most important thing in study skills is a review.

"The more you see the material, the more likely you are to learn it," Patterson says. "The mistake that most people make is they try to review too much in a limited period of time. [Some students call this 'cramming' for exams.] One of my patients told me once, 'You can eat an elephant with a spoon, if you take it one bite at a time.' When I teach study skills, I call it *intravenous learning* ... where they take information in one drop at a time."

Though they admitted to be experts in procrastination, many of the students surveyed for this telecourse were quite aware of the relationship between class notes, studying, and exam performance.

As instructional design student Mark Zempel observes, "It's an interesting way to look at an essay exam – to think of it as a research paper that you're going to write. But instead of going the library for all the information, the information should be everything that you've learned throughout the semester. That's why the instructor is asking the question: to see what you've learned over the semester."

Thinking and your health

It's easier to incorporate knowledge gained from reading and research into a term paper than into an exam, because the students responding to an exam must understand and *remember* a vast amount of information gathered throughout an entire course. Though it is a simple (and perhaps obvious) point, many students overlook the fact that both memory and clarity of thought are affected by mental fatigue and physical health.

John Lovas of De Anza College emphasizes how important soundness of body and mind can be when preparing for high-stakes writing situations. "It's good to prepare the same way you prepare for an interview to get a job. It's very basic. Like – get a lot of sleep the night before. That sounds like some parents talking, but ... to be well rested helps. The other thing that sounds really obvious is, eat something before taking tests. And take a walk around campus for fifteen minutes. Activity really clears the mind, and there's a real connection between activity and thinking. Paying attention to your physical condition before you take one of these exams is critical."

Summary

It is important to remember, as we wrap up this instructional unit, that the study of high-stakes writing strategy is not just designed as an exercise for your English class. Writing under pressure in English composition can help prepare students for the intense writing encountered in many out-of-class situations; high-stress occupations (including any form of science, medicine, law, journalism, or education) will require efficient writing on a deadline.

"Most colleges and universities have what are called placement tests, and those require writing under pressure," John Lovas says. "And many colleges, including mine, have occasions where at the end of the writing program you have to write a test to demonstrate you've achieved a certain level of mastery. Sometimes qualifying for [certification] in certain professions requires being able to write under pressure as part of your exam – a written exam for the law, for law enforcement work. There are other circumstances where you really have to be able to produce your thinking in a short period of time in a clear way."

Radio journalist Steve Scott and nursing instructor Julia Shovein, who both use writing on the job, review the main points of this instructional unit in the conclusion to this program.

As you watch Scott and Shovein talk about the high-stakes writing in their careers, consider how you can use the lessons of this course (and, specifically, of this program) to perform well when asked to write under pressure in your chosen occupation.

Integrating the Text

MINI-WORKSHOP E   "Writing Under Pressure: Midterms, Finals and Other In-Class Writing" (pp. 463–468)

Mini-Workshop E "Writing Under Pressure: Midterms, Finals and Other In-Class Writing" covers many of the same issues that this telecourse program covers, with a slightly different spin.

A Community of Writers, in the first 462 pages, emphasizes a style of writing where clarity of mind is *not* what you start out with; writing is a way to get to new thinking. That all changes with high-stakes writing assignments

According to Elbow and Belanoff, "The long and messy process [of standard composition] is a luxury you can't afford when you only have 30 or 60 minutes for en essay on an exam."

The authors recommend an approach similar to the one explained by teachers in this video. You must adapt an abbreviated version of the writing process that you are learning in your English course. Usually, composition courses tell you to invent, draft, organize, revise, and edit. In high-stakes writing situations, you practice much of the same in a condensed, confident, and efficient manner.

You are advised to read the question or prompt for an essay exam very carefully, looking for assumptions, implications, and "questions behind the questions."

Elbow and Belanoff also recommend quick sketch outlines, with each main point stated as an assertion in a complete sentence.

Finally, the authors explain that many essay exam situations require one-draft writing without much of an opportunity for freewriting or generating ideas. This is because much of the thinking should have been done before the exam, in the note-taking and studying phase.

Elbow and Belanoff also suggest that you should not worry *too* much about spelling – but, be sure to save time for some quick proofreading and corrections in mechanics before the clock demands that you stop writing.

Exercises

Check with your instructor for your formal assignments. You will be asked to do exercises from the *Telecourse Study Guide*.

EXERCISE 1 – WRITING UNDER PRESSURE

Spend two hours writing an analysis of any one of the video programs in this telecourse. (Since you are applying the lessons of the writing-under-pressure program, it might be better to pick any of the *other* twenty-five programs, so that you can master some new information.)

The goal of this exercise is to help you *practice* for writing-under-pressure situations in other classes or at work. (A side benefit of this exercise is that by the time you finish the exercise, you will probably absorb the lessons of this one unit better than any of the other twenty-five units in the telecourse.) Try to apply what you learned from watching the program, "Writing Under Pressure." Do not worry about a grade – the point of this exercise is to examine how you, personally, handle an assignment under pressure.

Dig deep, and work hard to make this as good as possible – but *make* yourself finish the exercise exactly two hours after you start writing. It would be best to watch the program you choose on tape, so you can rewind, pause, take notes, and so on.

This is a bit formulaic, but remember: You are trying to whip this out on a time deadline, in a style accepted in most classrooms. Your analysis of the program should do the following:

- The paper should start out with a main point or thesis. In other words, state a point that you want to make (or that the program tries to make) about the writing and reading process. It is best to include this thesis in the first paragraph, though it does not have to be the first sentence.

- Every subsequent paragraph in the essay should support the thesis. Each paragraph should be built around a topic sentence that relates directly to the thesis.

- The essay should quote and/or paraphrase comments from *at least three* of the people on the television program. These comments should support your thesis. Refer to your textbook for advice on paraphrase, quotation, and Modern Language Association (MLA) citation style. This will be good practice learning the process of bringing words (or thoughts) of others into your own writing – an important technique to master for research paper writing and argument/persuasion essay writing. Experiment with the difference between direct quotation, summary, and paraphrase.

- Summarize at least four of the main instructional points of the program as you interpret them. (Hint: The narrator in each program usually summarizes the main instructional points.)

- Conclude your essay with a summary of the main points of the telecourse program.

Some students claim to thrive on the "rush" of writing under pressure. If you are one of those, *have fun* with this assignment. Do not take it too seriously. When you finish it, see how many of the recommendations in this program on writing under pressure helped you – and consider which suggestions you ignored.

EXERCISE 2

As you write an essay on a deadline, note how you can use – or already use – some of the techniques recommended in the program about writing under pressure. Or, as an alternative, show how the techniques recommended in the program *do not apply* to your own high-stakes writing style.

Exercise just for fun

Shortly after final exams on your campus, do a quick informal survey of students at your school. Divide the students into two groups, based on the following criteria: One group should be students who partied – or crammed, – and slept little during final exam week. (On most campuses, it should not be difficult to find a representative sample.) The other group should have followed the advice of John Lovas, who suggested that sleep, exercise, and diet are all factors that affect how well a student performs in a high-stakes writing situation. Make a comparison between the groups and their final results on the exams.

Quick writing exercise

Your teacher may ask you to do a quick focused freewrite about the topic you are studying in this unit. Those of you who are taking the course through a distance-learning system may be encouraged to share your thoughts in a discussion thread or to post your ideas on an Internet bulletin board. If you are writing your thoughts out by hand in a process journal, you might use these questions to stimulate ideas. This is a freewriting exercise that will not be graded. You can use any of the following questions and statements to help you evaluate your personal approach to writing under pressure:

Write the first thing that comes to mind about your experiences with essay exams and other college writing-under-pressure situations. What is your personal reaction to timed writing assignments? Do certain strategies work particularly well for you? Is there something you do that seems to assure a better grade when you take an exam? What types of writing under pressure do you expect to be asked to perform after you leave school?

Is there *anything* you can get from an English class that helps in high-stakes writing, or does the English class seem like a completely separate, almost foreign, style of writing? Most students pick up at least one new idea from the program "Writing Under Pressure," and some students just reaffirm what they knew all along. What is your reaction? You can answer any of these question, or create your own spontaneous response.

Exercises related to *A Community of Writers*
In Mini-Workshop E, Writing Under Pressure: Midterms, Finals, and Other In-Class Writing" in *A Community of Writers,* the exercise "Practicing the Technique" of high-stakes writing (p. 468) is an excellent follow up to the points made in the telecourse.

Additional reading
What can you borrow from the writing style of Steve Shanesy, editor of *Popular Woodworking* (featured in the appendix), to help you succeed on an exam in a course such as chemistry, engineering, nursing, or computer science?

Quick Review

1. Instructors suggest that, given the time limitations of an essay exam,
   a. All attempts to organize with an outline should be avoided.
   b. There is probably not enough time to develop a clear thesis.
   c. Students should think "on the page," knowing that there won't be time for a major revision.
   d. Editing and proofreading will be a waste of time.
   e. All of the above.

2. When Beverly Moss recommends that students look for key word concepts, she is suggesting that you:
   a. Look for some word in the essay prompt that gives away the answer.
   b. Look for a key word that asks for a thinking/writing strategy (or rhetorical mode) such as *argue, compare, describe* or *define*.
   c. Look for how many points the question is worth.
   d. Look for how long the answer should be.
   e. All of the above.

3. The following strategies were recommended for effective writing under pressure:
   a. Keep healthy: exercise, eat well, and get some sleep.
   b. Approach lecture notes and reading assignments throughout the semester as if they were the "research" for your essay.
   c. Be aware of the audience and appropriate level of professional language, or jargon.
   d. None of the above.
   e. All of the above.

4. The telecourse and *Telecourse Study Guide* chapters said the following about writing under pressure:
   a. This kind of writing is limited to academia and the artifact of the essay exam and has little relevance to the "real world."
   b. A student should take care to freewrite and generate ideas that can later be organized into a coherent statement on an essay exam.
   c. A student should make sure to study as hard and as late as possible the night before an important essay exam, eating as much pizza as the human body can tolerate.
   d. All of the above.
   e. None of the above.

5. The following is good advice for performing well on an exam question that requires timed writing :
   a. The standard composition process of freewriting, drafting, and revising is an indulgence you can't afford when you only have a few minutes for an essay on an exam.
   b. Read the question for an essay exam very carefully and look for key words that suggest how the instructor would like you to organize your response.
   c. A quick sketch outline might actually save time.
   d. All of the above.
   e. None of the above.

6. In *A Community of Writers*, Elbow and Belanoff state that:
   a. The long and messy process [of standard composition] is a luxury you can't afford when you only have thirty or sixty minutes for an essay on an exam
   b. Read the question or prompt for an essay-exam very carefully, looking for assumptions, implications, and "questions behind the questions."
   c. A quick sketch, with each main point stated as an assertion in a complete sentence, is a good way to quickly organize your thoughts.
   d. Students should not worry too much about spelling – but, save time for some quick proofreading and corrections in mechanics.
   e. All of the above

"There are certainly some days when the words and ideas seem to swarm around me like bees, and there are other days when I have to coax them out of their holes with a stick and it's very frustrating and difficult. But sooner or later they always come. Freewriting, stream of consciousness, blank verse – there are many different ways to play with language. Take an idea and see how far you can push it, or take a couple of words that aren't normally associated and put them together in different sequences, different combinations, and then spin out from there. I have never been a victim of what is called writer's block.... On those days when things are difficult, you just start playing around with words. Play long enough and hard enough and with enough skill – just relax and have fun with language – sooner or later there's this rush where everything comes together and you just start flowing along."

TOM ROBBINS, novelist

Introduction to the Topic

With old-fashioned lawnmowers and boat engines, you have to pull and pull on that rope until the gears warm up and the beast suddenly roars to life. In case you haven't noticed, the human brain sometimes works the same way.

You can sit in front of the computer, fingers poised over the keyboard, and nothing comes. You chew your eraser off your pencil and doodle on the yellow pad of paper, but the sentences don't flow. The sludge in your brain feels like stagnant motor oil that

hasn't been changed in that old motor for at least three years.

Writer's block happens.

Perhaps you've left your brain in the storage shed to gather dust and cobwebs for the entire summer vacation. More likely, your thoughts are banging around in your head, ready to pour out in the essay – but your fingers are frozen, because your primary audience is an instructor who will scrutinize every word.

Students who find themselves in this

situation need to learn writing techniques that are the equivalent of replacing the spark plugs in that old engine. Even professional writers who rarely have problems with writer's block practice *prewriting* exercises designed to get the mind fired up with ideas. These techniques vary and come labeled with different names, but they all have one thing in common: They allow the writer to crank out words and ideas without fearing the grammar police and rhetoric instructors.

In the writing process, *freewriting* (and a related activity called *generative writing*) is part of the "invention" stage – the part of the composition process where you spend more time brewing up ideas and exercising the brain muscles than actually composing something you'll keep. You'll be typing out or scribbling down ideas, but most of what you write will be set aside. And that's OK. These prewriting techniques are designed to let you brainstorm and "think out loud" on the page before you start formally drafting the paper. This kind of verbal improvising takes a bit of courage; you should be able, willing, and eager to originate a pile of literary refuse, verbal compost, and rhetorical rubbish.

Instructor Peter Elbow puts it this way: "Freewriting is a way to produce garbage. Let garbage come. Freewriting is a way to produce total disorganization."

It's the freedom to be disorganized that eventually leads to clear thought, Elbow maintains. "If I start freewriting, my mind will jump around," he says. "It will be all disorganized at first. But after I go for a while, one of the paragraphs will say, 'Oh! This is what it is all about!' " Those who practice freewriting often find a gem in the pile of rocks – an original thought they didn't have before they just started playing with the words.

Those who learn to write freely (even if the thoughts are nonsensical at first) are taking a very important step: They are learning to think while they write.

Learning Objectives

After viewing the telecourse program and finishing the related exercises, you will develop strategies to churn out significantly more text than the minimum required for an assignment. In other words, you will learn how to generate a surplus of ideas in a prewriting stage. With sage advice from top fiction writers and English composition instructors, you will acquire techniques to overcome writer's block. You will also practice writing and thinking at the same time in a way that will allow you to get words on the page while forgetting about criticisms from an instructor or an audience.

These learning objectives work in harmony with Workshop 1, "An Introduction to the Variety of Writing Processes" (pp. 5–19) in *A Community of Writers*:

- Everyone can learn to become comfortable putting words and thoughts down on paper. Writing doesn't have to be a struggle.
- Writing is very different, depending on the situation – especially depending on topic, audience, and kind of writing. It helps to learn different "writing gears."

Throughout the textbook, Elbow and Belanoff recommend exercises of freewriting and generative writing designed to help you master the learning objectives of each individual workshop.

Before Viewing

Before you formally study this topic, consider the following questions: Who do you usually imagine as your audience when you draft an essay? Are you thinking of your instructor or your boss? Do you worry about your audience as you compose – and, if so, does that slow down your writing process? Are you one of those students who has trouble coming up with the minimum number of pages for an assignment – and is the fear of criticism slowing you down? Or, if you have no trouble writing, are you tapping as deep as possible into your creativity?

Read the samples of freewriting in Elbow and Belanoff (pp. 19–29) as well as "A Spectrum of Writing Tasks (pp. 6–12) and the section "Explaining Theory and Freewriting and Process Write-up" (pp. 15–18).

While Viewing

Take notes on how each writer, instructor, and student approaches the invention process. Keep in mind how they use freewriting and generative writing to break writer's block – or to just brainstorm ideas, if they don't experience any kind of block. Identify the attitude that comes closest to your own, and consider how you might adapt these writing techniques to your next writing assignment. Notice how similar the brainstorming techniques used by the Second City improvisational actors are to the free-form brainstorming you might do on a page.

After Viewing

Reread the "Explaining Theory" section (pp. 15–18) on freewriting and process writing in Workshop 1. Then, try writing an early draft of a writing assignment – with absolutely no self-censorship. Forget all the restrictions of spelling, structure, thesis, organization, coherence, and unity. Imagine yourself as the only possible audience, and don't take your fingers off the keyboard (or pencil) until you have written two or three times as much as required. This is an exercise in focused freewriting; it will lead naturally to a revision and editing stage that will require you to cut more than half of the writing. So have fun and write without restraint.

Viewing Guide

Even writers who usually have plenty to say experience moments when the words and ideas just won't come. As writer Himilce Novas explains, "The most frightening and yet the most wonderful thing in the world is the white page, because the moment you choose one word, you've already eliminated hundreds of other words that couldn't go near it."

As a writer-in-training, such moments will certainly happen to you. You may encounter a complete brain freeze, or your thoughts might seem plain and tepid. Many writers before you have discovered that certain activities can kick-start the brain much more effectively than snarling at your computer or chugging sixteen cups of coffee. These activities also beat waiting for inspiration to fall out of the sky.

Barriers that inhibit the thinking and writing process usually come from self-censorship, when you are worried about criticism from an audience or grades from an instructor.

The writers and teachers in this telecourse program will share their secrets about *prewriting* tasks designed to generate ideas or free up your imagination. Most of these techniques will encourage a state of mind that allows you to forget about the audience and just play with words for a while.

Mike Rose of UCLA explains why prewriting can be so important. "A lot of the students I work with find writing such a feared activity," Rose says. "They've not done well in it; they don't like it."

Rose observes that, strangely enough, the *same* students feel quite comfortable writing letters to girlfriends and boyfriends or e-mail to acquaintances. These documents are often very substantial and complex.

"The students may use writing in various informal ways all the time," Rose says. "But somehow or another, the minute that they're in a classroom, it seems like this really forbidding stuff."

Freewriting, generative writing, and other prewriting exercises (including reading, researching, and some forms of speculative outlining) can help bridge this gap between fun, uninhibited writing for friends and writing intended for an audience.

Elizabeth George, author of many top-selling mystery novels, observes that these prewriting techniques do not have to be limited to those who are experiencing writer's block. George sets a schedule to work on her books for a few hours every day and rarely experiences a lack of creativity. But she still uses freewriting to explore her "running plot outline."

"The purpose of this activity, for me, is to trigger the right side of the brain," George explains. "I am very, very strongly left-brained. I'm very much into organization, into details, into structure. But the creative part, the diving underneath the water of creativity and going with the flow – that's really what right brain does, and that does not come naturally to me at all. And that's the way I get into the freewriting."

Pure freewriting

Pure freewriting is used to reveal ideas. Professional writers use it to break through writer's block or to add creativity to an already successful writing session. Students use freewriting to explore what they are learning and to brainstorm ideas for course assignments. It's easier to tap the subconscious when you're writing only for yourself, freeing the mind from worries about grammar, spelling, or style. Pure freewriting has no audience, focus, or overt goal, other than to get something – *anything* – on the page.

In *A Community of Writers*, Elbow and Belanoff explain pure freewriting means, "writing privately and writing without stopping."

Changing topics is fine, they say. Writing pure garbage is fine; you don't have to show this writing to anyone. The privacy is important, because writing is usually judged. Freewriting is not. Pure freewriting is meant to get you comfortable with the process of thinking by putting words on a page.

Mike Rose, a widely read author as well as an instructor, explains how he uses freewriting. "I often find that the most effective thing I can do, when I'm stuck on a difficult intellectual problem, is to just start writing … not censoring myself, not editing myself, not worrying about whether it sounds right or wrong but just trying to work the thought out by letting the pen go. It's a handy strategy that we can pass on to our students, to get them to free up from years of perhaps feeling like that grammar policeman is right over their shoulder."

The point of freewriting, Rose emphasizes, is to let the pen connect directly to the thought processes. Later, after the thinking is finished, you can select passages that make sense, organize them, and edit them for surface errors.

Professional writers are comfortable with putting words on paper as a way of *thinking*. This strategy might feel foreign to students who are used to turning every written word in to an instructor for evaluation. Many students compose each passage painfully and slowly – constantly second-guessing each word choice, wondering what the instructor might think.

Megumi Taniguchi of the University of Hawaii explains a common reaction: "A lot of students do not feel comfortable with freewriting. They say, 'I'm going to write the paper, so why do you have to have me do this meaningless exercise beforehand?' What they don't realize is that, once they are *forced* to write, they're getting ideas down on paper … and they can keep them; they can use them later."

Some writers embrace the state of mind that true, unfettered freewriting can encourage. Science fiction novelist Kim Stanley Robinson says, "The surrealists called it automatic writing ... where you actually tried to keep your conscious mind out of the process and let there be a direct connection between your unconscious mind and the page."

Robinson says part of the technique is to write as *fast* as possible – fast enough to catch up with the thoughts flying through your mind. And, just as you don't worry what anybody thinks about the ideas going through your brain, you should not worry about the ideas that go down on the page. Your goal is to be as comfortable writing as you are when you say to a friend, "I'm only thinking out loud now."

Bill Walsh, former coach of the San Francisco 49ers, compares this writing process to the type of verbal improvisation we *all* use in spontaneous conversation. "In writing in that form [freewriting] you generally write as you think," Walsh says. "It's sort of verbal – but in a sense it's not verbal, because it's your thoughts that cross your mind ... and you write in those thoughts as you think of them."

Nursing instructor Julia Shovein notes that her nursing students use freewriting in a form of clinical log to unwind from a day in the hospital – to slow down and gather thoughts about what they are learning from the experience.

"It's very important, after you've had a new experience and you're very anxious," Shovein explains. "Things are happening that you are just learning about, so you really don't understand it all clearly. To go sit and just freely write helps you clarify, not only what actually happened in the professional nursing process. Freewriting also helps you clarify your feelings about what happened. And that helps you learn."

Generative writing

Generative writing is a natural outgrowth of pure freewriting, where the only object of the exercise is to get anything on the page. In generative writing, the writer attempts to generate a surplus of *ideas*. As with pure freewriting, the writer is not worried about spelling, grammar, organization, or audience.

Peter Elbow helps define the difference, saying, "By calling it generative writing, we're saying to ourselves, 'I need to produce a lot. I need quantity. Later on I'll push for quality. But for now I need quantity.' And it's generative also in the sense that I need my *own* ideas and I need *new* ideas."

This kind of writing can be used to rebel against the restrictions of academic writing, where almost every thought and every word committed to paper is to please an instructor.

"Students often feel like writing is just telling what the teacher wanted or writing what the teacher said in a lecture or reporting what's in some other book or article. And some writing does that," says Elbow. "But it's pretty sad when people conceive of writing as explaining ideas that don't belong to you. So *generative* also emphasizes the fact that you are generating this stuff. It's *yours*."

Chitra Divakaruni is just one of many instructors who encourage students to use this technique as a way to find something to say in an essay. It is a technique she uses to discover ideas for her own writing.

"I often use generative writing to figure out what is important," Divakaruni says. "And I have all my students keep a little notebook – their writer's notebook. As they're going through their daily lives, whenever they see something that excites them or interests them or perplexes them – anything that raises thought or critical thinking – I ask them to write it down. At the end of the week, I ask them to go through their writer's notebook and make a list of possible topics that they would like to address in papers. They bring those lists to class and we put them up on the board. Then we look at the connections between those lists and what we've been reading. Very often, we find wonderful connections. And then they have their topic. It gives them a real sense of empowerment, because I didn't impose that topic on them. They found it themselves."

An example: improvisation as generative writing

A brief part of every evening at Chicago's Second City comedy revue is dedicated to improvisation. The actors engage in an oral "invention process" that is very similar to generative writing. In the telecourse program, we see that, though these comic actors are not "writing" at a computer (or with a pencil and pad of paper), their spontaneous ad-libs are recorded and transcribed every day.

Comedy writer Kevin Dorff explains that what Peter Elbow and others describe as generative writing "reminds me a lot of exercises we do in rehearsal. Because directors will assign us exercises onstage that are meant to maybe sort of get us out of what we call 'being in your head.'... That implies that you're thinking ahead of the moment that's before you. We spend about twenty to thirty hours on stage a week. Everybody's keeping their own notes on what to remember; there's a record being built up of transcriptions based on what the director was interested in. And every once in a while, the director will say, 'Let's look at what we have.' "

The actors and directors study the transcripts, tossing out the weak moments and saving the best for a formal, scripted revue. This process is very similar to the way a beginning student might use freewriting to generate ideas for an essay or research paper.

How to freewrite and generate

All this talk about generating ideas might be interesting. But *how* does a student practice the art of freewriting? All writers have their own approach to the process. Here are just a few ideas recommended in the telecourse program.

JUST BE STUPID

Many teachers and writers suggest that freewriting is more about adopting an attitude than it is about learning specific techniques.

Thomas Fox of California State University jokes, "I tell my students, 'You just can't be stupid for that long.' It seems to be true. With graduate students working on an MA thesis, if it's been months and I haven't seen a word, I will often say, 'Will you write me a pile of garbage, please? If it's good, I'm going to hand it back.' It's sort of a joke and it's a way of getting them going."

Fox calls this process "a zero draft" – that is, it's a draft *before* the first draft.

This practice gives the student permission to write something (at first) that is disorganized and doesn't make a point. The sentences can come out mangled and the thoughts can take off on tangents. But the student will uncover some ideas – and will have something to show the instructor, even if it is a bit of an embarrassment.

"The truth is, most students *can't* write *that* badly," Fox says. "What comes out is usually a pretty good draft. But lowering the bar for yourself is really important, because writing starts somewhere. It doesn't start at the end; the first utterance is not in the conversation. That's what school is about, really. It's a bunch of practice runs before you enter into the *real* conversation, so there is a time to be stupid, and it's right at the beginning."

WRITE AN IMAGINARY LETTER

Humorist Tom Bodett uses a slightly different approach to freewriting and generative writing. He writes to an imaginary pen pal. This is especially effective, he says, if he is stuck in a variation of writer's block.

"One thing I do to get unstuck is, I start writing a letter to somebody. Anybody. It could be Richard Nixon; it could be my mom. I write something like, 'Dear Mr. President, I saw somebody kick a pigeon today....' And go on from there. And that will get me going, because all of a sudden, here's an audience. I know something about this person, so I'll start writing. Then, when it's all done, you take the 'Dear So-and-So' off the top and you've got an essay at the end of it."

Some instructors recommend a variation of the imaginary letter that starts with your instructor in mind. Of course, the essay should be edited and revised before you turn it in to the instructor for evaluation. But the idea of writing an informal letter can get you in the frame of mind to *communicate* to your instructor.

INVISIBLE WRITING

Many writers find that the very act of looking at the words, as they are composed, is what slows down their thinking process.

Teresa Redd of Howard University suggests turning off the computer monitor and writing with a blank screen. If you are a fairly adept typist, you'll make only a few typos, which can be easily fixed up later. For some writers, this is a way to make an even more direct connection between the freewriting process and the thoughts that are swirling around in the mind.

"You just start writing and you don't worry," Redd says. "It's freewriting. You don't worry about what you've already said; you just keep going. And then, when you turn the screen on, you've got all these words on your [formerly] white document screen. Half the stuff may be garbage, but that doesn't matter. Somewhere in there, there's going to be a nugget that you can then expand upon. So you're not faced with that blank page or that blank screen. You have somewhere to start."

Before computers were invented, writers sometimes practiced "invisible writing" with two pieces of paper that had a piece of carbon-copy paper in between. The writer could then us a pen without ink, or a pencil without lead. The purpose of the exercise was the same. Though no words appeared on the top page to distract the writer's mind, the carbon copy preserved the thoughts. (This works well for those who are uncomfortable with typing.)

In *A Community of Writers*, the authors also advocate a variation on invisible writing. In Workshop 1, "An Introduction to the Variety of Writing Processes" (p. 8), Elbow and Belanoff note the advantages: "Invisible writing increases your concentration. It forces you to focus better on what you have in mind – on the emerging meaning in your head. Invisible writing makes most people realize how often they get distracted from their topic in their regular writing; either because something else is on their mind or because they stop too often and look back at what they have already written."

CUT AND PASTE

In the telecourse program, Butte College instructor Michael Bertsch expresses his enthusiasm for freewriting on a computer. His advice is to open up two or more computer files on the monitor and to creatively use the cutting, pasting, and editing functions.

"Freewriting is a really easy way to open up," Bertsch says. "If you open up a separate window and do your freewriting – and then say, 'Oh, here's a neat sentence, or here's a neat phrase, or here's two neat words' – you just highlight them, copy them, and dump them into your alleged 'real writing.' So it's quite transparent. You can undo, redo – those kinds of things. It makes it really easy for students to generate stuff."

In the telecourse, we see Mark Zempel, a student who grew up feeling comfortable with computers and techniques like those suggested by Bertsch.

"I'll have paragraphs and some snippets of some freewriting in a text window in a text program that I have. And then I just click back and forth between windows and pull a paragraph out and paste it in over there – and then tweak with the sentence a little bit. Sometimes I'll have my text file program; I'll have my Internet site open as well, to find references. That's part of the fun of working on the computer. Sometimes when you're cutting and pasting stuff you've written, it's like you're *playing* with these programs. You're constructing something; you're composing something."

DON'T STOP

The best advice that can be given to a student who is practicing freewriting for the first time is, "Just keep writing."

It is *not* easy, for most students, to keep writing without stopping. But this is an essential aspect of freewriting. "In writing, there are a lot of constraints," says Peter Elbow. "With freewriting, you remove most of the constraints – except for, in a way, the *hardest* constraint, which is, *keep writing*! That's in a sense a very artificial, very difficult thing. Keep writing. Don't stop; keep writing. But in repayment for putting up with that [in a sense] horrible constraint, you take away all the other constraints."

Of course, the other payback often is a few good ideas that pop up as a result of the exercise. In fact, students who get used to pure freewriting often become so comfortable with this technique, they use it as the first stage of prewriting to generate ideas for every assignment they receive.

Focused freewriting: one subject only

An important distinction exists between unrestricted, pure freewriting (or writing completely for yourself) and the more focused freewriting that is designed to move you along on a specific writing task aimed at an eventual audience. Many instructors find it effective to have students practice both types of freewriting as often as possible.

In the telecourse, Peter Elbow introduces the notion of *focused freewriting* by suggesting, "Why not stay on the same topic? See if you can keep all your writing on the same topic. Yes, you'll digress, but after you've digressed a little bit, put yourself back on the track."

Pure freewriting, Elbow says, "is the way to get most easily at the kind of 'germ event' of writing."

Focused freewriting, he says, is when you are using "the freewriting muscle" to explore a particular topic.

In *A Community of Writers*, Elbow and Belanoff explain that "focused freewriting is especially useful for the hardest thing about writing: *getting started*" (p. 7). Throughout the book, they recommend focused freewriting as a method of getting started on a variety of workshop projects. It is a good technique to learn, for writing challenges in school and beyond.

Many professional writers, working against a deadline, use a variation of this technique, because they need to develop ideas on a regular basis. In the telecourse program, Himilce Novas explains how she uses the focused freewriting technique, saying, "Pick a subject. Then maybe you can freewrite on it, because at least it gives you visors. Visors are the things they put on the horses so they don't look from side to side – and they keep focused. If you pick a subject, you'll have visors, and then you can do a little bit of freewriting in a way that will be, perhaps, more fruitful."

Summary

The opening quote of this telecourse program features the wisdom of novelist Tom Robbins, who says that most days, the ideas buzz around his head like bees. However, even a professional writer like Robbins has frustrating days where he has to "coax ideas out of a hole with a stick."

Clearly, this is not a state of mind unique to first-year writing students. The difference is knowing how to use writing and language to create ideas.

Robbins says he doesn't experience writer's block. When the thoughts don't come as quickly as usual, he starts to amuse himself by playing around with written language on a pad of paper. Eventually, something emerges. His approach is not much different than what we are advocating in this chapter. Get some words on the page in any way you can. If the words are coming slowly, free yourself up a little. If the topic is slowing you down, write about *anything*. If the words themselves seem to stare back at you and impede your progress, turn off the computer monitor and *keep typing*. If you can't make any progress because you are worried about your grade, forget about being perfect, and just grind out a pile of garbage or a "zero draft."

Instructor Maria Madruga puts it very simply: "Writers write."

"Use your journal as almost a camera," she says. "You're just taking snapshots – snapshots of ideas. The best photographers carry their cameras everywhere. They see something that's rich and they grab it and they put it in their camera, they get it on film."

Use your freewriting to build a portfolio of ideas, she says. Take the time to jot down ideas in a notebook you carry around with you, or keep raw ideas stashed away in a special file in your computer.

Above all, write.

Write, even though it isn't going to be turned in for a grade. Write, even if nobody else will ever read it. Write when you are out of ideas; write when your brain is most active. You can edit and organize and revise later; you can forget, at least for a while, the *purpose* of the writing.

This stage is your prewriting. Keep the writing free.

Integrating the Text

Elbow and Belanoff mention in the process of freewriting and generating numerous times throughout *A Community of Writers*. The section "A spectrum of Writing Tasks" (pp. 6–12) in Workshop 1, "An Introduction to the Variety of Writing Processes," categorizes and explains various types of freewriting, including pure freewriting, focused freewriting, invisible writing, and public informal writing.

Public informal writing is a style of generative writing – designed for an audience and built around a topic – that is similar to the "zero draft" described by Thomas Fox in the Study Guide chapter.

The section "Exploring Theory: Freewriting and Process Writing" (p. 15) explains why Elbow and Belanoff believe freewriting is important. The authors emphasize that this is writing designed to get more directly to the thinking, saying, "Freewriting is an invitation to let words be less important and less careful than speech – and to see what you learn from them." This view contrasts with most writing *assignments,* because assignments are designed to be judged by a instructor. Students sometimes have trouble *expressing* themselves while writing, because they are always thinking about spelling, grammar, and grades.

Elbow and Belanoff point out that, while freewriting is a good device for blocked beginners, "skilled, experienced writers and teachers get even more out of freewriting. It is an exercise whose payoff increases with the expertise of the writer."

Several examples of actual student freewriting are published in this workshop (pp. 19–20), although it should be emphasized that most pure freewriting is usually just for the student's personal use and is not intended for an audience or instructor to view and comment on.

Exercises

Check with your instructor for your formal assignments. You will be asked to do exercises from the *Telecourse Study Guide.*

Exploring freewriting further

EXERCISE 1

Attempt to use focused freewriting for a passage of an essay that is due, especially if that passage is slowing your progress. Start a new computer file, pick a one- or two-paragraph section, and write about three or four pages of musings on the subject. Do not worry about spelling or grammar. Assume nobody will read the words in this new file. Read through your focused freewriting, and copy the sections that make the most sense. Paste them into a third file and revise the paragraphs until they are nearly perfect. Now, insert them into the main body of your essay, and keep writing!

EXERCISE 2

Use freewriting to help kick-start a term paper or research paper. Write everything you know about the subject. Then, after you have filled up as many pages as you can, go back and sort out the statements in categories. Here are some examples:

- Assumptions I have made
- Statements I can prove with facts and statistics gathered through research
- Questions I need answered through research
- Statements I can replace with quotes by somebody more famous (or more credible) who is saying a variation of the same thing
- Stuff that has nothing to do with my thesis

Exercise just for fun

Write for a half hour, without *any* constraints. Do not stop. Do not show the work to anybody. Read it a day later. If you find something useful, copy it, and paste it into a useful file in your computer. (If you found this exercise useful, try it again every day. Continue to copy the useful parts, and paste them into a file in your computer for future use.)

Revision exercise

Using the material you created and categorized in Exercise 2, write a preliminary draft of the paper. As you do more research, you will find material to fill in the holes you've discovered as well as find new areas of relevance with their own holes to fill. When you begin each new draft to incorporate this new information, make a copy of the previous draft and save it somewhere, but also keep a work copy open. You can push and squeeze new things into this work copy without fear of losing anything you've come up with in your drafts up to this point. You can freely experiment with where and how the new information fits.

After you've repeated this process as many times as it takes to cover all of the necessary bases for the subject matter, your most current working draft (with fine-tuning and editing) will be very close to your final paper.

Exercises related to *A Community of Writers*

Elbow and Belanoff introduce freewriting and generative writing in Workshop 1. The authors then ask you to use freewriting or generative writing in almost every workshop of the course, as a way of exploring what you are learning in each unit. In the units about description and narration, you may have already been asked to use freewriting to stimulate your imagination. Near the end of the course, you will use generative writing in the development stages of a research paper (p. 305), as a pre-writing technique that helps to select a topic and narrow down the research to a central idea.

It is quite possible, by the time you get to this unit, that you will have already had some trial runs with freewriting. Workshop 2, "From Private

Writing to Public Writing," contains an in depth exploration of how to use freewriting to generate ideas. This assignment starts with a practice exercise based on Sondra Perl's composing guidelines (p. 32) and concludes with advice on how to use your private writing to create a piece of public writing (p. 37). If you are inexperienced with freewriting and generative writing, work through these exercises and experiment with these techniques.

Quick writing exercise

Your instructor may ask you to do a quick focused freewrite about the topic you are studying in this unit. Those of you who are taking the course through a distance-learning system may be encouraged to share your thoughts in a discussion thread or to post your ideas on an Internet bulletin board. If you are writing your thoughts out by hand in process journal, you might use these questions to stimulate ideas. This is a freewriting exercise that will not be graded. You can use any of the following questions to help you freewrite about freewriting and generative writing:

Do you ever get writer's block? Is freewriting new to you, or is this something you have practiced before taking this course? How often do you write something just for yourself and not for an assignment? Are you able to think and write at the same time, or do you need ideas in your head before you start writing? Do you like to improvise? After watching this telecourse program, are you willing to try using freewriting or generative writing – or is the idea just too abstract? What is your personal reaction to the idea of freewriting?

Quick Review

1. According to guests on the telecourse program,
   a. Students should take care to spell correctly while freewriting.
   b. Freewriting is good for beginners but is rarely used by confident, professional writers who never get writer's block.
   c. It is always good to give your freewriting to someone else for feedback.
   d. All of the above.
   e. None of the above.

2. One difference between pure freewriting and generative writing is that
   a. Pure freewriting has no topic, purpose, or audience in mind, while generative writing is often used with a specific goal in mind.
   b. Generative writing should be grammatically correct and carefully edited, while pure freewriting often intentionally breaks most of the rules.

    c. Pure freewriting is aimed at impressing an instructor, while generative writing is aimed at impressing an audience.

    d. All of the above.

    e. None of the above.

3. Some of the advice given to students to practice generative writing is to

    a. Write an imaginary letter to someone, even if you never intend to send it.

    b. Try to write something silly or stupid – or just write a pile of garbage without worrying.

    c. Learn to freewrite with a computer and to copy and paste the best parts of freewriting into the main document.

    d. All of the above.

    e. None of the above.

4. Invisible writing is

    a. writing with absolutely no content

    b. writing in a way where you don't see the words as you compose

    c. writing that is so bad that nobody will ever read it

    d. all of the above

    e. none of the above

5. According to Peter Elbow, the only rule in pure freewriting is

    a. Make sure you write something that you can use in a final draft.

    b. Erase everything as soon as you finish.

    c. Keep writing; don't stop.

    d. All of the above.

    e. None of the above.

"The experience of writing – putting one word after the other, crafting sentences, crafting paragraphs – that that will remain the same. The *fundamentals* of writing are not going to change. The process may change somewhat, in that it will be much easier for you to stop in the middle of the writing and go back and find your research ... or grab an idea from another draft. It is much easier for you to stop and snap out to a Web site or some other resource and pull down the information. I wouldn't be surprised if college students are doing what I'm doing. All these windows piled up on top of each other – jumping back and forth between each one and always coming back to the thing I'm working on at that moment."

CHIP BAYERS, *Wired* magazine

Introduction to the Topic

Computers have changed the world.

Computers have changed the way some of us do our taxes. (Uncle Sam can dip into our wallets even *faster*.) Computers have changed the way instructors and students interact. ("My computer ate my paper" replaces "the dog ate my paper.") Computers have changed romance. ("I met this great girl on line, and then found out he played football for the Iowa Cornhuskers.")

Computers have also affected the way we write.

Those of us who prefer to write with a pencil and pad of paper can still find ways to ignore computers, though it is getting harder. You can always pay somebody to key the words into a computer and make the document look nice. Or you can peck the final draft in yourself; all modern computers have software that will check for typos.

It is fun to be derogatory and sarcastic about computers, but experienced writers find that the computer is *more* than a glorified typewriter. It is a composition tool that changes the process of writing.

If you want to freewrite a pile of garbage in an inspired state, you can save it to copy, paste, and edit the best parts later. If you write a great first draft, but the best paragraph is at the end (as it often is), you can simply cut and move that passage to the top.

You research quickly using the Internet, pop quotes directly into the document without retyping, and use your citation to link your reader directly to the source. You can edit, fiddle, and tweak. You can use an internal thesaurus, you can reorganize with an outline control, and you can collaborate with others – all with a few keystrokes and mouse clicks.

Then, if your computer does not crash (I *knew* I should have backed it up!), you can crank out a decent paper in a few hours. The paper will look nicer than the essays students hacked out few decades ago. Those papers of old – before 1984, when the personal computer became affordable – took gallons of Wite-Out. We wore our fingers down to nubs pounding a manual typewriter; if we procrastinated long enough, we even had to wait for the library to *open* so we could get a last-minute quote.

Think of these things the next time your computer crashes – and use this unit to discover what a great compositional tool the computer is.

Learning Objectives

After viewing the television program and finishing the writing assignments, you will learn several approaches to using the computer as a tool for composition. These techniques include using the hardware and software to brainstorm, draft, organize, revise, and collaborate. You will also consider how the computer changes reading, research, and the very way you present a "paper" – or a Web site of your thoughts – to an instructor.

These last learning objectives work in harmony with Mini-Workshop F "Doing Research on the Web," in *A Community of Writers* (pp. 469–477). In this workshop, Elbow and Belanoff explore how to use a computer connected to the Internet to find Web-based sources. The workshop also includes a discussion of how to evaluate and cite sources gathered through online research.

Before Viewing

Before you formally study this subject, consider your relationship with the computer. Does it slow you down? Is it a friend? Are you afraid of it? Have you been avoiding or resisting computers? Are you one of those students who grew up playing games and doing homework assignments with a computer since you can first remember? Can you turn your familiarity with the computer into an advantage in a composition class?

Read the Mini-Workshop F "Doing Research on the Web," on pages 469 to 477 in *A Community of Writers*.

While Viewing

Inventory the suggestions that the writers, instructors, and students make for using the computer as a tool. Compare the techniques they suggest to the techniques you already use. Think about your relationship with the Internet. Are you so familiar with the online world that you can make an easy transition to using the Web for research? Or are you so new to these experiences that you need a crash course to catch up with other students? Notice what the guests on the video say about how computers have changed the way good writers draft, revise, edit, read, research, and collaborate. Take careful note of what the video guests say about presenting "papers" on the Web, and imagine how those trends will affect the academic world.

As you watch the section on using the computer for research, reconsider Mini-Workshop F. Several of the guests on the video reinforce points made in this workshop about finding sources with a computer and evaluating online sources. Elbow and Belanoff also give additional advice about how to cite online sources.

After Viewing

Using the exercises suggested in this *Telecourse Study Guide* chapter, try some of the techniques suggested by the writers, instructors, and students in the video. Many of these suggestions are for using the computer as a device to aid composition. Determine how you can use the computer to be more creative with one *specific* essay you have written; in other words, use the computer keyboard much like piano players operate the keys of their instruments, as an interface to the creation process. Think of your most recent experiences with writing papers, and identify ways computers can improve your overall approach to the composition process.

Viewing Guide

The printing press put the written word into the hands of the common people. Before that invention, knowledge was stored on scrolls and controlled by society's elite: the church, the government, and the wealthy. In many ways, the typewriter was an even bigger technological revolution for the writing *process* than the printing press was. While the printing press allowed mass reproduction, the author still penned the original words with quill and ink. Setting the type for the printed pages was a tedious, time-consuming task. The typewriter changed that, putting the composition process at the writer's fingertips with a keyboard interface. With the easy availability of the personal computer, however, today's writers are finding that the typewriter actually limited their creativity – especially in the revision process.

Word processors versus typewriters

As writer and instructor Chitra Divakaruni points out, students are less resistant to revising because of computers. Word processing has caused nothing less than a revolution in the writing process, she says: "If they [students] had written a ten-page essay and I said, 'Now you really should change this and this and this' – and they had to retype it – well, they wouldn't! They'd just rebel."

Students weren't the only writers who benefited from the ease of revision on computers. Many of the professional writers interviewed for the telecourse told humorous stories of the days they were learning to switch from typewriters to computers. Essayist Tom Bodett admits, "The computer has made me a much better writer. I'd make a mistake [with my typewriter] at the beginning of a word; I would want to type *lazy*, but maybe I would type a *p* instead of an *l*, and say, 'Oh crap!' And so I would think of a word that meant lazy that began with a *p* – and think, 'Well, maybe he's not lazy after all. Maybe he's kind of *peppy*.' These are the kind of compromises I was making."

Dennis Richmond, an Emmy Award–winning news anchor from Oakland, California, was afraid he would lose his job when computers were introduced. Now he says, "Life is just so much easier with computers. With the typewriter, I would type something, and say, 'I don't like that.' Then – rip; just throw the page over my shoulder. And then I had to put in another page and start writing all over again. I'd make one little typo and say, 'Aw, man!' I'd look down, I'd have like fifty sheets of pages on the floor, each one with like five words."

Common computer functions

In the mid-1980s, most writers discovered that word-processing programs had distinct advantages over typewriters. It was suddenly possible to cut and paste paragraphs or to insert words in the middle of a passage, without having to retype. As if this wasn't enough, the computer also provided the author with startling innovations such as a built-in spelling checker and thesaurus.

Joe Harris, an instructor at the University of Pittsburgh, notes that the most obvious advantages of a computer are visible with just a glance at the keyboard and mouse functions. "Think about the set of function keys that are on a computer," he says. "You can add text to a document. You can hit the delete key and subtract text. You can cut and paste. You can actually rewrite text; you can highlight a sentence or a paragraph and you can change those words."

Many professional writers, including novelist Ernest Gaines, make use of such tools in their day-to-day work. Gaines, an old-school writer practiced in the art of cracking open a reference book when he needs to check a word, admits, "I have a dictionary in my computer; I have a thesaurus in my computer. It seems that this is where students will go from now on. They will not go to the open book. There's nothing wrong with going to the computer, if you have a dictionary or a thesaurus there. You can get the information just as quickly or even faster. There's nothing wrong with it, as long as you *use* it."

Many writing instructors caution students, however, against the overuse of such devices. Instructor Kimberly Wise of Cypress College warns, "People rely so heavily on a spellcheck nowadays that they think that's the only revising that they need to do. Revise does *not* mean spellcheck."

Humorist Dave Barry is also wary about spelling checkers. "The spellchecker doesn't have a clue which *there* you mean," he jokes. "Because we have so many *theirs* in our language, whatever random series of letters you write down probably is a form of the word *there*. And the spellchecker thinks, 'Fine.' Spellcheckers could start lying at some point; they're not stupid. They know how to spell more words than we do. At some point they'll say, 'Why should we spell it right? The humans don't know.' And they'll just start changing words around, inserting wrong words automatically. They can do it; they have the power."

Grammar checkers are even more difficult to manage than spellcheckers, but they do work for some beginning writers. Composition and computer expert Lewis Ulman of Ohio State University notes that grammar checkers usually deserve the bad reputation they receive. "They don't really understand grammar," Ulman says. Instead, "these primitive software programs run language through a mathematical algorithm that is only an approximation of real language rules." Since many of the rules are subjective, the computer still must rely on a human to make a choice about correct usage.

Computers and drafting

While some teachers and writers consider the computer's primary usefulness to be in the final editing stage, many others see it as a useful tool in just about every aspect of the writing process, including drafting, researching, outlining, collaborating – even inventing new ideas through freewriting.

In the telecourse, Teresa Redd of Howard University advocates using the computer to break writer's block. Redd encourages the student writer to type into a word-processing document after turning off the video display monitor. (The computer "brains" should be left on.) When the writing session is finished, the writer turns the monitor back on and saves the ideas.

"Half the stuff may be garbage," Redd says. "But that doesn't matter. Somewhere in there, there's going to be a nugget that you can then expand upon. So you're not faced with that blank page or that blank screen. You have somewhere to start. So many students [and even some professional writers] are afraid of that blank page or blank screen."

Instructor John Lovas uses a similar approach when he asks his students to freewrite ideas in short five-minute bursts, or "sprints." Though the computer screens are left on in this case, the results are similar. Students generate several files filled with random ideas that need to be organized.

The next step is to bring order to the chaos. Computers come to the rescue with a variety of tools.

Computers as organizing tools

After generating ideas, some writers prefer to use the built-in outlining functions that are common in word-processing programs; others invent organizational schemes, moving around blocks of text, highlighting key points, and connecting raw ideas on the screen like pieces of a puzzle.

Lewis Ulman suggests the following strategy for playing with a large block of unorganized text: "Start reading through it, and see a word that sort of keys onto an important idea, and use 'search and replace' to tell the computer to **boldface** all the instances of that word elsewhere in the text.

"Look for chunks of ideas, put paragraph breaks in, move those paragraphs around, and begin to experiment with the arrangement and organization of ideas in the text."

Instructor Michael Bertsch of Butte College recommends a variation on this approach. "You can make a map or an outline or a broken-down series of interactions by using the tab key only," Bertsch says. "Type out your word, and then you can tab over. You can make that in CAPITALS if you want; you can make it in *italics*; you can make it in **bold**. And if you have a *pattern* that repeats itself through your outline, you can use that. You can change the type size or you can change the color. All of those are things you can do at the computer with one or two points and clicks."

Computers can also be used as "sorting machines" to organize everything from research data to class notes. Mark Zempel, an instructional technology major, describes an approach many students use.

"I can't imagine doing the papers that I have to do now without the computer," Zempel says. "It's such a great organizing tool. All the ideas that I carry around on my little notebooks throughout the day – I bring them home and I put them on a notepad in the computer." As Zempel transcribes his class notes in the computer, he opens several windows and sorts them out according to topic. The various documents, he says, invariably match up with topics his instructors will target for writing assignments.

Computers and reading

Computers have clearly affected the writing process for professionals and students alike. Computers are *also* starting to affect the way we read, in everything from our posture to our attention span to how we bring what we read into what we write.

Chip Bayers, a senior staff writer at *Wired* magazine and former editor of the online-only magazine *HotWired*, suggests, "The experience of printed text is far different than viewing a story on your computer screen. So you have to put yourself into the mind of the person who's going to be reading or viewing your material. You have to understand that this is an experience for them, and it's an *interactive* experience. You're asking them not just to turn a page but to click a mouse or go on a hyperlink to another site. You might want them to view a little video, or listen to an audio track in one portion of your piece, but then return to some text you may have developed."

This vision is far different from the concept of the process of "reading" that most of us have been raised with. Cindy Selfe, an expert on composition and computers from Michigan Technical University, suggests our very definition of words such as *reading* and *text* will change because of computers.

"I don't think we can afford to limit our thinking of text to print text or book text or book reading anymore," Selfe says. "We're going to have to think of text as multimedia text, digital text, photographed text, moving images, computer games, the text of animation, and the text of simulation. English teachers are going to have to learn to be flexible about what they see as a document; we're going to have to start learning from students about what they consider the act of reading."

Presenting "papers" on the Web

Computers are even changing the way we present academic papers. Some instructors believe the medium itself will cause major shifts in the philosophy of structuring an argument. The very concept of a term *paper* may someday become outdated; students are already submitting research projects in the form of a World Wide Web site, and many more will follow.

Chip Bayers of *Wired* magazine points out, "There are already chunks of the academic community who are moving much more toward multimedia presentation, because they recognize the tools of the Web are very powerful. If you're a senior in an English department, and you're writing about Dylan Thomas, wouldn't it be great to have not only links to the full *text* of Dylan Thomas's works but audio, as well, of Dylan Thomas *reading* his own works? Won't you understand more, from the cadence of the poetry itself, if you're listening to the poet read his own work?"

The techniques of quoting and citing research sources will change as much as anything else when academic papers become commonplace on the Web. Lewis Ulman notices that his students at Ohio State are already learning how to deal with the changes.

"My students are already arguing serious academic work on the Web," Ulman says. "That allows links to sources. For example, if you're writing a paper about a community organization, you might be able to have links to that community organization's bylaws, or to news stories about it, and then come up with a readable, critical argument."

The links on the Web version of the paper would give the reader instant access to the evidence used to support the argument. In a traditional academic paper on the same subject, the writer would only be able to list the bylaws and the newspaper stories in the works-cited page. If readers wanted to read the full document, they would have to go to the library to access the original sources.

Of course, Ulman says, students will have to learn new methods to establish the *credibility* of evidence gathered from the Web and other online sources.

Research with computers

There is no doubt that the computer is a valuable research tool. In Mini-Workshop F "Doing Research on the Web" (pp. 469–477), Elbow and Belanoff discuss techniques for finding sources, evaluating online sources, and citing online sources. Most libraries today have completely indexed their resources with in-house computers; most colleges and universities provide students with direct access to their library archives.

This is an incredible boon to the student lifestyle. Are you stuck in your dorm room or apartment, cramming to finish a term paper at three in the morning? With enough coffee, it's no problem; you can dip into the school library database for a desperately needed quote or statistic at any time of day or night.

The public Internet is also a potentially valuable resource. However, students who quote Joe Bob's UFO Web site at <www.alienswillattacksoon.com> will likely not get grades that are as good as those who cite data from a respected source such as <www.nasa.gov>.

Librarian Sarah Blakeslee recommends using the Internet itself to judge the credibility of a source. "There are lots of sites out on the Internet – often from universities – about how to evaluate information you find on the Web," Blakeslee says. "It's very similar to evaluating information in a book, but there are some additional things you need to look out for. One of them is: 'Who put this Web site up?' Anybody can put something on the Web; not anybody can have something published in a scholarly journal."

It should be noted that many scholarly journals themselves are available on the Web; however, not all of them are free.

Blakeslee explains that the public Web is quite different from the private or the commercial Web. "The public Web is what people tend to refer to when they're saying the World Wide Web. These are documents that are available to anybody," she says.

"The private or commercial Web, we are just using the Internet as a vehicle of transportation or communication to access databases. The university pays money for these. They're only available to students and faculty and staff at the university."

Professional writers (and students willing to pay the fee) often find that specialized subscription databases are worth the price. While much of the information carried by these companies is available for free to those willing to do the time-consuming searches to find it, the ultimate search by someone who has a staff that has already collected and organized the data often costs the writer less in time and resources.

In the telecourse program, we encounter several professionals who use such databases.

Veterinarian Jim Esh uses the National Library of Medicine and a specialized search engine for journals about health and pets. Attorney J. Joaquin Fraxedas uses Westlaw and other legal research databases. And political satirist Al Franken uses an expensive (but powerful) database of news stories called Lexis/Nexis to wage war against his archrival, Rush Limbaugh. (Limbaugh, it should be noted, uses the same database to trade barbs with liberals.) Students in graduate school often use the same resources, and enterprising undergraduates are also using them more and more often – especially if the school provides the database free of charge.

Computers and collaboration

At first glance, the casual observer might assume that computers discourage social contact, luring the writer into a solitary relationship with a machine. But, as several teachers in the telecourse point out, the Internet allows writers to learn, socialize, and create together in a very interactive "virtual community." According to Chip Bayers, the very nature of the medium encourages collaboration.

"The description of the Internet has always been that it's a many-to-many network," Bayers explains. "I think that obviously automatically lends itself to collaboration, because it's not *one*-to-many, like broadcast television where there is one station sending out a signal that millions of people are receiving."

The Web provides students with a medium to invent and produce ideas together informally – in chat rooms, on electronic bulletin boards, or through e-mail. English instructors, who often emphasize collaborative writing and learning in the classroom, have started to experiment with the computer for enhancing opportunities in these areas.

At Stanford University, instructor Rich Holeton starts his students in a classroom with computers connected to a local area network. He eventually weans the students of their need to "attend class" within the same four walls and allows them to access the "virtual classroom" from their dorms or apartments.

Students continue "discussions" through an online "bulletin board thread." However, instead of being synchronous (in real time), many of the discussions are asynchronous. In other words, the students trade ideas at any time of the day or night; the interactions are preserved on the site for other students to view any time they visit the site.

"Threading is organizing the discussion by topics," Holeton explains. "You get a transcript. That transcript is already, by definition, a collaborative text. It's a text that everyone has produced together. It now becomes a new artifact – a part of the class and a 'document' that we can study and review. You can't do that with a face-to-face discussion."

In the online discussion threads, students post responses to other students' essays; then, other students post responses to the second level of responses. The discussions often become intense, with students quoting each other and supporting (or refuting) claims in an online debate.

Holeton observes, "If you quote your classmates from an in-class electronic discussion and cite them, you're starting to do that scholarly research – academic writing thing that we want students to learn. And you're starting to work as a true community of collaborative scholars, just like we do in the 'real' world."

In addition to collaborating informally, students develop a sense of audience, and they benefit greatly from peer feedback.

"When your work is published all the time, twenty-four hours a day, seven days a week, that gives you a different sense of audience than when the only way your work exists is to hand your essay to your teacher," says Holeton.

Though Holeton's Stanford model of online collaboration within an English composition class is centered around a localized university computer network, similar models can be set up on the Internet between students in different states or even different nations.

The collaborative document produced by Teresa Redd's students at Howard University and students at Montana State University (see the telecourse program "Collaborative Writing") is another example of what these online discussions and debates can produce, even when students live thousands of miles apart.

Megumi Taniguchi, an English instructor at the University of Hawaii who has experimented with collaboration between her students and students on the mainland, is enthusiastic about the possibilities: "I think that would be really neat, to have the students collaborate all over. I'd love if we can hook up with kids from India and kids from Japan and kids from the United States. What an enriching learning experience that would be."

Summary

Some instructors are skeptical about the popularity of computers and the acceptance of the online world into academia. It is easy to see their point; in our enthusiasm for the new technology, some may forget that the old ways of writing and composing work pretty well too. The computer is an interesting appliance, but it is not the only way to write.

Novelist Tom Robbins speaks for a minority with an important view when he says, "Writing by hand is so much more organic – particularly for someone who writes as slowly as I do. I love to watch that ink soak into the wood pulp. It sort of comes out of your brain and flows down the arm and onto the paper. There's a real natural rhythm there. I think ink is the blood of language, and paper is the flesh of language."

Some students (and instructors) relate to Robbins's point of view. Many more can see the advantages of computers and are using them as tools to compose.

And, as Selfe points out, even writers like Robbins are using a form of technology that was new to scribes at one time in our history.

"We don't have a choice, really, of whether we want to use technology to make meaning," Selfe says. "In fact, we're using technology right now, whether we use computers or not. The pen is a technology, and paper is a technology that we use to make meaning. Our real challenge is how can we look at the technology that we use to make meaning and to understand its limitations – and also understand its benefits. Even more important than that, we need to understand the implications that each technology will have for human communication."

Integrating the Text

Mini-workshop f "Doing Research on the Web" (pp. 469–478)

In Workshop 12, "Research," Elbow and Belanoff warn students that, "you can find informed, intelligent discussions of academic subjects [on the Internet], but these pages are in no way distinguished from less reliable pages. In short, when researching on the Web, you have to spend more time discriminating between what is useful and what is useless" (p.312). This passage refers students to Mini-Workshop F, "Doing Research on the Web" (pp. 469–478). In addition to giving advice on how to evaluate online sources, Mini-Workshop F explains how to use search engines to find sources and how to cite online sources correctly, using MLA style.

Most of the other points made throughout this telecourse show how the computer can be used in every stage of the composition process. Elbow and Belanoff support these points throughout the textbook, in passages about brainstorming ("Invisible Writing," p. 8), drafting and revising (p. 149), and editing (Mini-Workshop K, "Spelling," where homonyms are discussed on pp. 498 and 501).

Exercises

Check with your instructor for your formal assignments. You will be asked to do exercises from the *Telecourse Study Guide*.

Exploring computers in composition further

EXERCISE 1

Depending on the word-processing program you use, you may find it quite easy to insert within your paper an active hypertext link to an online source to which you refer in the body of your text. For example, recent versions of Microsoft Word will support this feature. Some word-processing programs allow you to browse the Internet from within the document itself. Failing that, you can simply highlight the URL (the stuff you type into the address bar of your favorite browser) and then copy and paste it into your document. When viewed digitally, the audience will be able to click on the link and see if what you're saying is supported by the facts in the linked document. Your audience will also be able to read the rest of the document to which you are linking, if the entire piece is of interest.

Take a paper you've previously written (in digital format) and find all of the places where you cite sources. For each citation, find a Web page that is related to either the author or subject of the text that requires the citation in the first place. If you've done research online for the paper in question, the sites to cite will be obvious from that step. One interesting aspect of hypertext is that the link the viewer sees on the screen does not have to consist of the same nonsensical string of characters that make up the URL. Here again, things depend on the word-processing program in use, but in most current versions you can highlight the existing words in your document that need the citation and make them the link to the address you wish.

EXERCISE 2

Open up a previously written paper in your favorite word-processing program, and find a section of the text in which you have attempted to verbally describe something. Now look on the Web for a photograph or illustration that shows rather than tells what you were describing. Play around with several different ways of inserting the picture in relation to the text with which it is associated. The formatting choice you make (where to put the picture) can be regarded as an extension of the composition process in much the same way as your choice of words. If your computer is capable of handling sound or streaming video, consider creating a link that will help illustrate an important point. For example, if you are writing about the rhetorical style of Dr. Martin Luther King, and can link to a speech on the Internet, this could be an important contribution to the paper.

EXERCISE 3

Consider the way the word *paper* is used in Exercise 2. Ask your instructor about the changing conventions of academia, and determine whether submitting a "paper" with links to pictures, sound, and video is appropriate, given the goals of the course. If appropriate, consider how the "paper" might be better if submitted as a self-constructed Internet site.

EXERCISE 4

1. *Writer's block exercise:* Try freewriting for fifteen to twenty minutes with your computer's monitor screen turned off. When you finish, turn on the screen and save the document. It will be, of course, filled with typographical errors and idle thoughts. That is fine. We will worry about organization later. Somewhere in the document, there may be a valuable idea or phrase or paragraph you would not have produced if you were reading as you were typing. Open a separate file; copy and paste the stuff that works into the new file. If this works well, consider trying it every day or two, just to get your writing kick-started.

2. *Disorganized essay exercise:* Take a look at an entire essay that has been criticized for being disorganized. Look for a key word. If a key concept is threaded throughout the document, highlight every use of the key word. Look for connections from section to section, to help you organize the threads of thought.

3. *Outlining exercise A:* Highlight the first sentence in every paragraph – and make it stand out in the document by increasing the font size or making the first sentence in each paragraph bold or italic. Highlight the thesis of your essay in the same way. Print out the document, and look at the rough outline created by the first sentence in each paragraph. Does the essay show a sense of organization this way? Does each new paragraph refer to (and support) the thesis? If the first sentence of the paragraph does not refer to (and support) the thesis, is there a topic sentence later in the paragraph that does – or does the paragraph need to be edited or deleted, to make the essay seem coherent and unified?

   Outlining exercise B: Using the outlining function in your word-processing program, try organizing the same passage of text.

Exercise just for fun

Students connected over a computer network are in an excellent situation in which to try what is known as the "Exquisite Corpse" method of story writing. As originally practiced, this method employed a single sheet of paper that was passed around a group of writers, each adding a sentence to the document in turn.

   If your class has a shared electronic forum where you can view and respond to each other's messages, start a thread called "E-Corpse" to which each student can add a sentence, either in an established order or whenever he or she happens to come into the "story." To do this by e-mail, print out and distribute a chart showing every student's e-mail address. Then decide by vote or by drawing straws who will write the first sentence. This person will write a sentence in an e-mail and send it to someone else on the chart. When that person gets it, she will cross off both her address and the sender's e-mail address from the chart, add her sentence, and forward it to someone else.

Rinse. Repeat. When every student has added a sentence, the "E-Corpse" is finished. The last person to add his or her sentence should e-mail the finished piece to the rest of the class.

Revision exercise

Use the "Exquisite Corpse" created in the "just for fun" exercise as a starting point for revision of your own version of the piece. Copy the text out of the e-mail and paste it into a new document in your word-processing program. You can cut and paste and drag sentences around and put them in any order that seems to make sense (or makes you laugh). Try to retain as much of each student's contribution as possible, but feel free to follow a tangent on your own, if you are so inspired. E-mail or post your finished revisions on the class bulletin board in the electronic forum, to share and comment upon, or set a day in class when you can exchange printouts to read and discuss.

Quick writing exercise

Your instructor may ask you to do a quick focused freewrite about the topic you are studying in this unit. Those of you who are taking the course through a distance-learning system may be encouraged to share your thoughts in a discussion thread or to post your ideas on an Internet bulletin board. If you are writing your thoughts out by hand in a process journal, you might use these questions to inspire a reaction. This is a freewriting exercise that will not be graded. You can use any of the following questions to stimulate your thoughts about using a computer to compose:

Does it help you write? Does it get in your way? What did you think of the main points made in the telecourse program? For instance, what do you think about spellcheckers, grammar checkers, using computers to freewrite, using computers to outline, or using computers to research? How can computers help you collaborate? Do you like to read on a computer? Is the computer your friend or foe? What do you think of submitting a research "paper" as a Web site? Would your instructor accept this departure from the traditional approach?

Exercises related to *A Community of Writers*

A Community of Writers offers two excellent exercises related to the use of computers in gathering information (pp. 475–476). The first is a six-step process designed to help an individual student evaluate the credibility of evidence gathered from a Web source. The second exercise is a collaborative group effort to explore some of the same issues. Read Mini-Workshop F, "Doing Research on the Web" (pp. 469–477), before attempting either of these exercises.

Quick review

1. Computers are helpful in the composition process
   a. While drafting
   b. while organizing
   c. while editing
   d. all of the above
   e. none of the above

2. The main advantage of word processors over typewriters is that
   a. Computer text is always much easier to read.
   b. Word processors make the revision stage easier.
   c. Computers always spell there words rite.
   d. All of the above.
   e. None of the above.

3. According to instructors in the telecourse program, computer interaction on the Internet,
   a. always creates isolation from real human contact
   b. provides students with many possibilities for collaboration
   c. inhibits creative writing
   d. all of the above
   e. none of the above

4. In research, computers
   a. allow students immediate access to sources on the Internet that are always reliable
   b. always link students to free information that could not be found in normal libraries
   c. allow students to link to very reliable databases that can cost average consumers a fee but are often provided to students for free through the university or college
   d. all of the above
   e. none of the above

5. According to guests in the telecourse,
   a. Academic papers presented as Web sites will soon become commonplace.
   b. Reading is exactly the same on the Web as it is in books.
   c. Just like most mass media, the Internet is a one-to-many communication model.
   d. All of the above.
   e. None of the above.

"Different organizational patterns are found in different kinds of writing. So if you're writing something for your manufacturing technology class, I would not suggest clustering. It seems like that's a very linear thing. You want to match how you organize your paper with the task at hand. In a freshman composition class, if it's a narrative, and if your teacher gives you a lot of freedom, it might make sense to cluster what's the main event or the main character. What are all of the things that happened around that character? Try to organize it that way. If you're doing a pretty structured research report, clustering might help. But, at some point, you have to get those bubbles in line. You need to be able to start with one thing, go to the next thing, go to the next thing ... and you have to move from clustering to something more linear. So I really think that the kinds of organizational strategies used depend on the kind of writing you're doing."

THOMAS FOX, California State University, Chico

Introduction to the Topic

Somewhere in a high school physics class, you probably came across the second law of thermodynamics (also known as entropy). It is, stated very succinctly: Chaos rules!

Think about how you are fighting this basic law of the universe every time you try to organize a pandemonium of ideas for a research paper or an essay.

It takes energy to make order of chaos, yet all writers must organize their thoughts and words. For some writers, it seems easiest to marshal the facts and quotes into neat little military ranks, like marching soldiers, in a traditional outline form. Other writers scribble a few sentences down on a scrap of paper; their "list-outlines" resemble a shopping list more than they do a tidy ordering of ideas.

Many writers think visually; they make drawings of ideas in a clustering of cartoon-like bubbles. Other graphically oriented writers gather their ideas around charts, photographs, pie graphs, and sketches.

Some writers organize at the sentence level – using a thesis sentence and a set of related topic sentences to somehow put a pattern to an anarchy of thoughts. Others use classic argument structures to organize their main points.

For centuries, instructors have been trying to tell students how to organize their ideas. Students, of course, follow their *own* laws of chaos and invent their *own* forms of organization. Some of these strategies are so good, we put fancy education jargon names on them – and now we can teach them as if they were invented by some textbook author.

Of course, students will continue to come up with their own unique ways of organizing that we haven't thought of – so we've decided to bring you to the smorgasbord and let you fill your plate with the styles that work best for you.

Take a look at the telecourse program, read this chapter in the *Telecourse Study Guide*, try a little of everything, and then decide for yourself what works best.

If you come up with your own strategy for organizing and it works really well, we'll coin a name for it and put it in the next generation of textbooks.

Learning Objectives

After viewing the telecourse programs and working on a variety of related exercises, you will become familiar with several traditional and nontraditional organizing strategies, and through doing this, you will start to learn what works best for you. You will achieve this goal by experimenting with linear outlines, graphically oriented non linear organizing strategies, sentence-level organizing devices, and the classic form of academic argument.

These objectives work in harmony with several sections throughout *A Community of Writers*. Elbow and Belanoff advocate using clustering to get started (Workshop 1, pp. 5–29), quick outlines when you need to write under pressure (Mini-Workshop E, pp. 463–468), and skeleton outlines during revision (Sharing and Responding, pp. 544–547).

Before Viewing

Think about your usual approach to organizing an essay or longer research paper. Recall whether you have accepted or rejected advice from your other writing instructors, including how to use a traditional outline to organize a paper. Imagine other methods of organization you have used or that you could think about trying.

Reconsider several sections in *A Community of Writers*, including the section on clustering in Workshop 1 (p. 7). In the passage on making and using outlines while writing under pressure in Mini-Workshop E (pp.464–465) and the segment "Seeing the Elements of the Argument" in Workshop 11 (pp. 279–281). Each of these sections connects with an important point in this telecourse program about organizing devices.

While Viewing

Draw a single line down the middle of a couple of pages in a notebook – creating two columns. In the first column, list the various methods of organization recommended by writers, instructors, and students in the program. In second column (alongside the first), add general impressions you have about each approach to organizing, including thoughts or comments on the videotape that made you think. Include in your impressions whether you have ever used this type of organization. If you have used the organizing device, note whether this approach helped your writing. If you have not used the organizing strategy, ponder whether it would fit with your thinking and learning style.

After Viewing

Using the exercises at the end of this *Telecourse Study Guide*, practice using several of the organizing devices discussed in the program, as you prepare for your next essay. Also consider how outlines, clustering diagrams, and other organizing devices can be used to revise your own work on an already-finished essay or how they can be used to help while giving feedback to another student.

In *A Community of Writers*, Elbow and Belanoff recommend using a variation of the skeleton outline as a vehicle to help evaluate another student's essay. See the section "Skeleton Feedback and Descriptive Outline" (pp. 544–547).

Viewing Guide

After they have generated ideas and gathered stacks of quotes and facts from their research, most writers find a way to organize the information *before* the formal drafting process begins. Please note that we said *most* writers. Some writers never do organize, and their work usually reads like they didn't. Others find that the best time to organize is *after* the first or second draft.

This chapter and unit of the telecourse offers a sample platter of approaches to organizing. One or more of them will work best for you.

A variety of approaches

Though some students hate the traditional approach of starting a paper with a formal outline, just as many students would feel uncomfortable starting *without* one.

Students learn in a variety of ways. As we'll see later, their preferences in organizing devices match up with different styles of thinking and learning.

As English instructor Joe Harris suggests, "It's important to acknowledge that everyone has a different kind of process. Part of what we have to do in a writing class is to experiment with many different ways of organizing material – and help students find the way that works best for them."

Starting with this observation, let us sample the many ways writers, students, and instructors organize their work.

The formal outline

For many, the formal outline method works best. It is a simple scheme most of us learn early in our lives – a linear, logical progression through the paper from the beginning to end, much like a football team advances from one end of a football field to the other.

Given that analogy, perhaps it is no surprise that someone such as Coach Bill Walsh would state in the telecourse program, "The only way I've written, all the way from junior high school, is in outline form. Point one and two and three, or point one, A, B, C, etc."

David Ellefson, bass player for the rock group Megadeth, also found the traditional outline convenient for organizing his book about the music industry. In the telecourse program, Ellefson explains, "I found out – as I was going back through and editing – the best material that I wrote was stuff that I actually had some sort of an organized outline [for]. And I actually do write with Roman numerals."

Ellefson uses a traditional approach most students learn in high school English courses. In the telecourse, Ellefson explains what his teachers taught: "Every Roman numeral should be a general topic or idea, and then you go down to capital letter *A* – that should be another paragraph. And within that paragraph you're going to have numbers one, two, and three – under which you may have other subideas of small letter *a*, small letter *b*, etc. I realized that when I started doing that [outlining], when I went back later to edit – the editing process really moved along a lot quicker. In other sections of the book, when I sat down at the computer and went and just started babbling [without an outline], the editing process was a nightmare."

Using this method, the first draft of an outline for a textbook chapter on organizing devices might be assembled in the following manner:

I. Organizing Before Your First Draft
  A. The Formal Outline
    1. Writers Who Prefer Formal Outlines
      a. David Ellefson – heavy metal rock musician
      b. Bill Walsh – football coach
    2. Writers Who Make Fun of Formal Outlines
      a. Janet Turner – police officer
      b. Dave Barry – humor columnist
  B. Alternate Approaches to Organizing
    1. Clustering & Mapping
    2. List Making
    3. Skeleton Outlines
II. Organizing After Your First Draft
  A. Unifying Sentences
    1. Thesis Sentences
    2. Topic Sentences
  B. Skeleton Outlines

This is a traditional approach that uses a linear thinking process and it works very well for many writers.

A high percentage of students rebel against the outline form – especially if they have been forced to organize this way by an instructor who does not recognize that some people are more comfortable with nonlinear thinking processes. These writers might like to freewrite first and find alternative methods to organize their thoughts midway through the drafting process.

Police officer Janet Turner represents many of these types of students when she confesses in the telecourse program that she hated the outline form in school: "Roman letters? A, B, C? Forget it. I can't operate that way. In fact, what's so funny is, in high school you'd always have to turn in your outline before your paper. Well, I'd write my paper and then go back and do my outline, because I could not think that way. It's ridiculous."

Though Turner defies the traditional advice for making a formal outline before writing, Peter Elbow of the University of Massachusetts suggests that her approach may actually be a good way to organize material. The trick is to use the final draft outline as a tool to evaluate the work and to consider writing one last draft if errors in organization are detected.

"Don't *start* by making an outline," Elbow says. "Then you're trying to make an outline with three main points, and you've only really got one point in your head. Outlines are a wonderful way to revise [after generating a draft]. First get a big fat mess; then make an outline."

Several successful writers in the telecourse program support Elbow's view. Charles Johnson (winner of the National Book Award for his novel *Middle Passage*) notes that he discards old plot outlines and starts new ones midway through the drafting process. Commentator Tom Bodett admits that if he doesn't like the way things are progressing in an essay, "the first thing to go is my outline."

Political science instructor George Wright goes so far as to suggest, "If you've got a twelve- to fifteen-page paper, you might actually write three, four, five, or even six different outlines. I think what is revised constantly is not the paper itself but the outline."

The problem, suggests Joe Harris, is that many English instructors have spent decades presenting outlines as the *only* organizing device.

"There were two problems with that," Harris explains. "One was that it asked students to map out what they were going to say *before* they had said it. If they were in a position to make that kind of outline, you would think they were done as a writer rather than beginning as a writer. The second thing was that it imagined that everybody went about the process of organizing their thoughts in the same way."

Alternate approaches to organizing

Quite a few writers have invented their own methods of organization. Some (such as the journalist's formula: who, what, when, where, why?) are verbal schemes. Others might have more in common with the way an artist would sketch an outline for a painting. The telecourse program offers a buffet of organizing devices to sample.

CLUSTERING AND MAPPING

Many nonlinear thinkers prefer visual or graphically oriented organizational schemes. In the video, Frank McCourt describes how he used one of these methods (called *clustering*) to organize the material for his Pulitzer Prize–winning novel, *Angela's Ashes*.

"I'm kind of a guerrilla writer," McCourt says. "I sift through all of my material, looking for an opening. I get these large artist's sketch pads, and I'll put down something like 'Mad Josey.' He was a character in my childhood – Mad Josey. Put things in circles. And I put down my mother, in the dispensary when she was on welfare, and make a circle. I have this big page filled with circles. Then I extract some of the circles, and I put them on the other page in clusters."

Joe Harris observes that clustering, mapping, and other visual schemes for organizing are effective because they help writers "think of a paper as radiating from a central idea" instead of making a linear, narrative progression. Using such a method, nonlinear thinkers might organize ideas while doodling on scratch paper just as effectively as a linear thinker might organize thoughts in a formal outline.

In *A Community of Writers*, Elbow and Belanoff offer an example of clustering on p. 7. They write, "A cluster diagram is…a 'map' of how concepts and ideas and feelings sit in your head. Cluster diagrams are often messy; sometimes you end up with a kind of spider's web of relations. But such diagrams are a good means for quickly getting down lots of possible subtopics and connections and also for giving a quick overview of a large conceptual territory."

Students who have been paying careful attention to the introductions of the telecourse programs will note that the concepts studied throughout the entire series are organized through a cluster diagram that appears on a green chalkboard during the opening sequence.

LISTS, SKELETONS, AND NUTSHELLS

List making, skeleton outlining, and nutshelling are organizing devices midway between the formality of the traditional outline and the free-form approach of clustering. These techniques can be effective for the most sophisticated professional writers as well as beginners.

John Lovas, English instructor at De Anza College, suggests: "Listing is one of the most powerful techniques a writer can use, and it seems like a throwaway. Most people sort of say, 'Make a list, big deal – anybody can make a list.' Well, that's exactly the power of it; anybody can make a list. You don't need a big piece of paper; you don't need a computer."

The next step, Lovas says, is just playing with the list. Some students, he explains, benefit from using three-by-five cards.

"So you write each thing you think you've got that you're going to write about on one of those cards … then you can actually start rearranging them," Lovas explains. "You say, 'Well, what if I did this?' If that doesn't make so much sense – just switch a card, just play around with it. Literally play around with it. You can do the same thing on computers with cut and paste lists … until you've got an order of ideas that starts making some sense to you."

Mo Collins, actress and writer for *Mad TV*, explains she how uses a similar combination of organizing devices to invent her famous characters: "I like to make lists about my characters – things I like about them, things that I don't like about them – how they make other people feel. I like to make collages on my characters. It's great to go through magazines and cut out ideas about a character; if you look at the piece of art, then it forms a personality."

Debra Wilson, also of *Mad TV*, compares the early rough versions of sketch comedy scripts to a skeleton: "I think that anytime you're writing, regardless if it's for comedy or a college course, you have to start with an outline. And that outline will be your skeleton…. A skeleton supports everything else around it." The improvisation done by the comedy actors is the "meat on the bones" of that script, Wilson explains.

Betsy Klimasmith, English instructor at the University of Washington, uses the skeletal structure as an important organizational device for college research papers.

"If you take out all the evidence, all the facts, and you're left with a thesis statement and topic sentences, that is an outline," Klimasmith explains.

"I like to think about a skeleton where the thesis idea is the backbone and then you have your ribs – those are the topic sentences. And then all the evidence is kind of the stuff that's in between."

Lovas explains a similar approach he calls *nutshelling*. "The idea is you have all this material, and you don't know exactly what to do. So the rule of the nutshell is this: In one sentence – it has to be a full sentence; it can't be more than one sentence – you must state the point you think you're going to make. And then you try to make three, four, or five other statements that you think support that. Putting it in a nutshell … that's the metaphor. The reason for stating each point in a sentence (and not two or three) is, it forces you to decide your focus.

"Then, once you've got that down, you can begin thinking about the sequence. The list is a very simple, quick way of doing it; the nutshell is a little more demanding because you have to write sentences."

SKELETON OUTLINE – AN EXAMPLE

- Thesis: Part of what we do in a writing class is experiment with different ways of organizing material and help students find out what works best for them.
- For many, the traditional formal outline works best.
- Many nonlinear thinkers prefer visual organizational schemes.
- Some organizing devices are midway between the formality of the traditional outline and the free-form approach of clustering.
- The most basic way to organize a paper is to narrow all of your raw information into one clear sentence.
- The classic academic argument itself is a kind of organizing device.
- You can change in the middle of a project; you are *likely* to change in the middle of a project.

Unifying sentence

The most basic way to organize a paper is to narrow all of your raw information into one clear sentence. Instructors call a one-sentence organizing device a number of different names: *premise, controlling idea, main claim, central point*, and *thesis statement*. Whatever you call it, this one sentence will help you get your paper started – and will help organize everything that follows.

Academic terms such as *thesis statements* give some students the impression this process is solely an academic exercise, with no practical application in the real world. Just the opposite is true.

Throughout the telecourse, we see that the difficulty of narrowing a complex idea down to one clear sentence is so common that it comes with a variety of different names – each popular with a specific profession. Journalists call it the *lead*; scientists call it the *hypothesis*; moviemakers call it *high concept*; sketch comedy writers call it *the joke*.

In the telecourse program, filmmaker Peter Farrelly explains the importance in his business of focusing an idea to one sentence, using one of his own films as an example: "There's a similarity between the thesis sentence and high concept. The movie *There's Something About Mary* is about a guy who tries to track down his high school girlfriend fifteen years later; he hires a private eye to find her, the private eye falls in love with her, and they both battle it out for her affection. That's the one line; that's the high concept of it. However, it does get way more complicated than that. And, in fact, if it were that story alone, it really wouldn't be very interesting. The high concept (the one sentence) is the thing that gets you in the door of the studio. They say, 'OK, I see where you're going.' But the thing that makes the movie work is the turns, the twists, and the character development."

Marine biologist Whitlow Au explains a similar organizing device used by scientists. In scientific methodology, the researcher will make a one-sentence hypothesis and then obtain data that supports or negates the hypothesis.

Student writers use a one-sentence statement, usually called the *thesis*, to serve a similar function. The thesis is "like the essay in miniature," writer and English instructor Duff Brenna explains. "It's the core of the essay; you make some kind of statement that you are going to support constantly in the essay. Everything that comes after (in the essay) should support the thesis statement."

John Lovas sums up the importance and the difficulty of writing the main point in one sentence. "It *sounds* easy. 'Oh, yeah, write one sentence.' What I find is, writers at the beginning will put their idea down in three or four sentences. But by using three or four sentences, you can kind of blur it. I think writers do that, because they're not confident of where they're going to end up. Try to write it in a single sentence – one clear sentence that says, 'This is what I want my reader to think when I've finished.' "

Often, a writer starts with a working thesis and *changes* the thesis as the paper takes shape. Some students fear that changing their thesis will only prove their thinking was faulty. However, the revising of a working thesis usually reflects the evolving thought process and critical thinking of the author.

As composition instructor Santi Buscemi points out, "The students have a preliminary thesis statement, and then they'll write a paper that won't fit the thesis statement, because writing is a process of *discovery*. And as they go through the drafting process, they start to learn. Something happens in their minds – they start to learn exactly what point they want to say about their subject. It becomes clearer to them and more focused. The actual process of drafting is a focusing activity. So, after they get to their first draft or their second draft, they haven't changed their thesis statement – the *essay* has changed their thesis statement – and that's fine."

Narrative and academic argument

The thinking/writing strategies we study individually in the telecourse can be thought of as organizing devices. For example, the narrative arc discussed in the unit on storytelling and narrative writing is a type of organizing device. A good writer can use Aristotle's classic "a beginning, a middle, and an end" – or the introduction of the problem, the complications of the plot, and the dénouement (or, resolution to the plot) to organize a story.

The formal academic argument is very similar in shape; the introduction, development, and conclusion form an arc of reasoning that is similar to a story. This thinking/writing strategy can also be seen as a kind of organizing device. The structure is so common that many instructors assume that written assignments will fit into this timeless formula.

The *introduction* usually contains the thesis. (The thesis is rarely the first sentence. Often, a paragraph or more gracefully leads into the thesis.) The introduction will also usually foreshadow the main subarguments in the paper.

The *development* section is expected to set out the evidence to back the thesis, in a logical, easy-to-follow manner.

The *conclusion* usually contains a restatement of the thesis – in slightly different words than the version of the thesis in the introduction. The conclusion usually summarizes (and ties together) the main points of the paper. A good conclusion also leaves some final thoughts for the reader to ponder – something that goes beyond the thesis. This could be a solution to the problem, a recommendation for additional research, or a final revelation that stimulates the reader to keep thinking.

Summary

As we close this unit, remember one final, important point. If your outlines, thesis sentences, clusters, lists, and topic sentences tend to evolve and change as you write, don't worry. If your conclusion in a formal argument turns out vastly differently from how you thought it was going to, that might have happened *because* you are a good student and a critical thinker.

You *can* change in the middle of a project. You are *likely* to change in the middle of a project. This should be a natural part of the writing process – as you learn, you change, you discover new ideas, and your original thoughts mature.

In *A Community of Writers*, p. 314, Elbow and Belanoff note, "The important thing to remember about outlines – whether generalized or specific – is that they're *only* outlines: You need not follow them like a robot. As you begin to write, you may discover some better structure. That may cause you to go back and revise your outline."

Santi Buscemi puts it this way: "I tell my students, the outline is not written in stone; this will change as you start to compose – as you start to put paragraphs together. You may think (two days down the line) that point four really should be point two. Make that change. You control the outline; the outline doesn't control you."

Integrating the Text

Peter Elbow and Pat Belanoff discuss organizing devices throughout *A Community of Writers*.

In Workshop 1, "An Introduction to the Variety of Writing Processes" (pp. 5–29), the clustering technique is introduced as a brainstorming method as well as a way to organize random ideas. An example of how clustering diagrams can help organize the essay appears on p. 7. Note that the brainstorming and organizing processes can overlap.

In Workshop 12, "Research" (pp.313–314), Elbow and Belanoff discuss strategies for outlining before or after a full draft and suggest, "Just don't agonize so long over your outline that you have little time and energy left to write the paper itself." The authors also note that writers should not be afraid to tear up their original outline and take a fresh approach to organizing their papers at any stage of the composition process. This advice can be applied to any of the organizing devices mentioned in *A Community of Writers*, including clustering diagrams, lists, outlines, topic sentences, and thesis sentences. In fact, a strong emphasis on the willingness to rethink an original premise (or "working thesis") is evident throughout the textbook as well as this telecourse.

In "Seeing the Elements of the Argument" (pp. 279–281), Elbow and Belanoff suggest that a student give feedback on another student's writing by analyzing an early draft and breaking the argument down to its main claim, reasons, support and assumptions.

This is similar to the advice given in the telecourse by instructors such as Betsy Klimasmith and John Lovas. If a reader can "summarize each reason [that supports the main claim] *in a simple short sentence,*" as Elbow and Belanoff recommend, then a teacher who is evaluating the work will also recognize the skeletal structure of the argument. If a reader has a hard time seeing the organizational structure in your paper, keep this in mind for the final draft.

Exercises

Check with your instructor for your formal assignments. You will be asked to do exercises from the *Telecourse Study Guide*.

Exploring organizing devices further

Work with two papers of your own writing. Select a paper you have already submitted to an instructor for a grade. (This can be a paper written for any class.) The second paper should be one that you are currently working on. Your assignment will be to use and compare organizational methods introduced in this telecourse program to rethink both papers. The idea is to see what method works best for you.

EXERCISE 1
Create a cluster diagram for both papers.

EXERCISE 2
Create a traditional outline for both papers.

EXERCISE 3
Use the journalist's who, what, when, where, why, and how to organize both papers. Ask and answer each of these questions about the papers' topics.

EXERCISE 4
Try variations of list making or skeleton outlines.

EXERCISE 5
Write a brief explanation of the organizing approach that works best for you.

Exercise just for fun

A QUICK "CONCEPT MAP"

Use a clean sheet of unlined paper. Write a main idea (word, phrase, or a couple of juxtaposed ideas) in the center of the page. Place related ideas on branches that radiate from this central idea. Some helpful formatting advice:

- The ideas should be brief, easy-to-read statements.
- Connect all elements with lines to the center or to other branches.
- For each new idea, start with a new "spoke" from the center.
- Write down everything you can think of.
- Go as quickly as you can; try to keep up with the flow of ideas.
- When you feel you've come to stop, look over your map to see if you have left anything out.

Revision exercise

Take a paper that you have almost finished, and create an outline. For many students, this is an unusual approach, because they have been taught to make an outline first, before drafting the paper. With only the new outline in front of you, try to imagine how a very demanding instructor would recommend that you revise the *outline* – as if you had not even started a draft. Tighten the structure, take out unnecessary points, consider the order and flow of topics, and add any important points that have been omitted. Now, using the revised outline, create the final draft of the paper.

Quick writing exercise

Your instructor may ask you to do a quick focused freewrite about the topic you are studying in this unit. Those of you who are taking the course through a distance-learning system may be encouraged to share your thoughts in a discussion thread or to post your ideas on an Internet bulletin board. If you are writing your thoughts out by hand in a process journal, you might use these questions to stimulate ideas. This is a freewriting exercise that will not be graded. You can use any of the questions listed here to activate your mind, as you freewrite about organizing devices.

Use this freewrite to spin some thoughts about your own approach to organizing a complex paper such as a research paper or term paper. The telecourse program discusses a number of organizing devices, including thesis sentences, traditional outlines, clustering techniques, skeleton outlines, listing, and the formal argument. When you studied the formal argument, you also heard the following terms: *controlling idea, main claim, working thesis*, and *thesis sentence*.

Every writer seems to use different types of organizing devices. What works best for you? Do any of the ideas make sense for your work? Do you have your own, self-invented style of organization? Or do you find that you can just sit down and write a successful paper, without any of these devices? It is OK to admit you don't use any of these approaches. (Did you notice how many writers made fun of the "traditional outline" in the telecourse program? Did you find anything in common with those who preferred a formal outline?)

When is the best time for you to start playing with these organizing devices? Do you start with an outline or with doodling of some sort, or do you find ways to organize your thoughts after the early drafting stages?

Exercises related to *A Community of Writers*
EXERCISE 1

A rather "traditional" research style term paper by Concetta Acunzo appears on pages 327 to 330 of *A Community of Writers*. This paper, written in the third person, has a clear-cut introduction, thesis, and academic argument, complete with identifiable topic sentences and a conclusion that restates the introduction.

This style of writing is rewarded by many teachers in many disciplines across the campus. To see how it works, do the following:

1. Identify the thesis sentence. (A variation of the thesis appears near both the introduction and the conclusion.)
2. Identify the key topic sentences (or controlling sentences) of the paper.
3. Construct a "skeleton outline" of the paper.

If time permits, create a more traditional outline of this paper.

I. Start with the Roman numerals to identify the main subjects.
   A. Use capital letters to show the main subheadings under each topic.
      1. Use Arabic numerals to show any additional subdivisions under this topic.
         a. Use small letters to show even finer subdivisions.

EXERCISE 2

After reading the descriptions of the different organizational methods in the textbook, apply each of them in turn to the Acunzo essay from Exercise1. Do you find that one of these methods works better for our understanding of the subject matter? You may find a mixture of parts from each of these methods works best. If so, put them together to create your own method.

Additional reading

As you read through samples in the appendix, consider: How do you think Steve Shanesy, editor of *Popular Woodworking*, organized his article about building book shelves before he wrote it? How would you organize a similar process analysis piece?

In the telecourse program, David Ellefson explains that he used a traditional outline form before writing his book, *Making Music Your Business*. Though his style comes off as very casual, can you detect the underlying structure? Do you think it would be possible to reconstruct his outline after reading his work? How is Ellefson's approach to organization different from Frank McCourt's organizational style, which is described in the telecourse program as being much like clustering? Is there a difference in the end result?

Read Dave Barry's piece in the appendix, "Business Memos." Though this piece is pure fun, it is organized very carefully. What are the organizing principles that make this excerpt from his book work? How is Barry's advice similar to the advice you have been getting for writing college-level papers?

Read the sample in the appendix from football coach Bill Walsh, "Establishing Evaluation Tools." The last sentence of the first section could be considered a thesis: "How well teams perform this task will have an impact not only on the effectiveness of their process for evaluating players, but also on their ability to be successful where it counts – on the field." List the organizing techniques that you think Walsh used to create this passage.

What are the similarities and differences in organizational techniques used for a television script (such as the excerpt from *Mad TV* in the appendix) and a formal argument, such as the essay in the appendix "Are Manufacturers of Caffeinated Beverages Targeting Children?" by Francine Taylor?

Quick Review

1. According to instructors in the telecourse program,
   a. All students should start a paper with a traditional outline.
   b. Once a student starts drafting with a good thesis, it should never change.
   c. It is important to experiment with different organizing devices and find what works best for you.
   d. All of the above.
   e. None of the above.

2. Some of the names given to one-sentence organizing devices include
   a. high concept
   b. the joke
   c. hypothesis
   d. all of the above
   e. none of the above

3. A student who is nutshelling or playing with a skeleton outline should include
   a. the full thesis sentence
   b. topic sentences
   c. ideas in complete sentences
   d. all of the above
   e. none of the above

4. According to the telecourse program:
   a. A student must stick to the outline very carefully when drafting.
   b. It is only an outline; if it doesn't work, toss it out and start a new one.
   c. The only appropriate time to outline is before the first draft.
   d. All of the above.
   e. None of the above.

5. In addition to traditional outlines, some of the other devices considered for organizing included
   a. the classic academic argument form
   b. informal, bubble diagrams – or "clustering"
   c. condensing the main point to one clear sentence
   d. all of the above
   e. none of the above

"During one class, students may be comparing texts – let's say a couple of descriptions of geophysical phenomena. Another time, they're comparing a couple of poems. Then, in yet another time, they're comparing a couple of theories about social behavior from psychology. The more that they try out these thinking/writing strategies with different kinds of disciplinary material – that is, they're actually trying these strategies out in real honest-to-God academic contexts – I think they get more proficient at using these thinking/writing strategies. They're able to leave that writing classroom and move into the world of the lower-division curriculum."

MIKE ROSE , UCLA

Introduction to the Topic

This chapter and telecourse program introduces two closely related thinking/writing strategies: comparison/contrast and division/classification.

The study of these skills dates to the time of Aristotle. These thought patterns (along with description, argument, definition, and other strategies we will study) have long been referred to as the rhetorical modes by some teachers and as genres by others.

Lynn Troyka of Queensborough Community College explains the history, noting that "people observed in ancient times how other people expressed themselves and solved problems; these kinds of so-called modes emerged from that kind of analysis."

In other words, Troyka says, people *think* by describing something, by telling how it works, by telling stories about it, and by comparing and contrasting.

Consider the following anthropological study of thought processes in the fifteen-year-old heavy metal music fan.

Assume this primate has only $10 in its pocket and desires to purchase a used CD of vintage heavy metal music. In the left paw, it holds a classic Led Zepplin recording; in the right paw, it ponders Iron Butterfly. Even with primitive intellectual capabilities, it considers basic comparisons of the recording acts: The thought "Zepplin shreds; all things metal start here" contrasts with the dim recollection "Iron Butterfly; one hit; really long drum solo; other songs hurl chunks."

If this biped is capable of a more complex thought process, it might notice that this section of the store has other choices; an elaborate division and classification scheme allows browsing of a plethora of other metal music acts. There's obese metal (Ozzy Osbourne), heavy metal lite (Def Leppard), Christian metal (Stryper), country metal (X), speed metal (Megadeth), and molten metal (Joe Satriani).

This *Telecourse Study Guide* assumes that the freshman college student, with a demonstrably advanced thought process, is capable of even more sophisticated uses of these thinking/writing strategies – and will be able to take them beyond the English composition classroom.

As marine biologist Chris Lowe notes, in his introductory statement on the video, "The basic skills that you learn in an undergrad English course are directly applied; they're the foundation."

Learning Objectives

When you complete this unit, you should know when the thinking/writing strategies of comparison/contrast or division/classification are needed in all styles of writing. That includes academic writing (including lab reports, exams, term papers, course assignments, etc.) and on-the-job writing. You will learn to adapt the techniques recommended by instructors, students, and professional writers who use comparison/contrast and division/classification and when these strategies are useful in your own writing.

As you study this genre of writing, you will realize how often the comparison/contrast and division/classification writing strategies are used in *A Community of Writers*.

Before Viewing

Before viewing this program, consider the skills you have already developed in using comparison/contrast and division/classification as thinking and writing strategies. Try to remember previous assignments from other classes that required these techniques.

The chances are high that you have an upcoming assignment in another class that requires one of these strategies. Try to imagine what skills you would need to succeed in such an assignment. Review Elbow and Belanoff's Workshop 9, "The Essay" (pp. 235–554) and the section on expository writing in Workshop 2 (pp. 48–49). While viewing the program, determine where the skills learned in this chapter and telecourse might apply.

While Viewing

Juxtapose the skills you already have in comparison/contrast and division/ classification writing with the techniques recommended by the instructors, students, and professional writers in the telecourse program. Note the skills that you have *not* already developed, and think about trying them in the next writing assignment that would benefit from such an approach. Become aware of the various styles of comparison/contrast and division/ classification writing used in different discourse communities. Notice how musicologist Rocky Maffit uses division/classification writing to develop his book. Observe how police officer Janet Turner compares and contrasts behaviors of methamphetamine and heroin users to establish accuracy in her police reports.

After Viewing

Look for good and bad examples of comparison/contrast or division/classification writing you encounter in recreational reading and reading you might do in the workplace. Look for variations of the strategies recommended in this telecourse program in the examples, and try to identify what is lacking in the poorly written examples. Determine what is considered appropriate (and inappropriate) comparison/contrast or division/classification writing within the discourse community of your chosen profession or academic major. Using the exercises in this *Telecourse Study Guide* chapter, practice techniques that can help you apply these strategies in an academic assignment or a real-life writing challenge.

In *A Community of Writers*, consider how Belanoff, Rorschach, and Oberlink use the thinking/writing strategy of division and classification in the piece "A Collage of Passages about Split Infinitives" (pp. 146–147). And, though it isn't strictly a comparison and contrast essay (most good writers combine thinking/writing strategies such as comparison, description, narration, and persuasion), notice how comparison is used in Melissa Fogel's essay "Be Brave Sweet Sister," pages 59 to 60.

Viewing Guide

Much of a writer's challenge is to organize random collections of information. Two common critical *thinking* strategies that also become important in *writing* involve comparing and contrasting or dividing and classifying ideas into distinct categories to make sense to the reader – and to the person doing the writing.

The telecourse program introduces comparison/contrast and division/

classification with examples of writing from the world beyond the English composition classroom. You'll see that a police officer, a scientist, a film producer, a musician, and a sports journalist all use these two thinking/writing strategies in their work.

The real-life examples of comparison/contrast and division/classification are introduced to avoid a common problem. All too often, students write such essays about meaningless topics, just to prove they know the form – and to get credit in a grade book.

Mike Rose, an expert on composition theory from UCLA, is aware of this phenomenon. In the video, Rose explains that if students try genres such as comparison "in real honest-to-God academic contexts" instead of just as abstract course assignments in an English composition class, they'll see the connection to actual writing challenges in upper-division classes and the world beyond the campus.

Common comparison methods

Some writers and students prefer to make up their own methods of comparing and contrasting. It is a fairly intuitive process. Since we all engage in these types of categorizations, consciously or subconsciously, on a daily basis, it is easy to improvise when writing in this style.

Other students prefer, at first, to use a predetermined pattern that has proved successful for other writers. The two most common patterns of comparison and contrast are fairly obvious.

- *Subject-by-subject comparison*: In this style of comparison, the writer uses the first half of the essay to examine and describe the attributes of one object and the second half of the essay to compare and contrast another.

- *Point-by-point comparison*: In this style of comparison, the writer alternates points – using a line or two for the first object, a line or two for the second object, a line or two for the first object *again*, and so forth.

In the program, you will see a student who is talking to her instructor about using comparison/contrast in a paper. University of British Colombia instructor Glen Downey counsels his student Sarah Zollinger to use a point-by-point strategy in her paper on the work of two architects. He clearly specifies the advantages of one approach of comparison over another.

"Would it be effective to talk about how the one architect does it in the early part of your paper and how the second architect does it later in the paper?" Downey asks his student. "No. It wouldn't be effective, because these two ideas then are completely dislocated."

Mike Rose says that it is important for beginning students to be exposed to these basic methods of comparison. "There may be times in particular classes where I may put on the board one of those kinds of cookie-cutter devices," Rose explains. "I may say, 'If you're having trouble getting started doing this comparison, here's a beginning sentence you might try: *There is a similarity between X and Y and it is such and so*. And then maybe in a follow-up sentence you might want to explain what you mean by this similarity. Then in a third and fourth sentence you want to give an example. After you've done that, you might want to move to a second paragraph that begins with a sentence that says something like: *Although there is a similarity, there is a difference as well*. Some students don't even have this strategy in their back pocket. They need it. It's providing them with a way to enter into this domain of thinking and writing comparatively."

A basic strategy, such as the one Rose describes, is valuable for experienced writers as well as students. Sportswriter Mark Ibanez explains that he uses the comparison/contrast strategy frequently in his writing, especially when he's on a deadline. For professional writers like Ibanez, comparison is seen as a convenient "gadget," or "a tool or a device to kind of set your piece off from a straight angle."

"It can also force you to be more creative, because you can't just leave it with one comparison/contrast; you've got to come up with a number to truly grind your point home," Ibanez says.

However, Ibanez also warns against allowing comparison writing to start sounding like a formula. "The only thing I worry about is just falling into a pattern of doing that all the time," he says.

Avoiding formula writing

Rose also cautions against writing too much with formulas, saying, "What we're talking about here is not *just* some sort of cookie-cutter rhetorical mode. That is, 'Here, dear student, is one way and only one way to write the comparison paragraph.' If that's where we [as instructors] stopped, then I think we'd be doing a tremendous disservice to students."

The next stage, Rose suggests, is to "complicate that simple process – to raise questions about what that little cookie-cutter device doesn't allow them to do. That's a real education in writing."

Creating a thesis

The risk in studying organizing techniques such as point-by-point or subject-by-subject comparison is that some students try to substitute the learning of formulas for actual substance in the writing. The skills of comparison and contrast should be used to address a need in the writing; the essay still has to have a strong thesis.

John Lovas, of De Anza College, gives this example: "Take high-cost and low-cost automobiles and compare and contrast. The papers will have all sorts of details and all sorts of well-formed sentences. At the end of three-and-a-half pages of comparing high-cost and low-cost cars, I'm sitting here saying, 'Why did you bother? So what? What's the *point* of all this contrast?' We never get to a point. Often, the writer has some point in mind but doesn't understand that the comparison is not an end in itself."

One approach an instructor can use to discourage meaningless, formula comparison/contrast essays is to require students to include a clearly stated premise similar to the main claim in an argument paper.

Another approach is to have students actually *use* the thinking/writing strategy of comparison/contrast as a way to *think* through a problem, instead of just using it to compose an essay. Teresa Redd, who teaches composition to a special section of students who are all engineering majors at Howard University, uses this method.

Her students must use comparison/contrast as a problem-solving strategy in their introductory engineering design course. The difference, in this situation, is that the problem solving comes *before* the writing. "They can see it as a critical thinking strategy," Redd explains.

"They can see language as a tool for accomplishing goals. Unfortunately, many of our composition texts and composition courses were so divorced from content and *purpose*, the strategies just seem like formulas to students. They think, 'Oh, I've got to write a comparison/contrast essay' – and the students don't realize this is a way to make *decisions* in a logical way."

Real-life examples

The telecourse program includes examples of writers who do use comparison/contrast to make a point. Police officer Janet Turner uses the strategy in her arrest reports every day; she isn't merely writing essays for an English composition course.

Notice how Officer Turner uses comparison/contrast to determine the behavior of subjects under the influence of either heroin or methamphetamines. Her reports feature both point-by-point and subject-by-subject comparisons, though the writing is not the result of a contrived formula. Comparison and contrast are also used as a problem-solving or thinking strategy to determine the source of a criminal's behavior.

Turner characterizes "crank users" (those who take speed or methamphetamines) as "very skittish, very restless, very talkative," with divided attention, jumping from subject to subject. She says they are likely to be "standing up, sitting down, constantly rubbing their hands, rubbing their faces." This is a stark contrast to a heroin user, who has droopy eyelids and answers questions a minute or two after he has been asked. The comparison/contrast clearly shows the difference between a speed user and a heroin addict.

Division and classification

The division/classification strategy is very closely related to comparison/contrast. It's also a way of organizing a chaos of ideas into categories, although the writers who use this tactic usually have a more complex task than simply comparing two objects.

The telecourse program uses an extraordinary book called *Rhythm and Beauty* to illustrate this writing genre.

Composer and percussionist Rocky Maffit explains that when he decided to write a book about his instruments, he put a lot of thought into the organization of the project. His natural thought process led him to a discussion of rhythm instruments in a classic division/classification style.

Maffit organizes his book about percussion instruments into four groups: drums; tonal percussion instruments; shakers, rattles, and noisemakers; and a category he calls "beyond tradition." Each classification is again subdivided, so that the author can help the reader explore complex variations of his subject.

As Maffit explains the subdivisions with each category of instrument, it is clear that his purpose demanded the form. In other words, the content came before the genre.

This is an important concept to bear in mind as you apply the lessons in this unit to writing an essay or research paper. Writing in the real world is almost never presented to the author like a course assignment; there won't be an instructor who assigns you a comparison/contrast or division/classification "paper." However, your real-life writing challenges will often require you to use these strategies.

Though it is good to practice these forms – to be familiar with them when the need arises – a formula essay, with too much emphasis on form over content, can be a hollow and meaningless exercise. Formula writing is not satisfying for either the student or the instructor who is stuck reading it.

With that thought in mind, this is a good point to reconsider Elbow and Belanoff's discussion of whether content should come before form. *A Community of Writers* explores this question in the section "Exploring Theory: *Are Genres Form or Content?*" on pages 53 to 55. Notice that the passage itself is a subject-by-subject comparison/contrast essay. The first half of the passage explores what might happen if the writer starts content only. Elbow and Belanoff then explore what might happen if a writer stars only with a form of essay (such as comparison/contrast or division/classification) as the primary goal, without thinking too much about the content.

Summary

We all use variations of comparison/contrast and division/classification in both academic and social discourse. The telecourse program ends with an observation by Donald Pharr of Valencia Community College, who emphasizes that these schemes of thought are *not* just formulas. If used correctly, they allow the writer to tap into creativity, humor – even deep academic-style thinking. They also work in on-the-job settings.

"If I'm working for my boss, Bob, and I'm sitting in my Dilbert-like cubicle, and Bob comes by and says, 'We've narrowed our search for a new company car down to two – the Buick and the Toyota. I've got all this information;

write me a report and let's try to come to a decision,' what kind of mode am I going to use? I'm going to use comparison/contrast," Pharr says.

"Do I have a choice? No. Did he assign me a comparison/contrast mode? No. He gave me a set of information that gave me no choice."

Pharr notes that "rhetorical modes weren't invented by English teachers." Thought processes such as comparison/contrast and division/classification have developed from the basic needs of communication.

Integrating the Text

WORKSHOP 9   "The Essay" pp. 235–254

The section on "Expository Essays," pages 48 to 49 in *A Community of Writers* explains why so many teachers assign comparison/contrast essays, as well as other genres such as definition and process analysis essays. After reviewing that section, re-read Workshop 9, "The Essay" (pp. 235–254), which thoroughly explores the difference between the personal and the impersonal essay. Workshop 9 also suggests several strategies for developing a formal academic essay.

At some point during the semester, your instructor may have asked you to write an expository essay using one of these "genres" or "rhetorical modes" (comparison/contrast, division/classification, definition, process analysis, etc.) – although you may be given the task of developing your own topic and deciding yourself which genre or thinking/writing strategy is most appropriate for the essay.

Several essays in *A Community of Writers* are exceptional samples of comparison/contrast or division/classification writing, and offer excellent opportunities to analyze how this style works. (Note: One exercise in Workshop 9 asks you to analyze an essay. Your instructor may also ask you to analyze an essay, based on the advice given in the telecourse program about comparison/contrast and division/classification writing). Consider how Belanoff, Rorschach, and Oberlink use the thinking/writing strategy of division and classification in the piece, "A Collage of Passages about Split Infinitives" (pp. 146–147). And, though it isn't strictly a comparison and contrast essay (most good writers combine thinking/writing strategies such as comparison, description, narration, and persuasion), notice how comparison is used in Melissa Fogel's essay "Be Brave Sweet Sister," on pages 59 to 60.

The essay "From Eve's Rib: The Biological Roots of Sex Differences" by Robert Pool (pp. 397–399) is an excellent example of how the comparison can be used in scientific writing. Notice that this essay contains an extended section using the point-by-point comparison strategy.

Exercises

Check with your instructor for your formal assignments. You will be asked to do exercises from the *Telecourse Study Guide*.

Exploring comparison/contrast further

Exercise 1

1. Take a moment to think of two items that are related but different. Examples could include two musical groups, two restaurants, two schools you've attended, and the like. Do a quick freewrite about the two items. Grammar and spelling are not important in this step; you should just try to get down on paper as many ideas as you can think of in relation to your subjects.

2. Go through the document created in step one and transcribe (or cut and paste) each idea you've written down into another document, taking care to separate them into at least two groups according to which of the two items they describe. *You may find that you need a third group for ideas that refer to both items in general, background/ explanatory information, or maybe your feelings about the overall subject matter.*

Exercise 2

Use the outline (or the product of whatever organizational method you used) created in Exercise 1 as a guide for a first draft of a comparison/contrast essay. Remember to begin with a thesis statement that identifies the subjects that you are describing. This draft can be very rough; like any first draft, you will be using it as a starting point to be refined in later versions.

Exercise just for fun – division/classification

This exercise can be done anywhere you find yourself with a little bit of extra time in a browsing situation, such as at a music store, library, or a video rental place. Before making a beeline to the section you would usually go to, take a moment to consider the sections you don't go to and the reasons why you don't. You will then be experiencing the *division/classification* phenomenon firsthand.

Revision exercise

In this exercise you will use the results of the freewrite performed in Exercise 1 and the rough draft from Exercise 2 as starting points for two different revisions. These will be as follows:

1. Write an essay that follows the *point-by-point* method described in the text. Take care to begin with a clear thesis statement that identifies for the reader what you will be talking about in the essay.

2. Write a version of the same essay by following the *subject-by-subject* method described in the text. Take care to begin with a clear thesis statement that identifies for the reader what you will be talking about in the essay.

   Note: Make sure to include the ideas that fell into the "other" category of your initial organization chart.

Quick writing exercise

Your instructor may ask you to do a quick focused freewrite about the topic you are studying in this unit. Those of you who are taking the course through a distance-learning system may be encouraged to share your thoughts in a discussion thread or to post your ideas on an Internet bulletin board. If you are writing your thoughts out by hand in a process journal, you might use these questions to compare your ideas with those presented in the telecourse. This is a freewriting exercise that will not be graded. Use any of the following questions to stimulate your thoughts about the comparison/contrast and division/classification writing:

Can you think of times when you have had to use comparison/contrast when you weren't assigned a comparison/contrast essay? Can you think of situations where you may have to use comparison/contrast (or division/classification) in a work-related writing assignment? Does this seem like just an academic exercise to you, or do you think there will actually be some sort of application for this type of writing in your future?

The questions in the "Process Journal" section of Workshop 9, "The Essay" (pp. 242–243), will be helpful in this writing exercise.

Exercises related to *A Community of Writers*

EXERCISE 1

Read Workshop 9, "The Essay" (pp. 235–253). Using the questions on page 241, analyze the following essays: "Be Brave Sweet Sister," by Melissa Fogel (pp. 59–60); "From Eve's Rib: The Biological Roots of Sex Differences" by Robert Pool (pp. 397–399). In your analysis, be sure to consider how each writer used the techniques of comparison/contrast.

EXERCISE 2

Analyze how Belanoff, Rorschach, and Oberlink use the thinking/writing strategy of division and classification in the piece "A Collage of Passages about Split Infinitives" (pp. 146–147).

Additional reading

Notice, in the appendix, how the excerpt from *Everything You Need to Know About Latino History* by Himilce Novas uses some of the techniques studied in this unit. Several thinking/writing strategies are combined. How many of those strategies can you identify?

How do the scriptwriters at *Mad TV* use comparison/contrast to create irony in the sketch about the "Spishak Home Theater"? (An excerpt from the script that appears in the telecourse is published in the appendix.)

In the telecourse, instructor and novelist Chitra Divakaruni talks about how she usually blends genres, or thinking/writing strategies. An excerpt of her short story "Clothes" appears in the appendix. How does Divakaruni use comparison/contrast to develop the narrative of this piece?

Quick Review

1. The main difference between comparison/contrast and division/classification writing is that
   a. Division/classification is rarely used outside of the classroom.
   b. Division/classification allows for a slightly more complex organizational scheme.
   c. Comparison/contrast is nothing more than a simple formula that can easily be used in a classroom.
   d. All of the above.
   e. None of the above.

2. According to this chapter, strategies that students can consider when drafting a comparison essay include
   a. point-by-point comparison
   b. subject-by-subject comparison
   c. a self-invented strategy
   d. all of the above
   e. none of the above

3. According to instructors in the video program,
   a. Comparison/contrast is also a critical thinking strategy.
   b. Writing merely to learn a formula can create essays that are devoid of content.
   c. Familiarity with comparison/contrast writing can help later, with real-life writing challenges.
   d. All of the above.
   e. None of the above.

4. In the video, percussionist and writer Rocky Maffit uses
    a. comparison/contrast to develop a book
    b. division/classification to develop a book
    c. subject-by-subject strategy
    d. all of the above
    e. none of the above

5. According to instructors quoted in this chapter,
    a. A comparison/contrast essay should have a main point or thesis.
    b. The content should determine the form, or genre, of the writing.
    c. Rhetorical modes, or thinking/writing strategies, are derived from the way people think.
    d. All of the above.
    e. None of the above.

"I think that one of the most valuable next steps, after just having students listen to each other, is just to have them read it and ask, 'What was the main point of what that person just said?' I want a writer to get multiple senses of what other people heard her say. Once they've received these summaries from other students, then you can say, 'Which one of these do you think hits best at what you were really driving at?' And they'll say, 'Well, this one does, but I'd want to change a few words.' And then you can move to the next step which is, 'I think the most *important* thing that you are saying is ...' "

PAT BELANOFF
State University of New York at Stony Brook

Introduction to the Topic

This telecourse is called *English Composition: Writing for an Audience*.

Here is one reason why.

In a common model of teaching, the student gives an essay to the instructor, the instructor puts red marks on it, the essay is handed back, and nobody ever reads it again. The student does not develop much of a sense of audience.

A writer-in-training *needs* audience feedback. According to those who conduct research on teaching effectiveness, students often learn more from other students than they do from the instructor.

In this telecourse program, students spend a great deal of time reading and critiquing papers by other students.

This peer feedback process can be accomplished a number of different ways – especially through modern approaches to distance learning, where the students can e-mail papers back and forth, post their essays on an Internet bulletin board, and use sophisticated peer feedback software. If other students read your essays, and give you feedback, you now have an audience – even if the class only has twenty other undergraduates just like you.

Writing is meant to communicate. If you are shy about showing your work to others, consider this: In the working world, your documents will be read by your boss, your coworkers, your business associates, and your clients.

All will give you feedback. Many won't hold back *anything*. Your feelings are not an issue when the business is at stake. Why not get used to the process now?

In the relatively safe environment of an English composition course, you can learn from even the gentlest feedback. You also learn about your own writing by finding flaws and gems in the work of others; in the process, you may build the skills of tact and diplomacy that will help you suggest improvements. If the advice from others is given with good intentions (the feedback in college is rarely mean-spirited), everybody benefits.

Learning Objectives

After viewing the television program and working on related exercises or assignments, you will learn how peer feedback is a normal part of any writing process – in college and beyond the classroom. You will practice the art of giving peer feedback and will also learn how to receive feedback in a way that will help you revise and improve your early drafts. You will also learn how to become an authority on your own work and gain confidence in your judgment as a writer, as you begin to judge the criticism of your work.

These learning objectives work in harmony with the concluding section of *A Community of Writers,* "Sharing and Responding" (pp. 511–557). Elbow and Belanoff's goal in this peer feedback section is "to help you become comfortable and skilled at asking for feedback and giving it."

Before Viewing

Before you formally study this topic, try to remember your previous experiences with peer feedback. Consider the following questions: Does it help once in a while to just have a friendly audience that gives you somebody other than the instructor to think about when you write? Have you been able to help others with peer responses? Were you so polite that the other writer barely learned anything about his or her flaws? Were you, perhaps, a little harsh? Or, as it is with some students – have you never even participated in peer feedback? Read the "Sharing and Responding" guide in *A Community of Writers* (pp. 511–557) to learn about different kinds of peer feedback.

While Viewing

Compare your preconceived notions about peer feedback with the attitudes expressed in the telecourse program. Learn *who* uses peer feedback, *why* they use it, and *how* they do it. Observe the various approaches to peer feedback mentioned by writers and instructors in this telecourse program. Compare them to the "Summary of Kinds of Responses" listed in *A Community of Writers* (pp. 511–515). Notice how the attitudes toward peer feedback change subtly from occupation to occupation, and imagine how peer feedback might be practiced in your own chosen career.

After Viewing

Using the exercises in this chapter of the *Telecourse Study Guide*, devise strategies to give (and receive) peer feedback on your next important assignment. Reconsider the passage in *A Community of Writers,* where Elbow and Belanoff encourage writers to avoid a passive or helpless attitude: "You as the writer get to decide what to do about any of this feedback from readers, what changes to make, if any" (p. 508). Elbow and Belanoff also suggest that writers should decide what kind of feedback they need and want form other students.

Viewing Guide

Peer editing is a form of collaboration. Although the brain is amazingly versatile in detecting and solving problems, it can't be trusted to recognize *every* mistake. This is especially true when the mind is attempting to evaluate its *own* writing. It is easier to see errors (and gems) in someone else's work, and the process of peer feedback allows the writer to team up with coworkers, friends, family members, or class members. Peer feedback is mutually beneficial, providing a "test audience" that can spot problems and strengths the original writer can't see. It's also one of the best ways in both college and the "real world" to turn out a document that is both clear and error free.

Feedback and tact
Professionals in every occupation surveyed for the telecourse said that peer feedback was a natural and necessary part of the working world.

In the video, marine biologist Chris Lowe explains how scientists use peer review relentlessly to improve their work. "One of the greatest ego blows you receive is when you spend hours, days, weeks, months working on a paper, polishing it, honing it to what you think is just perfect," Lowe says. "Then you give it to your professor or you send it out to your peers for review, which is a standard practice in scientific writing. You get it back, and it's just ripped to shreds. You need very thick skin because everybody has different styles [but] the idea is, the more people who read it, the more people who can improve it."

Feedback is tough-minded in fields such as research science, medicine, and engineering. Otherwise, the results from a minor mistake could be catastrophic. For example, if a paper started out calculating trajectory in inches and switched midway to centimeters, the research vessel sent to study Mars could easily miss by a few hundred thousand miles. Feedback from a peer group member (usually) can catch such an error.

In many writing environments, peer feedback is more casual. The ultimate goal is an atmosphere of inventiveness and free-for-all brainstorming in a group of cordial coworkers. The team of sketch comedy writers at *Mad TV* works hard to build such an environment.

Scott King, a writer and associate producer on the staff, explains the unspoken rule of his comedy-writing team: "One of the things that we have found that does *not* work is when you stop and say, 'Hmmmm, I'm not so sure about that idea!' Because it just kills the energy of the room. It's kind of like an agreement among the writers; when an idea doesn't work and nobody responds to it, you keep moving forward. So it's not too often that you see the writers say to each other, 'No, that's not funny.' It's more like, you just keep throwing out ideas until everyone laughs. You've really created an atmosphere that's just creating – not deciding right off the bat 'that's funny' or 'that's not funny.' "

The scene King describes is designed to help build confidence among the writers, allowing them to toss out silly (or even stupid) ideas without retribution. Many writing instructors try to create a similar attitude in the first-year writing course.

Feedback in the classroom

"The value of a peer response group is that it builds confidence," explains English instructor Santi Buscemi. "Most of my students are very supportive of each other, and they need that. That alone makes the small group worthwhile. It also allows them to work in a group, and in the modern world we need to work together; we need to cooperate with other people. When they get into the business world or the scientific world ... they're going have to work with teams of people. If you've got two or three friends sitting around you whom you trust, they will help you get it out. They will suggest things, and you will suggest things for them. For some reason it's easier to write somebody else's paper than if it's your own."

Many students feel uncomfortable about giving advice to peers, thinking they will come off as "critical" or "picky." If you are one of those students, turn the process around. If your paper has hidden mistakes, wouldn't you *want* another student to help you look for things you missed, before you submitted the document to the instructor for a grade?

There's no need to be rude about a document handed to you by a trusting peer. Still, your duty is to spot as many problems as possible and point them out *with tact*. Instructor Ariel Gonzales of Miami-Dade Community

College gives his students this advice: "I tell them, you're not helping the person out by being too nice. You're not helping the person out by being gentle. You're not grading it, so there's no penalty involved. The best thing you can do is rip it up. Then, whatever mistakes are there, when the person rewrites the essay, it will improve his or her grade. I think peer review is necessary, because it does introduce objectivity. They are obviously getting feedback on their own essays. But they are also practicing their own editing skills."

Of course, it is just as valuable to point out a paper's strong points. Often, an encouraging comment can help a writer gain the confidence needed to build on good work to make it even better.

Audience and peer feedback

Peer editing is part of the process of becoming a better writer. As you practice helping others find their strong points and weak points, you will get better at finding your own. More than just spotting errors, peer review gives the writer a sense of *audience* that helps change the writing. As you learn how your audience *reads* you, it becomes easier to make decisions about language use.

Michael Bertsch of Butte College explains how having even a small audience of peers helps the writer determine what the readers of the essay will actually *perceive*. "The writer thinks he or she has everything down. 'Oh, yeah, this is exactly what I mean.' But when the audience member sees it, the audience member has to say, 'Look, *this* is what I read. Is this what you *meant* me to read?' If the writer hears something different from what he or she intended, it must be edited. You can't get that unless you show it to your audience member."

Kim Stanley Robinson, who taught Composition before his success as a science fiction writer, had his students "publish" their work for the entire class, rather than turn it in for the instructor's eyes only.

The idea was to "make them write for the whole group," Robinson explains. This simple act often makes the writing process more real for the student. "They definitely blow it off when it's just for the teacher. The ability to vilify a teacher and say, 'That's someone I don't care about, they're a power figure, they're a danger, they're somebody I have to negotiate like a policeman' goes away. What it comes down to is that you were writing for an audience. You *need* to be writing for an audience. People care more, they work harder, they get more feedback. And a group teaches itself."

In *A Community of Writers*, Elbow and Belanoff agree completely with these observations. "In the long run, you will learn the most about writing from feeling the *presence of an interested reader* – like feeling the weight of a fish at the end of the line. It's hard for writers to prosper unless they give their work to a variety of readers (not just teachers) and get a variety of responses" (p. 510).

Elbow and Belanoff recommend starting with completely non-evaluative responses, where the reader simply becomes a good listener. Much later, as the students get more comfortable and experienced with the feedback process, they can "learn to write to the enemy – to write surrounded by sharks" (p. 508).

Learning through feedback

Students often discover (without the help of an instructor) that peer review is not *just* fixing grammar and spelling – although, it can help with that too.

Peer feedback is a way of learning and *discovering* new ideas together. In fact, the more you participate in the peer feedback process, the more you will personally realize what learning theory experts have been saying for decades: You can learn as much from other students as you can from the instructor.

Megumi Taniguchi of the University of Hawaii expresses the views of many instructors: "Students will pick up on stuff that I've entirely missed, because I was staying up until two in the morning trying to drink coffee to try to stay awake, or because I just didn't see it that way. They have a different perspective on things."

Beverly Moss, an instructor at Ohio State University, points out that, as you practice reading another student's work, you begin to develop new strategies to read your *own* work. "The students have this wonderful ability to read other people's essays and say, 'You know, I think that's a subject-verb agreement error.' or 'I think that you might organize this differently. I don't think this paragraph leads to the next paragraph.' But I don't think they ask those questions of *themselves* as writers. I think the more they do it with other people, the better they get at looking at *their own* text."

Mark Reynolds of Jefferson Davis Community College also uses peer review to build confidence in his students. If his students learn how to spot a comma splice or a weak thesis in another student's paper, they can approach their own work with conviction. Reynolds and other instructors even go so far as to appoint various students within a classroom as "the apostrophe expert" or "the czar of topic sentences." The idea is to let students know that *they* eventually become the authorities on their *own* work.

In *A Community of Writers*, Elbow and Belanoff suggest students can learn much more about the *impact* of the writing through peer feedback than they can learn about organizational grammatical problems if they merely use that feedback to "fix" an essay for a teacher to grade. "Evaluation and advice are not what writers need most," Elbow and Belanoff say. They suggest that a writer benefits more from hearing what the essay *almost* says, or from learning what is going on in the reader's mind as he or she reads the essay: "What you imply but don't say in your writing is often very loud to the readers but unheard by you" (p. 512).

Peter Farrelly writes scripts for movies with his brother Bobby. "My brother really helps me see what is funny, and I help him see what is funny as well," Farrelly explains. "He'll have a seed of an idea that's kind of funny. I'll say, 'I know where you're going with it; that's good, but what if we try this?' Then, badaboom. You switch something around and it's funnier."

Summary: knowing when you're right

Become an authority on your own work!

That is an excellent final thought on the subject of peer feedback. It is important to remember that the person giving feedback could be wrong and that *you* may be correct.

If the suggestions you receive for changing a document do not "feel" right – that's OK. It's all part of the peer feedback process. Whatever the suggestions for changes, *you* make the final decisions.

Betsy Klimasmith, an English instructor at the University of Washington, puts it this way: "You need the courage to say, 'It's my paper, darn it' – but you also must not be so wrapped up in your own paper that you're not able to listen."

If you think the act of rejecting feedback and sticking with your own decisions takes a bit of audacity in the classroom, imagine the implications it might have for writing on the job.

Several examples are offered in the telecourse. Even in the face of criticism from her boss, police officer Janet Turner resists *some* revisions. "There are times where the boss wants it edited, and I'll say, 'No. I like it this way. This is what I'm trying to get across.' And sometimes I'll just go to the sergeant and say, 'You made this comment, and that's fine. But let me tell you why I did what I did; this is what I'm trying to get across in my report.' And he'll go, 'OK' – *sometimes*. Other times he'll say, 'I don't care, change it. This is what I want to see.' And you change it."

Actress Debra Wilson explains that the process is similar in the collaborative writing process at *Mad TV*. "Aries Spears [an actor on the comedy team] came up with a sketch based on the Spike Lee movie *He Got Game*. The producers were like, 'Is it going to be funny or not?' They couldn't judge. Aries was adamant about it; he had such a clear vision of hearing the audience laughter and getting feedback from everybody that they finally said, 'We're behind you.' They gave in; it was shot, and it was hilarious.

"Now there were other times where I believed that [a sketch] was going to work – and I wanted to stick to that vision. You know what? The sketch fell on its face. And so it's finding that fine line between 'I have a vision for what I want to do' and having a new vision – or revision."

Kim Stanley Robinson emphasizes that seriously considering (and possibly rejecting) peer feedback can help build a writer's self-reliance. Robinson offers this final bit of advice: "One person will say, 'I thought that worked really well.' And the next person will say, 'Well, I thought that *didn't* work at all.' At that point, you begin to judge the criticism of your own work as being more than, 'The teacher/god says this, therefore it's true – and therefore I'm wrong.' You begin to get more confidence in your judgment as a writer, as you begin to judge the criticism of your work."

Integrating the Text

In *A Community of Writers*, Elbow and Belanoff value the peer feedback process so much, the dedicate an entire step-by-step "Sharing and Responding" guide (pp. 505–557) at the back of the book to the subject.

Elbow and Belanoff emphasize that the different *kinds* of feedback – ranging from easier to harder and from safer to riskier – can he helpful in different ways.

According to Elbow and Belanoff, evaluations and advice are *not* what writers need the most. "What writers need (and fortunately it's what all readers are best at) is an *audience*: a thoughtful interested audience rather than evaluators or editors or advice givers.

The Elbow and Belanoff guide to peer response lists several approaches to feedback. These include:

1. *Sharing: No Response* – The reader serves as someone who will just listen and enjoy.

2. *Pointing and Center of Gravity* – The reader lets the writer know which sections somehow seem important or resonant

3. *Summary and Sayback* – The reader tells the writer in his own words what the piece seems to say.

4. *What Is Almost Said? What Do You Want to Hear More About?* – The reader participates more, reading between the lines.

5. *Reply* – The reader tells the writer her thoughts about the essay.

6. *Voice* – The reader tells the writer what kind of voice and tone come across in the writing

7. *Movies of the Reader's Mind* – The reader tells the writer what is going on in his mind as he reads the piece.

8. *Metaphorical Descriptions* – The reader uses figurative language to describe the piece of writing.

9. *Believing and Doubting* – The reader plays devil's advocate, doubting, challenging, and agreeing with various points in the essay.

10. *Skeleton Feedback and Descriptive Outline* – The reader attempts to reconstruct the thought process behind the writing by creating an outline after the fact.

11. *Criterion-Based Feedback* – The reader critiques specific aspects of the essay, including clarity, organization, grammar, and spelling.

Notice that the very *last* of these approaches is what most students imagine will happen when they think of (and sometimes dread) peer feedback sessions in a composition class. Elbow and Belanoff emphasize that simply having a sense of audience is more important than having a classmate try to "fix" problems in an essay before it goes to the teacher.

The rest of the "Sharing and Responding" section includes samples of essays in various stages of drafting, and actual examples of the feedback given in each of the approaches above.

Exercises

Check with your instructor for your formal assignments. You will be asked to do exercises from the *Telecourse Study Guide*.

Exploring peer feedback further

EXERCISE 1

For this exercise you will need to exchange papers (in a format that can be written on) with another student in your writing class. As you read the paper, feel free to write down any comments and suggestions you may think of.

If the assignment is for a formal argument, a research paper, or a persuasion essay, answer the following questions on a separate piece of paper:

- Is there a *thesis statement*?
- Are there *supporting points*?
- Is there enough *evidence* for each point?
- Does each *paragraph* stick to one point?

If the assignment is for a narrative or short story, answer the following questions on a separate piece of paper:

- Is there a *central theme* or main point to the story?
- Are the lessons of the unit in *description* demonstrated in the writing?
- Does the *series of events* unravel with some sort of suspense or plot?
- Does the story end with a strong *dénouement*?

Your instructor may give you a more comprehensive "peer feedback form" for each genre.

EXERCISE 2

In this exercise you will be examining further each of the checklist items from Exercise 1. If the assignment is for a formal argument, a research paper, or a persuasion essay, make sure to include the following:

THESIS STATEMENT

- Assuming that you find one, does it clearly convey the main idea of the paper?

SUPPORTING POINTS/EVIDENCE
- Can you think of any evidence or support for the thesis that is missing?
- Is there any information that contradicts or is not clearly related to the thesis?

PARAGRAPHING/CLARITY
- Do the transitions between paragraphs help to connect ideas?
- Can you determine the paper's audience?
- Is the purpose of the essay clear?

If the assignment is for a narrative or short story, make sure to include the following:

CENTRAL THEME OR MAIN POINT
- Is there a moral to the story, or does it seem like a random, pointless series of events?
- Is the moral implied, or does the author come right out and say it?

DESCRIPTION
- Can you place yourself in the key scenes?
- Can you see, hear, taste, smell, and touch the action of the story?

DÉNOUEMENT
- Is the ending satisfying, or does the story leave you confused?
- If the ending leaves you wondering, is the effect intended and effective?

EXERCISE 3
In this exercise you will be examining the feedback about the piece of writing that has been returned to you by your fellow student. Briefly summarize in writing the feedback you've received, and document the changes you are considering for upcoming revisions. Remember, you need not make every change that your peer reviewer has suggested, but you may want to pay extra attention to those points on which you and your reviewer disagree.

EXERCISE 4
Following the guidelines and examples in *A Community of Writers* (pp. 544–547), use the skeleton feedback and descriptive outline techniques to give feedback to another student's writing.

Exercise just for fun
Rewrite the paper you have been given to review and exaggerate all of the weaknesses you have found in it, so as to illustrate the factors in question to your peer author.

Revision exercise

In this exercise, you will use the results of Exercises 1, 2, 3, and 4. Write a new draft of the paper in question, using the feedback forms and your summary as checklists. Be sure to address all of the points this process has brought to light.

Quick writing exercise

Your instructor may ask you to do a quick focused freewrite about the topic you are studying in this unit. Those of you who are taking the course through a distance-learning system may be encouraged to share your thoughts in a discussion thread or to post your ideas on an Internet bulletin board. If you are writing your thoughts out by hand in a process journal, you might use these questions to stimulate ideas. This is a freewriting exercise that will not be graded. You can use any of the following questions to kick-start your thoughts about the peer feedback:

How does feedback work for you? Can you distinguish between the different types of feedback? Do you feel there is value in having a test audience that just reads your paper without offering critical comments? If so, how can this type of neutral audience help you? Full explanations and samples of different types of feedback are given on pages 521 to 550.

Can you give feedback easily yourself, or are you feeling pretty shy about the process? Do you think other students will feel offended if you suggest improvements in their papers? Have you discovered strategies for responding to another writer's work? What can *you* get from giving feedback to others?

How do you feel about showing your work to other students? This model of instruction is much different than the kind of class where the only person to ever read your paper is an instructor. How do you personally react when another student offers suggestions for improvement? Would you prefer one of those "nice essay" types of comments or a response from a student who really digs in and looks carefully at your paper? Have you ever changed or revised a paper because of feedback you have received from another student? Procedures for giving and receiving responses are discussed on pages 516 to 520 of Elbow and Belanoff's *A Community of Writers*.

Do you think you will be able to apply the lessons learned in this unit to other courses or to writing situations you encounter beyond school? If so, imagine what those circumstances might be like.

You may use the questions in the "Process Journal" section of Workshop 7 "Revision Through Purpose and Audience: Writing as Doing Things to People" (p. 199) in *A Community of Writers* as an additional source of inspiration for this quick writing exercise.

Exercises related to *A Community of Writers*

Using peer feedback is so central to Elbow and Belanoff's philosophy that *A*

Community of Writers has a peer feedback, or "Sharing and Responding," exercise in each of the primary workshops. By this point in the course, if your teacher is also a strong believer in peer feedback, you may have already been assigned many of these exercises, and you are already familiar with the peer feedback process.

While the textbook describes most of these exercises from the point of view of a traditional classroom, many of these exercises can easily be adapted to a distance learning environment. They work particularly well in a course that uses the Internet and allows students to share and respond via e-mail, bulletin boards, and collaborative software.

If you are learning in an environment where formally assigned peer feedback is difficult to achieve, it is a good idea to analyze the samples of peer feedback published in the book (pp. 523–549) to see how effective the process can be in real-life writing challenges).

If you have no other experience with peer feedback in the entire semester, you should at least once try the "Sharing and Responding" exercise in Workshop 7, "Revision through Purpose and Audience: Writing as Doing Things To People" (p. 199). The exercise makes clear that in order to revise your paper based on what it does to people, sooner or later you will have to see how an audience actually responds to it.

Additional reading

Several student essays are featured in the appendix. They reflect different levels of writing ability, and several of the papers could benefit from revision. Consult the "Summary of Kinds of Responses" in the "Sharing and Responding" section of *A Community of Writers* (pp. 503–520). Imagine how you might give feedback to Gregory Andrus, Corie Cushnie, Ethlyn Manning, and Francine Taylor, if they were in your own class and they were asking for help in creating a final draft.

One of the hardest things for a beginning student to do is to give feedback to a writer who is much more experienced. Assuming musician David Ellefson is a peer, how would you give peer feedback to him for his excerpt from his book on the music business, featured in the appendix? Use the same approach for any of the professional writers featured in the appendix, including Rush Limbaugh, Kalle Lasn, Bill Walsh, Dave Barry, and Steve Shanesy. Remember: All writers could use some help in improving their work.

Quick Review

1. When giving peer feedback, it is good to
   a. Be as blunt and matter of fact as possible when pointing out errors.
   b. Learn how to deliver criticism with tact and diplomacy.

   c. Always be as nice as possible, and avoid pointing out errors if it will hurt the other student's feelings.

   d. All of the above.

   e. None of the above.

2. Peer feedback is an important and common part of writing in
   a. the workplace
   b. upper-division college courses
   c. the field of research
   d. all of the above
   e. none of the above

3. An important side benefit of peer feedback is that
   a. Students learn how to read their own papers better after reading the papers of others.
   b. Students gain a sense of self-confidence after learning when to accept or reject feedback.
   c. Students gain an actual sense of "audience" instead of just handing in an assignment.
   d. All of the above.
   e. None of the above.

4. When students get peer feedback to change a document, they are encouraged to
   a. Make all the changes recommended to fix the paper and make it perfect.
   b. Learn to judge the criticism of their own work, and decide what suggestions to accept or reject.
   c. Smile, and ignore most of the suggestions for change.
   d. All of the above.
   e. None of the above.

5. In the telecourse program and study guide chapter, one or more instructors made the following observation about peer feedback:
   a. The more students give feedback to other people, the better they get at looking at *their own* text.
   b. Students will often pick up on errors that the teacher entirely missed.
   c. You need the courage to say, 'It's my paper, darn it' – but you also must not be so wrapped up in your own paper that you're not able to listen.
   d. All of the above.
   e. None of the above.

6. According to Elbow and Belanoff,
    a. What you imply but don't say in your writing is often very loud to the readers, but unheard by you.
    b. Evaluation and advice and help fixing grammar are *not* what writers need most through peer feedback.
    c. In the long run, you will learn the most about writing from reeling the presence of interested readers.
    d. All of the above.
    e. None of the above.

"Defining, for me, becomes a very exciting intellectual and writing task. Because it's not simply looking up in the dictionary the two or three sentences that supposedly define in stone what something means. The very act of defining is a very fluid activity loaded with social and political implications. A definition is always open to question, and it is always open for students to think hard about, to push on, and, in fact, to re-create."

MIKE ROSE, UCLA

Introduction to the Topic

Throughout your college career, no matter what your major will be, you will have to write and read definitions. Teresa Redd, who teaches a composition course for engineering majors at Howard University, says that the inability of students to master this genre of writing is a big concern among her colleagues.

According to Redd, "One of the main complaints from instructors across the campus has been, 'These students don't know how to define.' Math and engineering students, for instance, have to define a lot of concepts. And they define in the social sciences. A lot of the short answers on those exams in those courses are definitions. So the instructors in the other disciplines are very concerned about those definitions."

After college, you will no longer write *just* to satisfy an assignment from an instructor or get a correct answer on a test. It is unlikely that the boss will pay you overtime to go home and write a definition essay. However, you may need to demonstrate your skills of definition writing during normal working hours, just to *keep* the job. For instance, you will have to define key terms when familiarizing coworkers with a new piece of technology. Or, if you are working with patients in an emergency room and explaining medical procedures, you will need to define with compassion and clarity.

Your definition may be perfunctory. Robert Stansberry, a student and diesel mechanic, explains that he often adds brief definitions of the terms he uses when writing a repair report on a big-rig truck. Marty Wallace, a graduate student in chemistry, says that brief definitions of new terms are a mainstay in his discourse community. In fact, he thinks a chemist may learn more new vocabulary terms than a language major.

Your definition may be complex. As we'll see from several examples in the telecourse, you may have to define your role in society or your position at work. Or you may have to define an abstract concept, such as "sanity" or "relativity." These definitions can become full-length essays, twenty-page grant proposals, or even entire books.

In this unit, you will become familiar with all aspects of definition. In the end, you'll be prepared to respond skillfully when you are asked to write something that requires this thinking/writing strategy.

Learning Objectives

After viewing the television program and finishing the writing assignments, you should know when definition is needed, in everything from the precise technical definitions used in the academic disciplines of engineering, chemistry, law, computer programming, or psychology to extended definitions of complex concepts, such as when people "define themselves" in society or when someone defines a feeling, concept, or theory. You will also learn *how* writers create effective definitions.

Before Viewing

Before you formally study this topic, consider the techniques you have already developed in using definition. Try to recollect assignments you have had from other classes that required definition writing. This type of writing is quite common; chances are you will have an up-and-coming assignment in another class that requires definition. Try to imagine what skills you would need to succeed in such an assignment. Review Elbow and Belanoff's section on expository writing in Workshop 2 (pp. 48–49). Consider where the skills learned in this chapter and telecourse might apply.

While Viewing

Compare the skills you already have acquired in definition with the techniques recommended by the instructors, students, and professional writers in the telecourse. Note the skills that you have *not* considered, with a goal of using these methods in the passage that requires definition in your own writing. Notice how

Keena Turner (sports broadcaster and former football player), Marty Wallace (chemistry student), Himilce Novas (writer and multicultural history instructor), Gordy Ohliger (musicologist and performing musician), Jim Esh (veterinarian), and others featured in the course use definition in their on-the-job writing. Become aware of the various styles of definition used in different occupations. Consider how you might use your awareness of definition to improve your writing in other classes, to define yourself in your world, or to improve your understanding of work-related issues.

After Viewing

Using the exercises in this *Telecourse Study Guide*, practice the art of definition. Also look for strong definitions and weak definitions in the writing you encounter in assignments from other classes, recreational reading, and reading you might do on the job. Try to find variations of the methods recommended in this telecourse program in the good examples, and be on the lookout for what is lacking in the bad examples. Look for examples of definition in the writing of your academic major. Determine what is considered appropriate (and inappropriate) definition style within that discourse community. Gauge what level of jargon (or professional language) is accepted as automatic and necessary, noting the terms that are understood by all and the vocabulary that needs to be defined within the discourse.

In *A Community of Writers*, consider how William Zinsser uses definition techniques in his essay "Writing Mathematics and Chemistry (pp. 331–333) and compare his technique to the way both Susan Faludi ("Speak for yourself," pp. 140–142), Minh-Ha Pham ("How Can I, A Vietnamese Girl ..." pp. 142–144), and Charles Miller ("About Being a Man," pp. 63–64) all use definition.

Viewing Guide

From the opening sequence of this telecourse program, there should be no doubt in your mind that definition skills are needed in almost every academic major and profession. In quick succession, you will meet a veterinarian, a football player, a chemist, a musician, a police officer, and a political activist who all use definitions.

Definition, as an abstract exercise, often means very little to a student. To understand why you define, you'll need a reason to define. This will also help you learn how to define.

In the video, English instructor Akua Duku Anokye of the University of Toledo supports this point, emphasizing that the writer (and reader) will care if the definition has a clear purpose.

That purpose may be to persuade. As Chitra Divakaruni of the Foothill College points out, many definition essays have an agenda.

To illustrate Divakaruni's point, the video features two controversial definitions of the word *welfare*. Conservative radio talk-show host Rush Limbaugh uses his definition to make a political point, calling welfare "a scheme devised by liberals to persuade as many people as possible to give up on themselves ... thereby transferring power to those who are in charge of passing out the benefits."

Film producer and liberal political activist Michael Moore offers an alternate definition of welfare, claiming, "We spend fifty billion dollars a year on social welfare, AFDC [Aid to Families with Dependent Children], food stamps, etc. We spend one hundred and seventy billion dollars a year in corporate welfare. Those are free handouts of our tax money, to corporations for things they could otherwise pay for themselves."

The idea that two people could define a word differently might surprise students who are in the habit of simply *accepting* the definitions handed down by instructors and textbooks. In academia, you will soon discover that students are expected to participate in the interpretation of words and concepts.

Mike Rose of UCLA explains, "Most folks think in terms of a dictionary defining meaning – as if the meaning is fixed, and it's written down someplace and all we've got to do is look it up. Think about it. So much of our lives are structured around the ways that institutions have already created definitions for us.

"One of the powerful things that can happen in a writing course is when we get students to the place where they realize that they can *challenge* definitions. That they even can try to *create* alternative definitions of anything – from defining [words like] *intelligence* to defining one's ethnicity to the way one interacts with others."

Rose is talking about *extended definition*. This is a form of writing that goes beyond the few sentences you will find in a dictionary. It is a creative tradition that allows the writer to tell a story, persuade, have a little fun – and, in the process, create meaning.

Extended definitions

According to Santi Buscemi of Middlesex County College, "An extended definition really covers an entire essay. It's a long definition and it includes a lot of different kinds of writing.

"When I teach definition, I like to tell my students that writers will use illustration; they'll use cause and effect. They may use narration or description – you name it – to extend the readers' understanding of that term."

An extended definition allows the writer to make a more profound statement about a term or concept. Mike Rose continues to explain the concept of an extended definition, using the definition of the word *intelligence* as an example.

"Let's talk about defining something like intelligence," Rose says. "Intelligence, in traditional Western culture, is defined through something like an IQ test. Is that the way to define something as complex as intelligence? Could we complicate the definition – even overturn it?"

Defining, in this context, is an act of critical thinking. It is *not* simply looking up a term in a reference book.

This type of extended definition writing can be used to teach, to provoke thought, to persuade, or to prove a point. An extended definition can be lively and even fun – because the reader ultimately has to arrive at his or her own conclusion of what the word really means.

Both Michael Moore and Rush Limbaugh have written entire books that could be considered extensions of their definitions of the word *welfare* – each spinning the definition to persuade and to make a point. (Moore's book: *Downsize This*, Crown Books, 1996; Limbaugh's book: *The Way Things Ought to Be*, 1992, Simon & Schuster)

We see several other examples of extended definitions in the telecourse program when

- An athlete uses an extended definition to define his role on the team.

- A musician reinvents his career by creating a new concept and defining himself in such a unique way that he is awarded several prestigious grants.

- A Chicano studies instructor uses extended definitions to embrace the positive aspects of being a Chicana and to explore how cultures mingle by sharing different approaches to cooking.

- A veterinarian uses definition to explain the diagnostic technique of ultrasound.

- A social activist defines what it means to be a "culture jammer."

Each of these writers uses a variety of techniques (including definition by example, definition with figurative images, definition by negation, and definition by comparison) to flesh out her or his extended definitions. Let's look at some of these strategies more closely.

Negative definition/defining by negation

A writer can often start to define a term by explaining what it is *not*. Some instructors call this definition by negation, or negative definition.

In *Making Music Your Business*, David Ellefson defines the role of the manager of his rock group, Megadeth, by using a negative definition.

"In my chapter about managers, I put in some specific things that I *don't* do. I try *not* to call my managers outside of business hours. I try *not* to arrange for them to ship flowers to my wife, when I can do those things myself. In the music business, there are some managers who pamper rock stars. I'm *not* really one of those people."

Keena Turner uses the same strategy to define his former role as a defensive football player, saying he was *not* allowed to use his hands in certain ways. Janice Peritz of Queens College starts her definition of a dreidel by saying it is *not* an insignificant object. Organic gardener Sharon Casey explains that chocolate peppers are *not* sweet peppers, even though the name and hue make them appear delicious. And veterinarian Jim Esh explains that his ultrasound diagnostic technique is *not* like an x-ray.

In each case, the writer is able to communicate much to the reader by eliminating possible misconceptions and thereby narrowing down the definition of the term.

Avoiding circular definitions and using figurative images

Of course, defining by telling what something *is* can be more direct than saying what it is *not*. But a straight-on look at something doesn't reveal all sides.

When a writer looks at an object, it is nearly impossible to see anything *but* that object; it is therefore difficult to avoid a circular definition, or defining something by itself.

"I love you – well, because I love you," is a classic circular definition. So is, "My house is a home."

Often, it is better to define with a sideways glance by using a figurative image – a metaphor, a simile, or an analogy. This type of language is usually considered the domain of the poet or the literary novelist. But we all use images to define. Some of us are just more aware of how effective they can be.

The great philosopher and bard Neil Young once ruminated, "Love is a rose; better not pick it."

Though his goal is not as poetic, Keena Turner uses this same kind figurative language in defining his former role as a defensive football player by saying, "As a smaller player, getting around a three hundred pound-offensive lineman is kind of *like* a physics experiment."

English instructor Janice Peritz uses figurative images to define a dreidel, saying, "It is like a kiss, an excess, a gift – like a child's laughter." J. Joaquin Fraxedas, a novelist, says the Gulf Stream is like a thousand Mississippi Rivers.

Engineering student Larry Thompson uses an analogy (somewhat of a more straightforward comparison) suggesting a cutting fluid is "like soap."

In each case, the writer expands the definition by allowing the reader to see the object through peripheral vision, instead of with a straight-on stare.

As Elbow and Belanoff point out, in Workshop 14, "Text Analysis through Examining Figurative Language" (p. 371), "Figurative language appeals to the mind at a deep level. When figurative language tells us that something is *like* rather than what it is, it's taking a path that is natural for the mind. It's in the nature of the mind to see things *like* other things or standing in for other things. Indeed, that is how we *do* see."

Definition by comparison and contrast

Straightforward comparisons work in definitions too. Peritz compares a dreidel to a similar toy: a spinning top. And veterinarian Jim Esh uses comparisons when he defines the term *ultrasound*. He compares the process to sonic radar (sonar) used by submarines and contrasts the term with x-rays (using a bit of definition by negation).

The straightforward comparison gives the writer a tangible idea or object to use as a foundation on which to construct the definition of the new term. A contrast allows the writer use the polarity of opposites to create new meanings.

In his book *Downsize This*, Michael Moore uses comparison and contrast to define *terrorism*, expanding the traditional notion of the word to mean "when a company throws people out of work when it is making a record profit." To illustrate, Moore shows two nearly identical photos in his book: the Oklahoma City Federal Building, destroyed by terrorist bombs in 1995, and a General Motors plant, destroyed by the corporation in 1996.

Moore says, "The obvious definition [of terrorism] is when somebody blows up a building and kills people. I would like to expand that definition to mean when a company throws people out of work – at a time when they're making record profits. We don't usually think of terrorism in that way, yet many of those people lose their jobs, and their lives are completely ruined."

Though comparison/contrast is a genre of writing you will study separately, this is not the last time you will see writers blending thinking/writing strategies to create effective writing. In fact, the thinking/writing strategy of description also blends quite effectively with definition.

Definition by describing qualities and characteristics

Our discussion moves from the sideways glance to the straight-on inspection with the strategy of defining by describing qualities and characteristics.

Veterinarian Jim Esh describes characteristics of ultrasound. At the same time, he contrasts the diagnostic technique with the x-ray (or radiograph) technique: "Air completely blocks ultrasound. If you want to look at a lung, ultrasound is worthless and an x-ray is excellent. Fluid is the opposite. Fluid enhances and clarifies ultrasound and totally obscures everything on an x-ray.

"On the ultrasound, we'll be able to take a very careful look for tumors and evaluate the heart. The other nice thing about the ultrasound is that it's in real time – you can watch the heart beat; you can watch the rhythm; you can see the walls contract. The x-ray is just a momentary image."

Notice that, as Esh defines, he *describes*. It is rare that any writing is *purely* definition. As you will discover throughout the telecourse, good writers frequently blend thinking/writing strategies such as definition, description, comparison, and persuasion.

Defining by example

The most direct definition tactic is to use an example.

In the telecourse, political activist Kalle Lasn, editor of *Adbusters* magazine, defines the political movement of "culture jammers."

Lasn uses a concrete example of a corporate interaction with society to illustrate the "culture" his group wants to "jam" – or obstruct and impede – through its activism.

The example is a corporate intrusion into the tradition of a child's neighborhood lemonade stand.

"It's really quite a good example of what's happened," Lasn explains. "Children have done that for a hundred years. Suddenly, Kool-Aid now gives you the kit – the signs and the containers."

Through a photo of the Kool-Aid sidewalk sales kit, featured in his magazine, Lasn shows how the corporation is attempting to "brand" the neighborhood tradition.

A similar corporate takeover process, Lasn says, is happening "in every nook and cranny of our culture. So 'culture jamming' is an attempt to reclaim that culture. To take it back from the people who have taken it away from us."

With one simple example, Lasn begins to define a very complex notion.

Himilce Novas takes a similar approach to define the phrase "fusion cooking." She starts with a delicious example: a restaurant in Chicago that serves Puerto Rican and Mexican food on the same plate. The "jalapeño bagel" is another example of fusion cooking – though the combination might not be as appetizing to some.

Keena Turner also uses examples to define his role as a linebacker, explaining that his defensive position must be able to battle three hundred-pound offensive linemen, tackle fleet-footed runners, or cover an elusive pass receiver.

Summary

Many of the writers in the telecourse define *themselves* in one way or another.

This is a very practical use of the skill. You can define your role on a team (as Keena Turner does), your place in society, or your role at work. Those who learn to define themselves – instead of letting others set the definitions for them – gain a significant amount of power and control over their own lives.

In one example, Himilce Novas explains how César Chavez "took the evil power out of the word *Chicano*" and taught Mexican Americans to transform a word that originated as an insult into something that showed pride in their heritage.

In the final example on the video, musician Gordy Ohliger explains how he defined himself as the "banjo-ologist" and earned a grant from the California Arts Council in the process.

As Ohliger explains how he wrote the grant proposal, notice that his narrative reviews every key point in this unit.

Ohliger uses negative definition when he explains that the "banjo-ologist" is not just some guy who plays bluegrass. He defines by comparison, by showing how his concept of a "banjo-ologist" is similar to a musicologist or historian.

Ohliger uses figurative language to describe his act, saying, "I am like your Thanksgiving dinner, where you have the grandfather that tells stories of the old days and the twenty-two-year-old stand-up comic. I'm also the little kid being silly – I'm like everybody at the dinner table, all at the same event."

Describing the qualities and characteristics of his show, Ohliger says, "I do children's shows where I bring some comedy bits that I wouldn't do for an adult crowd, such as a presentation at a museum. I'll play music on a lunch bag and do a lot of physical comedy – and the presentation is completely different."

In his shows for adults, Ohliger explains, he displays antique instruments, gives a bit of a history lesson, entertains with rip-roaring ragtime, and spins funny tales of "what it was like when your great-grandparents were dancing to these songs."

"I absolutely have to redefine who I am on stage and how I present myself. It's an ongoing process," Ohliger says. He concludes with the most important reason for learning definition.

"As I was defining what I am, I *realized* what I am – and also realized what I wanted to be. It was fascinating."

Integrating the Text

Elbow and Belanoff's *A Community of Writers* includes several excellent examples of definition writing. For example, the entire section, Mini-Workshop B, "Double Entry or Dialectical Notebooks" (pp. 450-453), can be read as a definition of a reading technique. Other essays in the book that use definition include Susan Faludi's "Speak for Yourself" (pp. 140–143) and "How Can I, Vietnamese Girl ..." by Minh-Ha Pham (pp. 142–145). Both of these pieces are variations of the type of writing identified as "defining yourself in the world" in this telecourse and Study Guide.

Exercises

Check with your instructor for your formal assignments. You will be asked to do exercises from the *Telecourse Study Guide*.

Exploring definition further

EXERCISE 1

After hearing the definitions of *welfare* in the telecourse program provided by Michael Moore and Rush Limbaugh, create your own definition of *welfare*. This exercise often sparks a vigorous discussion in the classroom or in the distance-learning forum. Before you get too caught up in the emotion of your response, don't forget the advice given in the telecourse program for writing a complete definition:

- Can you provide an example? (A context for the reader)
- Can you provide a negative definition? (Something to dispel common misconceptions)
- Can you provide a metaphor or simile?
- Can you provide a description of qualities and characteristics?
- Can you provide a direct comparison or analogy?

Though you should not forget the advice offered by instructors and writers for writing a complete definition, your definition *may* have an agenda or a point to prove. The definitions provided by Limbaugh and Moore are provided in this exercise, so you can think of a response:

RUSH LIMBAUGH:

Welfare. WELFARE. A scheme devised by liberals to persuade as many people as possible to give up on themselves, invest instead in the government for their daily needs. Which thereby transfers power to those who are in charge of passing out the benefits. I think welfare is demeaning; I think it's destructive. Welfare is the absolute opposite of compassion. As long as we're doing definitions, I think a good companion definition to welfare would be compassion. A lot of people will define compassion by scouring the country and counting the number of people who are receiving some sort of largesse, some sort of aid. I, on the other hand, think that a more productive and accurate definition of compassion would be to scour the country and count the people who no longer need it because they've been taught (educated) how to acquire, not just personal things, but how to acquire knowledge, how to make the most of themselves. How to get the most out of themselves. They've been taught how to access the opportunities that this country provides. They've been taught how to acquire the things necessary to access those opportunities. Compassion ought to be the number of people that have been motivated and inspired to go out and fend for themselves.

MICHAEL MOORE:

I want people to consider these words: Welfare. Say *welfare*. What do you think? Single mother, lots of kids, living in the ghetto. Well actually the average welfare recipient lives in the suburbs and is white, and has only two kids. And they're not on welfare usually for more than two years. Those are U.S. government statistics. Yet that's not the image that is presented to us from the politicians and from people in charge. Because they really like to manipulate us with

this kind of hatred and fear and bigotry. And I'm really kind of tired of it. And I
wish when we say the word welfare we would think about corporate welfare.
We spend fifty billion dollars a year to social welfare, AFDC, food stamps, etc.
We spend 170 billion dollars a year in corporate welfare. Those are free handouts of our tax money, to corporations for things they could otherwise pay for
themselves. Yeah, we just dole it right out and we never talk about it when we
use the word welfare."

EXERCISE 2
Write a quick draft of an essay using the ideas created in Exercise 1. Don't
worry about grammar or spelling for this draft. Don't worry if you can't find
a response to each of the points in Exercise 1. Get down on paper whatever you can; this material and the connections you come up with in this step
will prove useful in later drafts of this essay.

EXERCISE 3
Try to informally define an emotion, a concept, a theory, or an interesting
vocabulary word. Show the draft of this definition to a few classmates, and
see if your peers have similar or different definitions of the same term. You
should use the questions in Exercise 1 to help you get started.

EXERCISE 4
Define yourself in the world, using the definitions by Gordy Ohliger (the
"banjo-ologist"), Keena Turner (the former linebacker), or Himilce Novas
(the multicultural history instructor) as models. You should use the questions in Exercise 1 to help you get started.

Exercise just for fun
Sometimes the easiest definitions can be expressed by using examples of
what your subject is not. Start by identifying a subject to write about that
you have somewhat strong feelings about ("Football is so boring!" or
"Country music rules!" or "Body piercing is …") Whatever subject you
come up with, write a short essay about everything it is not.

Revision exercise
In this exercise you will use the rough draft created in Exercise 2, 3, or 4
as a starting point for revision. As you read the rough draft, transpose (or
cut and paste) the most important ideas and clever phrases, and weed out
any unrelated material that you find. Looking at what's left, check to see if
you have covered all five of the points suggested in Exercise 1, and then
write your next draft of the essay.

Quick writing exercise
Your instructor may ask you to do a quick focused freewrite using definition. Those of you who are taking the course through a distance-learning

system may be encouraged to share your thoughts in a discussion thread or to post your ideas on an Internet bulletin board. If you are writing your thoughts out by hand in a process journal, you might use these questions to conjure up ideas. This is a freewriting exercise that will not be graded. You can use any of the following questions to stimulate your thoughts about definition writing:

Can you think of times when you have had to use definition writing when you weren't assigned a definition essay? How would you define yourself in the world? Do you agree with Chitra Divakaruni that many definitions have an agenda? What is the difference between an extended definition and a dictionary definition? Are any of these techniques recommended for an extended definition new to you?

Exercises related to *A Community of Writers*

EXERCISE 1

A Community of Writers contains an interesting example of definition in Mini-Workshop B, "Double Entry or Dialectical Notebooks" (pp. 450–453). The entire workshop can be viewed as an extended definition. As you read, look for techniques recommended in this telecourse Study Guide chapter and the telecourse program "Definition." Underline examples of negative definition (or definition by negation), definition with figurative (find a simile *and* a metaphor), definition by describing qualities and characteristics, and definition by example.

EXERCISE 2

Read Workshop 9, "The Essay" (pp. 235–245). Using the questions on p. 241, analyze "Speak for Yourself" by Susan Faludi (pp. 140–143) and "How Can I, Vietnamese Girl ..." by Minh-Ha Pham (pp. 142–145). In your analysis, be sure to consider how each writer used the techniques of definition.

Additional reading

Notice, in the appendix, how the excerpt from *Everything You Need to Know About Latino History*, by Himilce Novas uses definition. How is this an example of "defining yourself in the world"?

How does football coach Bill Walsh use definition writing, in "Establishing Evaluation Tools," the sample of his writing that is included in the appendix? How is this different from the way Novas uses definition?

David Ellefson uses several thinking/writing strategies in the excerpt from his book *Making Music Your Business*. As you read this sample in the appendix, do you notice any of the techniques discussed in the instructional unit about definition writing?

How does Corie Cushnie use the thinking/writing strategy of definition, in the essay, "What's Your Name?"

In the telecourse, instructor and novelist Chitra Divakarui talks about how she usually blends genres, or thinking/writing strategies. An excerpt of her short story "Clothes" appears in the appendix. How does Divakaruni use definition to develop the narrative of this piece? (The short story is from a collection of works called *Arranged Marriage*.)

Quick Review

1. According to instructors in the telecourse program,
   a. Definitions are more effective if the author has a purpose.
   b. Definitions often have an agenda.
   c. Students can challenge existing definitions and create their own.
   d. All of the above.
   e. None of the above.

2. Writers can use the following rhetorical modes to expand their definitions:
   a. persuasion
   b. comparison
   c. description
   d. all of the above
   e. none of the above

3. The following techniques can help an expanded definition:
   a. definition by negation
   b. definition by example
   c. definition with figurative language
   d. all of the above
   e. none of the above

4. Circular definition is
   a. a good way to "define the self"
   b. recommended as a way to extend a dictionary definition
   c. often used in research
   d. all of the above
   e. none of the above

5. Rush Limbaugh and Michael Moore use their definitions in the program
   a. exactly as the terms are explained in a dictionary
   b. to substantiate in-depth research
   c. to persuade and to promote an agenda
   d. all of the above
   e. none of the above

"In the real world, collaboration is the rule as opposed to the exception. Collaboration is really advantageous, because if every person knew everything about everything, we could all write in isolation and make the well-formed text. But that is not what the real world is all about. Each person has specialized learning. So we get together a team of people who know a bunch of different things, and then we make a project. And that project is a well-researched, well-formed piece of text (or multimedia presentation) and it's the result of everyone's input. We can teach that to our students ... by creating opportunities to collaborate."

MICHAEL BERTSCH, Butte College

Introduction to the Topic

Some instructors do not include units about collaborative writing in their composition courses. Recently, however, more teachers have incorporated both collaborative learning and collaborative writing into their first-year writing courses.

Peter Elbow of the University of Massachusetts, Amerst, is a strong advocate of collaborative learning and peer feedback. But, even he observes, "If you go too far in that direction, it's sort of leaving out the fact that it's a pain to write something with somebody else."

The flip side of the agony, however, is the reward.

Two or more writers *do* discover more, in the learning and research phase. With a built-in test audience, it is possible to find out how the early drafts read. The various tasks – drafting, research, revising, fact-checking, editing – can be shared, and divided, and assigned to the writer who has special talents. Technical accuracy improves. And, in the best collaborations, previously elusive creative sparks are magnified exponentially.

If the team members don't end up as quibbling lunatics, throttling each other in frustration, or divorcing in the process, the resulting documents are almost always better than what could be produced alone.

In fact, through the process of collaboration, relationships often are strengthened. If the document is published with success (positive feedback, good reviews, best-seller lists, cash grant, box-office hit, or major award), the team gains confidence and builds on the accomplishment the next time around.

Learning Objectives

After viewing the television program and finishing the exercises and assignments related to this unit, you will acquire strategies for working on collaborative documents in a variety of different styles and situations. You will achieve this goal by hearing about several models of collaborative writing from guests in the telecourse program and reading about various approaches to collaborative writing in the *Telecourse Study Guide*. You will also become aware of the benefits (and potential pitfalls) of collaborative writing.

These learning objectives work in harmony with the general philosophy of *A Community of Writers*, which contains collaborative exercises in almost every workshop of the textbook. One essential premise of Workshop 3, "Collaborative Writing: Dialogue, Loop Writing, and the Collage" is a mirror image of the main point of this telecourse program: if two or more people come at the same topic, they don't just add to the thinking (two heads are better than one), they *multiply* the thinking through the interactions of ideas. Dialogue is one form of collaborative writing.

Before Viewing

Before you formally study collaborative writing, reflect on your own experiences with (and attitudes toward) team writing experiences. Consider: Was the group given any models or strategies for collaboration, or did you just wing it? Try to remember what worked, and what didn't work in your past experiences with writing in a team.

Read Elbow and Belanoff's Workshop 3, "Collaborative Writing: Dialogue, Loop Writing, and the Collage" (pp. 67–99).

While Viewing

Compare your past experiences in writing as part of a team with the various models of collaborative writing mentioned in the telecourse program. In addition to the methods of collaborative writing, notice the attitudes expressed by various writers, instructors, and students toward the practice of writing with a team. Pay careful attention to the section about "negoti-ating" differences with a team.

As you view this segment of the video program, reconsider the section "Down-to-Earth Suggestions for Working with Others" in *A Community of Writers* (pp. 81–83), in which Elbow and Belanoff discuss strategies for nego-tiating problems within a collaborative writing team. Elbow and Belanoff don't necessarily agree with the views of everybody in the telecourse pro-gram. Note the similarities and differences in approaches to collaboration expressed by the guests on the telecourse and the authors of the textbook.

After Viewing

Using the exercises in the *Telecourse Study Guide*, practice writing with at least one other writer. (You may be given an assignment by your instructor to create a collaborative document.) Think about the opening quote by Michael Bertsch, of Butte College: "In the real world, collaboration is the rule as opposed to the exception." Ask yourself how you will react to your first on-the-job collaborative writing assignment? How will you adapt the lessons from this unit to future college writing assignments that will require you to work with a team?

Viewing Guide

If you think writing by yourself is tough, just wait until you have to write with a team. Collaborating with others can be a challenge in many ways; it also has many rewards. The resulting documents – whether they are group reports, stories created by a news team, novels created by more than one author, or scripts for a movie – are often stronger that something written by one person. Academic documents can also turn out better, because they combine the strengths of several individuals.

As Elbow and Belanoff point out, "If two or more people come at the same topic, they don't just add to the thinking (two heads are better than one), they *multiply* the thinking through the interactions of ideas."

As you work on your first collaborative exercises in class, keep in mind that the instructor is preparing you for the world outside of school. As com-position instructor Akua Duku Anokye of the University of Toledo points out, "We know that in the industrial world, in the corporate world, people are collaborating more and more. You have groups working on projects, and they produce these projects and each of them shares responsibilities."

The telecourse introduces the subject with a few examples of collabora-tive writing on the job.

Though she holds a high-ranking position, Federal District Judge Helen

Gillmor is quite dependent on the collaborative process. "Because I spend a great deal of my time in court actually presiding over trials and various proceedings, I can't possibly write all of the things that I'd need to write," Gillmor says. "So I have two law clerks who are recent law school graduates and they do research. And they do writing at my direction."

Scriptwriter Peter Farrelly (*There's Something about Mary*) is just as dependent on collaboration for his comedy films. In his case, the collaboration is a family affair. "When I'm writing a screenplay, I find it much easier to collaborate than to write alone," says Farrelly, who coauthors scripts with his brother Bobby. "In fact, I tried to write a screenplay alone one time when I was on vacation. I had a very hard time, particularly for comedy, because, as my brother put it, 'If you come up with a joke in your head, you don't laugh.' You think, 'Maybe that's amusing.' But if there's another guy there, and you come up with a joke and you say, 'How about this?' – suddenly you're *hearing* the laughs."

Chris Lowe, a marine biologist associated with the University of Hawaii, agrees that collaboration is an everyday activity in the sciences too. However, Lowe points out, writers who need teamwork skills in his discourse community are often not exposed to collaboration in their first-year writing classes; they frequently arrive at graduate school unprepared for the experience.

"Basically, we're trained to write as individuals," Lowe says. "I think it's important to kind of develop your own style first. But once you reach a certain level in your science career, you *have* to learn to write collaboratively. The idea is that you can still feel comfortable with what you've written – and everybody feels as though the text that you've put together conveys the same message that everybody had originally envisioned."

Division of labor

Communicating a message that reflects the single vision of a group of individuals can be difficult. Ironically, one common method of creating a collaborative document that appears to have one voice is to divide the tasks so that every member of the team has a different role to play.

Richard Aregood, winner of the Pulitzer Prize for his editorial work at the *Philadelphia Inquirer*, describes how each member of a newspaper staff performs a separate task.

"Division of labor is important in newspapers," Aregood says. "We have a slot man … a copy editor who is very good at envisioning the whole thing. We have a headline writer who is superb at that little art. We've got editorial writers. Some are very facile, but need backup for getting all their facts; others will just absolutely bury you with facts and make you wonder what it is they're trying to say."

The eloquent writers work with fact checkers, and the writers who are good at research work with editors who make the articles more interesting for readers. The goal, Aregood explains, is to get all of these different personalities to blend together so that the paper presents a unified voice. It is, in essence, a daily exercise in collaborative writing.

Himilce Novas, who has collaborated successfully on several book projects, also feels that separating tasks is the most successful collaborative model. "I think people *have* to have a division of labor," Novas says. " I don't think that two people can be doing exactly the same thing."

Working on a book called *Latin-American Cooking Across the USA*, with her partner, Rosemary Silva, Novas explains that the tasks were efficiently divided. One writer focused on research; the other composed the narrative. Both worked on editing.

Like many other instructors, speech and communications teacher Robb Lightfoot of Shasta College introduces collaboration in his speech and debate classes. Rather than *telling* students exactly how to collaborate, Lightfoot allows them to discover the models that work the best for them.

"When we're a week or two into it, we'll talk about the idea of a division of labor," Lightfoot explains. "We'll talk about the fact that in some groups, a *leader* emerges – but not always. And we talk about the dynamic of leadership emergence – and that it can be messy. It can be frustrating. It's not always fun."

Lightfoot, like most other instructors, knows there will be moments when collaborative groups of students will struggle for a direction. But students learn the most when they have to figure things out on their own. When they come to him for suggestions, Lightfoot says, he smiles and asks, "Gee, what are you going to do?"

Other models of collaboration

Division of labor is only one model of collaboration, and it might not work well if a group does not have a natural leader, editor, or researcher. Though it is good for students to figure out how to collaborate on their own, there is no need to reinvent the entire process. Many teams of writers have collaborated successfully before them, and we have some idea of what works and what doesn't work in collaborative projects.

Everyone does everything

The methods used to collaborate are as varied as the different types of groups that collaborate – and they can differ quite a bit, as marine biologist Whitlow Au points out.

"In terms of collaborating on a writing project, you can do it several ways," he says. "One way is to have specific individuals write about specific areas of an article. Another way is to have one individual write the whole article, and then the other individuals critique the article and begin to make changes or begin to rephrase things that they feel ought to be rephrased – or begin to add materials that might have been left out."

In either approach described by Au, every member of the team contributes to every aspect of the document, including researching, drafting, and editing.

Judge Gillmor also uses several different models of collaboration in her work, though the most common is similar to the one described by Au.

"When you work in a law firm, you may have several people working on the same project," she explains. "You may divide up the different parts of a particular brief – and someone would write one part; someone would write the other. And then you're going to have to read it and make sure you haven't contradicted each other, and you may help each other with that."

The final step, Gillmor says, is to have the entire team of lawyers edit the manuscript together and present a unified voice.

PARTNERING AND DIALOGUE

Author William Gibson has won every possible honor in his specialty area of science fiction. To add a shot of midcareer creativity to his work, he decided to experiment by writing a collaborative novel with fellow science fiction writer Bruce Sterling. The result was an extremely successful book called *The Difference Engine*. The novel had many of the best aspects of both Sterling's and Gibson's individual styles, but it was quite a bit different from what either would have written alone.

The partnership "literally created a third entity who was *neither* author," Gibson says.

In a way, he claims, the book "was in the control of this stranger. When people ask how collaborations work, it's like asking how marriages work. Nobody knows; they're all very individual deals. But I think that it's a very, very interesting creative modality."

Student Mike Gratton, who is shown in the video working with a student partner who has opposite views on an argument paper, explains that the creative tension helped both to create better papers – one from each side of the issue. "Collaboration (next to research) is probably the most important thing in my writing," Gratton says. "You can't think of all the different possibilities in your paper that two people might see. So collaboration is really important, and I'm glad that it's embraced in college."

In *A Community of Writers*, Elbow and Belanoff describe a style of partnering called "Writing a Dialogue." This technique is a very effective way for student writers to explore the process of collaborating in a team of two.

As Elbow and Belanoff explain, "You won't have trouble if you realize that you are just 'having a conversation on paper.'" The goal of a rough draft of a dialogue should be to have an exchange of ideas as free as any gabfest. Later, the dialogue can be revised to focus the ideas and emphasize the most interesting parts.

COLLABORATIVE COLLAGES

As Elbow and Belanoff point out in *A Community of Writers*, "If you use a collage structure, you can communicate more richness and complexity in a piece of writing – even contradiction – and still give the readers a sense that the piece hangs together." According to Peter Elbow, the collage is an excellent way to work up to more difficult types of collaborative writing that *do* require a unified voice.

"Supposing four of us have to write a piece together," Elbow explains. "Instead of us having to agree on our thoughts and agree on our voice, *all* we have to agree on is the topic. We all write whatever we want to write about that topic."

The goal, Elbow suggests, should be to produce a collage that does *not* have a single point of view; it should be a *collision* of various views. The main collaborative exercise should be in the organizing and revising stages.

"We do have to agree among the four or five of us about which bits, which blips, which chunks to use, because we probably will have to throw away five-sixths of what we have," Elbow says. "Then we also have to agree on the ordering of those things. Which ones shall we start with and which comes next? So we have to do this job of working together and agreeing on *certain* things, but it's not as hard as agreeing on the thoughts and the language and the voice."

Though this kind of collage breaks all kinds of rules for traditional documents (the paper is not unified, the paragraphs don't support a thesis, and the voices are *intended* to collide), it provides a lively forum to showcase a variety of ideas.

"It's a very effective and pleasing document to have a piece of writing that consists of four or five different voices, chunks of thought that don't agree with each other (in fact, bounce off each other) in whatever kind of order, whether it's imaginative or logical," says Elbow.

The collaborative collage, according to Elbow, is in a sense "doing push-ups" to build strength for writing in a more difficult collaborative style – but it is a wonderful genre in itself. Though this might sound like an artifact of academia, the collaborative collage is actually quite common in the writing of the workplace. For example, when several police officers add different views to a report on a crime scene, the result is expected to be a "collage" of several voices; the opinion/editorial section of a good newspaper also features, by design, a collision of different voices to show more than one side of a controversial issue.

In the program, two students are working on a collaborative collage. All class members have posted their own definitions of the word *welfare* in response to the definitions of *welfare* proposed by Rush Limbaugh and Michael Moore. Each of the individual essays is rather one-sided; the students in the program are attempting to provide a more complete definition, by creating a collaborative collage that features snippets of thirty different views of the word *welfare*.

Edited and revised collages

In a way, the telecourse programs are collaborative collages that have been carefully edited and revised. Though the programs are unified and back a theme with a carefully designed sequence of ideas, each half-hour presentation carefully strings together a narrative of different instructors, writers, and students to talk about one subject. A scriptwriter has glued together the various comments with narrator tracks that are the equivalent of topic sentences in a research paper. In this type of collage, each guest has a different voice, and some have contradictory views.

For example, one telecourse program features many different approaches to defining the concept of "critical thinking." Though some of the views are contradictory, the *combination* of ideas leads to a comprehensive understanding of critical thinking.

In a way, the scriptwriter's job is to help "negotiate" the different views, much like a team leader would assist the various personalities to wrangle about their views, if the guests in the television program were all collaborating on the program together.

Negotiating with a team

Writers who are working collaboratively must learn to build a strong team. In college, and in the real world, that sometimes means picking your partners. If you don't have a choice, it means *negotiating* who will do what in the collaborative process.

Beverly Moss of Ohio State University says that the process of interacting with others is important for students to learn at the undergraduate level. Moss explains, "Not only do they have to learn how to write with a group, they've got to learn how to negotiate in a group – as part of the planning, as part of the drafting, as part of carrying out the project."

The skill of dealing with cooperative (and uncooperative) classmates translates directly to the workplace, Moss says. "But I don't think students see that right away. So I think that one of the values in collaborative work is the whole idea of negotiating. They don't understand that the boss isn't going to ask if Sally did her part of the project. The boss is going to look at the *project*. And Sally's part better be done by somebody, even if it doesn't get done [by Sally]."

In college, of course, working in a collaborative group means that the work (or lack of work) by one or more others can affect your grade. For many, this is an uncomfortable situation. Instructor Robb Lightfoot notes, "A big part of making [a collaborative] class work is simply creating an ethic and an environment where people realize that we *can* work together. There's a real legitimate fear of ... 'If this person over here working with me in a collaborative setting goofs up, it's going to hurt my grade.' If someone's goofing up, you need to talk to them about it – but where there's some protections built in. And rather than being a real negative thing ... you have this basic ground of understanding that … you do what you're supposed to do, you make an honest effort, and you'll be OK."

And, Lightfoot emphasizes, when you get away from worrying about *grades,* and realize that collaborative learning can produce documents that surpass the quality of any possible individual effort, you will truly appreciate the process.

Novelist and instructor John Morgan Wilson warns that the collaborative process is very tricky, and he recommends that collaborators think carefully about picking partners. "I would advise you to pick someone you communicate well with – someone with whom you have no axe to grind. It should be someone whose skills you respect. Ideally, your partner would be someone whose strengths complement your weaknesses and vice versa."

This doesn't mean that all members on a team must have the same opinions and attitudes. In fact, in college (and in the working world), you are often *assigned* to a team. And, members of that team may have attitudes diametrically opposed to your own.

Sometimes, writers who have opposite views can actually collaborate on a pair of essays to make *both* papers stronger – as in the example in the telecourse, when two students from Butte College take different views on the minimum-wage laws. Computer science student Mike Gratton explains, "A lot of the times we would sit there and fight about his point and my point.… And just from fighting about our papers (and finding the strengths of each one) we were able to figure out what we were lacking in each of our papers."

The model of writing where all writers on the team take part in the drafting, revision, and editing cycle *assumes* that all members can contribute equally. Everyone on the team brings ideas during the drafting stage, and, presumably, every team member will find a way to negotiate the differences as the piece is revised. Since egos often get involved, this approach to collaboration could lead to a disaster, with each writer defending her or his contribution against perceived attacks by other team members.

One way to avoid such problems is to set up an ongoing collaborative atmosphere of cooperation before the writing even begins.

Kevin Dorff, who writes for Conan O'Brien of Second City Comedy Revue, explains how the sketch comedy troupe creates an creative ambience that allows the team to function without too much strife. "A principle of our collaboration is that any person's idea should be treated as a *gift.* And we actually *call* them a 'gift.' I use the gift, and then I add something to it, which ends up being a gift back to you. We can go through all the re-writes – we can just change this, pull this out – so that the whole show, from beginning to end, is a *completely* group written thing."

Summary
There's no doubt that collaboration is a skill needed in upper-division classes

and in the world beyond college. It's a good idea, in the relatively non-threatening environment of the English composition classroom, to learn how the process works. Once you get beyond the skepticism about writing this way, you may find that the resulting documents *are* much more powerful; you'll also discover there are many other benefits to working with a team.

Robb Lightfoot gives just a hint of the many advantages: "It is possible, in a classroom – through collaborative learning – to have moments that change people forever in ways that give them confidence, that bond them to one another. I don't tell people you're going to come out of this class finding the person you're going to marry in here. But I generally predict that in situations where people work together not only will they produce a superior product – but they will also come away with friendships and associations that'll last them a lifetime. What a deal – all for the price of a college education."

Integrating the Text

WORKSHOP 3 "Collaborative Writing, Dialogue, Loop Writing, and the Collage" (pp. 67–98)

Throughout *A Community of Writers*, Elbow and Belanoff advocate a variety of collaborative exercises that support the points in this telecourse program. In fat, in almost every unit, there is a section of exercises called "Suggestions for Collaboration."

Workshop 3, "Collaborative Writing, Dialogue, Loop Writing, and the Collage" (pp. 67–98), offers a clear process on analysis of several types of collaboration, with step-by-step instructions on how a team of students can assemble such a document. Of special interest is the collaborative collage, a central idea in the telecourse program.

The techniques of collaboration introduced in Workshop 3 are designed as much for developing ideas as they are for creating a "group-authored document." In fact, the emphasis is *not* on the type of collaborative project that attempts to create a document with a unified voice.

Elbow and Belanoff also address several key concepts, such as how to negotiate and "harness the power of disagreement." They offer down-to-earth suggestions for working with others (pp. 81–83). The authors explore the theory of "taking chances" by writing without knowing what you are going to say first. In other words, they suggest you try the "dangerous method" often pursued by collaborative team: starting the process of composing a document before you know what you want to say. This philosophy runs counter to conventional wisdom advocated by many writing instructors, who insist students figure out what they have to say *before they start writing*." Elbow and Belanoff's approach is quite similar to the method advocated in the telecourse by the staff writers and actors at *Mad TV*.

At the end of Workshop 3, several examples of collaborative projects give students ideas of how such experiments might come out.

Exercises

Check with your instructor for your formal assignments. You will be asked to do exercises from the *Telecourse Study Guide*.

Exploring collaborative writing further
EXERCISE 1
Get a group of students together. Decide on a hot topic. Have everybody write the most opinionated statement they can about the topic. Create a collaborative collage of different views on the topic to get a broad look at the issues from *all* sides.

Example: In the unit about definition writing, you may have been asked to give your own definition of the word *welfare* as a response to two radically different definitions offered in the program by Michael Moore and Rush Limbaugh. This exercise usually elicits a wide variety of responses that show positive and negative views of the welfare system. Use these responses to create a collaborative collage that gives a complete definition of the word – showing as many views and attitudes as possible.

EXERCISE 2
Working with a team of people, try to pick a controversial topic that is likely to inspire a wide variety of views. Use the loop writing process in *A Community of Writers* (pp. 70–71) to generate short bursts of writing about the topic.

Using the definition of *welfare*, again, as an example:

1. List first impressions, prejudices, and preconceptions about welfare.

2. Do another short burst of writing that includes anecdotes, stories, memories, moments you have about welfare.

3. Explore some dialogues about welfare.

4. Try writing about welfare for various audiences – or for people of a different time of the century.

5. List the lies, errors, and common sayings you know about welfare.

This is an exercise that can be done by one writer, but it works especially well in a group. The loop writing will generate a wealth of ideas for a collaborative collage – or raw material for a more unified style of collaborative document.

Exercise just for fun

Pick another student in the class, and start sending e-mail messages back and forth about a specific topic you want to explore. (You might consider one of the techniques you are studying about writing – or a topic you would like to debate and explore with someone else who has an active mind.)

The goal of these exchanges will be to build a collaborative document in the "Writing a Dialogue" style of Plato and Socrates, described in *A Community of Writers* on page 68.

Keep all messages (and responses to your messages), as you exchange the e-mail. Set a date to get together and revise the document. Your goal in revision should be to find the most interesting parts and bring out the focus of the discussion.

That might include a creative discarding and rearranging of the messages. (The final version does *not* have to be chronological.) See pages 69 to 70 in *A Community of Writers* for advice on revising dialogue.

Revision exercise

Using the collaborative collage created about the subject chosen in Exercise 1 as a starting point, decide within your group how best to revise it and put it in the form of an academic essay about the subject. Among the factors you will need to discuss and come to agreements about are

- What sort of voice to employ

- How to divide work among the group members

- What points are in need of support and documentation

The group should be prepared to set aside time outside of class to meet, resolve these and other issues, and to complete the actual final draft of the essay.

Quick writing exercise

Your instructor may ask you to do a quick focused freewrite about the topic you are studying in this unit. Those of you who are taking the course through a distance-learning system may be encouraged to share your thoughts in a discussion thread or to post your ideas on an Internet bulletin board. If you are writing your thoughts out by hand in a process journal, you might use these questions to help produce ideas. This is a freewriting exercise that will not be graded. You can use any of the following questions to stimulate your thoughts about collaborative writing:

When placed in a collaborative group, are you usually a team member or a team leader? Have your experiences in collaborative learning environments been comfortable or uncomfortable? Why? Do you anticipate that you will need collaborative skills in your upper-division classes or in your career? If so, what kinds of activities can your instructor provide to help prepare you for these experiences? What can you do to learn to be a better collaborator?

You may use the questions in the "Process Journal" section of Workshop 3, "Collaborative Writing: Dialogue, Loop Writing, and The Collage" (p. 84) in *A Community of Writers* as an additional source of inspiration for this quick writing exercise.

Additional reading

How is the excerpt in the appendix from David Ellefson's book, *Making Music Your Business*, relevant to the main premise of this telecourse program?

One student essay in the appendix, "Are Manufacturers of Caffeinated Beverages Targeting Children?" by Francine Taylor, is presented as a formal academic argument. Using a division of labor model, how would you go about assembling a team to create an in-depth, expanded document based on Taylor's thesis? (Imagine you are going to submit this document to Congress and the U.S. surgeon general.)

Exercises related to *A Community of Writers*

The emphasis on collaborative learning is so central to Elbow and Belanoff's philosophy that *A Community of Writers* has a "Suggestion for Collaboration" exercise in all 16 of the primary workshops. By this point in the course, if your teacher is also a strong believer in collaboration, you may have already been assigned many of these exercises, and you may be familiar with many aspects of the collaborative writing process.

While the textbook describes most of these exercises from the point of view of a traditional classroom, many of these exercises can easily be adapted to a distance learning environment. They work particularly well in a course that uses the Internet and allows students to share and respond via e-mail, bulletin boards, and collaborative software.

If you are learning in an environment where formally assigned peer feedback is difficult to achieve, it is a good idea to at least read the suggestions for collaboration. In graduate school, and in the working world, mastering the skills of collaboration can be quite important.

If you are in a learning environment that is friendly to collaborative writing, survey the "Suggestions for Collaboration" assignments from the 16 workshops in *A Community of Writers*, and work with your instructor to select one to focus on for this unit of collaboration. The teacher will also help break the entire class up into several smaller groupings of students. Your goal will be to write an essay about the similarities and differences between collaborative learning and collaborative writing, using the workshop you have selected from the textbook as a starting point. Each group will probably focus on a different workshop.

Quick Review

1. According to instructors in the television program:
   a. Collaborative writing is easier than writing as a solitary individual.
   b. Collaborative writing is only found in the classroom environment.
   c. Collaborative writing often leads to a better document.
   d. All of the above.
   e. None of the above.

2. A division of labor model
   a. has all writers contributing equally on every aspect of the writing
   b. assigns a different task to each member on the team
   c. is never used in academia
   d. all of the above
   e. none of the above

3. A collaborative collage
   a. should always have a unified voice
   b. should always be built around a unified thesis
   c. might showcase a collision of voices
   d. all of the above
   e. none of the above

4. A collaborative dialogue
   a. should get both writers to agree on all points in a unified thesis
   b. allows two writers to have a conversation on paper
   c. is usually very carefully outlined
   d. all of the above
   e. none of the above

5. According to instructors in the telecourse program:
   a. We know that in the industrial world, in the corporate world, people are collaborating more and more.
   b. Not only do students have to learn how to write with a group, they've got to learn how to negotiate in a group.
   c. The dynamic of leadership emergence in a collaborative group can be messy. It can be frustrating. It's not always fun.
   d. All of the above.
   e. None of the above.

6. According to Elbow and Belanoff:

   a. If two or more people come at the same topic, they don't just add to the thinking – they *multiply* the thinking through the interaction of ideas.

   b. A collage structure should never show contradiction of views; otherwise, it will give the readers a sense that the piece doesn't hang together.

   c. The collaborative dialogue is a relatively new and trendy classroom device invented by modern-day English teachers to give students something to take up classroom time.

   d. All of the above.

   e. None of the above.

"I think what works to persuade people is to find a way to immediately say, 'I understand this from your point of view' – to be on the other side of the argument, to use a voice that proves that to them, to address things in a way that sees the issue through their eyes. It starts with the understanding of who is going to be persuaded."

JEFF GOODBY, advertising executive

Introduction to the Topic

We deal with persuasion every day.

Let's face it: The only real reason we parade around in some of the silly-looking fashions we wear and drive some of the gas-guzzlers we own is because someone *persuaded* us to.

Don't believe it? Check out how much of every month's paycheck it costs to drive that pollution-spewing hulk – and look at some old photographs to see what you wore a decade ago. (For even more fun, check out what you parents were wearing at your age.)

But we aren't sheep following a shepherd. This practice goes both ways. We actively persuade other people every day of our lives too. Imagine your dad or mom begging for those bell bottoms, disco outfits,

or whatever else was in style when they were thirteen – or yourself lobbying heavily for the T-shirt that cost $50 just because it had a designer logo or emblem of a sports franchise on it.

Persuasion is so pervasive in our lives, we all have a strong intuitive sense of how to do it. When it is time to sit down and write a persuasive essay, many of us find the writing quite natural. In fact, most students find that the assignment for this instructional unit is not only fun, it's also an opportunity to air passionate views or champion a pet cause.

This *Telecourse Study Guide* chapter and the related telecourse program will teach you the basics of how to write a persuasive essay like this.

Learning Objectives

After viewing the television programs and finishing the writing assignments, you will know when informal persuasion is the appropriate thinking/writing strategy to use in college writing tasks. You will also consider the *type* of persuasion you might use for other types of writing outside of college. You will learn the art of persuasion with expert guidance from instructors and some of the most persuasive writers in the country, and you will practice the techniques for writing a persuasive piece of writing.

These learning objectives work in harmony with the essential premises of Workshop 10, "Persuasion" (pp. 255–275), in *A Community of Writers*, in which Elbow and Belanoff state

- The first step in persuasion is getting someone to listen.
- Persuasion relies less on formal rational argument than on reaching out to an audience and getting their interest by appealing particularly to experience and feeling.

Before Viewing

Consider if you have ever been persuaded to change your mind, specifically because a good writer urged you to action. Try to determine what moved you and how you could create a similar effect with your own writing.

Read Elbow and Belanoff's Workshop 10, "Persuasion" (pp. 255–275), with a special emphasis in understanding the section "Persuasion as Informal Argument."

While Viewing

Compare the techniques you already have in persuasive writing with the methods recommended by the instructors, professional writers, and students in the telecourse program. Imagine how you might borrow some of the secrets of how to sway opinions that are shared by the successful persuasive writers included in the telecourse program. Learn how to hone your own expertise in winning over readers. Also notice how the instructors, students, and professional writers persuade by becoming aware of common assumptions they have with an audience, hammering away at a focused central point, and mixing in a little logic with their ethical and emotional appeals.

Reconsider the section "Exploring Theory: Informal Persuasion and Formal Argument" (p. 267), in which Elbow and Belanoff contrast this "intuitive and experimental" style of writing with the style of formal argument (which is more appropriate for an "expert and professional audience") that we will explore in the next unit.

After Viewing

Using the exercises at the end of this *Telecourse Study Guide* chapter, practice the art of persuasion. Also identify several examples of persuasive writing you are exposed to, in college and day-to-day life outside of school. It should not be hard to find examples; we are constantly surrounded by persuasion. Determine whether the persuasion writing you recognize is convincing, and consider if any of the points made in this telecourse program contribute to the effectiveness or lack thereof. Develop an awareness of when you are being exposed to persuasion and of how you react as a critical thinker to this kind of communication.

Viewing Guide

Writing to cause social action, to persuade others to change their thinking, or to do something that affects their world is a direct application of the skills learned in this course. Persuasive writing borrows a bit of storytelling here and a bit of definition there. It might use a touch of comparison/contrast, spiced with a heavy helping of opinion.

If you have ever learned how to entice, cajole, or influence your parents, siblings, or friends, you will find this writing style to be intuitive.

Though related to the formal academic arguments common in classroom work, persuasive writing is usually more casual and spontaneous.

Persuasion is an important style to study in a composition course, especially when you consider how many different kinds of writers practice persuasion to promote social action in writing beyond the classroom.

Persuasion all around us

The telecourse program introduces several people who use persuasion outside of the classroom. This is a writing style that permeates our society, and it's not difficult to find examples.

Jeff Goodby, an advertising executive responsible for the award-winning "Got Milk?" campaign, observes, "I work in a business where persuasion is not usually welcome. What we try to do here is to raise things to the highest common denominator – to presume that people have a sense of humor, to presume that they're intelligent enough to be able to follow this argument and have fun with it. And I think humor gets them on your side, so that when a piece of persuasion starts to occur, they're more open to it."

U.S. District Judge Helen Gillmor explains that, although a trial that is heard only by a judge is built around carefully reasoned arguments, a trial that goes to a jury is a stage for emotion-laden persuasive appeals.

"An attorney who is speaking to a *jury* with respect to the facts has two burdens," Gillmor explains. "He has to stay within the laws, but he has twelve people who are not lawyers to persuade."

Novelist Kim Stanley Robinson reminds us that science fiction, mystery, and other pop culture novels can be extended forms of persuasion.

"Fiction is social action," Robinson explains. "The writing of a story and giving it to other people is a social act that will influence their opinions of what's going on in their own lives." In fact, Robinson's famous novels *Red Mars*, *Green Mars,* and *Blue Mars* do just that. Though presented as science fiction thrillers, the books are also intended to provoke readers into thinking about the environment on their own planet.

Radio personality Rush Limbaugh builds his talk show around persuasion. His goal is to incite others with similar conservative political beliefs to action; along the way, he hopes to change the minds of the liberal listeners who dial in to the show to take issue with everything he says. Limbaugh's technique is to get listeners to come to their *own* conclusions in the debate.

"If I am successful, they think *they* have come to that conclusion, maybe with my assistance but not totally because of me," Limbaugh says. "They'll be much more inclined to accept their own conclusion and rely on their own intelligence, rather than to say, 'I used to think something, but Limbaugh convinced me.' People don't want to say that somebody convinced them they were wrong; they would much rather tell you they figured something out on their own."

Before we get too serious about the implications of persuasion in politics, law, and other arenas, actress and writer Mo Collins, who uses social satire on the comedy show *Mad TV*, reminds us that persuasion should be *fun*. Participating in the process can also help you see several sides of an issue; if you can laugh at yourself, she says, you can sometimes get closer to understanding.

"What I like about great satire is that it plays both fields," Collins explains. "Whatever your own opinions are, it's best to play devil's advocate and argue the other side. In my experience, I found that is always fun. Because I *did* form very strong opinions of my own. And because I looked so far to the other side, many times I would be swayed – which is really cool."

Persuasion versus formal argument

Persuasion, as we are defining the term in this course, is informal. The process depends on getting people to listen to you. The best persuasive pieces have a clear purpose, state a claim that addresses that purpose, and back the claim with believable evidence. Good persuasive writers are aware of their audience and think a great deal about the implications of tone, language, assumptions, and voice.

These are all important aspects of good academic papers, but many instructors take care to distinguish between a formal academic argument and a piece of persuasion that emphasizes emotional and ethical points, even though the goals and overall structure are quite similar.

English instructor Betsy Klimasmith of the University of Washington describes the distinction between the two styles: "There are some differences between the idea of persuading and the idea of a formal argument. And I think that the words *persuasion* and *argument* in this sense are confusing, because when you usually think of argument [outside of an academic setting], you're thinking of something that's much more confrontational."

Outside of school, the use of the word *argument* has an almost violent implication, she says, while the word *persuasion* implies subtle pleading.

An academic's view, Klimasmith says, reverses this notion. Argument is considered more subtle and more carefully reasoned. The term *persuasive writing* implies something that is more "in your face" – and perhaps charged with more raw enthusiasm than logical reasoning.

Elbow and Belanoff support this differentiation between persuasion and argument in *A Community of Writers* (p. 255). "Persuasion relies less on formal rational argument than on reaching out to an audience and getting their interest by appealing to experience and feelings," they write.

"Sometimes people are persuaded by long formal arguments that somehow 'prove' or 'settle' an issue by means of incisive reasoning and evidence. But sometimes these good arguments don't work; that is, the reader is somehow not persuaded even though the argument is impressive."

How to persuade

One key to influencing readers (and even changing their minds) is to understand *how* people are swayed, shaped, sold – and persuaded. You can begin by reflecting on what sways *you*.

The next step is to consider your audience. As Judge Gillmor noted earlier, an attorney might argue a case formally if the judge is the only person deciding a case; the same attorney would have to carefully study an audience of twelve people, to determine what would persuade a jury.

In a classroom setting, the judge is your instructor and the jury is your classmates.

Of course, in this unit, you will most likely be asked to read and consider the writing of other students in your class. That task allows you to feel what it is like to be persuaded – or *not* be persuaded. Skillful writers learn to translate that experience by asking, "How would I react, as a member of the class, if I were asked to read my own work?"

AUDIENCE

Every instructor surveyed for the telecourse said that awareness of audience is an important aspect of good persuasive writing.

Elbow and Belanoff agree. "Extended, careful argument is what you might be expected to write for an audience that is expert and professional," they write (p. 267). "Informal persuasion, at the other extreme, is the kind of thing you find in editorials, leaflets, advertisement, short spoken interchanges, and of course letters to the editor in newspapers."

Sometimes, the best way to revise a persuasion paper is to visualize yourself as a member of the audience for a moment. For that reason, Elbow and Belanoff recommend you read and analyze several persuasive letters to the editor in order to gain objectivity about your own work. In analyzing a persuasive piece you are *reading*, Elbow and Belanoff ask you to consider: "Do you think you're the audience the writer had in mind? How does that affect whether or not you're persuaded? If you're the wrong audience, what sot of an audience do you think the writers *had* in mind?"

Many student writers never even consider the audience; they are just doing the writing to get the course assignment over with. Those who excel, however, are the students who understand how much awareness of audience plays a part in the writing beyond school.

Kalle Lasn, the self-described "culture jammer" featured in the telecourse, is the publisher of a magazine called *Adbusters*. *Adbusters'* mission is to persuade readers to consume less and to resist corporate takeover in their lives. Those objectives require *complete* understanding of the audience. This is not an easy challenge, especially considering that even Lasn's most supportive readers are used to the comforts of a consumer society. Lasn says that, as a writer whose every sentence is intended to persuade, he thinks often about the audience.

"I do see everything that we do as being a kind of a contest with the audience. I see it as like a battle of the mind – there are people in the audience with in a certain frame of mind, and I have a chance to grab their attention. I must ask, 'How do I engage in this battle of the mind with the audience in such a way that after the battle is over, they will have changed a little bit?' "

Lasn's challenge is daunting. He is dueling with advertisers who spend millions of dollars to create an accurate profile of the consumer audience.

Advertising writer Jeff Goodby explains, "We have these people who are called strategic planners, and they don't do anything except go talk to people who are going to be like the ones that we have to persuade. And we talk to them about the way that they see the world, the way that they see this particular product fitting into the world. And we learn about the parameters of what they *will* believe."

In the telecourse program, instructor Michael Bertsch explains how he gets students to put the equivalent amount of thought into the audience.

"Writing the urge-to-action paper, you have to disarm the fear in the readers. You want to bait them with something that they agree with and bring them slowly in. There's a certain moment that they won't realize that your opinion has closed around behind them and you've got them in your nice warm little arms of rhetoric. Let's say I wanted to persuade

244

someone to recycle. I wouldn't say – 'You dog! You had best recycle!' That isn't the way to get someone to do something because they'll just move away. What you want to do is entice them into some idea of participating in a greater good or perhaps making money for your city or perhaps reducing the cost of goods and services they purchase. These are the things that disarm fear."

ASSUMPTIONS

To be an effective persuasive writer, you should consider whether the *assumptions* you start with are the same ones the audience has. An effective persuasive piece will state or imply common points that both writer and audience are likely to agree on – before exploring new territory.

Pat Belanoff of the State of New York at Stony Book gives the example of a student's paper that advocates the freedom to buy guns from the perspective of the National Rifle Association.

"I can look at that and say, 'Yes, that's well reasoned' ... and I might have to give the student a very good grade on that paper. But, it wouldn't persuade me because the person who wrote that and I started from different assumptions. My assumption might be that there are too many dangerous guns floating around in this world and that I want to get rid of as many as I can, and they're starting with the assumption that guns can be used safely.

"I don't buy that assumption. I would more likely be *persuaded* by a story in which something awful happened to somebody because they didn't have a gun to protect themselves – something that perhaps is not such a closely reasoned argument."

An unethical writer might try to slip in implied "assumptions" that are false, trying to trick the reader into accepting as "given" some idea he or she wouldn't ordinarily embrace. For example, a persuasive article about immigration might insert an unwritten and hidden assumption that "all foreigners are unwelcome in our society." While only a very small percentage of the audience would agree with that statement, a larger part of the audience might partially swallow a piece of persuasion where that philosophy is the hidden agenda.

The ethical writer will build on *mutual* assumptions to make the essay more persuasive.

Thomas Fox of California State University suggests that you will not only become a more persuasive writer – you might actually learn more as you come to understand the opposition's strongest points.

"If you're going to persuade others to change their stance, you really do have to understand their legitimate point of view," Fox explains. "It might be common assumptions. It might be weighing different consequences. Those are the kinds of things that I always think are really interesting topics for you to write about – where your own values might be in conflict with the others'. Then you learn a lot, and you think a lot, and you get new places. You can persuade new audiences."

Effective persuasive writers work hard to find the common assumptions with their potential audience, Fox says. "Otherwise, they're not going to listen to you. They won't respect you; they won't think you have anything to offer."

Finding and highlighting the assumptions that the reader and writer have in common can be an excellent place to start creating an effective tone for your persuasive piece.

TONE

A writer can consciously affect the tone of an essay by finding a friendly place – a mutual assumption, a laugh, a definition – in common with the person he is trying to persuade.

Instructor Michael Bertsch puts it this way: "The writer has to affect an *accessible* tone. Sometimes humor can be good; sometimes just pure information can be good. Sometimes mildly miffed instead of argumentative can be good. Indignant can work, but you don't want to make your readers afraid or defensive – especially if you're trying to *persuade* them to do something."

A paper's tone, or attitude, manifests itself at the most basic level, with conscious word choices. Many words have hidden meanings, or connotations, that can subtly (or not so subtly) spin a sentence toward a particular feeling.

For example, the sentence "He told a little white lie" attempts to tone down the fact that someone lied. Consider how a public relations person or editorial writer might change the verb to affect each of the following short sentences:

> She fibbed. He deceived. She bent the truth. He manipulated. She twisted the truth. He told a tale. She fabricated a story. He beguiled. She misrepresented. He falsified records.

As the writer is trying to imply a more damaging or less harmful deceit, the choice of the verb becomes quite important.

Even the basic choice of a pronoun can affect the tone of a persuasive piece. For example, *formal* academic arguments are often expected to be in the third person to give the impression of objectivity. It is common for an instructor to mark on a formal research paper, "We don't care what you feel. Don't use 'I feel' or 'I believe' statements. State your thesis, and back it with evidence – in the third person!"

Ariel Gonzalez, an English instructor at Miami-Dade Community College, says, "I tell students that there's one thing that I guarantee will lower their grade. "That is, if they ever begin a sentence with 'In my opinion.'"

Persuasive papers *can* be third person, but since they are less formal, they can also be written from the writer's point of view. First-person statements such as "I feel" are much more likely to be accepted by a general audience. The second-person pronoun is also acceptable in certain circumstances, such as when the writer addresses the audience directly.

As we learned in Chapter 6 (the unit about voice), the pronoun *you* can imply a friendly tone, as in, "You've probably felt the same emotions I have."

The writer who uses the second person should be careful, however. It is just a subtle shift to create an accusatory tone, with a sentence such as, "You are probably one of those responsible for this pollution problem."

Voice

Advertising executive Jeff Goodby points out in the telecourse program that the persuasive writer should be aware of all aspects of voice.

"I think what works to persuade people is to find a way to immediately say, 'I understand this from your point of view.' To use a *voice* that proves that to them. To address things in a way that sees the issue through their eyes."

Advocacy journalist Tim Bousquet explains that it helps in his business to adopt a voice that sounds like you're just talking to the guy next door.

"I try to have a conversational tone in my stories," Bousquet explains. "Especially local stories dealing with the local city council and local people. I'm writing as if I'm speaking to someone and I try to say what's going on. When I was in school, I tried to *sound* smart. And if you have to *try* to sound smart, you're not smart. And now I just write what I feel and what I think – backed with research."

The results, he says, are much more persuasive.

It is just as important to have a tone that does not waver as it is to have a tone that conveys the right mood. Michael Bertsch explains, "When the voice is inconsistent within the paper, the reader feels the writer's point of view is inconsistent and waffling. So that paper is less persuasive, less hard hitting."

Purpose and claim

Like the formal academic argument, the persuasive paper should demonstrate a clear purpose. Readers are unlikely to change their minds if the author has no idea *why* he or she is writing the piece. Many attempts at persuasion often do in fact read as if the author's only purpose was to vent some frustration.

The purpose is usually clarified during the drafting process, as the writer determines the key point of the essay and figures out how to support the main claim.

Unlike the formal academic argument (which usually states the thesis in the beginning, supports it systematically with evidence, and restates the thesis in the conclusion), *some* persuasive communications, including speeches and newspaper editorials, save the main point, claim, or thesis until the end of the piece.

"Suppose you are making a claim that you think is going to be so offensive or just so problematic for your reader that you don't want to come out first with that main point," Teresa Redd of Howard University explains. "You want to present the evidence to the reader so that that reader will gradually come to the conclusion. You might want even want to withhold your thesis till the end. It depends on your purpose."

Speech and debate instructor Robb Lightfoot agrees with this tactic.

"In most forms of persuasion where you expect a negative audience response, you're better off to build up to it," Lightfoot claims. "The actual one-sentence statement of what you're talking about probably will come late enough in the speech that you've already hooked people. Because, if you lead off with that, you'd lose them right off – 'Hi, I'm here and I want to raise taxes.' Nobody's going to buy that. You've got to create a feeling of concern, of a general sense of need, and then you pop them with your solution."

Usually, the premise, thesis, or main claim is stated early in an essay – especially in a persuasive piece that is not extremely controversial. But no matter what, there is almost always some sort of one-sentence summary that explains the main point you are trying to convince the readers to accept. As Jeff Goodby explains, even a commercial has something like a main claim. The unifying device is a technique used in almost every type of writing.

"We spend a lot of time talking to people before we make a commercial to address them," Goodby says. "Eventually, I think we narrow everything down to have a single, simple thesis sentence to work with."

Sometimes, of course, the thesis is not effective, and the writer must reconsider the piece in the revision stage.

"If it doesn't work, the only choice you have is to go back and rewrite the original thesis and rethink it," Goodby says.

Balancing emotional, ethical, and logical appeals

The persuasive essay usually makes a series of loosely connected key points in support of the thesis. However, the structure is not as methodical as the argument essay, and the points don't have to always follow logically.

Elbow and Belanoff write, "Informal persuasion may make 'points,' but more often it succeeds by conveying experience or affecting feelings.

"The essence of persuasion in today's world is often embodied in advertisements. Advertisers usually have only one goal: to get you to buy their products" (p. 267).

Writers who intend to persuade (including those in advertising) do use the logic of facts and statistics and other forms of hard evidence to state a case. However, they usually rely more heavily on emotional and ethical appeals to influence opinions.

"Good persuasion is logical and emotional at the same time," says Goodby. "I think that the logical part is really, in many cases, the easiest part. The hard part is the emotional part. And the way that you get listened to is the emotional part. You have to get somebody's attention, you have to lead them through it, you can't just lead them through it through their heads; you have to lead them through their heart too. And it's the emotional part, I think, of advertising that really makes it work."

English instructor Geoffrey Philp of Miami-Dade Community College suggests that if a persuasion paper is purely logical or ethical, the reader will might be bored, thinking, "Yes, it's good, but what the heck? There's no emotion behind it."

According to Philp, it is just as important to prove the persuasive piece has an ethical basis as it is to prove the logic; the writer has to justify that the point is morally right.

"There has to be a blend of all three [appeals]," Philp says. "Show the basis of your ethics; then prove it logically. Now after you've proven it logically (using your value system) – then the passion comes in. *Show* it to me. Show me the reason *why*. Because we don't react unless there's *desire*."

Summary

Ultimately, a writer must decide *why* she or he is writing a persuasive paper. Often, the reason is to promote some sort of social action – to create a change in society, to make a bad situation better. Persuasion can also cause different kinds of social "actions," including getting people to open up their wallets for a cause, getting people to vote, or merely making your readers *think*.

Conservative radio personality Rush Limbaugh explains his purpose for persuading. "When I finish my radio career (when they write an epitaph, or some historian judges my achievement), if somebody were to say, 'He opened more people's minds and allowed more people to end up thinking for themselves, rather than accepting whatever is presented to them in the media and the textbook' – then that would be the greatest thing I would think I could accomplish."

Liberal newspaper editor Tim Bousquet has a similar attitude about the purpose of the persuasive writing he publishes in a small-town newspaper. "The vote you cast for your local city council person has way more of an effect on your everyday life than a vote in a national election," he says. "I am trying to produce a publication that underscores that reality. If the readers, over time, understand that, then they're more apt to be involved politically one way or the other. They don't necessarily have to agree with my take on it – but I think that they'll see that their vote actually is very important in terms of how it affects their own lives."

Though Bousquet and Limbaugh have almost no political views in common, they both have the necessary passion to cause social action. Both are trying to use persuasion to make things happen; both are trying to lead the readers to their own interpretation of the truth.

English instructor Cynthia Selfe hopes to inspire her English composition students to the same level of motivation and caring in their writing.

"If we can work with others to identify those truths and to come to some mutual understanding of the basis of different positions and different ways of solving problems, we might actually be able to solve some of the major problems that confront our world today," Selfe says. "That would be an accomplishment."

Integrating the Text

WORKSHOP 10 "Persuasion" (pp. 255–276)

Elbow and Belanoff's approach to this subject in Workshop 10, "Persuasion" (pp. 255–276) is quite similar to that of the telecourse.

Elbow and Belanoff first ask you to consider (through freewriting) times when someone's words played a role in changing your mind or actions. Thinking about how you were actually *persuaded* by something will give you some insight into how easy or difficult it is to do this in writing yourself.

The second exercise in *A Community of Writing* is a very practical one: to write a letter to the editor of the school newspaper or local newspaper.

This is an excellent assignment, one that is not merely a homework exercise. Letters are usually published with byline, and the student suddenly has a real audience. The prospect of publication usually inspires you to focus on the subject; you will think about how readers will judge your grammar, spelling, organization, and tone as well as your premise and evidence. Suddenly, you are not *just* writing a paper for a teacher.

This exercise has two stages. In addition to the letter to the editor, Elbow and Belanoff recommend a second document an explanatory piece for the teacher and classmates that clarifies the letters purpose and audience. This is also an excellent exercise, because all too often writers of letters to the editor have no clue as to their audience or purpose.

Workshop 10 clearly delineates the difference between an informal piece of persuasion and a formal academic argument. (The formal argument will be studied in an upcoming program of the telecourse and in Workshop 10 in *A Community of Writers.*) Elbow and Belanoff make the point that formal arguments, while well reasoned and impressive in their logical approach, rarely move readers to change their minds. The trick of persuasion, however, is to get the reader to *listen.* To illustrate this point, Elbow and Belanoff examine the persuasive techniques used in advertising; their approach works in harmony with the interview in the telecourse featuring advertising executive Jeff Goodby, designer of the "Got Milk" campaign.

The point is, many of the same techniques used to make advertising persuasive will work in a short persuasive essay. Workshop 10 asks students to first dissect a few sample advertisements, and then to use the same criteria to construct (and later evaluate) their own persuasive writing.

Exercises

Check with your instructor for your formal assignments. You will be asked to do exercises from the *Telecourse Study Guide*.

Exploring persuasion further

Exercise 1

While watching television or surfing the Internet, try to find two different advertisements for the same product (or the same type of product) that are aimed at two different audiences. Write a short paper describing your ideas regarding:

- Who are the target audiences of each of the advertisements?
- What different forms of persuasion are attempted?
- What is the purpose of each advertisement?
- How is each of the ads specifically targeted for an audience?

Exercise 2

Take a minute to think about the methods of persuasion you employ in your everyday life. Write a short paper describing the differences in methods used when trying to persuade an instructor as opposed to those you would use with your peers.

Exercise 3

Consider times when someone's words played a role in changing your mind or actions. Thinking about how you were actually *persuaded* by something will give you some insight on how easy (or difficult) it is to do this through writing. If you cannot think of a specific time you were persuaded in this manner, look in the editorial pages of magazines or newspapers. Write a short paper about the methods employed in these situations or articles that worked to persuade you.

Exercise 4

Try to list as many "purposes" for writing a persuasive piece as you can. You can start off with variations of

- To make someone else as angry as I am
- To get someone to open up his or her wallet and spend some money on my cause

Have fun with these purposes. You can stretch and exaggerate. When you finish, determine what the real purpose of your own next persuasive essay might be.

Exercise 5

Take any premise that you want to build a persuasion piece around, and list at least two ethical points, two logical points, and two emotional points that would support your claim.

- Take the same main point you used, and list several assumptions that you and the intended audience are likely to agree upon.
- Write a brief character profile of the audience that this persuasion piece might be aimed at.
- Characterize the tone and voice that would be most effective for persuading that audience.

Exercise just for fun

Write an essay that persuades your instructor that you already know how to write a persuasive essay.

Revision exercise

Using the six questions about purpose, audience, assumptions, voice, claim, and decisions in the section "Writing Your Explanation" (p. 264) in *A Community of Writers*, reread and revise an early draft of your persuasive essay.

Quick writing exercise

Your instructor may ask you to do a quick focused freewrite about the process of persuasion. Those of you who are taking the course through a distance-learning system may be encouraged to share your thoughts in a discussion thread or to post your ideas on an Internet bulletin board. If you are writing your thoughts in a process journal, you might use these questions to stimulate ideas. This is a freewriting exercise that will not be graded. You can use any of the following questions to start thinking about what persuades:

Have you ever been persuaded to change your mind? What persuaded you? What makes the difference between writing an essay that is merely aimed at others who believe the same as the writer and a paper that can really change opinions? What do you think about the points made in the telecourse program about assumptions, tone, and balance of logical, ethical, and emotional appeal? Are these concepts you never thought of, when asked to write persuasive papers in the past, or are they already quite familiar to you? What is the difference between the persuasive technique you used as a young teen to persuade your parents and the technique you might use to persuade an instructor or a classmate in an essay?

You may use the questions in the "Process Journal" section of Workshop 10 (p. 266) in *A Community of Writers* as an additional source of inspiration for this quick writing exercise.

Exercises related to *A Community of Writers*

A Community of Writers offers several exercises for practicing and analyzing the art of persuasion. The nine-point analysis of the effectiveness of an advertisement (p. 259) is a good exercise to learn *how* people are persuaded. Many of the points, including purpose, focus, language, assumptions, audience, and voice, are *exactly* the same as those made by the writers and teachers in the telecourse program.

The exercise to evaluate letters to the editor (pp. 259–262) looks at persuasion that is a little closer to the type of essay you might generate for a college class. Notice that most of the criteria are essentially the same.

The suggestions and questions in the "Process Journal" for looking at the material generated in the section "The Main Assignment: Writing A Letter To The Editor" (pp. 263–266) offer an excellent guide to follow for any assignment to write a persuasive essay for class – whether the target audience is your teacher or the general readers of an op-ed page in a newspaper.

Use these exercises to generate and revise your persuasive work, even if they are not assigned formally by your teacher.

Additional reading

What assumptions does Himilce Novas make about her audience in the excerpt in the appendix from *Everything You Need to Know About Latino History*? How does Novas balance logical, ethical, and emotional points? What is the implied thesis from this section of her book?

What techniques of persuasion do you recognize in the writing of Kalle Lasn (a self-described "culture jammer") and Rush Limbaugh (conservative radio talk-show host) in the pieces that are included in the appendix? Are either Lasn or Limbaugh effective in reaching people who don't sympathize with their views? Why?

One student essay in the appendix, "Are Manufacturers of Caffeinated Beverages Targeting Children?" by Francine Taylor, is presented as a formal academic argument. Is it also persuasive? How is this different from the informal persuasion you have been reading? How might Taylor's piece be different, if it were written as a letter to the editor of a newspaper?

Quick Review

1. A good persuasion piece should use
   a. logical appeal
   b. ethical appeal
   c. emotional appeal
   d. a blend of all three types of appeal
   e. none of the above

2. The difference between an academic argument and a persuasion piece is that
   a. Persuasive pieces do not have a clear thesis like an academic argument has.
   b. Persuasive pieces are more informal and based more on feelings than logic.
   c. Persuasive pieces don't use evidence to support the claim.
   d. All of the above.
   e. None of the above.
3. The persuasive writer is aware of
   a. audience
   b. tone
   c. assumptions
   d. all of the above
   e. none of the above
4. Tone is potentially affected by
   a. word choice
   b. pronouns
   c. voice
   d. all of the above
   e. none of the above
5. The premise, main point, or thesis
   a. is always stated at the beginning of a persuasive piece
   b. is always saved for the end of a persuasive piece
   c. is not even a consideration in the persuasion of advertising
   d. all of the above
   e. none of the above

"The kind of reading that students encounter in college – I'm talking about the work in sociology, in history, in women's studies, in astronomy, zoology or biology – the reading is often quite difficult. It's quite academic and it's grounded in some sort of research tradition. What I hope students in my class begin to experience is: no matter how hard a reading is, if you give it time, and if you're lucky enough to be in a setting where you've got somebody else who can read it with you, talk to you about it ... you realize that even a very difficult reading *can* be understood. It can be unpackaged. In fact, you can criticize it. There are very interesting ideas imbedded in readings."

MIKE ROSE, UCLA

Introduction to the Topic

In the opening segment for this telecourse program, Loren Goerhing expresses his enthusiasm for freedom of the press as he demonstrates an old fashioned printing press in the Benjamin Franklin museum.

"Funny ideas come from reading books," Goerhing says. "So, after the printing press became available, Thomas Jefferson was able to get the books of Locke, Henry Russo. Thomas Jefferson was able to get funny ideas, like, 'All men are created equal. We are endowed by our creator with certain inalienable rights.' Those funny ideas became the Declaration of Independence."

Our democratic society is dependent on the ability of its citizens to read like thinkers. In school, we are asked to read textbooks, handouts from the teacher, and the work of other students. When we graduate to life beyond school, most of us continue to read, although the material isn't assigned.

With luck, an element of critical thinking is assimilated into that process of reading. Without critical thinking, how would we mind-wrestle with the editorials in the daily newspapers or make any sense of the fine print found on our voters' pamphlets?

From time to time, we need to stand back and question our reactions to these kinds of readings.

Do we tend to accept statements simply

because they are printed in a book or magazine? Do we apply the same standards to an official-looking web site, sample ballot, or brochure? Do we give up if we don't understand something the first time we read it?

Just importantly, if we are presented with valuable new ideas from credible sources, do we know how to digest those ideas and blend them with our own thoughts?

Take this process one step further, and ask yourself: if you absorb knowledge, arguments or values through other sources – including television, movies, songs, advertising and the internet – can you still apply the same strategies of critical reading to the ways you interpret those funny ideas?

Learning Objectives

After viewing the television program and finishing the exercises assigned by your teacher, you will have a new view of the way you read a homework assignment, a newspaper, or a web site. You may also change the way you "read" a situation, an argument, or even a person. In the "Reading as a Writer" unit of this telecourse, you explored reading for pure enjoyment and reading to emulate a style. In this unit, you will focus on reading as a student and as a critical thinker – reading as a seeker of new knowledge and reading as a skeptic, in search of truth. You will practice techniques that will help you become a reader who thinks critically – and, hopefully, if you embrace the process, you will continue to be a student (and thoughtful reader) *beyond* the formal limitations of a college credit course.

These learning objectives work in harmony with the essential premises in *A Community of Writers* by Elbow and Belanoff. Workshop 13, "Interpretation as Response: Reading as the Creation of Meaning" (pp. 337–361).

- When we read, we don't so much *find* meaning as build and create meaning – just as we build and create meaning when we write.

- It's helpful to capture our reading process in more detail by observing it closely, which we can easily do by stopping periodically in midprocess and writing what we find in our heads.

- We automatically create an interpretation of a text whenever we *say* it out loud with full meaning or expression. The interpretation we create by entering into a text in this way is often more interesting than the one we come up with if someone asks us directly for "our interpretation."

- One of the most satisfying ways to write a poem – and it is the method that many poets use – is to take a germ or structural element from an existing poem we like and use it as the generative seed for a new poem.

Before Viewing

Before formally studying this subject of reading as a thinker, consider every-thing you have read since the beginning of the school year. Include recre-ational reading, reading at work, reading homework assignments, reading for research, reading instructor's handouts, reading the writing on a chalk board during lectures, reading of e-mail or web sites on the internet – all of it. Determine how you read differently in specific situations. Consider if you consciously or subliminally accept or question the ideas, values, arguments, and hidden agendas you encounter along the way. Think about how you "make meaning" from the text you encounter.

While Viewing

Take note of the strategies for thinking and reading advocated by the writ-ers, teachers, and students on the television program. Determine if any of those strategies reinforce skills you have already developed for reading as a critical thinker. List any new strategies for critical reading that you have not encountered before, and try them out the next time you read.

Think about the similarities (and differences) in attitudes about reading as a *thinker* that are expressed by various guests in the telecourse pro-gram, and compare those views to the attitudes expressed by Elbow and Belanoff in the section "First Activity: Giving Movies of your Mind as you Read" (pp. 339–344) in *A Community of Writers*.

After Viewing

Try any of the activities in *A Community of Writers* (pp.339–348).

Use the exercises in this *Telecourse Study Guide* that are designed to improve your critical reading skills. Read some writing that is representative of your academic major or future profession. Reflect on the way you accept or question each statement; think about why you react the way you do. Consider the attitudes of your discourse community. Are you encouraged to question and challenge your readings, or are you expected to absorb and regurgitate the information, without dispute? Answer this: How do you, as a student, react to the challenges outlined in the program "Reading as a Thinker"?

Viewing Guide

A broad range of professionals were surveyed for this telecourse program, including political analysts, musicians, professional athletes, and scientists.

All agreed that to be successful in school and in the world of work, it is necessary to master the process of reading as a thinker.

For example, to win debates with others on an intellectual or political playing field, it is absolutely necessary to read and think more than your opposition does.

Political talk-show host Rush Limbaugh prepares for his skirmishes on the radio this way, every day. In fact, he says, those phone callers who hope to spar with him on the air had better keep up on all the recent political developments by consuming everything they can in newspapers and magazines, or they'll likely end up sounding pretty uneducated: "The only way I have found to learn more than anybody else is to read," Limbaugh says. "Everybody else just watches television. Even when I'm on vacation, if I don't have at least three or four newspapers, the day isn't right. I feel unworthy."

Musician and writer David Ellefson, bass player for the heavy metal rock band Megadeth, found early in his career that reading as a thinker was essential in his business – especially when he had to deal with contracts and lawyers. "The first time that I read a contract, I was frightened," Ellefson explains. "My father always used to tell me, when I was a teenager, 'Don't ever sign a contract without having read it first.' So I'd get these contracts. I couldn't understand them, and I'm like, 'I don't know what it means, but does it qualify that I read it?' I found out how naive I was about music publishing."

Every scientist interviewed for the telecourse said that reading and thinking were essential for survival in scientific discourse communities. As with many reading and thinking challenges, the biggest hurdle was learning how to decode the dense text. "Any scientist needs to do a lot of reading before he even does a project," says marine biologist Whitlow Au. "You have to read to keep abreast of what's happening in your field. Reading scientific articles is hard work, because you have to concentrate.... It's not like reading a novel."

Most college students begin to develop thinking/writing strategies early in the freshman year and continue to refine those strategies throughout their upper-level classes and their careers. Good reading habits clear a path to success in and out of school. Learning theory experts say these habits start with recreational reading and evolve into reading that challenges the intellect. This transition becomes easier if you make reading an everyday activity.

Freshman accounting major Xavier Pino notes that the intensity and sheer volume of reading in college is significantly more than he was accustomed to in high school. Not surprisingly, those who adapt to college lifestyles find ways to enjoy challenging reading assignments, even if the prose is dense and formidable.

Talking about his first year in college, Pino says, "I've read more books than I read in the last six or seven years of my life. I've never been a reader for enjoyment, but I found myself doing it lately. I'm gathering up information in my mind that will allow me to make the transition from an immature twenty-one to a mature twenty-three or twenty-four-year-old."

Reading for fun

From Pino's view, the key was learning how to have fun, even with coursework. He explains that if he could not find some way to take pleasure from his reading, he would not remember or understand much of the information.

Kim Stanley Robinson, author of the award-winning *Red Mars*, *Green Mars*, *Blue Mars* trilogy, knows that some students Pino's age gobble up his science fiction books for recreation. English instructors rarely assign these books as "literary classics" for reading and analysis; however, students who voluntarily read science fiction, mystery, westerns, romance, thrillers, and other paperback novels are more likely to succeed with more difficult types of reading.

"I found that when I was teaching writing, shockingly, you'd find many college students who don't read for fun – and have rarely read anything except what they were forced to in schools," Robinson says. "Those people are in trouble, because writing is a process of doing things on the page with sentences, as opposed to just talking. Whatever students read is their own business, and it's good for their writing."

Donald Pharr of Valencia Community College in Orlando, Florida, laments: "Most of our students don't read. They read when they *have* to for classes that require reading. They don't read for fun; they don't read the newspaper for information when all they have to do is watch the TV."

Pharr agrees that the first step toward handling more difficult reading is reading for amusement and diversion.

"Any type of reading – books, magazines, even reading 'zines – is going to improve your writing skills," Pharr says. "Even if you read some stuff that's not written properly, eventually your mind will distinguish what is good from what is bad. You'll know when something sounds right or sounds wrong. And this is how one learns to be a better communicator."

From light to challenging reading

The best English instructors teach strategies designed to help students make the transition from recreational reading to the difficult and complex reading encountered in most college-level classes. Mike Rose of UCLA suggests, "The important thing is getting students to see the value that reading can have for them." Rose encourages students to read whatever interests them. "It doesn't matter if the teacher thinks it's good or bad stuff. What matters is that they're getting something from it. They're reading to escape, or they're reading to learn things. They're reading just for wild pleasure; they're reading to kill time. It doesn't matter. They're reading. Now the challenge is to figure out how you help people move *beyond* what they are reading to something new."

259

ACKNOWLEDGE THAT IT'S HARD

Many instructors emphasize that college reading assignments are *supposed* to be complex enough to require several readings. This is, after all, higher education. Some concepts are going to require deep thought and rigorous interpretation. If you can plan on reading something two, three, or even four times – much like you would plan on watching a favorite movie more than once – the reading experience will not be as frustrating the first time through.

Joe Harris of the University of Pittsburgh suggests a simple but important approach to helping students make a transition from recreational reading to more challenging academic works: "The first thing in getting people to read difficult texts and helping them to read difficult texts is to *acknowledge* that they're difficult. This is not necessarily only their problem; these are complex materials and they're going take some time to get through."

Harris encourages instructors to let students know it is common for everybody (even instructors) to have to read difficult text at least twice before making sense of it.

Time and energy are necessary to get through difficult college reading; in some circumstances, that could mean having to read during every spare moment. For example, a pre-med or pre-law student should expect to read volumes of technically oriented material before receiving the prestige that comes along with the degree. Any other attitude would just invite failure.

Beverly Moss of Ohio State University says, "I think we have to give students *permission* to say, "This reading is hard." Then we have to tell them that part of being in college is understanding that you might have to wrestle with the text, get a little frustrated with the text and *not give up* on it. Sometimes that means putting it away for a couple of hours and then coming back to it."

TRANSCRIBE AND EXAMINE WHAT YOU DON'T UNDERSTAND

Thomas Fox of California State University, Chico, recommends several strategies to help students understand difficult texts. The most obvious is to make an educated guess. "When I give them something difficult, I ask them to cite the part they don't understand," Fox explains. "I say, 'Pick the thing you don't understand or that you felt like you understood least.' And I ask them just to transcribe it and then take a wild guess what they think it means; it's unbelievable what happens. They're never wrong; they always understand it."

This is a very good exercise for a number of reasons. First of all, Fox says, it assigns *not* understanding. Students can acknowledge that initial confusion is a normal part of the reading and thinking process.

"You have to *not* understand some part in order to complete the assignment," Fox says. "So it makes legitimate the fact that they may not feel like they understand every single word. That's important. And then, when I hand them back, I say, 'See? You did understand!' It shows them that their strategies for guessing are reliable."

Explore your feelings about the text

As Writing Center Director at Ohio State University, Beverly Moss works with many students who are struggling with difficult texts. She suggests that one key to understanding tough reading is just to admit you don't like it.

"I think we have to talk to students about finding an opening," Moss says. "Sometimes that opening is, 'I don't like this text.' Then the next question is, 'OK, tell me why. What is it about this text that bothers you?' Because that may be the starting point of the discussion."

The following sequence of questions helps Moss's students make meaning from the text they did not like:

- Do you have an ideal text in mind?
- What would a better (or more accessible) text do?
- Why isn't this text accessible?
- Are there points in this text where you think the writer might be trying to make the content accessible?

With this exercise, Moss says, "The students now have to go back to the text and look. So we have to give them openings that are comfortable for them. One of those openings might be *not liking* it or not understanding. But also the opening is to make them understand that we all don't sit down and read from front to back cover and get it the first time. Or the second time. Or the third time."

Read collaboratively

Sometimes it takes more than one person to unravel a difficult passage of reading. Often, instructors set up class discussions for that very purpose: to allow a group of students to make meaning of a difficult piece of reading – collaboratively.

"We so often do reading alone, just like we do writing alone," says Mike Rose. "We tend to think of it [reading] as a very solitary and alone kind of an activity. But once we unpack a reading in a group, what we're talking about is a very communal, exciting, conversational possibility. I think everybody enjoys that; think of all the late-night sessions you have. Everybody enjoys talking about controversial ideas or ideas that somehow touch our lives. Reading is about unpacking ideas and using them to engage in conversation with each other. That's the way I try and get students in my classroom to come to understand collaborative reading."

Questioning the text

Reading is a way for students to learn – to dispute personal assumptions and to discover new ideas. And, many students discover, it's not only OK to question their reading assignments – they are *expected* to challenge college reading materials.

Charles Turner, a history instructor at Butte College, says that too many college students have not been trained to read *critically*. He admits he will purposefully tease the students by playing devil's advocate on a controversial topic in order to provoke reactions. This is a common approach used by instructors at higher academic levels, and students are *expected* to open up to a new world of critical analysis that includes questioning each other, challenging the instructor, and possibly disputing the text.

Turner starts his class lectures assuming that all students have read the assignment. Then, he says, "I'll change the facts."

"I'll change the issues; I'll throw in different points of view; I'll bring in another author's analysis that's diametrically in opposition to the point of view they just read. It causes them to have to think. Not everything that they read in print is accurate, and not everything in print is correct – and their analysis and their challenge of that material is a worthy challenge."

Akua Duku Anokye of the University of Toledo also trains her students to challenge written materials. "We *want* our students to interact with the text," she says.

"Anything is open. You can say what you liked; you can say what you *didn't* like. You can say where you thought they went off; you can say what you thought was valuable. You can pass all kinds of judgments; there's all kinds of reactions – positive and negative – that we get out of that kind of reading."

Interacting with the text
ANNOTATE THE TEXT

Many instructors suggest a key to understanding difficult text (as well as a method to grapple with a text you don't agree with) is to physically interact with the printed page.

Kay Halasek of Ohio State University encourages her students to *talk back* to the text. Simply highlighting a text is not enough; that reading technique is too passive. "If you simply highlight the words of the author that seem important, you're not articulating *why* you find those particularly important," Halasek says.

Instead of merely highlighting, Halasek encourages the student to use a pencil or pen and write remarks in the margin. "Ask a question. Indicate a disagreement with the author. Interact with the text."

In the K-12 schools, where books are recycled, it is common to punish students for writing in a textbook. Textbooks are treated as if they are sacred. The attitude in college is *quite* different.

Many instructors feel it is so important to get students to rethink how they interact with a book that they actually *assign* the act of writing in a book. Teresa Redd of Howard University is one. "I'll go around the room and see how they've marked it up," Redd says. "Some students don't like that, because they want to return their book to the bookstore and sell it as a used book. But I think annotation of the text is so essential! You should look at English teachers' books. They are riddled with our comments … with emotional reactions, with allusions or references to other things that we've read. With questions. We are constantly interacting with that text."

Santi Buscemi of Middlesex County College also doesn't worry too much about desecration of a textbook. "Aren't the best books the ones that are dog-eared and marked up and torn apart?" Buscemi asks. "That's what a book is for. I really like my students to take those notes [in the books] and transcribe them in a variety of ways: freewriting, listing, brainstorming in small groups. I have them write all this material down; as they digest this material, it helps inspire them."

DOUBLE-ENTRY NOTEBOOKS

As an alternative to writing in the textbook, several instructors interviewed for the telecourse advocated the use of a double-entry notebook. (Some instructors call this a dialectical notebook.)

Akua Anokye explains how they work: "I use one of those double-entry journals. On one side students have to summarize what the author is saying, using their own words. Then, on the other side, they have to react to that. How do they interpret the meaning that they extract? What is the author saying? What do they think about that? That's a reading strategy to get them to organize their thoughts around what the author is conveying and how they interpret it."

A Community of Writers contains an in-depth, step-by-step examination of how these notebooks work, in Mini-Workshop 8, "Double Entry or Dialectical Notebooks" (pp. 450–453). This section also explores the theory behind double-entry notebooks and the parallel between reading and writing.

Thomas Hilgers of the University of Hawaii advocates a combination of double-entry notebooks and writing in the text, as well as small group collaboration about the readings. The point, Hilgers says, is that students should not read passively; they should do *something* while reading to interact physically, mentally, and even socially with the words: "One of the things I would recommend to any student is start taking notes, either in a margin or in a journal that you just call 'my reading journal.' So if I'm reading something from the philosopher Locke, for example, and I'm having problems with a particular paragraph, I just write down in the margin, 'What's this saying?' Or I try to summarize, in my reading journal, what I think it's saying. I'll have one of my friends check it. This works best in a small group where students can keep reading notes on what they're reading, as part of their homework assignment. Then, at the beginning of the next class session, they exchange their reading notes. If they find that they agree on lots of things, there's a good chance that they're part of the community. They're understanding, in common. Or, if they disagree, it's a good jumping-off point for discussion."

Reading for research

Of course, there are many different types of reading, for different types of situations. Reading during the research process is different from both recreational reading and reading textbooks for course assignments – though much of the advice given in this unit, "Reading as a Thinker," applies to both types.

In preparing to write his novels, Charles Johnson reads thousands of pages to get historical background and the texture of the time he is writing about. He is aware that this kind of research is different from the reading he does for entertainment.

"I'm reading as a researcher," Johnson says. "I'm reading with a pencil, and I'm marking things that are going to be useful, marking in the margins, asking questions of the author as I go along. So I'm reading with a far more focused intention. I'm *looking* for something."

English instructor Michael Bertsch puts it this way. "When you read a novel, you want to read from beginning to end, and you want to read mostly every word to get all the juice out of it. When you're researching, you're not really reading; you're trying to *notice* things. You notice key words that you've already written down on a note card. This allows you to very quickly process a tremendous amount of text, by opening your eyes big and just turning the pages of that particular article until you find those words. Kind of like speed reading; it's more like noticing."

Teresa Redd, aware that research work is limited by time constraints and deadlines, recommends that students learn how to skim, mining the books for the relevant material and then carefully reading those parts more than once.

"You can't possibly read these books cover to cover to get the information that you need," she explains. "If you have to do this research, how are you going to do it? What aids do you have here? Of course, we talk about some of the obvious things – like the index, the table of contents – but we also look at chapters and look for previews that most good authors will put in. We'll also check the introduction and summaries that most authors will put in toward the end of the chapter."

Once the relevant passages are identified, research sources are often difficult to understand. The earlier lessons in this unit (techniques for reading complex texts) need to be applied to make sense of the evidence.

Librarian Sarah Blakeslee explains, "The authors use the lingo or the verbiage of the discipline, so you won't *understand* what they're saying unless you understand a little bit about the field. You cannot expect to read this just once; you may have to read that article several times to really understand what it is they're talking about. It's not light reading."

This does not mean that all research reading is boring. Once you find a topic you care intensely about, you'll find all the work of reading to understand worth the effort.

For example, musicologist Gordy Ohliger reads everything he can about his craft, because he is intensely interested in the subject; his performances benefit from the knowledge. For Ohliger, the hours spent in the library are pure delight.

"I realize that it sounds like homework," Ohliger says. "But I don't need somebody to tell me to go out there and do it; I'm excited about it. I quite literally read *every* book in the university library on vaudeville and then went to the county library and read all those too. I was reading all those books for my own pleasure, getting all excited about studying this totally obscure information. Who could care about that except me? But it's so exciting to assimilate this information and then hand it out again, through my performances."

Many researchers, including scientists such as marine biologist Chris Lowe, spend even more hours reading on the Internet than they do in the library. Lowe explains that learning how to scan for just the right material is even more important online, since the Internet contains such an overwhelming amount of information.

"Reading is a prerequisite of any academic study," Lowe says. "So you spend a lot of time reading things. But one of the great things about the information sources now is that you don't necessarily have to go to a library to access information. You can access a lot of information electronically now, which makes it more convenient. There's an inherent danger to that, in that you might be taking information out of context. So you have to be able to get to the point where you have confidence in your ability to interpret something that someone's written – and take it for what it's worth."

Summary

From hieroglyphics to hypertext on a computer screen, the technology of displaying written communication will change as long as humans evolve. What doesn't change is the process of reading to assist in thinking. The strategies you study in this unit will remain essentially the same even if most of your reading is absorbed from an electronic device instead of from a book.

However, many instructors suggest that digital communications will change some of the ways we look at traditional approaches to *presenting* the text. Critical "reading" these days requires the audience to interpret words, sounds, and moving images transparently blended in one cohesive presentation.

Chip Bayers, an editor at the internet-only magazine *HotWired*, observes that the Internet is rapidly evolving into a completely flexible, multi-media presentation format. Though the smooth integration of text and video will require higher bandwidth connections than are available to most consumers, near-daily innovations will soon make it possible for consumers to produce and broadcast television programs from their own home computers.

In fact, by the time you hold this book in your hand, high-speed hookups to the Internet (allowing two-way video transmission) may well be available in your neighborhood.

"I think more and more of reading is going to migrate to pure electronic form that comes on a tablet, an e-book, what ever you want to call it," Bayers says. "The academic community is going to be more and more electronic; this will probably happen faster than other chunks of society. But, to me, reading is part of processing information ... that's what the human brain does; it processes information and tries to create something coherent out of it. So, I don't see how the reading experience actually is changing very much because it's always been the same thing."

Akua Duku Anokye closes this unit on Reading as a Thinker by asking student to reconsider the definition of "reading," considering how quickly the written word is being integrated into such multi-media presentations: "We're talking about visual literacy. That's become a very big thing. How do you read – not just text – but how do you read a painting, or a movie? We've expanded our definition of reading."

Integrating the Text

Workshop 13 "Interpretation as Response: Reading a Creation of Meaning" (pp. 337–361)

In Workshop 13, "Interpretation as Response: Reading a Creation of Meaning" (pp. 337–361), Elbow and Belanoff emphasize that reading is an active exercise.

"Reading may *look* passive," they write. "We sit quietly and let the image of the words print itself on our retina and then pass inwards to our brain." However, each reader's brain actively creates an interpretation of the text, and those interpretations may vary quite a bit. This is why it is important to see yourself not as a sponge, but as a dynamic attentive participant while you are reading.

Workshop 13 emphasizes many of the key points in this telecourse and Student Study Guide. To read like a thinker, you must be *critical* and learn to develop your own interpretation from the text as you interact with it.

"In fact, when we have trouble with reading, it's often because we are mistakenly *trying* to be passive," Elbow and Belanoff write. "We've been trying to become perfect little photographic plates on which the meanings on the pages print themselves with photographic accuracy. But, since reading doesn't work that way, we don't understand the words very well."

Exercises

Check with your instructor for your formal assignments. You will be asked to do exercises from the *Telecourse Study Guide*.

Exploring reading as a thinker further

EXERCISE 1: EDUCATED GUESSING

Read the text assigned by your instructor. This is likely to be a very challenging piece of text. Don't worry if you get lost during the reading; that's what this exercise is all about. Now, find one or more passages within the text that are difficult to follow, or are unclear to you, and transcribe them onto a separate piece of paper. For each passage you have transcribed, write down your best guess at what you think the passage means.

EXERCISE 2: COLLABORATIVE READING

After reading the text from Exercise 1 and writing down your guesses, form into groups of three or four with your classmates and discuss each of your guesses.

EXERCISE 3

Think about your least favorite form of text to read. In the library (or in your backpack), find a text that meets this criterion. From within the text, identify a passage that illustrates one or more of the reasons that cause you to dislike it. Write a brief response explaining what it is about the text that you dislike. While writing, consider these factors:

- Do you have an ideal text in mind?
- What would a better text or more accessible text do?
- Why doesn't this text do this?
- Are there points in this text where you think the writer might be trying to do that?

EXERCISE 4

Read a passage of persuasive or argumentative writing by a writer you generally agree with – and a passage by a writer you do *not* agree with. Consider the sample essays "Got Violence?" and "The Great Campus Goof-Off Machine" (pp. 272–274) in Workshop 10, "Persuasion" and "Aiming a Cannon at a Mosquito" (p. 293) in Workshop 11, "Argument' in *A Community of Writers*. Try to determine differences in the way you read each sample.

Exercise just for fun

At the beginning of a new semester or section of study in one of your other classes (a particular period in history, a distinct field of thought in philosophy, etc.), ask the instructor to suggest a "difficult" reading. Read the text and make notes to yourself to document your best guesses of what is being said. At the end of the semester or section, revisit the text and your notes to see how close your guesses were.

Quick writing exercise

Your instructor may ask you to do a quick focused freewrite about the topic you are studying in this unit. Those of you who are taking the course through a distance-learning system may be encouraged to share your thoughts in a discussion thread or to post your ideas on an Internet bulletin board. If you are writing your thoughts out by hand in a process journal, you might use these questions to help you evaluate the way you read. This is a freewriting exercise that will not be graded. You can use any of the following questions to stimulate a response about reading as a thinker:

How is reading as a thinker different than other types of reading? How do *you* read differently, in different situations? Are you a skeptic? Do you believe everything you read? Do you scan for high points, mine for good quotes? How do you read research material? What happens when you have too much research to absorb? How do you read something you do *not* agree with?

How do you read in a chat room? Is this a whole new meaning of reading? For instance, can you *read* a personality? If you are trading papers and participating in discussion threads, are you getting to know some of the students in the forum and chat room in a different way than if you just talked to each other?

You may use the questions in the "Process Journal" section of Workshop 13, "Interpretation as Response: Reading as a Creation of Meaning" (p. 349), in *A Community of Writers* as an additional source of inspiration for this quick writing exercise.

Exercises related to *A Community of Writers*
EXERCISE 1
Read the entire Workshop 13, "Interpretation as Response: Reading as the Creation of Meaning," (pp. 337–361). Apply the strictest criteria for critical reading, based on what you have learned, as you analyze Elbow and Belanoff's writing in this workshop. Use any of the lessons you picked up from the telecourse, writing down your thoughts in a double-entry notebook as if you were engaged in a dialogue with the authors.

EXERCISE 2
Read the essay, "The Social Consequences of Voicelessness" by Linda Miller Cleary (pp. 229–231). Apply the lessons you learned in this unit to the reading of this essay. Connect your thoughts to the lessons learned in the telecourse program 6 on "Voice."

Additional reading

Two samples of persuasive writing – one from Kalle Lasn (a self-described "culture jammer") and one from Rush Limbaugh (conservative radio talk-show host) – are included in the appendix. As you read these pieces, consider: How do you approach reading something by somebody you obviously disagree with? How is that different than when you read a piece by a writer who has political views similar to your own?

As a reader who is practicing critical thinking, how would you react to the student essay, "Are Manufacturers of Caffeinated Beverages Targeting Children?" How would you read this essay, as published in the appendix, differently than the pieces by Kalle Lasn and Rush Limbaugh? Why?

Quick Review

1. According to guests in the telecourse program, reading in the future
   a. will include digital media that seamlessly combine text with audio and video images
   b. might include an expanded definition of what we consider "reading"
   c. will just be an extension of the multimedia already available on the Web
   d. all of the above
   e. none of the above

2. Instructors in the program suggest that, when reading for research,
   a. Students should read every word very carefully.
   b. Students should memorize as much as possible.
   c. Students learn how to skim, mining the books for the relevant material.
   d. All of the above.
   e. None of the above.

3. Instructors in the telecourse program expressed the following attitude about books:
   a. Books should be treated with reverence and should be never be abused or marked.
   b. Students should read carefully and should take care to memorize as much as possible.
   c. The best books are the ones that are dog-eared and marked up and torn apart.
   d. All of the above.
   e. None of the above.

4. Instructors in the telecourse program said that to learn how to read academic textbooks,
   a. It is OK to admit you are bored by or don't like a textbook.
   b. It is OK to admit that a textbook is difficult and confusing.
   c. It is OK if you have to read difficult books two or more times to understand them.
   d. All of the above.
   e. None of the above.

5. In the telecourse program, the following guest said that reading was essential for his or her career:
   a. radio talk-show host Rush Limbaugh
   b. musician David Ellefson of the heavy metal band Megadet
   c. research scientist and marine biologist Whitlow Au
   d. all of the above
   e. none of the above

"In your freshmen composition class (in fact in a lot of academic situations), most of the genres are kinds of arguments. They *do* something. Even a really descriptive piece – say, you're doing a lab report, where you're describing what you saw – in a sense you're arguing for the fact that this is what you saw and not something else. Almost everything is an argument, in my opinion. I think that writing teachers get in trouble when they try to create an assignment that's out of context, and I think students get in trouble if you imagine that your task is to do an abstract argument, and you don't ground it in a real purpose. The kinds of arguments across the disciplines vary broadly, but in the academy as well as in life, a big part of what we do is argue."

THOMAS FOX, California State University, Chico

Introduction to the Topic

In Chapter 17, we emphasized that most persuasion is an intuitive writing style that leans heavily on emotional and ethical appeal to change the views of the reader. Most formal academic arguments are carefully constructed pieces that are designed with a different purpose. Formal argument attempts to logically support a theory or claim in the form of a scholarly discussion.

This chapter doesn't disavow the techniques used in the unit on persuasion. You'll discover in this chapter that formal argument borrows from and builds on some of the same basic structures of persuasive writing.

In argument writing, your intent may not be to change everyone's mind – any more than a Democrat filibustering on the Senate floor thinks he will change the minds of all the Republicans in the building. Similarly, a defense attorney does not dream that he or she will change the prosecuting attorney's mind in a hotly contested trial. The defense's well-reasoned argument might not even sway the judge, though it might "prove" (within the letter of the law) reasonable doubt.

The formal and logical argument *does* have a long-term effect. The carefully reasoned plea in a court case may sway a judge's opinion; the cumulative effect of objective arguments on the Senate floor might eventually influence public opinion.

In this unit, you will learn the basic structure of a formal academic argument. But you should be aware that each academic discipline has its own set of conventions for this style of writing. In other words, writing an argument paper in the style of the political science department for an engineering professor might be just as inappropriate as trying to do some fancy hip-hop moves in a crowd of people who are shuffling along in a country line dance.

Your goal should be to build on what you have learned about persuasion, carry forward the lessons of this unit on formal argument, and continue the learning process by eventually practicing within the discipline you plan to pursue. One day, your papers will stand right alongside those written by other graduate students and professors who use argument as the primary communication style within their academic discourse community.

Learning Objectives

After viewing the television programs and finishing the writing assignments, you will know when formal academic argument is the appropriate thinking/writing strategy to use in an assignment. You will consider how argument is used in your academic discourse community and in the occupation you might pursue after college. You will also learn the form of an argument with expert guidance from some of the best writers and instructors in the country, and you will practice the techniques for writing a formal argument.

These learning objectives work in harmony with the essential premises of Workshop 11 (pp. 277–302), "Argument," in *A Community of Writers*:

- There is no single, magic right way to argue, with all other ways being wring. In fact, the nature of argument differs from field to field.
- There are powerful procedures for working on argument that don't depend on the formal study of logic.
- Good arguments don't have to be aggressive or confrontational.

Before Viewing

Before you study how to write a formal argument, think of the assignments you have had in other courses that asked you to make a statement about a topic and, through writing and research, create a defense of that statement. Consider what your teacher's expectations were for that kind of writing, and evaluate how you met those expectations.

Read Elbow and Belanoff's Workshop 11, "Argument" (pp. 227–302), with a special emphasis in understanding the section "Building an argument" (pp. 283–286).

While Viewing

Compare the techniques you already have developed in argument writing with the methods recommended by the instructors, professional writers, and students in the telecourse program. Try to determine the skills you need to improve in this formal style of writing. Become aware of the subtle differences in approaches and attitudes toward argument writing, as expressed in the telecourse program. Notice how the instructors delineate between different types of arguments. Also check out how the instructors, students, and writers form their arguments, analyze assumptions, evaluate evidence, create tone, and balance logos with ethos and pathos.

Reconsider the section "Exploring theory: Nonadversarial Argument, Reasoning and Grammar" (pp. 287–291), in which Elbow and Belanoff discuss the power of this style of writing as a way "to create a foundation from which both the writer and the reader can build knowledge."

After Viewing

Using the exercises at the end of this *Telecourse Study Guide* chapter, practice writing in a formal argument style.

With assistance from your instructors, locate samples of formal academic argument that will be similar to the type of writing you will compose in courses related to your academic major. Using the exercises for evaluating argumentative style in *A Community of Writers*, reflect on how effective these arguments are within the context in which the writing was submitted. Determine the type of formal argument writing that is considered appropriate (and inappropriate) for your discourse community.

Viewing Guide

Argument

Don't get misled by the title of this unit. Argument, in an academic context, does *not* refer to angry, confrontational bashing of words.

This unit focuses on a nonadversarial approach to writing that we call "argument" in academia. Most scholarly debates or discussions (on paper) are conducted with this polite, formal style of writing.

This doesn't mean that the writer is completely avoiding strong disagreement. Certainly, a formal academic argument about racism, the death penalty, or the environment can be written with passion; however, the same argument can be a carefully structured, informed paper that begins with a clear thesis and develops with a logical sequence of quotes, statistics, facts, and other forms of evidence to support the thesis.

This is the favored writing style "of the academy," as some instructors put it. We write in this style frequently, in every discipline across the campus.

As English instructor Kathleen Bell of the University of Central Florida explains, "Argument, in its broadest sense, is a way to enter the conversation. Because the argument essay, as a genre, is a way to put forth new ideas – or to look at previous ideas in new ways. But argument is not a fight, not even a debate. It is a way to find your place in an [academic] conversation."

Like many other instructors, Robb Lightfoot, a speech and debate instructor at Shasta College, suggests that formal argument writing is designed to encourage critical thinking. The challenge is to put forth an opinion or observation that is then supported with evidence found through research. Argument is the essence of doctoral dissertations, master's degree thesis projects, scientific research, and the vast majority of undergraduate student papers. It is also the underlying structure for argument and debate classes. Lightfoot alerts his students to put the emphasis on debate, not on the word *argue*.

"When students come to argumentation, one thing they think [is] it's unpleasant. Being in an argument means yelling at people and calling names. That's not it. It's simply committing to something very difficult, which is a pursuit of the truth as best we can know it."

Types of argument

There are many types of argument and persuasion papers, and the genres often overlap. Some instructors assign "cause-and-effect papers" as a type of argument. Others insist that even a good narrative should have an underlying main point, thesis, or "moral to the story" – that is, an argument.

Butte College instructor Michael Bertsch narrows argument and persuasion writing down to these two very general categories:

"There's two broad kinds of argument paper: the problem/solution, where you define a problem, and then solve it as defined; or there's what I call the thesis/defense, where you advance some controversial topic like, 'All handguns should be banned,' and attempt to prove the thesis with evidence."

Kathleen Bell favors problem/solution arguments. "The strongest thesis sentences for arguments are based on cause-and-effect relationship," she says. "I use it when I need a little magic with a student who is so frustrated – who can't find a subject he or she is really involved in. I say, 'Let's put it in terms of a cause-and-effect relationship,' because there's tension. Cause and effect evokes the question, 'Why?' Once you ask why, you have people caring about it."

The problem/solution paper is an excellent opportunity to find the link between the argument writing we practice in the classroom and the writing you will be expected to do on the job, Bertsch explains. He uses the writing of a criminal investigation as an example: The crime is "the problem." The criminal evidence is analogous to the evidence a student gathers in the library to "argue" an academic-style paper. The "solution" is proving who committed the crime.

"That's a straight problem/solution argument paper to my mind," Bertsch explains. "The student – say, a criminal justice major – can look at the extant evidence and try to decide how this thing worked out. And then he builds his case: Here's my evidence, and this led to this led to this led to this. Obviously, that person did it."

Argument writing in the real world

As scholarly as this style of writing might sound, many occupations outside of college also favor the formal argument style. Scientists use a variation of argument writing as their standard approach to prove a theory. Lawyers use a formal argument when appealing to a higher-court judge. (Though, as we learned in the persuasion unit, they would use a more emotional, persuasive style with a jury.) Even members of the agricultural community are apt to use such a writing style, such as in an environmental impact report, or in an issues paper about pesticide use.

Agricultural sciences instructor Dave Daley explains that, in his business, argument writing is an essential skill, and he teaches several agriculture courses that require practical application of this genre. "The focus is primarily on writing skills and issues – and delivering an argument paper," he explains. "We teach a fairly traditional approach in terms of stating a thesis, developing the evidence, and summarizing with conclusions and recommendations."

A variety of formal argument is also used in the world of finance and business. Any proposal for investors and any business plan is usually a variation on a carefully reasoned argument, where the thesis is, "Our idea is worthy of the risk you take for investing in our company, for it will surely generate a healthy profit."

Newspapers also routinely publish several different forms of argument.

The editorial writing of more conservative, mainstream daily newspapers is usually part persuasion and part argument. Dorothy Rabinowitz, editorial writer for the *Wall Street Journal*, explains that she uses a style that is very close to the structure of a college term paper.

"You know the famous thing, called the topic sentence, in a paragraph? Well, you have to have that in an editorial too," Rabinowitz says. "It matters that editorials read gracefully. They're the hardest thing of all to get readers to read, because they are also a closely reasoned argument."

Though the newspaper editorial form of an argument may retain more elements of persuasion than other styles we have mentioned, it is usually a vivid contrast to the "letters to the editor" published in the same section. Letters from readers tend to use more emotional and ethical appeal; the newspaper's official editorials traditionally rely more on logical points.

In a way, even journalists writing news stories see their work as related to the formal argument. Though they are not trying to prove a thesis, news reporters pride themselves on using facts instead of emotions or personal opinions to recount an event. This type of "argument" is closely related to the argument of a scientific discourse community: The facts are revealed in a logical order to support the writer's interpretation of a series of events.

Chip Bayers, senior writer at *Wired* magazine, explains, "As a journalist, you're trying to make a point all the time. You're trying to convince people that this is the truth about this story. So even what seems to be the most objective reporting, in my experience, is an argument. Because you're arguing that these are the most important facts for the reader to pay attention to."

In *A Community of Writers*, Elbow and Belanoff also emphasize that this is not merely an academic exercise; in the world of work, they say, you will be expected to write carefully reasoned reports, memos, position papers, and grant proposals that organize facts into an argument-like shape.

"For friends and general readers we need to write short informal pieces of persuasion, "Elbow and Belanoff explain (p. 278), "but as professionals we need to analyze and write more formal and explicit arguments.

As Elbow and Belanoff put it, this type of writing is not grounded in a "If I am right, you have to be wrong" stance (p. 287). It is a reasoned dialogue, one that assumes author and audience are seeking common ground. A good argument doesn't have to be aggressive or confrontational. Instead, an argument should be carefully reasoned to fit within a scholarly or professional context.

Tone and audience

As we discovered in Chapter 17, tone is a key element in persuasive writing. An effective persuasion piece can be humorous, gently insistent, even indignant. It can lean heavily on emotional and ethical appeals, and the tone can vary quite a bit, depending on the audience.

There is less flexibility of tone in a formal argument, which assumes that your readers will seriously consider your views. Formal argument requires a tone of mutually-accepted, scholarly (or professional) dialogue. As Elbow and Belanoff emphasize, "The challenge is to write in such a way that a reader is neither passive nor resistant but encouraged to become a part of a dialogue. You can show your awareness of opposing opinions, of opposing voices, without belittling them. Once you've set up a tone of dialogue, your reader is far more likely to listen to you" (p. 288).

In a way, there is less flexibility in formal argument, because the audience is less likely to vary. As Elbow and Belanoff note, "Sometimes you are lucky enough to be writing to readers who are ready to listen...." When you write essays for most teachers, especially essays in subject courses, they won't buy an informal burst of persuasion: They're usually asking for a full, careful argument" (p. 278).

Novelist and English instructor Chitra Divakaruni sees a relationship between tone used in formal, expository writing and writing that is used to entertain or enlighten. In many ways, she says, the connection for the beginning writer is simply being *aware* that the tone has such a profound effect on the reader.

Divakaruni explains that her novels are intended to persuade and cause readers to think and react but that she is also able to bring a touch of that into her academic and scholarly writing as well.

"I think I do write for social action," she explains. "I hope my books and stories will have an impact on people; certainly, they have a social purpose behind them. I think with expository writing too, one has to be careful to achieve just the right tone, so that you draw the reader in and the reader feels along *with* you and is not in a skeptic's position *against* you."

Many writers and instructors feel that a self-assured, positive tone is the result of more than the successful use of language. This desired effect comes naturally from a writer who has confidence in the evidence used to support the argument.

In other words, a calm, objective aura of self-assurance is projected by a thorough knowledge of the facts and issues being argued.

In the telecourse program, broadcast journalist Dennis Richmond talks about projecting a similar, well-reasoned tone in his newscasts. "If you know more than your audience, you can stand there [at the news anchor's desk] confidently; that feeling of confidence will translate to your audience," he explains. "They will listen to every word you're saying. And they will get the feeling that you know what you're talking about. But if you don't know it, and the way you're going to deliver is going to be in an unsure tone, they'll know. If you deliver in that tone, then you aren't going to gain the confidence of whoever you're trying to tell the story to."

It is this same self-assured tone that a student might convey in a well-written academic argument, knowing that the research, without question, supports the thesis.

Evidence

A self-confident tone might be projected because you have faith in your evidence. However, it should be noted that not all kinds of evidence are considered credible. Your instructor might automatically find some *types* of sources (such as peer-reviewed academic journals) more significant than others.

Stephen Browning, an English instructor at the University of Washington, is very clear with his students about the kinds of evidence he values. His views mirror those of most other instructors across the campus, not just those in the English department.

"On the first day of all my classes, Microsoft Encarta [and other similar generic information sources] is banned. It's far too easy to take information from that type of source without doing any critical analysis, such as, 'Why am I using this here?' Encyclopedias are so neutral that you can't get much energy or authority out of them. If you're writing to an academic audience, usually there's a specific discipline involved. There's an index of people, of journals, of books, of linked knowledge that you can go to. If you're writing for a sociologist, cite a sociologist. If you're writing for an anthropologist, cite an anthropologist. That all goes to ethos, and authority, and knowing who your audience is going to listen to. If you cite people who your audience admires and listens to, then they're much more likely to listen to you and what you have to say."

Librarian Sarah Blakeslee says that from her perspective, the sound academic argument starts with decisions made by the student during the research phase.

"I think choosing the articles that you will use to write your paper is very much a part of critical thinking. You need to gather together a number of articles, read through them, and pick out the best and the most pertinent, using all kinds of criteria for evaluation.

"On the Web, of course, you can find all kinds of information that is incorrect and plain wrong. *Any* type of information tool that you're using, whether it's a book or an article or on the Web, you do need to evaluate the information to make sure that it's still credible. For example, it may have been credible when it was written and no longer credible at the time that you are writing your paper."

The unit on research in this *Telecourse Study Guide* offers some advice for evaluating evidence.

However, no matter how good the evidence is, a student who carelessly plops a bunch of facts, quotes, and statistics into a document without a clear main point (or a series of reasons that support the main point) will create an ineffective paper.

Joe Harris, an instructor at the University of Pittsburgh, has observed many student writers in this predicament.

"I think one problem with student writing, particularly in research-oriented writing, is that students turn themselves into kind of human Xerox machines," Harris says. "They find information and they reproduce it on the pages of their paper. Any paper needs something more. Sometimes it's called a thesis; sometimes it's called a central idea. I actually prefer a slightly different metaphor than central idea; I say the papers need an edge to them."

Oftentimes, the edge comes from a clear understanding of the paper's form – and of what the paper *does* to the reader.

Form

Elbow and Belanoff warn against relying too heavily on the formula argument, in an argument essay of their own (pp. 287–291).

They characterize the formula essay as follows: Construct a thesis; state it forcefully; line up evidence to prove that your thesis is correct; prove that contrary opinions are wrong; conclude by restating your thesis.

This type of formula begs for an either/or, right/wrong, good/evil attitude, they argue. Elbow and Belanoff push for a different conception of argument, one that is less aggressive and less adversarial. They are not suggesting that such traditional approaches to arguments are wrong, however. In fact, they write, "As one form of argument, they are worth studying and mastering."

They also note that there will always be situations (in school and in the real world) where a person has to argue for absolute acceptance of his or her point of view – for example, when a lawyer argues against a death sentence, or when a teacher has required a formula argument as the accepted method of writing a paper for a class.

Our advice is to learn the traditional formula for an academic argument and to ask your instructors when it is appropriate to improvise your own variations on the standard approach. It is also important to determine the favored form of an argument in the discourse community you are writing for.

THESIS OR MAIN POINT

The most common approach to academic, nonadversarial argument writing is to introduce an organizing statement early in the essay. That sentence controls and directs the supporting elements introduced throughout the rest of the paper. This all-important sentence is commonly called a *premise*, *theory*, a *main claim* – or *thesis statement*.

This sentence is the main point of your argument. It is so essential that the preferred form is to restate a variation of this sentence again, with slightly different wording, in the conclusion.

You learned in Chapter 17 that the writer of a persuasive paper might *save* the sentence that states the main point until near the end of the piece, especially when the target audience might react negatively to the author's premise.

Most instructors prefer a more traditional approach for argument, where the first paragraph or two leads the reader gracefully into the thesis.

In fact, many instructors become quite irritated if you save the thesis until the end of a formal argument paper. English instructor Donald Pharr of Valencia Community College in Orlando, Florida, is one of them.

"I've always really distrusted and disliked clever pieces of writing that tell me their thesis at the very end," Pharr says. "They're making me trust the skills of the writer a great deal. What if I don't like the composite effect of that thesis and I am disgusted at the end of the thing? I'm probably going to be more unhappy with the writer than if I had had the thesis where it logically should be – up toward the front of the paper. Readers have expectations. That classical pattern of the introduction, the discussion, and conclusion – this is what we expect in a paper. Even the person who's never been to college and does not read very well expects it. We all have this pattern built into us somehow. Why violate expectations unless you have an awfully good reason?"

A small minority of instructors will encourage a style of formal argument that builds to the thesis at the end. If the instructor has made the expectations for the placement of the thesis clear, it is appropriate to ask before submitting the assignment for a grade.

No matter where the thesis sentence is placed, a well-written argument will leave the reader with little doubt about what the main point is. To satisfy most instructors, the academic argument should be focused on an easily supported idea that can be stated in one clear sentence – presented, *not as a question* but as a central idea the student is ready to defend.

Geoffrey Philp, English instructor at Miami-Dade Community College, offers two examples of thesis sentences – one too general and then one that has been sufficiently narrowed down:

"A weak thesis sentence is merely a sentence that is a statement of fact. 'Bob Marley was a great musician.' That's *just* OK. 'Bob Marley was the greatest reggae musician of his time.' Ah hah! Now we have something, because now we're getting into something that you can *defend*. You have to be able to back this up with facts."

REASONS OR TOPIC SENTENCES

The common way to structure an argument is to forcefully state the main point of the overall essay and then use several subpoints to support the main idea. The subpoints are usually spread out throughout the paper at key transition points, summarizing each section of the document.

Instructors might call the subpoints "topic sentences." The idea is that each subpoint, reason, or topic sentence can function as a unifying device for a section of the paper. In a sense, if that section of the paper is one or two pages long, the topic sentence can function as a "mini-thesis" for that passage.

In evaluating an argument paper by one of your classmates, Elbow and Belanoff recommend that you *look* for these topic sentences and create the skeleton outline that you see emerging. This allows the writer to see if the structure of the argument, as he or she envisions it, comes across to the audience. (In *A Community of Writers,* peer feedback through skeleton outlines is explained on p. 514. Examples of how to use skeleton outlines to give peer feedback are on pp. 544–547.)

Elbow and Belanoff suggest that in order to evaluate a good argument, students should "Define and refine the main claim. List the main reasons. Play with the ordering of points as you restructure the piece." They recommend an intuitive approach, rather than trying to follow a logical step-by-step set of rules for structuring an argument.

Betsy Klimasmith of the University of Washington explains the shape and structure of an argument to her students this way:

"The way that I think about an argument is, you have a thesis statement, a main idea, the main point that you want to make. One of the ways that you *know* that it's a thesis statement is that you *need* to support that with reasons and evidence. A thesis statement really *isn't* a thesis statement if it's so obvious or you don't need to write the paper to prove it; that's really not good enough. So your thesis statement is really the backbone of the paper; that main idea is carrying the whole thing. Then the topic sentences are supporting ideas. They are also making a claim; they're not facts, because the facts come as evidence to support each of those topic sentences."

Like Elbow and Belanoff, Klimasmith also uses the skeleton metaphor to describe the structure of an argument. She compares the thesis sentence to the backbone and the topic sentences to the ribs. The support and evidence between the topic sentences, she says, then become the meat of the essay.

Ethos, logos, and pathos

We touched on the need to balance ethical appeal (ethos), logical appeal (logos), and emotional appeal (pathos) in the unit about persuasion. Academics have a slightly different spin on the need to balance these different types of argument. The formal study of arguments dates to the days of Aristotle – thus the Greek names.

Instructor Thomas Fox explains that the need to weigh all three kinds of argument is still important in a formal paper – though the emphasis is more heavily weighted on the logos.

"Somebody can string together some logic that makes sense to me, saying, 'Here's the reasoning behind my opinion. This is why this is better than this.' They give me evidence; that's called logos," Fox says. "And then other times, when someone I really, really respect has an opinion that's different from me, I rethink my position. That's called ethos."

This notion of ethics is slightly different that the concept of ethics that was explored in the unit about persuasion. Instead of establishing that the writer is a conscientious person, using virtuous standards to support the argument, the formal academic argument might use quoted opinions from *others* who are highly regarded to shore up the reasoning. The quotes might be from writers, researchers, academics, or others that readers are likely to *also* respect for their integrity, wisdom, and ethical standards.

"Pathos is when somebody makes an appeal to get me to *feel* something," says Fox. "In the end, most people combine these approaches. As a writer, you need to create that sense of respectability. Like you really know your stuff, like you're really a good person, like you have an ethical reason for your stance. You construct that in your text and therefore the reader is more likely to be persuaded by your thought. I think that there's a lot of pathos in advertising (and other kinds of persuasion), to appeal to the emotion of the reader."

But Fox and others emphasize that logos should be the primary basis of an academic argument.

Elbow and Belanoff agree, pointing out that formal argument writing "permits us to consider things more carefully – to help us see whether we should follow our feelings and experiences where they lead us. Writing, in particular, permits us to figure out reasons carefully and fully, to stand back from them and consider them one by one. In short, we need to be able to analyze and build arguments in order to make our own minds work well" (p. 278).

Assumptions or warrants

The telecourse program on persuasion pointed out the importance of knowing your audience's assumptions. Scrutinizing assumptions may be even more important in formal academic argument. In fact, some textbooks recommend that in the introduction, the writer should build up to the thesis by noting a list of assumptions, or warrants, that the paper will start with. These are "givens" that the reader and writer can agree on before they enter into the dialogue represented by the paper.

Stephen Browning explains how he introduces the concept of assumptions to his students. They are, he says, "what you can assume that you *don't* have to argue for your audience. Something like, 'Democracy is a good thing,' or 'Honesty is a virtue.' These kinds of things – you can take these as givens or warrants or assumptions."

Finding common assumptions is also a way to build a kind of relationship with your audience, Browning explains.

"If you can get your audience to agree with you, even on an unconscious level, then you've made a bond with your audience," he says. "That is very important, if you want to create shared values, shared knowledge, this kind of thing."

Political science instructor George Wright explains the notion to his students who are writing papers about governmental controversies.

"Regardless of what the other person's views are, whether it's liberal, mainstream, or conservative, if you find yourself in a position where you're in disagreement, you cannot just know *your* argument; you also have to know where that other person is coming from," Wright explains. "You have to know what *their* assumptions are."

Part of effective argument *and* persuasion, then, is looking for those assumptions that the reader and writer have in common. Stating common assumptions establishes the common ground in the introduction. It is an excellent place to start to set the tone and stance of a well-constructed argumentative paper. This is also an effective technique for building up to the point where the dialogue about possibly disputed points might begin.

Summary

As we've learned throughout this telecourse, rhetorical thinking/writing strategies rarely work in isolation. Many good arguments blend elements of other modes of discourse, including description, narration, comparison, and definition – all mixed in with good research.

Ku'ulei Rodgers, a marine biology graduate student, explains that argument papers in her field tend to mingle the modes. "We read journals upon journals, and a lot of other articles and papers, and then we have to pick out what's relevant to our project. Those are the things we'll use to compare and contrast various points."

Robb Lightfoot says that the formal arguments of his debate classes frequently use an element of definition to frame a discussion and to help set an emotional tone. You have already learned, in Chapter 15 of the *Telecourse Study Guide*, that definitions often have an argumentative agenda. You will learn in the critical thinking unit that formal debate includes considering how definitions can be manipulated.

Finally, no matter how dry and academic the writing of a college argument paper might be, a strong underlying narrative can bring the reader into the piece, just like a good story line can draw a reader into a suspenseful novel.

"Along with organizing the research project based on an argument, what is also very important is good writing and good storytelling," political science instructor George Wright says. "Fundamentally, what you're trying to do as a writer is to tell a story. This is not some bland bureaucratic report; this is something that you're trying to sway or enlighten or inform another person about. So the narrative is very important."

Since argument is the most common kind of writing on a college campus, it is a vital skill to master in this course. Most English composition classes introduce the argument paper toward the end of the course so that the student can combine and apply all the other skills that have been studied. For example, by this point, you should be able to employ all aspects of the writing process (including freewriting, drafting, organizing, revising, and editing) as you compose your first college argument papers.

One way to excel in argument writing is to build on the lessons you have learned throughout this course on persuasion, definition, narration, description, and comparison and contrast. If you can weave those lessons together into a piece that supports your main idea with a combination of logical, ethical, and emotional reasoning – along with solid evidence – you will do well.

Integrating the Text

WORKSHOP II "Argument" (pp. 277–301)

The section "Building an Argument" (pp. 283–285) in *A Community of Writers*, Workshop 11, works splendidly with this telecourse.

A key premise of Workshop 11, "Good arguments don't have to be aggressive or confrontational," links up with a similar premise in the telecourse. For many students, we are creating a new meaning for the word "argument." The term argument is used by teachers to indicate a thoughtfully reasoned, formal academic paper that supports a thesis with evidence.

Elbow and Belanoff point out that, "When you write essays for most teachers, especially essays in subject courses, they won't buy a short, informal burst of persuasion: They're usually asking for a full, careful argument."

Though argument is often paired with persuasion, it should be noted that persuasion will not be the *primary* goal of argument writing. In a formal argument, you need the "best reasons and evidence to help you make up your own mind," and you are expected to communicate them in a reasoned, scholarly manner.

Of course, this does not mean that you must make an either/or decision about persuasive and argumentative writing. As we have discovered throughout this course, good writing combines many of the genres. And as Elbow and Belanoff point out, "Even though you will now be working on a longer, more careful argument, that's no reason to forget the skills you focused on in the persuasion workshop to get readers to listen and to try to make your position human."

Of course, Elbow and Belanoff point out, "There is no single, magic right way to argue, with all other ways being wrong. In fact, the nature of argument differs from field to field." Still, some basic approaches to writing argumentation to writing arguments can give some structure to your writing. (See the section, "Exercises related to *A Community of Writers*.")

If your assignment is to write a traditional academic argument essay, Elbow and Belanoff recommend you "isolate significant points in your dialogue and build an informal outline" before completing your draft.

After encouraging students to write a quick, informal draft, Elbow and Belanoff then offer extensive advice for revising the draft (pp. 284–285).

Notice that Elbow and Belanoff advocate the blending of genres or rhetorical modes by saying that the end result of the argument is "presenting a *narrative* of the development of your thinking." This is the most valuable aspect of an early, informal draft. The structure can be added to the explanatory writing in the revision.

In the revision, the authors recommend you do the following: Define and refine the main claim; list the main reasons; play with the ordering of points as you restructure the piece. (Elbow and Belanoff recommend an intuitive approach, rather than trying to follow a logical step-by-step set of rules for structuring an argument.)

In the section "Exploring Theory: Nonadversarial Argument, Reasoning and Grammar (pp. 287–291), Elbow and Belanoff encourage the type of argument paper that is more likely to be effective – a paper that states,

"This is what I believe, and this is why I believe it," rather than an "I'm right and you're wrong" approach. (It should be noted that, although you are supporting a "this is what I believe" type of statement, many instructors prefer the formal argument to be stated in an objective third-person voice, leaving out the first-person pronoun "I.")

Elbow and Belanoff question the value of a traditional argument that uses the formula: state the thesis, support it with evidence, knock down the opposition's view, restate the thesis. This is *one kind of argument worthy of studying and mastering,* they say, but they favor a more subtle approach that encourages the reader's active participation in a dialogue that brings writer and audience closer to a mutual understanding. The crux of the style recommended by Elbow and Belanoff is a nonadversarial approach to argument. The idea is to show an awareness of opposing opinions and voices without belittling them.

Finally, don't forget to read the passages from the "Readings" section in Workshop 11 (pp. 292–301), paying special attention to "Aiming a Canon at a Mosquito," by Mona Charen (p. 292) and the pair of essays about grades, "Testing in Schools is Part of the Problem," by Michael Greenbaum (p. 298) and "Measuring Students' Progress Is Not Antithetical to Learning," by Gary Stoner and Bill Matthews (p. 300).

Note: Several of the sample readings in Workshop 12, "Research" (pp. 326–336) are also formal academic arguments. However, since they are intended to illustrate the importance of good research, these essays rely more heavily on evidence gathered from reading in the library and on the Internet.

Exercises

Check with your instructor for your formal assignments. You will be asked to do exercises from the *Telecourse Study Guide*.

Exploring argument further
EXERCISE 1
The following exercise is designed to help you make a rapid, bare-bones sketch of an academic argument. Try this for a hypothetical paper, and do the exercise as quickly as possible.

On actual assignments, students sometimes stretch this process out over a period of weeks, procrastinating until it is too late to spend the proper amount of time drafting and revising the paper. This exercise is designed to show you that the prewriting stage of an argument is not as difficult or painful as you might think.

Try to do a this a couple of times, spending about five minutes per topic. Of course, you can take more care to work out an actual paper if one is assigned. The idea of this exercise is to get you acquainted with the process.

(A variation of this can be used in writing under pressure situations. See Chapter 9 of the *Telecourse Study Guide*.)

1. Write a hypothetical main claim, or thesis, that you could defend.

2. Decide what type of argument you will use to defend the claim. (Examples: thesis/defense or cause and effect)

3. Describe the discourse community the argument will be aimed at.

4. Describe the types of evidence you will use to support the claim.

5. List several subpoints or reasons based on logos.

6. List at least one subpoint or reason that uses ethos. Consider the type of person you might quote to back up this point.

7. List at least one subpoint or reason that uses pathos.

8. List the warrants, or assumptions, that you will start the paper with.

9. Restate the thesis in slightly different words. (The thesis or main claim is usually stated at the beginning and restated at the conclusion of a formal argument.)

EXERCISE 2
Building upon your responses to questions 4, 5, 6, and 7 from Exercise 1, list your subpoints or reasons or topic sentences that will unify various sections of the paper and will support the claim. These should be in the form of full sentences.

Exercise just for fun
Using the same topic you explored in Exercise 1, write a dialogue between characters having opinions that include your own and as many differing opinions as you can. Have fun making up the names of these characters and the dialects you supply in writing their responses.

Revision exercise
Revise an informal paper you wrote in the persuasion unit using the formal academic argument style.

Quick writing exercise
Your instructor may ask you to do a quick focused freewrite about the topic you are studying in this unit. Those of you who are taking the course through a distance-learning system may be encouraged to share your thoughts in a discussion thread or to post your ideas on an Internet bulletin board. If you are writing your thoughts out by hand in a process journal, you might use these questions to stimulate ideas. This is a freewriting exercise that will not be graded. You can use any of the following questions to provoke thoughts about the formal academic argument:

Have you had assignments in other classes where it wasn't clear whether the instructor expected a formal argument or an informal persuasive paper from the students? Persuasion and argument are very different. What do you see as the primary difference between the two genres? What techniques can you use to bring out your personal voice in a formal argument? Do you ever dream of getting a master's degree? If so, what lessons can you carry forward from this instructional unit to work on a bigger project such as a two hundred-page master's thesis?

You may use the questions in the "Process Journal" section of Workshop 11 (p. 286) in *A Community of Writers* as an additional source of inspiration for this quick writing exercise.

Exercises related to *A Community of Writers*

The "Main Assignment" in Elbow and Belanoff's Workshop 11, "Argument" is "Analyzing or Writing an Argument" (p. 285). If you can break down the individual elements of another writer's formal argument, you will develop a better feeling for constructing your own. You will also gain insight into how a reader will *react* to your argument.

While the analysis exercises in Workshop 11 are useful for the study of how an argument is written, many teachers will expect you to go one step further, and will assign you the task of writing your own argument paper.

Elbow and Belanoff recommend one practical approach: revising an informal persuasive piece you have already written, strengthening the argument for a particular audience. In the section "Building an Argument" (p. 283), Elbow and Belanoff build on the analysis you have been asked to perform and offer an exercise for direct application of what you are learning. The authors recommend (as one approach) starting with an issue you have not decided upon – and beginning the drafting of your paper with an imaginary dialogue between two people who represent extremes of the position. In other words, if you start with an issue that you have strong feelings about, the next logical step is a dialogue with someone you "*imagine* disagrees with you." This act will help you pinpoint the audience the argument is aimed at.

This imagined dialogue will help you draft the essay and will naturally reveal the claims, reasons, evidence, support and assumptions. This exercise can help you get started, if your primary assignment for this unit is to produce a formal argument paper.

Additional reading

One student essay in the appendix, "Are Manufacturers of Caffeinated Beverages Targeting Children?" by Francine Taylor, is presented as a formal academic argument. How is this piece different from the informal persuasive writing in the appendix? How does Taylor use evidence to prove her point? What is her thesis, and where is it located in the paper? Does Taylor use ethos, logos, or pathos? Does Taylor reach beyond the thesis, to propose a solution, or does she just point out the problem? Why?

Is this paper a "research paper" or an "argument?" What is the basis of your response to this question?

Two samples of persuasive writing – one from Kalle Lasn (a self-described "culture-jammer") and one from Rush Limbaugh (conservative radio talk-show host) – are included in the appendix. Summarize the thesis of each of these pieces, in one clear sentence.

How would you rewrite either of these pieces in a formal academic style, to present to a political science instructor such as George Wright, who is featured in the telecourse program?

Quick review

1. Formal argument writing
   a. is called that because the stance is often confrontational
   b. is rarely used outside of the campus community
   c. is the primary writing in academic settings
   d. all of the above
   e. none of the above

2. In an argument paper, a thesis sentence should
   a. be so obvious, you don't have to provide too much evidence to support it
   b. have little to do with the topic sentences or the evidence
   c. should be primarily based on feelings and experiences
   d. all of the above
   e. none of the above

3. In argument writing, the primary type of appeal should use
   a. logos, or logical appeal
   b. ethos, or ethical appeal
   c. pathos, or emotional appeal
   d. all of the above
   e. none of the above

4. Argument papers could use
   a. some of the skills we studied in the unit about comparison/contrast writing
   b. some of the skills we studied in the unit about narrative writing
   c. some of the skills we studied in the unit about definition writing
   d. all of the above
   e. none of the above

5. A warrant, or assumption,
   a. is a stereotype you might make about an audience that is essentially a bunch of idiots
   b. is something "given" that the reader and writer will start with before they enter into the dialogue
   c. is a mistake made by writers who have not double-checked their facts
   d. all of the above
   e. none of the above

"You have to learn how to do internal citations correctly because when you incorporate somebody else's ideas or words into your paper, you have taken their intellectual property. You don't have to pay for that property, but you do have to give them credit. Because this is not your original thought, it's somebody else's, and it's only fair that they get credit for it. It's as simple as that. Otherwise, it's called plagiarism."

SANTI BUSCEMI, Middlesex County College

Introduction to the Topic

Recently, a flurry of television and newspaper reports told of software developers who had been experimenting with new programs that could detect plagiarism in student papers. The designers tested the products with professors who taught upper-division classes at the University of California, Berkeley.

The students had plenty of warning that the professors had a new way of detecting passages of text that weren't properly cited in their research papers. However, they were apparently unprepared for how well the software would work.

The professors ran the papers through the programs, which had mechanisms to make an Internet-wide search to find passages with matching text. The software discovered nearly a third of the students had passages that would be considered plagiarism.

This is a rather shocking result, considering that the attitudes of most instructors mirror that of English instructor Michael Bertsch, who says in the telecourse, "If you steal somebody else's writing and don't give credit, you're going to fail my class and you're going to get kicked out of the school. I get paid the same whether you do or don't, so it's your choice!"

Plagiarism is a very serious matter. Intentional plagiarism is simply unethical, and as instructor Santi Buscemi notes, "There have been people who have pursued Ph.D. degrees who have copied things right out of textbooks and claimed it as their own research – and they've lost the Ph.D. and were drummed out of academia. Whole careers have been ruined because of that."

However, Buscemi says, most freshman English students are honest. When they do use the words of others without giving proper credit, he says, "Most of the time what they commit is unintentional plagiarism. They just forget and they have to be reminded."

This chapter of the *Telecourse Study Guide* and the related telecourse program will address the most important aspects of how to *correctly* bring quotes gathered through research into your own writing by giving credit through accepted citation style.

Once you master these lessons, you'll never plagiarize unintentionally. More important, you'll practice the art of blending the words of others with your own thoughts to create new ideas. This is a very valuable skill, necessary for your growth as a scholar.

Learning Objectives

After viewing the television programs and finishing the writing assignments, you will become adept at the process of using the words of others in your work. This will include learning how to avoid unintentional plagiarism, how to quote directly, and how to summarize and paraphrase the words of others. You will also learn the basic mechanical aspects of citing a quote within the text of your paper and listing your sources in a works-cited page at the end of your document.

These learning objectives work in harmony with the "Documentation" section on pages 314 to 322 of Workshop 12, "Research", in *A Community of Writers*. In this section, Elbow and Belanoff explain the rules of internal text citation and works cited pages, pointing out that proper documentation "lends authority to your research paper."

Before Viewing

Think about the experiences you have had with bringing in the words of others to your own writing, through quoting, summarizing, or paraphrasing. Try to remember how you gave credit to the original sources of those words. Review your knowledge of college-level citation style and construction of bibliographies or works-cited pages.

Check the guidelines of your MLA citation and Works Cited Style on the inside front jacket cover of your textbook, *A Community of Writers*.

While Viewing

Listen to the attitudes expressed about plagiarism by instructors, writers, and students. Consider if you have ever accidentally plagiarized the words of others and learn how you are expected to correctly cite sources in academic writing. Notice the difference between direct quotes, paraphrased quotes, and summarized quotes. Pay careful attention to the attitudes expressed by instructors toward all three methods of bringing the words of others into your writing.

After Viewing

Using the exercises in this *Telecourse Study Guide*, practice summarizing, paraphrasing, and quoting various passages of reading materials. Determine whether Modern Language Association (MLA) or American Psychological Association (APA) style is more appropriate for the discourse community of your academic major, and learn how to create an internal text citation in the style that works best.

Check with your textbook, *A Community of Writers*, for accuracy. Guidelines for MLA and APA citation style and works cited are on the inside of the front cover. Documentation of on-line sources is discussed on pages 474 to 475.

Viewing Guide

Many of the documents you will create, in college and beyond, require you to both read and write. After examining and absorbing research, you are expected to gracefully blend the words others have written with your own thoughts. Part of learning that skill is understanding *why* certain types of writing rely so heavily on quotes, citations, and attributions.

Instructor Michael Bertsch points out that many students think the only reason they have to cite sources is to get a decent grade. While practical, this is shallow reasoning. Writers cite sources to substantiate their claims. Good quotes become evidence to support your main theory or premise. Your citations show you did not make up the evidence; they also show where you found the information you used to support your argument.

In a way, you are providing a service to your readers. If they become interested in your topic from examining your work, they can follow the threads from your citations through the works-cited page to the original source. With an online document, you can even provide a direct link to the articles you read.

Think of your work as something more than a mere assignment that will *only* be read by an instructor. Your work *could* be considered a research source some day. In other words, students may cite *your* words and follow the threads you create (through proper citations) to find evidence for *their* papers.

Though you are in the very early stages of your college career, this process of sharing ideas through in-text citations happens regularly at higher levels of academia. Biologist Whitlow Au, who specializes in research about dolphins, explains that correct citations, or references to ideas and data traded with other scientists, are very important in his discourse community.

"If I'm writing a paper that's on an experiment that I've just done, I'll probably have about ten or fifteen references," professor Au explains. "If I am doing a review paper, reviewing not only my work but the work of other people, then I might have about one hundred references. But no matter what, there are always references."

The references are necessary, he says, to conduct a academic-style "conversation" (as explained in Chapter 21, about research) with others who study across the globe.

Using quotes: beyond the classroom

Some students view all of this concern about quotes, citations, and plagiarism as a bunch of silly, worried hand-wringing that is only practiced in school by instructors and college students.

However, as English instructor Cynthia Selfe observes, "There are many tasks in the real world, outside the classroom, that require you to write from sources – to take those experiences [of everyday life] and to weave them into the text of your writing."

It's also important, Selfe points out, to acknowledge "the intellectual work of others" when ideas in your writing clearly originate from a source other than your own imagination. These tasks all bear a similarity to quoting library books in a research paper.

In his book *Making Music Your Business*, musician and author David Ellefson often quoted others or used information from research sources about the music industry. When he did, he always gave credit, he says, "So that I could walk away from my computer feeling good – knowing that I did not have to look over my shoulder and think, 'I sure hope so-and-so never reads my book to see that I had stolen something.'"

Plagiarism

If you are a writer-in-training, it is critical to learn how to attribute the words and ideas of others that you have incorporated into your own work, so you won't be accused of plagiarism. As David Ellefson points out, this is vital in the real world for maintaining a good reputation. In the academic world, where the exchange of written words is sometimes the entire basis for evaluating a student's grade, a clear understanding of what it means to have *original* thoughts on paper is essential.

In the video, history instructor Charles Turner states, "Many students don't understand what it means to plagiarize work. They have no clue. They'll say, 'Well, if I change the words, a word here or there, then that's not plagiarism.' They don't know what to cite."

Students interviewed for this video seemed to confirm Turner's observations. The scene of Butte College students discussing plagiarism is fairly typical of what we encountered in other classrooms; roots of the problem can be traced back through high school and grade school.

Computer science major Mike Gratton observes, "We were plagiarizing a lot when we were younger. Our teacher would just say, 'Here's some books; make a report.' So we figured the easiest way to do it was just copy straight out of the book. We put some stuff together; there's our paper! And then once we got into high school, they said, 'You can't really do that.' But in high school, they'd never really check for it. So you're thinking, 'As long as I'm not getting caught, what difference does it make?'"

Gratton and other students interviewed for the telecourse all said that one of the first lessons they learned in college was that the instructors were stricter about citations. Plagiarism is considered a much more serious offense.

Avoiding plagiarism

In college, it is *not* a problem to use the words of others in your papers.

In fact, you are *encouraged* to use the words of others – often, and with confidence. You simply must attribute those words and clearly distinguish your own ideas and phrases from those borrowed from others.

Joe Harris of the University of Pittsburgh explains: "There are two writing conventions that help distinguish plagiarism from simply dealing well with sources. The first would be the conventions of documentation."

Students must learn how to document (or cite the source) *within* the text, giving the reader a quick idea of where the quote came from.

The second half of the formula is to create "a kind of acknowledgment section" at the end of the paper, Harris says. This is most often in the form of a bibliography or a works-cited page.

In a way, a works-cited page is similar to the credits at the end of a movie. The author of the paper saves the end of the document to acknowledge where ideas, quotes, and statistics used to bolster the argument originated.

In *A Community of Writers*, Elbow and Belanoff explain the difference between internal text citations and works cited pages (pp. 314–322). They also provide a model on the inside front cover of the textbook, for students to use as a quick reference.

Different types of quotes

DIRECT QUOTES

There are several different ways to display the words of others in a new piece of writing. The simplest is to use the exact words from the source in a direct quote. (For an explanation on how to punctuate direct quotes in a research paper, see Mini-Workshop J in *A Community of Writers*, pp. 494–496.)

There are advantages and disadvantages to using direct quotes. "If you use too many direct quotes, your paper will appear to be a hodge-podge of styles," observes instructor Michael Bertsch. "There'll be several different writing styles in there and it interferes with the flow of your paper. But sometimes a writer will create the perfect sentence and there's no better way to say it. That is the perfect direct quote to select. Short and sweet – just a nice phrase that turns it perfectly."

Some students assume that instructors prefer direct quotes, where the exact words are being used, to paraphrased quotes, in which someone else's words have been rephrased, because the direct quote is more accurate. However, this is not always true.

Instructor John Lovas speaks for many instructors when he says, "A paper that consists entirely of one quotation after the other [in other words, you went to five sources, you got five related quotes, you just put the quotations down] makes me say, 'That's an interesting organizing of somebody else's material.' But where are your ideas? Where are *you* in this?"

The same attitude holds true in the world of work beyond college. Newspaper editors often tell their reporters to paraphrase more often and to use fewer direct quotes, with the admonition, "We're paying *you* to write the story, not some guy you interviewed."

In the video, Judge Helen Gillmor describes a similar problem with her new law clerks. The young clerks often want to quote a lengthy passage from a law book in an important legal document, Gillmor says, "because then they feel safe. And I say, 'No, no, no, no! If you truly *understand* the subject you will be able to put the rule of law into your own words.' "

PARAPHRASING QUOTES

Often, the exact words of a direct quote are not graceful enough or are too long-winded to include in a paper. In such cases, it is best to paraphrase – to recast the quote into your own sentences. This is an important process; to paraphrase correctly, you must understand the essence of the quote.

Student Mike Gratton explains it this way: "When you're paraphrasing, you're forced to think about what's going on in the paper you're quoting; and, when you're forced to think about it, it kind of makes you put in your *own* ideas."

Many instructors prefer this approach. The use of paraphrased quotes demonstrates that the students are engaged in some critical thinking, finding a way to combine the thoughts of others with their own musings. The very act of paraphrasing requires this process. A paper with a high percentage of direct quotes indicates, instead, a high percentage of cutting and pasting.

As Michael Bertsch observes, "Too many direct quotes make the reader think that the writer doesn't really have anything to say. It looks like the writer is assembling a patchwork quilt paper. There's no unity, the flow is interrupted, and the point is obscured by stylistic considerations. So I advise writers to not use too many direct quotes."

Some instructors refer to the act of understanding and paraphrasing as "owning" the concept. In other words, the student has studied the ideas that are being quoted well enough to internalize the meaning.

Judge Gillmor says this process is important when you are through with being a student. She tells her law clerks, "Make the concept your own; then you are able to say in your own words what it is."

SUMMARIZING QUOTES

The techniques of summary and paraphrase allow you to translate ideas you have gathered from reading and research into your own words. There are subtle differences between the two techniques; summary usually involves reducing longer passages into a few sentences. In some college courses, you might be asked to condense, or summarize, an entire book into a few sentences. Beyond school, the boss may ask you to summarize volumes of data and reports into a few pithy lines.

"So it's a summary process, it's a digesting process," John Lovas says. "It's being able to read the material with some care, and being able to figure out the key ideas, and then being able to state them clearly."

The work of law clerks is again used as an example of the quoting, paraphrasing, and summary process in the world beyond school.

Lovas asks, "What do law clerks do [for the boss] before they get to do big-deal lawyer work? They go off to the law library, and their task is to find the precedent-setting cases and to summarize them."

Though the law clerk may think he or she has been assigned the "grunt work" while the boss gets all the glory, the summary may be the most important (and mentally challenging) part of the entire case.

As Mike Rose of UCLA observes, "Summarizing two or three or four sources, or a big set of data, can be a profound intellectual challenge with an important sort of argumentative point to it. In summarizing, you have to make decisions about what you're going to put in and what you're going to leave out.

"What gets silenced or lost, as you make those decisions to leave things out? These are a series of very important decisions that show that even an act that's seemingly as dry as summarizing is as vital and alive and dynamic as any other kind of writing or social act."

Synthesis of ideas

You always bring preconceived ideas to a piece of writing before you read it. As you read, you gain new ideas and combine them with your own. Some instructors refer to this process as *synthesis*. The idea is that, by blending your own thoughts with the concepts you absorb through reading, entirely new ideas emerge.

As Chitra Divakaruni of Foothill College explains, "One of the biggest tricks of the research paper is how to use outside information but process it through your own intelligence and your own thinking so that it becomes part of your own argument."

This is why many instructors recommend starting a paper with a working thesis. It is through the synthesis process that you will discover how to refine – and state succinctly – the main point you are trying to make with the paper. Most instructors agree that the only way you can learn to paraphrase and synthesize ideas is to practice the process over and over until you have a feel for it. This is one of the most important skills to learn in an English composition course. Students who learn how to synthesize ideas and think critically as they develop the main points of their papers in upper-division courses will prosper in academia.

Correct citation styles

The final skill to practice in this unit is the attribution, or internal text citation style.

It is essential to learn learn the proper internal text citation style for your discourse community. Most English courses use MLA style, since it is the accepted style in the department.

However, since students of all majors from across the campus learn how to write in the composition course, it is important to acknowledge that many academic disciplines have style guides that require a different approach. (We'll look at one of those styles – the APA style – later in this chapter.) We recommend learning one style in this course, and learning how to adapt citation technique to your academic major, in upper-division classes.

Learning how to cite a source is often a confusing task for students who have never practiced the technique.

As librarian Sarah Blakeslee observes, "There are more questions at the reference desk about that than about anything else. I try to tell my students to not get too wrapped up in it; know the purpose behind the citations or the works cited. It is so that somebody can come after you and find the source that you're referring to."

Though there are so many rules for correct form of internal text citations and works-cited pages that it takes an entire book to detail them all, the *most common* conventions are actually quite simple.

BASIC MLA CITATION

The Modern Language Association style is favored by English instructors and many other instructors in the humanities. The MLA style emphasizes the page number of the book or magazine.

For example, this is the correct citation for quoted material in MLA style:

> According to one astronomer, "The atmosphere on Mars could support life" (Smith 9).

If the material is a paraphrase or summary instead of the exact words, the parenthetical citation remains the same, but the quotation marks are eliminated.

> According to one astronomer, the Martian atmosphere could support life (Smith 9).

Notice that only the author's last name and the page number are included in parentheses, after the quote. This citation tells us that the quote from Smith can be found on page nine of a book, magazine, newspaper, or journal. To find the exact publication, the reader can look up Smith in the "Works Cited" section of the paper. Notice, in MLA style, there is no comma between the author's name and the page number and that the period for the sentence comes after the citation.

A variation of this basic MLA citation would be:

> According to astronomer William Smith, "The atmosphere on Mars could support life" (9).

In this example, the writer of the paper identifies the person being quoted within the sentence. Therefore, it is not necessary to put the name within parentheses, in the citation. Only the page number is listed in the parenthetical citation.

For a paraphrase or summary, the citation would be the same but without the quotation marks.

> According to astronomer William Smith, the Martian atmosphere could support life (9).

VARIATIONS ON BASIC MLA RULES

These are only the most basic rules of parenthetical citation style. To write successful papers, students should always get in the habit of consulting a style guide or handbook.

Here are some variations on the basic rules:

- Citations of works written by more than one author:

    (Smith and Jones 119)

- Citations where the paper quotes two or more works by the same author:

    (Smith, *Chemical Analysis* 235–37)

- Citations from the Internet (Note: MLA guidelines recommend listing author or title of the Web page as an internal text citation and the URL in the works-cited page.):

    (Smith and Jones)

BASIC APA CITATION

As we mentioned previously, many academic disciplines use different citation styles.

The American Psychological Association (APA) style for internal text citations is frequently used in natural science and social science courses, where it is important to know how recently the evidence supporting a claim or hypothesis has been published.

In APA citation style, the reference looks like this:

> According to one astronomer, "The atmosphere on Mars could support life" (Smith, 1999, p. 9).

Notice that the citation emphasizes year of publication. In this case, there are commas between the author's last name and the year.

If you are writing a term paper that emulates the style of your academic major, ask your English composition instructor for permission practice the APA style (or other citation style) instead of MLA.

WORKS-CITED PAGE

It is just as important to learn the rules for the works-cited page at the end of your paper as it is to learn the internal text citations. The listing should be alphabetical by author, and – generally – each listing should have the following features:

1. Name of author, editor, translator, or compiler (last name first, followed by a comma and the first name)
2. The title of the article or book cited
3. The title of the larger work (periodical, journal, or other work) you are citing
4. The edition (or volume number) and, if it is a book, the city and publisher
5. The date of publication
6. The page number or numbers

Here's an example of MLA journal citation style::

> Smith, William Z. "Atmospheres of the Planets."
> Journal of Humans Who Use Telescopes 17 (1999): 9

For a work you found on the Internet, use the journal citation form, and add the name of the organization sponsoring or associated with the Web site, as well as the date you found this resource, and the URL in angle brackets:

> Smith, William Z. "Atmospheres of the Planets." Journal of Humans Who Use Telescopes 17 (1999). the Astronomy Barn. March 23, 2001 <www.astronomybarn.com>.

If you can, provide the complete URL that will take the interested reader directly to that article, and be sure that spelling and capitalization are correct.

Both the MLA and APA style guides list separate rules for works-cited page references for quotes gathered from interviews, speeches, television programs, newspapers, the Internet, and other types of sources.

Many of these guidelines are also available on the Internet. Inexperienced students are well advised to find good models for citations and works-cited pages, by reading other academic papers or publications that use these conventions.

A Community of Writers provides a similar summary of conventions for MLA and APA citation style and works cited pages on the inside of the front cover. The textbook also features an excellent section on documentation for on-line sources (pp. 474–475).

Summary

Though the introductory information in this chapter will help you get started with internal text citations and works-cited pages, it is important to consult your textbook for details and additional instruction. Many instructors place a high priority on learning the technical aspects of proper citation, and sloppy documentation can often lead to a bad grade on an otherwise well-written paper.

Frequently, students put off creating the works-cited page until the last stages of the final draft. This can pose quite a problem if the student is working on the paper Sunday evening and it is due Monday morning. At this point, the library is closed and it is too late to ask the instructor for advice – although an enterprising procrastinator could still find MLA guidelines on the Web.

Students who work ahead and learn the conventions well in advance of the due date will find that most of the mechanics involved with citations are fairly easy to learn from reference books or with a little friendly help from an instructor. The MLA and APA handbooks are available in any college library, and most composition textbooks have a section that clearly explains the conventions of quoting, paraphrasing, summarizing, and citing sources.

It is also important to remember that the process of incorporating quotes into your paper is more than an exercise in mechanics. You are expected to learn how to gracefully incorporate the words of others into your own work and to avoid accidental (or intentional) plagiarism by giving credit to those whom you are quoting.

Integrating the Text

Workshop 12 "Research," (pp. 314–322)

Workshop 12, "Research," in *A Community of Writers* introduces the topic of documentation for a research paper (pp. 314–322).

As Elbow and Belanoff point out, "from a pragmatic point of view, documentation lends authority to your research paper." This is important for research papers and for just about any other type of paper you will have to write in courses after English composition.

The phrases "term paper" and "research paper" are considered quaint by many teachers; Elbow and Belanoff point out that all college-level papers are expected to have correct documentation for quoted materials.

Elbow and Belanoff also point out that "you should integrate and internalize what you learn [from reading and research] into your own thinking" but that you should also let readers know that other authoritative sources have said things about your topic that support your claims: "Quotations that allow these voices to come through to your readers will give them a feel for the texture of research on your issue."

Several sections in *A Community of Writers* will help you learn the mechanics of incorporating such quotes into a paper.

Mini-Workshop J, "Quotation and the Punctuation of Reported Speech," has formatting and punctuation advice (pp. 494–496).

Mini-Workshop F," Doing Research on the Web," has advice about how to cite online sources (pp. 474–475).

The inside cover of *A Community of Writers* contains basic rules for parenthetical citations of standard print sources. It also has rules for creating a works cited page.

As Elbow and Belanoff point out, "Footnotes aren't footnotes any more." The style you may have learned in high school (with notes at the foot of the page) has fallen out of favor in most disciplines on a college or university campus, though there are a few exceptions.

Exercises

Check with your instructor for your formal assignments. You will be asked to do exercises from the *Telecourse Study Guide*.

Exploring quotes and citations further

EXERCISE 1

Write down a thesis or main point that you are attempting to prove. Select an article in a magazine, newspaper, or journal that you know will agree with your thesis. Or, if you have time, read an entire book that supports your view. In part one of this exercise, you should summarize the main point of the article or book in one or two sentences. This summary should be written in such a way that it supports your thesis.

Example: Thesis: It would be possible, in the not too distant future, to colonize Mars.

Summary: Science fiction writer Kim Stanley Robinson, in his books *Red Mars*, *Green Mars*, and *Blue Mars*, shows how it would be possible, over centuries, to add enough oxygen to the atmosphere of the red planet to support human life.

In part two of this exercise, select a passage that supports your thesis, and paraphrase the writer in your own words.

Example: According to *Washington Post* columnist Joel Achenbach, much of the speculation in Kim Stanley Robinson's books is based on solid scientific evidence.

In part three of this exercise, select a passage where the exact words support your thesis, and use them in a sentence that is punctuated to show you are using a direct quote.

Example: According to Achenbach, Robert Zurbin, leader of the Mars Society, assembled an impressive team of NASA scientists, because "he knew he needed a good screening process, because advocating human migration to Mars was strange enough" (25).

Notice that the final example uses MLA internal text citation style. The fastidious student will practice citation while working on this exercise.

Exercise 2

Go to the library and find examples of writing from the academic discourse community in which you hope to earn an undergraduate degree. You can usually find these in the peer-reviewed journals from that discipline. Identify the documentation method employed by the author. Compare how the internal text citation and works-cited pages look. Is the paper written with a variation of the MLA or APA styles previewed in this chapter? If not, list the differences.

Exercise just for fun

One of the biggest problems students have is setting up an attribution. This is for the students who need a little practice – especially the ones who just plop in a quote with no setup at all.

Try to create at least ten different ways of introducing a quote, even if they are silly. Some examples:

According to one know-it-all ... (Berkow, 2000)

Student Mark Zempel claims, in spite of his lack of experience, that ...

On the other hand, one researcher accidentally discovered, "Saccharine was as sweet as sugar" (Jones 4).

Revision exercise

For this exercise you will need to exhume a piece of your own writing that has included in-text citations and sources cited. Since you discovered the citation documentation that is preferred in the writing of your chosen discipline, this piece should be properly formatted to meet that system's requirements. If your discipline uses MLA citation style, and you have documented the paper correctly, take the day off. Go fishing or work out.

Quick writing exercise

Your instructor may ask you to do a quick focused freewrite about the topic you are studying in this unit. Those of you who are taking the course through a distance-learning system may be encouraged to share your thoughts in a discussion thread or to post your ideas on an Internet bulletin board. If you are writing your thoughts out by hand in a process journal, you might use these questions to stimulate ideas. This is a freewriting exercise that will not be graded. You can use any of the following questions to evaluate the way you use quotes and citations:

Are you comfortable taking a direct quote and paraphrasing the author's words into your own words? Why do most instructors prefer paraphrased quotes to direct quotes? Do you have problems introducing the quoted material? Some student essays read as if the student simply plopped huge hunks of words from some other document into the paper; do your papers ever come off this way? Do you ever feel that you are using so many quotes that your own voice in the paper is becoming overwhelmed? Or do you feel that your paper is so much you, and uses so few quotes, that it doesn't sound "scholarly enough"? What is the right balance between quotes and your own words? Do you know any students who have intentionally plagiarized? How do you think the institution should treat these students, if they are caught plagiarizing? How would you feel if another writer used some your words in his or her paper?

You may use the questions in the "Process Journal" section of Workshop 12 (p. 323) in *A Community of Writers* as an additional source of inspiration for this quick writing exercise.

Exercises related to *A Community of Writing*

As you build your own research paper, your teacher may ask you to use the guidelines in Workshop 12, "Research," to practice internal text citation styles that will show where you found the evidence used to support your thesis. You will also need advice for building a works cited page at the end of your paper. A detailed explanation of rules for documentation and works cited pages appears on pages 314 to 322. A quick reference guide for both of these tasks can also be found on the inside front cover of *A Community of Writers*.

A Community of Writers offers two excellent exercises related to the use of computers in gathering information (pp. 475–476). The first is a six-step process designed to help students evaluate the credibility of evidence collected from a web source. The second exercise is a collaborative group effort to explore some of the same issues. Read Mini-Workshop F, "Doing Research on the Web" (pp. 469–477), before attempting either of these exercises.

A related exercise might be to evaluate (by yourself or in a group) the credibility of the evidence and sources used in the sample essays in Workshop 12, "Research," including "When a Child has Cancer,' by Kymberly Saganski (pp. 326–327) and "Devoured: Eating Disorders," by Concetta Acunzo (pp. 327–330).

Additional reading

One student essay in the appendix, "Are Manufacturers of Caffeinated Beverages Targeting Children?" by Francine Taylor, is presented as a formal academic argument. How does the use of internal text citation and a works-cited page factor into the construction of this essay? Is Taylor using MLA or APA citation style? Do the internal text citations detract from the flow of the paper, or do they help the credibility of her work? If you were working on an essay about a similar topic, how would you use Taylor's paper as a springboard to dig up research? How does the author use attributions to work the quotes into the flow of the paper? Does the Taylor use direct quotes or paraphrased quotes? Why?

Quick Review

1. According to the telecourse program,
   a. Direct quotes are *always* better than a paraphrase or summary, because the writer is using the actual words from the source.
   b. A writer can often paraphrase or summarize evidence in a manner that is clear and easy to understand.
   c. There is no difference between paraphrasing and summarizing.
   d. All of the above.
   e. None of the above.

2. According to the telecourse program
   a. Plagiarism is stealing the words of another writer without permission.
   b. Plagiarism is using the words of another writer without proper citation.
   c. Plagiarism can be ground for failure in many universities.
   d. All of the above.
   e. None of the above.

3. According to the telecourse, in MLA citation style:
   a. The page number (not the date of publication) is emphasized.
   b. The citation is after the quote, not at bottom of the page.
   c. The author's name is included within parentheses, unless the author's name is introduced before the quote.
   d. All of the above.
   e. None of the above.

4. According to the telecourses, in APA citation style:
   a. The year of publication is emphasized. The citation is after the quote, not at bottom of the page.
   b. The author's name is included within parentheses, unless the author's name is introduced before the quote.
   c. All of the above.
   d. None of the above.

5. According to the telecourse, when assembling a works-cited page, you should be sure that
   a. All items are alphabetized, using the authors' last names first.
   b. The title of the work you are citing is the second item; book titles are underlined, whereas article and chapter titles are enclosed in quotation marks.
   c. The title of the larger work (for example, the periodical in which the article was published or the book in which the chapter appeared) comes next.
   d. For books, the editor, edition, number of volumes, city of publication, publisher, year of publication, and page numbers are also included; for journal articles, the volume number of the edition you are using, full date of publication, and page numbers.
   e. All of the above

"This is a college survival skill. You're going to need to write research papers for many, many courses that you take for college and hopefully beyond if you go to graduate school. As a matter of fact, research writing is an important business skill as well."

SANTI BUSCEMI, Middlesex County College

Introduction to the Topic

Why do research?

To answer that question, you must look beyond the assignment in your first-year writing class. In a typical freshman composition course, you are likely to have an end-of-semester assignment or "term paper" that is longer than your shorter essays. You might be asked to compose a substantial academic argument that cites evidence to support a thesis, and the syllabus could call for this paper to be a minimum of ten to twenty pages. Instructors typically ask for a works cited page that shows a minimum of ten to twenty references; students are expected to demonstrate that they know how to find credible evidence from a variety of sources, including peer-reviewed academic journals, on-line resources, books, magazines, and newspapers.

Students who think of such an assignment as a mere chore necessary to get credit in the class are missing the point. Sadly, this is all too common.

English composition instructors introduce research in a first-year course to prepare you for upper-division classes where the instructor announces on the first day of class that a research paper will account for half the grade. That future instructor will expect you to know college-level research techniques. As you have discovered through this telecourse program, many on-the-job writing challenges also require research skills. The time to learn these skills is *now*; it is unlikely someone else will take the time to show you later.

Students who succeed at research often do so because they learn how *gratifying* the process can be. Step back from the chore for a moment, and listen to librarian Sarah Blakeslee's take on research.

"I see it as being a detective; it's a treasure hunt," Blakeslee says. "I'm like a pit bull. I get a question and I won't let go; I get a question and will keep going until I find the answer. It's the thrill of the chase."

If you can pick up on just a little bit of Blakeslee's enthusiasm, your research will be much more rewarding – and enjoyable.

Learning Objectives

After viewing the telecourse program and finishing the writing assignments, you will understand why research is an integral part of the writing process in academic writing and in many styles of writing beyond the academy. With capable guidance from respected instructors from across the nation and writers who research at work, you will acquire new research techniques. You will also practice the recommended methods of research in preparation for your own writing in this course.

These learning objectives work in harmony with the essential premises of Workshop 12, "Research," in *A Community of Writers* (pp. 303–336).

- Research is an integration of what one already knows (through observation and conversation) and what one learns from additional sources.
- The kind of research one undertakes depends entirely on one's purpose and the availability of sources.

Before Viewing

Think about your previous experiences with writing in high school and first-semester college courses that required something called research. Consider how your definition of the word research might change as the stakes get higher and you advance to upper-division courses with more academic rigor. Imagine what you might start to learn about research at this stage of your education, and think about how those lessons might help you in future writing challenges.

Read the main assignment in Workshop 12, "Research," in Elbow and Belanoff's *A Community of Writers* (pp. 303–322).

While Viewing

Compare your previous experiences in research with definitions of research, techniques of research, and attitudes about research expressed by the instructors, writers, and students in the telecourse program. Notice the similarities between the way Elbow and Belanoff discuss research as part of "joining the conversation" (Exploring Theory: The Ongoing Conversation, pp. 323–325) and the way guests in the telecourse program, such as Thomas Fox and Charles Johnson, also talk about research.

Note how research can be used at several stages of the composition process – from finding a topic to final revision. And take notes on the surprising aspects of college research that you might not have considered before this program.

After Viewing

Evaluate your personal approach to research as you learn more about how it is conducted in a college and university environment. Spend some time in the library, learning where the scholarly journals are stored and where you can find other types of research sources appropriate for your academic discipline. Locate a friendly librarian, and discuss what you have learned in this unit of our telecourse. Make a list of questions provoked by this program, and ask the librarian for assistance in discovering the secrets of your own college library.

Using the exercises in this Telecourse Study Guide chapter, practice some of the skills of research discussed in this telecourse program and in the A Community of Writers. Consider the readings in Workshop 12 of A Community of Writers, and notice how the authors incorporated research into their work..

Viewing Guide

No doubt, you wrote some sort of "research paper" during high school, even if your only support was a few quotes copied and pasted from an encyclopedia and a Web site into a three-page report about William Shakespeare.

When you land on a college or university campus, don't be surprised when you hear students in upper-division classes or graduate school mention something like, "I have a course that requires five research papers this semester." You can be sure the standards for those assignments will be much higher than in high school, and the expectations for original thought will vary quite a bit as your academic career advances.

If you are lucky, you will be introduced to the research process in increments. In your early undergraduate experiences, the "term paper" assignment is usually meant to train you to look for quotes, facts, statistics, and other types of evidence to support a thesis or main claim. These will all be combined into some sort of paper designed to show that you are actually learning something.

Though the instructor may assign the subject of the paper, you are often expected to find a topic yourself, one that is worthy of your inquiry for knowledge.

To many instructors, a worthy subject means avoiding hackneyed topics that require little more "research" than popping a key word into an Internet search engine and quoting the first few easy references that show up on line.

Chitra Divakaruni speaks for many English composition instructors when she says, "Research papers *teach* students how to come up with a thesis and how to come up with a project."

This is a key point. The very act of finding an appropriate subject to write about may take some research; narrowing that topic down to a defensible thesis will require even deeper research.

In the video, instructor Chitra Divakaruni describes an approach many instructors use: keeping the research topic open. The effect is to allow the students to write about something they *care* about. The open-ended research paper assignment also emulates many writing challenges in upper-division undergraduate classes, where the goal is to demonstrate initiative and originality of thought.

This process intensifies in graduate school, where you will be required to do even more; the graduate-level research paper should show a contribution of original ideas to an ongoing field of study.

In many disciplines (including the hard sciences), the skills learned while creating a traditional term paper are absolutely necessary for success. As chemistry graduate student Marty Wallace points out in the telecourse, it is essential that a student practice research papers in an English composition course. "Hopefully, by the time you're a junior or senior, you're not *learning* those skills," he says. "You're *applying* them and refining them a little bit."

Though you will not be required to write this kind of research "paper" beyond academia, many tasks in the working world require you to adapt the skills of inquiry you pick up in college.

The opening sequence of this telecourse program is designed to help you learn more about the expectations you will encounter when you are asked to do research work. It should lead naturally to an important question. If it is not acceptable to grab a few quotes from your electronic encyclopedia, or snag a few statistics from the first few Web sites that pop up on your Internet search, then what *is* research?

Defining research

One way of looking at the process is to think of research as a way of entering a conversation that has lasted for years. Much of this conversation has gone on before you, the student, arrive. The way to catch up, and add your own contribution to this "conversation," is to gather as much information as possible – by reading books in the library, searching documents on the Internet, watching television documentaries, talking in person to experts in the field you are researching, or reading the writing of those experts in peer-reviewed academic journals.

As you discover information, you will add these bits of accumulated knowledge and wisdom to your *own* thoughts. The facts and quotes gathered should not just be random ideas, however; you should only hold on to the discoveries relevant to the conversation.

Charles Johnson, a novelist and instructor at from the University of Washington, suggests that entering the conversation is the essence of scholarship. Research, he points out, is as important to a novelist as it is to a philosopher, a scientist, or an engineer.

"If one is doing scholarly research, you are entering into a dialogue that might be two thousand years old," Johnson says. "It might go back to the ancient Greeks. And it's impossible to 'enter into the room' where the dialogue has been going on if you don't know what's been said. Your whole point of entering in the dialogue is that you have something to say. And you won't know what to say unless you see what's been said previously. So it's clear. You have to do your homework."

In *A Community of Writers* (p. 324), Elbow and Belanoff reinforce this view, stating, "When you do print-based research in a library, you are entering into a conversation with those who wrote centuries ago or thousands of miles away. But, to situate yourself within that conversation and to make valid contributions to it, you need to know what has been said in it. This is the basic purpose of most education; to help you find our place in the ongoing flow of history."

This definition of research might sound intimidating. It would be easy to say, "What contribution could I possibly make? This is only my first year of college."

Betsy Klimasmith of the University of Washington has these encouraging words of advice: Take responsibility for finding out how to do research, and don't assume your questions are stupid. Usually, an instructor or librarian will be eager to help a student who is genuinely interested in learning.

"It can be difficult to get past those feelings of – 'Oh geez, I was already supposed to know this' – and feel that you were the only one who didn't know the way this works," Klimasmith says. "As a teacher, I try to remember that academic work can be a very intimidating thing; your professors and instructors have been doing research for a long time. For them, that feeling of newness and that feeling of intimidation may be way in the past. You'll find that people are very helpful and very willing to answer questions that you thought were stupid – that nobody else was going to ask. That's part of it too: figuring out how to take that responsibility."

One important aspect of learning how to do a research paper is to find out what your instructor's expectations are. Some instructors prefer an introspective, personal accounting of observations mixed with quotes and anecdotes gathered from research.

For an example of this kind of approach, see the research paper "When a Child Has Cancer" by Kymberly Saganski in *A Community of Writers* (pp. 326–327). Saganski's personal experiences are an integral part of the paper.

Other instructors insist on an impersonal, third-person, objective point of view. They will lower the grade if you chance a first-person statement such as "I believe" or "I think." These instructors want papers written in the style of a formal academic argument that states a thesis early and supports the claim with evidence you gather from research.

The research paper "Devoured: Eating Disorders" by Concetta Acunzo in *A Community of Writers* (pp. 327–330) is closer to this style of presentation.

It is part of your job as a student to learn from the instructor the *style* of research paper that is expected in a given course or assignment.

The formal academic argument

There are several types of research papers, including purely informational reports that gather, summarize, and somehow organize the random data available on a given subject. However, the academic conversation you join is most likely to be in the form of an academic argument, as we have studied in Chapter 19 of this *Telecourse Study Guide*. Instructors in every discipline across the campus value this form of research writing.

"I like to distinguish between writing a 'report' and doing a research paper," says John Lovas of De Anza College. "Most students have written reports from elementary school; the report is a kind of writing that says something like, 'Find out what the most important product in Peru is and tell us about it.' You can go to a couple encyclopedias, and you find out that the most important product is something like tomatoes, and you describe how they're grown and you produce a nice report. This is a useful kind of thing but it's *not really research*. It's searching, gathering information and putting it down on paper."

True research, Lovas says, has additional steps beyond the gathering of raw information; these steps involve critical thinking, a claim, and evidence to support the claim.

Thomas Fox of California State University, Chico expresses a similar point of view:

"In your freshman composition class or in your other classes, in fact, in a lot of academic situations, most of the genres are kinds of arguments. They *do* something. Say, you're doing a lab report; in a sense you're arguing for the fact, 'This is what I observed' – and not something else. Almost everything is an argument, in my opinion."

Political science instructor George Wright notes that the kinds of arguments across disciplines vary quite a bit. One secret to learning how to compose a successful research paper is to understand how arguments in your academic major are constructed.

"You have to understand how your argument fits within a body of literature," Wright explains. "To know within political science literature or sociology literature or elite theory literature what is old and what is new related to your idea."

It is the research – the reading and referencing of ideas that came before your own – that allows you to understand where your own argument fits within that body of literature.

Learning research techniques

How do you conduct this research?

The most obvious starting place is the library. It is easy, however, to become overwhelmed by the volume and variety of choices in a college or university library.

You can seek scholarly writings through peer-reviewed academic journals, you can read books, and you can browse through decades of magazines and newspapers. And as you bring quotes and statistics back to an instructor to support your point of view, you quickly learn that certain types of evidence carry more authority than others. Part of your job as a student is to learn how to find the most credible evidence in the library on your campus – evidence that will convince your instructor and peers that you have considered the topic thoroughly.

A good librarian can help you figure out where the best resources are.

Students who dig deeper will find many supplementary types of information available in the college or university library, including government documents, abstracts, CD-ROM databases, and historical archives. Elbow and Belanoff list a variety of additional sources in *A Community of Writers* (p. 310).

A primary goal of the research paper assignments in an English composition course is to familiarize you with the types of evidence available; instructors in upper-division courses will always spot students who do the minimal amount of research, using only the easiest and most obvious sources. It is important at this stage of your development to experiment with a variety of research techniques to discover what types of evidence carry the most weight in an academic environment.

Librarian Sarah Blakeslee explains a common blunder: "People will stop at the first things that they find. So if you have a computerized database, they'll stop at the first articles that they find; the teachers see the same articles again and again and again. It is really important for students to understand that they need to evaluate the information that they're finding and get the *best* articles."

Instructors tend to reward students who find the strongest sources. And instructors often favor scholarly journals of academic research. Most students have never even seen one of these journals before entering college. The diligent ones will be quite familiar with them by the time they finish their English composition courses.

PEER-REVIEWED JOURNALS

What is a "scholarly journal" or "academic journal" or "peer-reviewed" journal? And why do instructors value the quotes and evidence gathered from them so much?

All three terms refer to essentially the same thing: publications of writings from scholars, academics, and researchers who are writing for *other* scholars, academics, and researchers.

These publications are also sometimes called "refereed journals" because when a professor or scholar submits an article to the editors for publication, that article is sent out to other peers in the field to review. Those experts, or referees, make a judgment as to the merit of the article; if they report that it does not measure up to the standards of the publication, the article will not be published. Since your research paper is, in essence, joining a written "conversation" with this elite group of folks, it is a good idea to read and quote the articles that they deem worthy.

You've probably seen newspapers and television stations quote articles from one of these journals every time a new medical study is announced. The *Journal of the American Medical Association* (*JAMA*) is a great source for health-beat journalists, especially when a new study about cancer, heart disease, or dieting is released.

There are journals, no less scholarly, for every possible field of study, including journals for spud farmers (the *Journal of Agricultural Science*), journals for rocket scientists (*Annales Geophysicae, Journal of Aerospace Engineering*, the *Astrophysical Journal*), journals for folks who study sanitation systems (*Journal of Environmental Engineering, Journal of Environmental Science and Technology*), and so forth. These journals don't receive as much publicity as the *JAMA*, and it is likely a freshman-level student has never heard of most of them. However, within a specialty field (such as potato farming), a quote or statistic from the related journal is often the most valuable evidence you can cite.

These journals are important sources in your scholarly research papers. In the hierarchy of evidence, most instructors will consider these journals much more reliable than popular magazines such as *Time, Newsweek*, or *Psychology Today*, which are aimed at the general public.

As librarian Sarah Blakeslee explains in the video, many students approach her reference desk confused about the difference between a scholarly article and an article from a popular periodical. Their instructors have insisted, "You need to have evidence from a scholarly journal." However, the students have no clue where to start looking.

In the video, Blakeslee illustrates the difference between types of articles with two examples. One is an article from The *International Journal of Sports Psychology*. The other is a piece of fluff from a popular golf magazine. The popular magazine is filled with garish advertisements and colorful layouts. The peer-reviewed journal is filled with columns of black type, broken up from time to time with a mathematical analysis or chart.

The lead article in the golf magazine is "The Only Way to Fix Your Slice Is Right Here." The article is designed to entertain and, perhaps, teach the amateur golfer.

The article about golf in the *International Journal of Sports Psychology* is titled "Differences Between Actual and Imagined Putting Movements in Golf: A Chronometric Analysis." This article is aimed at other scholars and academics who study sports psychology.

While each article might provide interesting quotes for a research paper, the quotes from the academic journal are more likely to impress the instructor grading the assignment.

Nonprint sources

Most academicians emphasize gathering ideas from printed materials. The value of talking face to face with other humans is an often-overlooked opportunity.

While talking to a random person on the street might not seem like a great way to get "evidence," public opinion surveys are often quoted as legitimate research. Students should be aware that the procedures for accurate and thorough surveys represent an entire academic discipline. It is *not easy* to conduct a survey as primary evidence for a first-year writing course research paper, though a casual survey might provide informal, anecdotal evidence to support your thesis.

What *will* impress a reader you are trying to convince is a quote gathered directly from a phone conversation or personal meeting with a person of authority in your field. Though many students are too shy to call an "expert," the obvious question might be, "Why not call?"

Consider what might happen if you phoned the author of an article that sparked your interest. The investment would be meager, even for a long-distance call (less than the cost of gas to drive your car to the library) – and often the person on the other end of the phone is flattered to have an undergraduate student interested in her or his writing.

Gathering quotes in person is actually a time-honored research technique. Journalists, for instance, thrive on in-person interviews. Though they sometimes dig through libraries and government archives for documents, most of their quotes, observations, and statistics are gathered by talking directly to the newsmakers.

As a matter of fact, much of the research for this telecourse was in the form of in-person interviews gathered on video and presented as "evidence" to support the points made in either the television programs or in this *Telecourse Study Guide*.

In *A Community of Writers*, Elbow and Belanoff praise the in-person research technique: "We hope you'll believe as we do that individual research (observing and interviewing) and textual research (print, library, Internet) are equally valid; which to use depends on what you want to know" (p. 303). The authors discuss this approach to research in the "Interviewing and Observing" section of Workshop 12, "Research" (pp. 308–309).

ELECTRONIC RESEARCH

It wasn't that long ago that all research was done with paper indexes to periodicals and cardboard filing cards lovingly sorted into long wooden drawers. The notion seems quaint today.

By this century, the paper library has almost completely evolved into an electronic database. (A few specialty libraries retain the paper/cardboard/wood model.) Within the realm of "online research," there are several ways of looking for information. For example, you could search data in your local library electronically; you could look through the free information available on the World Wide Web. You could also pay for an electronic service that has collected and organized much of the information for you.

Many of the databases that would normally cost the public money are free through your college or university library.

Librarian Sarah Blakeslee explains the importance of knowing the difference in types of Web-based information sources: "There are two kinds of information, from a librarian's perspective, on the World Wide Web. There's the public Web, and there's the private [or commercial] Web.

"The public web is what people usually refer to. These are documents that are available to anybody. If you have a URL [Web address], you can type it in, go to a site, and read what's on the site. On the private, commercial Web, we're just using the Internet as a vehicle of transportation or communication to access *databases* that used to be on paper. The university pays money for these. They're only available to students and faculty at the university. There are periodical indexes such as Academic Search, PsycINFO, or MEDLINE – databases that are going to give you access to the scholarly journals and other kinds of specialized publications."

Many of these databases (such as Westlaw, a database of legal research used by attorneys, and LEXIS/NEXIS, database of legal decisions and of newspaper and television news stories) are expensive and impractical for first-year students to use – especially if the school library does not subscribe to the service. And it is quite possible to find excellent information for free, on the public Web, if a student is discriminating.

In *A Community of Writers*, the excellent Mini-Workshop F, "Doing Research on the Web (pp. 469–477) advises students on how to find information on the web and how to evaluate the credibility of online sources.

Students will find online research an easy-to-use resource to do preliminary (and even in-depth) research. It is almost *too* easy.

As Thomas Fox points out, "The problem with the Internet is there's *so* much information out there that it's easy to get anything to support *any* point of view. This is different than when I used to teach research fifteen years ago, when I taught was how to *find* information. Well, we have a search engine now. That takes about five seconds to teach."

Instead of teaching how to get information, the modern-day instructor's bigger challenge is to teach students how to discriminate.

"Is somebody's personal Web page as reliable as a Web page from a professional organization?" Fox asks.

"There are many college professors who would really want you to find a *book*, because it's gone through an editing process. Somebody has decided it is worth publishing; anybody can put any information up on the Internet."

Of course, this isn't a completely new problem. As Fox points out, "There's all kinds of bad information in the library [in books and journals] as well as on the Internet. It is good to *mix* sources."

Research-style reading

The chapter and telecourse program "Reading as a Thinker" emphasizes careful, in-depth critical reading skills. It also introduces a much different style of reading, aimed at gathering information in a short amount of time.

Elbow and Belanoff describe this type of reading in *A Community of Writers,* p. 311: "You can tell in a few seconds from a title or an abstract whether something is worth tracking down – then tell in a minute or two whether an article or Web site or book is worth spending an hour trying to 'mine' (not necessarily read)."

Of course, you have to do some *careful* reading, too, they emphasize. The main task might be trying to find the best pages to read carefully and not waste time reading the wrong pages.

In the telecourse program, author Kim Stanley Robinson describes a similar process. "I have a form of reading I call strip mining," Robinson explains. "You use it for researching to try to get what you *need* for the project you have at hand. And you don't get distracted by the stuff in there that you might be interested in but is not germane to what your project is. In this kind of strip mining, many nonfiction books are organized in basically a scientific basis where they have the equivalent of an abstract that tells you what the book's about and where the information is located; the abstract gives you five sentences at the top of the article that tell you what the article is going to tell you, in a classic expository writing style."

Research and composing

It is important to realize that research is part of the writing *process*. You are not simply gathering data to plug into your typing. In a good project, your investigation and inquiry will affect every stage of your writing. As you review various stages of the writing process already studied in this course, you will see that the reading material you gather will affect every aspect of the way you compose.

In *A Community of Writers*, Elbow and Belanoff recommend starting off with a series of questions about at topic that will give you reason to find the answers through your research (pp. 305–308). The answers you discover through your treasure hunt will become tools to help focus the subject matter.

FINDING SOMETHING TO SAY WITH RESEARCH

Before you even *start* a paper, research can be part of finding a subject to write about.

"Before grabbing onto a topic and holding onto it and deciding you're not going to write about anything else, I would encourage you to come into the library and do a little bit of research first," Sarah Blakeslee says.

It's possible, she points out, that there will be very little information on the topic that you thought you wanted to write about.

"Rather than struggling and trying to keep finding things that really don't exist, you'll find *other* things while you're doing your research that could be just as interesting," she advises.

Thomas Fox adds that it is important to avoid the clichéd topics and to instead look for something that actually requires research – instead of choosing a subject matter that *anybody* can tell you were able to research in less than ten minutes. In other words, your instructor will reward the student who uses critical thinking to find an interesting topic.

"There is a really bad example of research papers out there, where somebody picks a topic that everybody's pretty tired of hearing about and says something that nobody's surprised about hearing," Fox says. "And I would really counsel you away from doing that kind of paper, because it's boring to read too. That's why a lot of teachers don't want you to do gun control or abortion. The opinions are all out there; it's not real research, you're not *discovering* new things, you're not making a new point."

FOCUSING THE TOPIC WITH RESEARCH

Even after you've found a topic, it can be a challenge to narrow the rough idea down to a defensible thesis, main claim, hypothesis, or other focusing device. After you develop the main thesis, it is usually necessary to find a mini-thesis for each subsection of the paper (or, in more traditional terms, a topic sentence for each main section of the paper).

One way to accomplish this task is to use the data gathered in your research to clarify your fuzzy ideas. For example, as we studied in Chapter 12, "Organizing Devices," many writers *start* a paper with a "working thesis" and change the perspective as they learn more.

Kimberly Wise of Cypress College explains: "Even though you go into a research paper with a preconceived arrangement for your thesis statement, your research is going to determine the organization of your paper. And that thesis statement is tentative."

Some instructors prefer to think of the original set of ideas that you take into the library as a "controlling idea" that gives you reason to start browsing through books, journals, and databases.

Says instructor Michael Bertsch, "The controlling idea is merely a collection of words from which we work. Out of the controlling idea we get the thesis statement that will actually appear in the final draft. But the controlling idea just controls our research; the controlling idea gives a general direction."

Bertsch emphasizes that it is OK not to know where you are going until you have done some actual reading on the subject. It is possible (and expected) that your original idea for a thesis may actually change drastically as you open up your mind and let the ideas pour in.

DEVELOPING THE WORKING THESIS WITH RESEARCH

"When you start writing a paper, you will hear your topic referred to as a 'working thesis.' As you write, and learn more through research, your thesis changes," Sarah Blakeslee explains. "It may be that the change is ever so slight, or it could be that you totally reverse what you originally set out to prove through the research that you're doing.

"I think that [when a writer changes his or her mind] is something incredibly fun for a professor to see," Blakeslee adds. Fun, because the instructor has stimulated a student to think about an issue, and through research, the student has learned enough to think critically about the conclusions.

Donald Pharr of Valencia Community College notes that continued research is intertwined with the process of drafting and revising. "Another virtue of research is it will help you shape your thoughts," Pharr observes. "You might have a strong opinion about something, but it will never have occurred to you that you got this opinion from your family or our church or your friends. You go to the library and start reading actual *facts* on a subject, and you think, 'I'm not so sure I believe the way I used to. I'm going to have to think about this.' And very frequently your opinion does change."

REVISING THROUGH RESEARCH

One difficult lesson for writers-in-training to learn is that research can be part of the revision process. If a writer is bogged down with a disorganized paper – even if the paper's due date is looming dangerously soon – it could be a sign that another trip to the library to gather more data is in order.

"Revision comes after new knowledge," Thomas Fox observes. "It's after you think through something differently; you have changed your mind a little bit so you have to revise your piece. Otherwise you're merely fixing it."

The best revisions, Fox explains, come after an early draft is blocked out – and when the writer continues with new reading, new observations, and new experiences. In other words, an effective revision only comes after you have a *reason* to revise. That reason often comes from additional research.

Summary

Ultimately, research is part of the *discovery* process. The typing is only a small part of the work. And, as you learned in Chapter 20, "Quotes and Citations," using direct quotes is a very small part of writing the research paper. You are encouraged to *think* after reading, so you can paraphrase and summarize your research rather than simply reproduce the insights word for word.

Writing is mostly *thinking* and learning. A student who is a critical thinker should always be aware of the differences between strong and weak evidence, truth and falsehoods, opinions and facts.

Charles Johnson observes, "What's interesting to me about the process of creation is that it really is a process of discovery – and you may find your ideas transformed by the end, just as a scientist's ideas are transformed by the end of a laboratory experiment.

"The same is true of research. The problem with the student who says, 'I think abortion is bad' and then goes and writes an essay, selecting only information that will support that argument – well, then what we have is rhetoric. The process of discovery is cut off if the student does not look at other evidence that might be contradictory. In other words, it is like looking at two sides of a debate and trying to give credit to both sides — to be open as one goes through the research."

Integrating the Text

WORKSHOP 12 "Research," (pp. 303–336)

In Elbow and Belanoff's *A Community of Writers*, Workshop 12 "Research" examines research and related issues.

The authors emphasize that research should be a process of integrating what the student already knows with ideas gained from additional sources.

The sources recommended included non-text interactions (interviews and personal surveys), although Elbow and Belanoff also discuss the importance of learning how to master on-line resources and libraries.

In the section "Using the Library" (pp. 309–312), the authors recommend spending time just browsing and learning to feel comfortable in your school library. They point out that a student cannot be expected to "master" a college library information system on the basis of one English composition term paper.

"The trick is not to feel intimidated," they say. "Realize that it's legitimate to ask librarians for help – and don't be afraid to ask dumb questions. Most are happy, as long as you treat your questions as occasions for learning, not as requests for them to do the work for you."

This is very sage advice.

Librarians tend to get cranky with students if it appears that there is no true seeking of knowledge. If you treat the librarian like a humanoid search engine, you'll get nowhere. If you express a genuine curiosity about your research, they will be happy to assist you in learning your way through the library archives.

On page 311, Elbow and Belanoff also discuss how reading for research is different from most of other types of reading you have experienced in college and university life.

"The essential skill for doing library research is to learn a *different relationship to the printed (or electronic) word,*" Elbow and Belanoff explain. Students should discover how to glance, browse, and leaf through material, with a goal of finding the right pages to read carefully "and not waste time reading the wrong 50 to 100 pages."

Workshop 12 also emphasizes that learning how to decide on a topic is a key objective of any research project. The sections "Deciding on a Topic" and "Designing a Research Plan" (pp. 304–305) complement the points made in this telecourse program about using research to come up with ideas.

The strategy is to create a list of questions that will give you a reason to go to the library and seek answers. The various stages of *answers* to these questions will become the equivalent of a "working thesis" and, eventually, "thesis statement" that would normally appear in a formal academic argument.

The processes of "Writing an Exploratory Draft" and "Moving Toward a Final Draft" described in *A Community of Writers* (pp. 312–314) also mirror the processes of creating a working thesis and a final thesis statement.

Elbow and Belanoff's suggestions on making a quick outline for a research paper (pp. 313–314) are similar to recommendations in the Student Study Guide Chapter 12 and telecourse program "Organizing Devices."

The advice in the sections on "Documentation" (pp. 314–322) directly supports the main instructional points in the Student Study Guide Chapter 20 and telecourse program "Quotes and Citations."

Finally, the section "Exploring Theory: The Ongoing Conversation" (pp. 323–325) supports points made by Charles Johnson, Tom Fox, and others in the telecourse program and viewing guide section of this Student Study Guide called "Defining Research."

Exercises

Check with your instructor for your formal assignments. You will be asked to do exercises from the *Telecourse Study Guide*.

Exploring research further

EXERCISE 1

Find a quote from a peer-reviewed journal (also called a scholarly journal or an academic journal) in a field you are interested in. Find a quote from a consumer-oriented magazine about the same subject. Compare the difference in jargon and sentence structure in the two quotes. Determine which you personally consider the more credible evidence. Imagine what your instructors might consider the more credible of the two.

EXERCISE 2

1. Find at least five articles about the American president of your choice.

2. Write a paper incorporating the articles you found. To do this, refer to three or four issues from your articles (either good, bad, or both) and write your piece to represent a balanced view of these issues.

EXERCISE 3

To discover a research topic that you are interested in, do a five- to ten-minute freewrite about things you care about. Afterward, read through the text you have created and make note of any topics that have been suggested therein. For each of the topics you've listed, think of and write out a list of questions that would need to be answered in a research paper about that topic.

Next, to help decide which of these topics will work best for a research paper, go to the library or the Internet and do some preliminary research based on the questions you have listed. If you can't find anything that relates, you may want to consider another topic.

EXERCISE 4

Repeat Exercise 3 – but just before you freewrite, spend a half-hour browsing through the specialty magazine section of a very good bookstore. This works best if you go to one of those bookstores that has a coffee cafe attached. Grab a cup, open your notepad and start freewriting. If you hit on a topic, go back to the specialty magazines in that area of the bookstore, and see if you can find some articles that will help you focus on a thesis or main point for the paper.

Exercise just for fun

Meet with a group of other students in the library and take turns thinking of outrageous topics to research. For each topic, group members must return with at least one piece of reference material and defend their reasons for why it is applicable to the topic.

Revision exercise

To improve your evidence in a research paper, highlight each quote that you use to support your thesis. Find the original article or book that you read, and look at the works-cited page to see what articles or books *that* writer used as evidence. Locate those same articles or books in the library, and see if you can find even stronger quotes to support your thesis.

Quick writing exercise

Your instructor may ask you to do a quick focused freewrite about the topic you are studying in this unit. Those of you who are taking the course through a distance-learning system may be encouraged to share your thoughts in a discussion thread or to post your ideas on an Internet bulletin board. If you are writing your thoughts out by hand in a process journal, you might use these questions to stimulate ideas. This is a freewriting exercise that will not be graded. You can use any of the following questions to stimulate your thoughts about the research process:

Assuming you have a research paper due soon, have you found it easy or difficult to find the sources you need to provide evidence that will help prove your thesis? If you have had success, share what worked for you. If you have had difficulties, what kinds of problems are you running into. Have you found way too much information? Have you found no evidence at all that will help prove your thesis? Based on your early results, do you think you have picked a good topic to research? Will you be able to find the evidence you need to support your thesis? Is your thesis starting to change because of new ideas you have picked up through your research? Is your college research experience different, or is this the same old same old thing you have been doing since grade school?

Have you been able to find a peer reviewed journal that addresses the topic you are trying to research? Some teachers require evidence from these types of journals. How easy or hard was it to find a quote or two from this type of source? What kinds of research sources do you personally consider to be strong evidence? What kinds of research sources do you personally consider to be weak evidence?

You may use the questions in the "Process Journal" section of Workshop 12 (p. 323) in *A Community of Writers* as an additional source of inspiration for this quick writing exercise.

Exercises related to *A Community of Writers*

The primary exercises in this unit will be linked to a research paper assigned by your teacher. In *A Community of Writers*, the main assignments in Workshop 12, "Research," focus on finding information from a variety of sources, including print, electronic media, personal interviews, and the Internet.

The "Main Assignment' in *A Community of Writers* (p. 304) is:

1. To develop a research topic out of a previous piece of writing you've done for this class

2. To design a research plan that calls for individual research (interviewing and observing), library or print research, and – if resources are available – Internet research.

3. To write a research paper that combines this information. Your final paper will need to include appropriate documentation.

The various stages described in the section "Main Assignment: Writing a Research Paper" (pp. 304–314) will guide you through various stages of completing a research paper, including: Deciding on a topic, Brainstorming [through freewriting], Designing a Research Plan, Using the Library and Internet, Writing an Exploratory Draft, and Moving Toward a Final Draft.

Additional reading

One student essay in the appendix, "Are Manufacturers of Caffeinated Beverages Targeting Children?" by Francine Taylor, is presented as a formal academic argument. How does Taylor use evidence, gathered through research, to support her thesis? How could Taylor extend the research, to expand this paper into a twelve-page research paper? What types of sources would you recommend for further research? Could Taylor's paper be viewed as part of an ongoing, scholarly "conversation" about caffeine in our society? How would you imagine a student could build on the ideas started in a paper like this (composed in the freshman year) and pursue more in-depth research that could eventually become a graduate-level master's thesis?

How would you use the excerpt in the appendix from *Everything You Need to Know About Latino History*, by Himilce Novas, as a source for a research paper? How would you go about determining the type of research did Novas to create her book?

Read Dave Barry's piece in the appendix, "Business Communications" Though it is stated satirically, how is the formula similar to the standard structure of an academic research paper?

Quick Review

1. According to instructors and writers interviewed in this telecourse unit,
   a. All evidence is created equal.
   b. A peer-reviewed academic journal may not be a strong source for evidence.
   c. Research is much like joining a conversation.
   d. All of the above.
   e. None of the above.

2. Research papers that are formal academic arguments
   a. usually have many "I believe" and "I think" first-person types of statements
   b. state a thesis early and support it with evidence gathered from research
   c. avoid the impersonal, objective third-person point of view because it seems stuffy
   d. all of the above
   e. none of the above

3. Quotes and statistics gathered from research sources found on the Internet
   a. are very rarely considered strong, because Web pages are usually assembled by an assortment of hackers, lunatics, wannabes, and other undesirables
   b. can be evaluated for credibility by sets of guidelines offered various places, including on the Internet itself
   c. are always free and easy to access
   d. all of the above
   e. none of the above

4. Instructors you encounter are likely to
   a. weigh the credibility of quotes and statistics presented to support a thesis according to a hierarchy of evidence – where some sources are considered more valid than others
   b. ask for a mixture of different types of sources
   c. value hard-earned evidence over quotes gathered from the first few sources that come up on a quickie Internet search
   d. all of the above
   e. none of the above

5. According to instructors interviewed for the telecourse program and Study Guide chapter:
   a. Research papers *teach* students how to come up with a thesis and support an argument.
   b. It is really important for students to understand that they need to evaluate the information that they're finding and get the *best* articles.
   c. The problem with the Internet is there's *so* much information out there, that it's easy to get quotes that support *any* point of view.
   d. All of the above.
   e. None of the above.

"I firmly believe that the only way that you learn to write and the only way that you're going to learn spelling, punctuation, and grammar is to rewrite your own writing. Some people will understand those rules by reading. But most of us have to rewrite our own writing."

PATRICIA SCULLY, Pleasant Valley High School

Introduction to the Topic

Sentences can get mangled in the typing process. As writers pass their thoughts through their fingers, sometimes mistakes are made. Often, those literal gaffes go undetected, only to appear in time to embarrass the author, as well as lower the grade of the paper.

Example: I ran outside to grab my cat in my socks. (The instructor's question: Why was your cat wearing your socks?)

And then, there are those phrases that, even though they look fairly silly on paper, we have no trouble using in casual conversation, I'm like sure you know what I mean, and everything. Whatever. Know what I'm saying?

Since the process of composing sentences allows the author to edit, proofread, and correct mistakes, such blunders tend to stand out more in a document than they do in spontaneous chatting with a friend, instructor, or business associate.

In college you are expected to learn how to fix sentence problems in the final stages of revising and editing your manuscript.

This unit will give you some strategies for spotting and correcting errors in sentence constructions. You won't master all sentence-level difficulties in this instructional unit, but you will be given a brief tour of the most common mistakes.

These are important strategies to practice. Ignoring them could mean the difference between getting an F or an A on a paper – or, even more important, could mean squandering an employment opportunity in the world beyond school.

Learning Objectives

In this unit, you will learn proofreading strategies to identify and fix the most common sentence-level errors. You will focus on editing of fused sentences, comma splices, run-on sentences, sentence fragments, and sentences with misplaced modifiers. You will also learn how to detect and correct nonparallel sentence constructions and develop a personal editing checklist that will help you copyedit papers for writing challenges you'll encounter in upper-division classes and in the working world.

Before Viewing

Think about the following terms – they may be familiar as correction marks on papers returned by an instructor: *fragment, run on, comma splice, fused sentence.* Also ask yourself: Have you ever seen a comment about a sentence with a parallelism problem or a misplaced modifier? Try to recollect the lessons learned in high school about these types of sentence problems.

While Viewing

Draw a single line down the middle of a couple of pages in a notebook – creating two columns. In the first column, list the types of sentence structure problems that are explained in the program. In the second column, list techniques you can use when editing a paper that has sentence structure problems – even if that paper was written by someone else and you were given the task to detect and correct the problems.

After Viewing

Create a personal editing checklist that features the errors you are most likely to make in a paper. Use this checklist the next time you proofread an important document that might determine your fate: a job application, a plea for a presidential pardon, or a paper that will determine your final grade in a class. Using the exercises in this *Telecourse Study Guide* chapter, practice detecting and correcting errors in sentence structure.

Read Mini-Workshop J, "Quotation and the Punctuation of Reported Speech," in *A Community of Writers* (pp. 494–496). This is important supplementary material for understanding how to punctuate sentences – especially those in research papers, where quoted materials are used extensively. The material covered in Mini-Workshop G, "The Sentence and End-Stop Punctuation" (pp. 481–485), is also helpful in understanding how to punctuate effective sentences.

Viewing Guide

Most problems with sentence structure come from a simple lack of proofreading.

A high percentage of students put off writing their papers until the last minute, leaving almost no time for the editing process. "I write so much better when I'm under pressure." "Procrastination is a family trait; I've inherited it." "I was so busy, I didn't have time."

Students use these clichés because they've heard them used by other students.

Instructors have heard those phrases too. They translate them directly to "I didn't bother to proofread."

The best way to avoid sentence-level problems is to finish your paper far enough in advance so that you can put it away for a few hours (or even a few days) and read it with a fresh eye. The problems addressed in this unit can be solved by students who use common sense – and who learn to *see* and *hear* each individual sentence.

Of course, some students leave plenty of time for proofreading and still have problems with sentences. If you have more difficulty than most, try this proofreading technique:

First, make a checklist of your most common sentence problems, based on feedback received on previous papers. Then, read one sentence of your paper at a time, out loud. Try starting at the end of the paper, and read the sentences in reverse order.

If each sentence does not stand on its own, or if a sentence doesn't sound right to your ear, the chances are that it is in need of fixing. Students often catch these problems more easily if they consider each sentence in isolation. A sentence that seems right within an essay often sounds awful by itself.

The chances are very high that the problem with the awkward sentence is on your list of most common mistakes. One of the remedies in this unit of the telecourse and chapter of the *Telecourse Study Guide* may cure the error.

As Peter Elbow of the University of Massachusetts explains, "The best copyediting involves turning off much emphasis on the actual meaning. People say the best way to copyedit is to read the last sentence, and then the next to the last sentence, and then the third to the last sentence. Read your essay in reverse order to try and check the sentences and spelling."

This approach is unlike revision, Elbow observes. "It is not good for thinking about the essay content," he says. But it is a good way to look for surface-level errors.

Nonparallel sentence constructions
(Correction symbol: //ism = correct the parallelism problem)
If you read the following sentence out loud, it probably will sound wrong:

> Chocolate makes me gain weight, lose my appetite, and breaking out in hives.

To fix it you would say:

> Chocolate makes me gain weight, lose my appetite, and break out in hives.

To most students, this is just plain common sense. You don't need jargon or a page full of rules to spot the problem and edit the sentence. Technically, this is a nonparallel sentence construction – the verbs don't work together. Your instructor may scrawl the red word *parallelism* or the correction symbol *//ism* on your paper.

English instructor Geoffrey Philp of Miami-Dade Community College speaks for many English instructors when he says, "One of the biggest problems I have with students is in parallelism."

Philp offers this example:

> He hopped, skipped, and jumped. (CORRECT)
>
> He hopped, skipped, and was jumping. (INCORRECT)

English instructor Santi Buscemi explains the problem, using the following sentence as an example:

> Many people get up early to jog along country lanes, to observe the wonder of nature, or just watching the sun come up. (INCORRECT)

In the telecourse program, Buscemi explains, "If the student was editing carefully, he or she would have looked at it and said, 'Oh, there's an infinitive – 'to jog.'

"What's next in the series? 'to observe' – another infinitive.

"But there's an 'ing' word (a gerund – that's a technical term for an 'ing' word.)"

As Buscemi points out, the student should realize that something is wrong. To solve the problem, Buscemi says, "It doesn't matter what type of construction is used, as long as you're consistent."

The sentence would be correct if all three verbs were gerunds (verbs that end with 'ing').

> Many people like jogging along country lanes, observing the wonders of nature, or just watching the sun come up.

The sentence would also be correct if all three verbs were infinitives – verb forms that start with the word *to*.

> Many people like to jog along country lanes, to observe the wonders of nature, or to watch the sun come up.

You don't have to know what gerunds and infinitives are to fix a problem like this. Commonsense editing can fix the problem if you use your ear and read the sentence out loud.

A final thought: Sentences that contain skillfully written parallel verb constructions *can* be used effectively to create a rhythm. Consider the following sentences:

> I learned to detect surface errors, I studied how to correct them, and I came to expect a good grade.

> I came; I saw; I conquered.

Misplaced modifiers and dangling modifiers
(Correction symbol: mod = correct the modification)
Another standard English instructor's complaint is the sentence with the misplaced modifier or dangling modifier. As Dave Barry (in his alternate persona, "Mr. Language Person") observes, this is not exclusively a problem with student essays.

Barry says he often finds misplaced modifiers in the newspapers that publish his columns. This includes sentences such as

> Walking down the street, the lady's hat blew off. (INCORRECT)

> Being in a dilapidated condition, I was able to sell the house cheap. (INCORRECT)

Santi Buscemi uses a famous quote from a Marx Brothers film as an example.

> Yesterday I shot an elephant in my pajamas. How he got in my pajamas, I'll never know.

Groucho Marx is using a dangling modifier to create a laugh. The sentence wouldn't be funny this way, but it would be correct:

> Yesterday, while I was in my pajamas, I shot an elephant. (CORRECT)

Instructor Donald Pharr points out that this type of sentence-structure error can become an embarrassment if the writing is not *intended* to be funny. Pharr uses this example:

> Snoring peacefully, Mr. Martin saw his son lying on the couch. (INCORRECT)

If Mr. Martin is snoring peacefully, he can't see, because he's asleep. Obviously, the son is snoring peacefully. The modifier has been misplaced. The correct sentence would be:

> Mr. Martin saw his son, snoring peacefully, lying on the couch. (CORRECT)

Comma splices and fused sentences
(Correction symbols: cs = comma splice; fs = fused sentence)

Perhaps the most frequent first-draft sentence-level errors are comma splices and fused sentences.

The fused sentence occurs when two sentences (or two independent clauses, each complete with a subject and verb) are jammed together without any punctuation at all.

The comma splice occurs when two sentences (or two independent clauses, each complete with a subject and verb) are jammed together with a comma.

Students who do not learn to detect and correct these common surface errors during the editing process will confuse the readers and annoy their instructors.

Examples:

> There were no other people around Jill played alone.
> (INCORRECT – FUSED SENTENCE)

> There were no other people around, Jill played alone.
> (INCORRECT – COMMA SPLICE)

Both of these sentences are punctuated incorrectly, and the meaning has been obscured.

Was Jill being shunned as she played by herself in a crowded room?

Or were there no people around, anywhere – so that Jill had to entertain herself to keep from being lonely?

A semicolon would fix the sentence, especially if the two ideas are meant to be connected:

> There were no other people around; Jill played alone.

Using a simple period to create two sentences will work just as well:

> There were no other people around. Jill played alone.

Sentence Fragments
(Correction symbol: frag = correct fragment)

The sentence fragment is a part of a sentence punctuated as if it were complete. As instructor Michael Bertsch explains in the telecourse, sentence fragments are usually caused by gaps of thought between your brain and your fingers. For example, a student might be thinking this sentence:

> Wearing my blue coat, I walked to the store.

An inexperienced writer might write:

> I walked to the store.

A sentence fragment is created when the less important thought is written as a discrete and separate phrase.

> Wearing my blue coat. (FRAGMENT)

Detection and correction of this problem are very simple. All sentences must contain at least one verb and one noun. If the phrase lacks either – and is punctuated as if it were a complete sentence – you have created a fragment. To fix the problem, either attach the phrase to the thought, or add the missing verb or noun.

Run-on sentences

(Correction symbol: ro = correct the run-on)

The run-on sentence is closely related to the sentence fragment. Both involve cramming too many ideas into one poorly punctuated sentence. Santi Buscemi defines the run-on sentence as, "two or more independent clauses without a conjunction or without correct punctuation."

Often, an inexperienced writer will attempt to string *many* more than two clauses inappropriately, with a confusing string of extraneous conjunctions, missing conjunctions, poorly placed commas, and other errors that create a rambling mess of ideas.

One solution is to simply break down the message to two or more sentences. The run-on is difficult for some students to notice, since they often talk in run-on sentences. Example:

> We, like, went to the mall I'm all, "There's a SALE at the GAP," but, there's like this cute guy, he's all, "Let's get some ice cream," so, you're not going to do ANYthing but get ice cream with a heckacool guy like that, so we're like going to miss the sale and I might as well get a doublescoop, unless you're like gunna spill it on your sweater, and then, OMYGAWD, its like, gottta go NOW to get a new sweater, because there's still a sale at the GAP, and I'm so SURE.

This example is only a slight exaggeration of the many run-on sentences that actually turn up in student papers.

The following example is from a paper turned in for a grade. Though this writer's paper had many good ideas, the reader would have had an easier time understanding them if the run-on sentence had been separated into individual thoughts.

Example:

> To be a hotshot, it not only takes a well-defined physically fit body you'd better have a good head about you because not only do you work with the other members but you also have to live with them for forty-five days at a time away from home.

The simple solution is to use several sentences to separate the ideas. A more elaborate solution is to connect ideas in a complex sentence with correct punctuation, using semicolons, conjunctions, and commas.

Summary

It is *not* a crime to have problems with comma splices. If your early drafts have sentences with nonparallel sentence constructions or misplaced modifiers, it does *not* mean you are stupid. You are *not* necessarily a bad writer if you compose a paper that has a run-on or a fused sentence.

You *are* expected, at the college level, to proofread for these errors.

In *A Community of Writers* (p. 162), Elbow and Belanoff note that, "Instruction in grammar cannot serve as a substitute for writing." They add, "Students should be required to submit final copies of their pieces that are free from errors in typing and usage. We believe in giving students some help in achieving this, but what's most important is making them realize that they have to find whatever help they need."

Most instructors feel students *can* catch the types of sentence problems identified in this unit by learning to recognize their patterns of error. This is important for building strong editing skills for future classes. Some students would benefit from working closely with an instructor or a tutor to develop strategies for detecting and correcting such problems. Often, colleges and universities have writing centers with tutors who can help with these skills.

Teresa Redd of Howard University notes, "Proofreading is abnormal reading. Good readers will chunk what they're reading; in other words, they read in phrases for meaning."

"A good tutor or a good teacher can also read over your paper without marking it and then hand it back to you and say, 'Look! I see a pattern of fragments in this essay. Let's work on that problem, and then you go back to your paper and you find those errors.

"It's really important to practice detection as well as correction. It's not enough for a teacher to circle an error, because then the student doesn't have any practice in finding that error."

Integrating the Text

The material in Mini-Workshop J, "Quotation and the Punctuation of Reported Speech," in *A Community of Writers* (pp. 494–496), is not covered in the telecourse program. However, some students have trouble with punctuating sentences with dialogue of sentences in research papers, where quoted materials are used extensively. Students who experience difficulty with these issues will benefit greatly from reviewing this portion of *A Community of Writers*.

The material covered in Mini-Workshop G, "The Sentence and End-Stop Punctuation" (pp. 481–485), is also essential in understanding how to communicate with effective sentences. Though many students understand these basic rules, those who have trouble remembering or applying basic punctuation marks should review this workshop.

Exercises

Check with your instructor for your formal assignments. You will be asked to do exercises from the *Telecourse Study Guide*.

Exploring editing sentences further

EXERCISE 1

Each of the following sentences features a problem with modifiers that are in the wrong place. Write a version that makes more sense.

Jimmy looked at the dog that he bought last Thursday carefully.

Walking down the street the lady's hat blew off.

Being in a dilapidated condition I was able to sell the house cheap.

I only feel like playing golf nine holes today.

After graduating from high school a job is the next step.

EXERCISE 2

Each of the following sentences features a problem with parallelism. Write a version that makes more sense.

He was good at running, jumping, and to shoot the free throw.

I wanted to study medicine, to save lives, and earning a good income.

He's learning golfing and to play tennis.

EXERCISE 3

Each of the following sentences is a comma splice, a fused sentence, or a fragment. Identify the problem and write a version that makes more sense.

I ordered eggs she ordered a hamburger.

The Democrats won the election, taxes went up.

The Republicans won the election. Raising taxes.

The Green Party won the election General Motors moved to Mexico.

I drank five cups of coffee, later I typed an entire paper. Feeling the buzz.

Exercise just for fun

Try to put a verb and a noun together without forming a sentence. Try this exercise with any random verb and noun. Make absurd combinations. (They will still be sentences.) After playing around with this exercise, ask yourself, "What causes a sentence fragment? Why would any student in his or her right mind try to write a sentence without a verb or a noun?

Revision exercise

Editing is not revision. After you proofread a paper for sentence structure problems, look at it one more time. Read your thesis out loud, and judge the strength of the sentence, not just grammatically but for the clarity of thought that this sentence represents. Many instructors consider this the most important sentence of your paper. Consider: Is your thesis, by itself (without the rest of the paper), as strong as it possibly can be?

Quick writing exercise

Your instructor may ask you to do a quick focused freewrite about editing sentence structures. Those of you who are taking the course through a distance-learning system may be encouraged to share your thoughts in a discussion thread or to post your ideas on an Internet bulletin board. If you are writing your thoughts out by hand in a process journal, you might use these questions to come up with ideas. This is a freewriting exercise that will not be graded. You can use any of the following questions to stimulate your thoughts about editing sentences:

What techniques have you used to proofread your papers in the past? As you progress to upper-division classes, how do you expect your proofreading techniques will change? What do you think of instructors in other disciplines – sciences, humanities, business, engineering – who still take off points on a paper for grammar errors, even if the course content does not include the study of writing? Is this an aspect of your writing that you prefer not to think about? If so, why?

Exercises related to *A Community of Writers*

A Community of Writers emphasizes punctuation in the workshops about editing sentences. These exercises are complementary to the *Telecourse Study Guide* exercises in this chapter, since they emphasize other aspects of sentence construction.

Mini-Workshop G, "The Sentence and End-Stop Punctuation," concludes with an exercise for students who need extra practice with marking sentence endings in writing (p. 485).

Mini-Workshop J, "Quotation and the Punctuation of Reported Speech" contains exercises especially helpful for students who are having trouble with punctuation of quoted materials in research papers (p. 496).

Additional reading

Several student essays are featured in the appendix. They reflect different levels of writing ability, and they have been published in early draft form without final editing. How would you help Gregory Andrus, Corie Cushnie, Ethlyn Manning, and Francine Taylor, if they were in your own class and they were asking for help in spotting sentence-structure problems?

Quick Review

1. Which sentence does *not* have a misplaced modifier?
   a. Before changing into my hospital gown, the nurse took my temperature.
   b. Before I changed into my hospital gown, the nurse took my temperature.
   c. Walking down the street, the lady's hat blew off.
   d. None of the above.
   e. All of the above.

2. Which sentence has the problem of nonparallel construction?
   a. She enjoys hunting, fishing ,and to cook the results.
   b. She enjoys hunting, fishing, and cooking the results.
   c. She enjoys to hunt, to fish, and to cook the results.
   d. None of the above.
   e. All of the above.

3. Which sentence is punctuated correctly?
   a. We traveled to New Orleans I gained seven pounds.
   b. We traveled to New Orleans, I gained seven pounds.
   c. We traveled to New Orleans; I gained seven pounds.
   d. None of the above.
   e. All of the above.

4. Which of the sentences is punctuated correctly?
   a. I had gumbo and pecan pie but my wife liked the shellfish and I was also intrigued by the local music scene.
   b. I had gumbo and pecan pie; my wife liked the shellfish. I was also intrigued by the local music scene.
   c. I had gumbo and pecan pie, my wife liked the shellfish. I was also intrigued by the local music scene.
   d. All of the above.
   e. None of the above.

5. Which of the sentences has correct punctuation and grammar?
   a. The volcano erupted, tourists fled for their hotels.
   b. Belching blue smoke, I was barely able to drive the car to the muffler shop.
   c. We went to the island to swim, to get sun, and for some relaxing.
   d. None of the above.
   e. All of the above.

"It's very important as a researcher to learn both the pros and cons of your own opinion: the one you walked in with at the public library. And very often you are converted to whatever it is you didn't believe in when you went in there. That's part of the process and the beauty of research and the beauty of writing. The moment you open that door to see what other people are thinking and believing and feeling ... if you're willing to walk in other people's moccasins, then you have opened the door for your own instruction and growth."

HIMILCE NOVAS, historian and novelist

Introduction to the Topic

An English composition course is supposed to teach you how to string words together. It is not supposed to teach you how to think. Right?

If you accepted the opening statement of this chapter, simply because it is in a text-book, perhaps you are not thinking critically. If the statement gave you pause – and you took a few moments to consider its authenticity – perhaps you are *already* a critical thinker.

Some would say it is nearly impossible to separate thinking from writing. The argument goes like this: We write to learn; we discover as we write.

As we write, we read, research, and originate new ideas. We confront our personal assumptions and convictions; we challenge the unproved theories of others.

Along the way, we learn the compositional skills of thesis and support; we learn how to spot logical fallacies; we learn to judge the credibility of sources; we learn how to balance logical appeal with ethical and emotional arguments.

And we learn that critical thinking is part of *life* – not just an abstract concept taught in a college course.

Perhaps we should modify that opening statement.

How does this sound?

A writing course is supposed to teach you how to string words together. It is not supposed to teach you *what* to think.

Learning Objectives

After viewing the television program and finishing the exercises in this instructional unit, you will develop a sense of what educators mean when they use the term *critical thinking*. You will develop your own definition of critical thinking, and you will prepare to practice critical thinking during the rest of this course, throughout your academic career, and in the world beyond college. This will include an awareness of how to read critically, when to question authority, when to challenge your own assumptions, why some forms of reasoning are false, and how to evaluate evidence.

The learning objectives work well with the many critical thinking exercises included in *A Community of Writers*, "especially the section "Analyzing an Argument" (pp. 278–283). One goal of this section, in Workshop 11, "Argument" (pp. 277–30l), is to get students to critically consider counter arguments or attacks that could be made against each reason, support, or assumption.

Before Viewing

Before formally studying the concept, think about the times you have heard the phrase *critical thinking*. Mull over what the term meant to those who used it. Imagine what your own definition of the term *critical thinking* might be, before reading this *Telecourse Study Guide* chapter and before hearing what the guests in the telecourse program tell you what the phrase is *supposed* to mean – in *their* view.

While Viewing

Listen to the various definitions of the term *critical thinking* offered by instructors, writers, and students. Judge for yourself the interpretations that ring true – as well as those that might seem off-base. Pay close attention to the views on critical thinking expressed by English composition instructor Mike Rose and by speech and debate instructor Robb Lightfoot. Notice how the ancient notion of "logical fallacies" connects with the concept of critical thinking.

After Viewing

Using the exercises in this *Telecourse Study Guide*, develop your own definition of *critical thinking*. Evaluate your own attitude about critical thinking by answering these questions: Do you keep your mind open to other points of view? Are you inflexible in your world view, or are you easily swayed from your original opinion? If you are *likely* to change your mind in an argument, what types of evidence or emotions can change your thinking? If you *almost never* change your mind in a debate, is it because your convictions are inflexible or because the other side has failed to persuade you? Become aware of your critical thinking process, and consider how you might carry your awareness of critical thinking to writing challenges beyond this course.

Viewing Guide

The concept of critical thinking is as important to understand as it is difficult to define. Most of us think critically, every day of our lives. We just need to recognize, refine, and *improve* our critical thinking skills, both for success in our academic pursuits and for life beyond the classroom.

Mike Rose of UCLA puts it this way: "Think about how many times in the day each and all of us have to make some kind of decision, sometimes in a split second. How many times a day we say one thing rather than another. We stop ourselves from using one kind of language rather than another. We go down one street rather than another. We ask this person rather than that person. Each and every one of those moments calls for a split-second decision ... some kind of critical thought, some kind of reflection. All of us are thinking critically all the time."

Ask Pat Belanoff, coauthor of *A Community of Writers*, and you'll get a completely different take on the subject. Critical thinking; that's a real buzword," she says. "Critical thinking for me is the white spaces on the page. When I come to a period, that's where I critically think. How did that writer get from this sentence to that sentence? That's why punctuation is important; it's a matter of stopping at the comma and simply saying to myself, 'How did that person get from this word to this word?' For me, not allowing myself to be passive [as a reader] is critical thinking."

Chitra Divakaruni of Foothill College sees the ability to organize ideas as the main application of critical thinking in academic work: "I think critical thinking is when you look at the information available to you – whether it's written or whether it comes to you in verbal form – and you can see past a group of disconnected events or a group of disconnected facts. You see the connections. You begin to see how things fit together. And you begin to see inner meanings."

While these ideas are related, the definitions of *critical thinking* proposed by Rose and Divakaruni are quite different. As you watch this telecourse program, you will realize that the phrase *critical thinking* means something different to each person interviewed. The ideas expressed by our diverse group of instructors, writers, and students will give you a broad overview of the many uses of the term – in a definition format similar to the "collaborative collage" that we studied in Chapter 16.

That definition starts with an assumption agreed upon by all of those interviewed: Reading and writing are part of the discovery process. We write not merely to get a paper done but to *think* and learn!

Critical reading

History instructor Charles Turner represents the views of instructors from many disciplines across any campus when he laments: "They [students] haven't been taught to read critically, and I have to explain to students what that means. They read passively."

Psychologist and instructor Pat Patterson suggests that some students don't really read – they just do eye exercises. "When they get to the end of a chapter, someone will say, 'What did you read?' and they'll say, 'I don't know.' And that's because it just went through their eyes and not into their heads."

The solution to this problem, according to many instructors, is to find a way to actively engage with the text. That can mean doubting and even "arguing" with the author by writing notes in the margins of the book or in a journal as you read.

Ariel Gonzalez of Miami-Dade Community College suggests, "You cannot teach critical thinking without close reading. Students are taught to speed-read. I really emphasize and force them to read with a pen in their hands – to underline, to take notes, to make notes on the margins, to really just go through the text line by line, and then underline any key word that may have meaning within it."

Pat Belanoff emphasizes that an important part of the critical thinking process is making meaning from the words on the page. The active reader is an equal participant in this communication model; it is *not* a process like a photocopy, where the brain just soaks up the exact information on the page: "Too often, students think of reading as if their brain is like a template – that what they want to do is just ingest the printed page in front of them. In fact, the page is only a blueprint. We know that our eyes translate – so when those little neurons fire into our brain, we *construct* the meaning that's on the page."

A significant part of that critical reading process, therefore, is questioning or challenging what is on the page – not just accepting the words because they have been published.

Pat Belanoff emphasizes that an important part of the critical thinking process is making meaning from the words on the page. The active reader is an equal participant in this communication model; it is *not* a process like a photocopy, where the brain just soaks up the exact information on the page: "Too often, students think of reading as if their brain is like a template – that what they want to do is just ingest the printed page in front of them. In fact, the page is only a blueprint. We know that our eyes translate – so when those little neurons fire into our brain, we *construct* the meaning that's on the page."

A significant part of that critical reading process, therefore, is questioning or challenging what is on the page – not just accepting the words because they have been published.

Challenging personal assumptions

Instructors such as Turner, Gonzalez, and Patterson suggest students need to question texts as they read. In the composing process, critical thinking also requires you to challenge your *own* beliefs. Oftentimes, that means starting out with an idea or a gut feeling (in academic terms: a working thesis) and being willing to modify your initial assumptions as you read, research, and gather more information.

Ecologist John Merz works as an environmental advocate for rivers and wildlife. His job involves arguing legal issues in the courts and in the legislature. Merz knows that he still must constantly reassess his own beliefs, attempting to keep an open mind, no matter how committed he is to the cause. "It's not just *'Are they are wrong?'* It's, *'Am I wrong?'* It's an educational process," he says.

Scientists usually incorporate this aspect of critical thinking in their work as a matter of course. The essence of the scientific method revolves around questioning your own thesis (or hypothesis) as you look for results that prove or disprove a theory. Marty Wallace, a graduate student in chemistry, adds that it is not necessarily a disappointment when the scientist's experiments show a hypothesis to be false.

In his composition classes, Wallace remembers being instructed to "write the thesis and then support it afterwards."

"It's not quite that way in chemistry," he says. "There's plenty of ideas that you chase that turn out to be bad leads. But that's OK, because that work has to be done some time too. So there's nothing wrong with publishing it and saying, 'Well, it's not this. So we won't waste any more time pursuing that.'"

Many composition instructors urge students to have more of a scientific approach, as Wallace describes. They suggest starting out with a working thesis that can evolve or change direction as the student thinks critically about the *evidence* that emerges through the research.

Historian and writer Himilce Novas supports this approach, adding that it is not necessarily a bad thing to find research that contradicts your original thesis.

"If I find something that debunks or opposes my original belief, it may even help me with my original belief," Novas says. "Because you always have to know what your enemies think, in order to make a better case. In a sense, as a writer, you're a lawyer too. You're pleading your case. So you've got to know what the opposition has in their pockets. By knowing what they think, then you can oppose it, attack it, and look at the issues."

Questioning the norm

The critical thinking process might require you to doubt conventional wisdom or defy authority. In school, that process starts with reading critically – and understanding that not everything in print, even in textbooks, is necessarily true. The process continues with learning how to critically "read life," carefully examining and confronting the attitudes and opinions that swirl around us.

Charles Turner, like many good college instructors, is concerned that students learn to question what they read – in textbooks, in the newspapers, or on the Internet. "That's another transition that my students have to make in college," Turner says. "Knowing not everything that they read in print is accurate and not everything in print is correct – and that their *challenge* of that material is a worthy challenge. That's what academicians do. It's a difficult one for some students. They're not accustomed to that kind of academic environment, but it's necessary. It's necessary for their own growth and for them to become scholars."

Robb Lightfoot, an instructor who specializes in teaching speech, debate, and other critical thinking courses at Shasta College, urges students to be wary of the types of evidence they bring into research projects – especially if the evidence comes from an online source.

"When a student comes to me and says, 'I found it in the library' – my common response is, 'Well, was it in the stacks or was it written on the wall of the restroom? Where did you find this?' They might say, 'I don't know. I found it on the Internet.' Well, there's all kinds of stuff on the Internet. Where did this stuff come from? There are lots of Web pages put together by people who have an agenda."

In *A Community of Writers*, Elbow and Belanoff also urge students to challenge the accuracy and validity of material they gather through research, especially through the Internet. In the section, "Evaluating Online Sources," in Mini-Workshop F, "Doing Research on the Web," (pp. 472–475), they recommend asking the following questions about each site that you visit:

- Is the source authoritative?

- How impartial is the source?

- Is the source presented in a professional manner?

- Is the source useful?

The same criteria, of course, can be applied to printed materials.

Evidence

A first step into critical thinking is learning how to consider the validity of an *argument*. This process starts with the abilities to distinguish between strong and weak evidence, between a fact and an opinion and between a truth and a falsehood.

As Geoffrey Philp of Miami-Dade Community College suggests, judging an argument also means separating out the various uses of logical, ethical, and emotional appeals: "If you become too emotional, then you're becoming like a con man. Any con man can con you out of anything, because the argument is based solely on the emotional situation."

While most instructors emphasize the balance of emotional, ethical, and logical appeal in persuasive writing, the critical analysis of an argument or a persuasive piece will deemphasize the emotion and carefully scrutinize the logic.

"Emotions are a part of argument and they're a legitimate part of an argument," says debate and speech instructor Robb Lightfoot of Shasta College. "But they can't overshadow the fact that you must have some substance – which is evidence. I council students to realize that Aristotle talked about the credibility of the speaker, the emotions of the audience, and the actual substance of speech. And those are still the things we look for. Thousands of years haven't dulled that truth."

In many academic contexts (including formal academic research papers), students are *expected* to avoid first-person statements such as "I feel" and "I believe." Instead, they are encouraged to *state* their opinions as a truth and then to prove the statement (also called a thesis) with evidence. This is usually done in an objective, third-person voice.

Ariel Gonzalez has a view about academic argument that might sound harsh at first – but it is actually similar to the view held by many upper-division instructors: "I tell students that there's one thing that I guarantee will lower their grade: if they ever begin a sentence with 'in my opinion.' That's when the critical thinking comes in. Because critical thinking requires them to go through the text – whether it's a film, a story, poem, novel – and they have to now find the *evidence*. And not only must they find the evidence, they must analyze the evidence."

John Lovas of De Anza College continues this thread of thought, saying, "This critical discrimination between what supports your idea and what doesn't – the techniques for doing that – they are essentially what's involved in critical thinking."

There are two important aspects of critical thinking, says Lovas: "Learning how to decide the difference between good and bad information, and knowing some basic skills of logic."

Logical fallacies

The basic skills of logic include learning how to identify propaganda, innuendo, and other forms of faulty reasoning. The formal study of reasoning is so important that entire critical thinking courses are built around the study of logic. An English composition course usually only introduces the subject.

Starting with the ancient Greeks, who categorized types of bad logic, academics have identified and separated "logical fallacies" into distinct categories.

Sometimes a logical fallacy simply represents lazy or incoherent writing. However, fallacies are often used intentionally, to seduce and persuade the listener or reader. If the audience being persuaded is passive and not likely to use critical thinking skills, it is quite probable that the fallacy will be accepted without question.

As part of your own analysis of critical thinking strategies, carefully read the following statements by conservative spokesperson Rush Limbaugh and liberal comic Al Franken. Then consider instructor Robb Lightfoot's discussion of the classic logical fallacies. Can you connect any of his observations to these examples?

LIMBAUGH:

I do not regard myself as a name caller. What I do is construct labels for people that I think aptly describe their views. I've used the term *femi-nazi* – it's been the most distorted term I've ever come up with. There are about twelve femi-nazis. And a femi-nazi is simply a woman, a feminist, to whom the most important thing in the world is an abortion. Every abortion possible must happen. There aren't very many of them, but those women do exist. And femi-nazi, I think, is an adequate description of what they're attempting to accomplish and what they're attempting to do. My other labels (or name calling that I'm accused of engaging in) is not about people's personal characteristics. You can call me fat all you want – calling me fat will not clue anybody in as to anything meaningful about me. All the labels that I've come up with attempt to hit the nail on the head as descriptions of people's views. As simply another means of communicating using as few words as possible. If all you've got is thirty seconds and you've got to resort to calling me a name that has nothing to do with anything relevant, then you're smoked. But see, I'm a big boy, this is the arena of ideas, and I just think that the Franken book [*Rush Limbaugh Is a Big Fat Idiot*] and all similar things like it are only the result of my effectiveness – and the desire on the part of Franken and others to discredit me, because I'm effective.

AL FRANKEN counters:

A logical argument to prove that Rush is a hypocrite is to take his draft status. First of all, he says "Never trust a draft dodger." He always calls Clinton "the draft dodger." Then you say, "Where were you [during Vietnam] – in the rice paddies?" And then you discover that he's said different things that contradict each other. And that's always fun to show.... The thesis (of my book) seems to be stated in the title, *Rush Limbaugh Is a Big Fat Idiot*. However, in discussing it – he's really a big fat hypocrite and liar. But I thought that would be too confrontational to call it, *Rush Limbaugh Is a Big Fat Lying Hypocrite*. So I just say big fat idiot. And I pretty much prove the lying hypocrite part; he's not an idiot, but he says a lot of idiotic things.

In his analysis of these two statements, Robb Lightfoot notes that they both are riddled with the fallacy of ad hominem, or attacking the person instead of the issue. "There is an element to them where you can be out-raged – or you can just think they're great sport. And the people – whether it's Rush Limbaugh or Al Franken – are doing it and kind of winking at you. We all know this is not really being taken seriously. That's one thing. But if it's creeping in, and it's a part of getting us [the listener or the reader] to ignore the fact that often they're not really attacking what's being said – in other words, they're just harassing the person – then it's a problem."

Though this program is too short to list all of the categories of logical fal-lacies, Lightfoot identifies two other common ones – using both their pop-ular names and Latin names.

JUMPING ON THE BANDWAGON

"Most of these things have Latin names because the Romans were the ones who catalogued these things by the scores," Lightfoot explains. "The *ad populum* fallacy is: Everybody believes this (I should too). We've all done it. But it doesn't change the fact that just because a whole bunch of people believe something, they can be wrong."

FALSE CAUSE

The fallacy of false cause – or in Latin, the post hoc fallacy – is faulty rea-soning based on the following assumption: If one event precedes another, the second event is caused by the first. For example, you might hear some-one say that there was a full moon before the last big earthquake and jump to a conclusion that earthquakes always come after a full moon.

Lightfoot warns that it is more important to use common sense to spot the bad reasoning than it is to know all the fancy names. "For someone to say to you, 'Oh, well, that's the fallacy of post hoc' – that's not going mean anything," he says. "You may not know the Latin name of the fallacy, but you'll eventually be able to figure out you've been had if you buy the argu-ment at first and see the holes in it after careful scrutiny."

Synthesis and analysis

Ultimately, the study of composition is designed to teach the student the process of synthesis and analysis. In a research paper, that means con-suming and digesting a pile of information, ideas, statements, and assump-tions – and learning how to come to your own conclusion. Clearly, this is also a form of critical thinking.

Veterinarian Jim Esh uses this type of critical thinking when he writes articles for scholarly journals about animal health care. He explains the thought process, saying, "Before you ever put a word on paper, you've read everything you can on the topic. There is rarely a general consensus of opin-ion, where everybody agrees. So you've read and you've analyzed and said, 'OK, this is the part of it that makes sense to me. And these five people ... these papers that I'm summarizing are the ones that I really think have the kernel of truth that applies to my paper.' You are attributing things to other people, but there's also a whole process of *analysis*."

The college student is expected to use critical thinking in the same way, starting with short essays and culminating with longer research papers. Mark Reynolds of Jefferson Davis Community College tells his students, "Initial research is always a walk in the dark; you sort of have to have faith that if you keep walking, or keep reading and keep taking notes, keep summarizing the sources, then things will become clear. And that's the way they [students] *own* their material. They own it through actually filtering it through their own brains. And letting it come out of their pens, and out their fingers as they type it on the computer. The ideas then become theirs. It's an excellent way to teach the old concepts of synthesis and analysis in terms of synthesizing the notes, and analyzing the ideas of others."

In other words, Reynolds says, you know when you are thinking critically when you can truly say, "These ideas – though backed with evidence from the writing and thinking of others – are now my own."

Summary

Since each instructor, writer, and student in this program expresses a slightly different take on what the phrase *critical thinking* means, it would be unfair and counterproductive to ask you to regurgitate a quick definition on an exam.

We won't do that. However, we might suggest that you start to create your own understanding of the phrase, beginning with the ideas expressed in this telecourse. That definition is likely to combine an understanding of the concept of synthesis and analysis – along with the willingness to question authority and challenge your own assumptions.

You might include an awareness of logical fallacies and what it means to *read* critically. And you will certainly mix in your own ideas. Ultimately, the very nature of critical thinking requires active participation in the definition – not passive acceptance.

Integrating the text

In the introduction to Workshop 11, "Argument" (pp. 277–301), Elbow and Belanoff distinguish between emotionally based persuasion and carefully reasoned argument, pointing out that it takes thinking critically to evaluate your own response. "Feelings often influence us more than careful reasoning," they say (p. 278). "For that reason, we need careful argument as an antidote. Experience and feelings can fool us."

The goal of Workshop 11 is to "help you see through any essay to the skeleton of the reasoning at its heart, in order to better evaluate the arguments of others and to construct better arguments of your own" (p. 277).

A secondary goal is to "become more sophisticated about the nature of arguments, to become more critical as you read and listen to arguments."

In the section Analyzing an Argument (pp. 278–283), Elbow and Belanoff start with the assumption that instead of a simplistic series of critical thinking "rules," students should draw heavily on common sense and tacit knowledge to analyze an argument.

Elbow and Belanoff's approach is to first get you to analyze the reasoning behind someone else's work. You might be too close to your own argument, as you are writing it, to put it through a rigorous critical evaluation for effectiveness. As you learn how to analyze another's work, you may be able to stand back from your own work to objectively apply these principles to your own writing.

Workshop 11 is built in two stages:

You are asked to break down an argument into several parts: the claim, the reasons, the support, the assumptions, and the implications about the audience.

You are asked to assess the effectiveness of the argument, to evaluate the reasons, evidence, and assumptions.

The emphasis of this study is on seeing the elements. Elbow and Belanoff state that, "Evaluating an argument is usually a matter of unending dispute, whereas seeing it clearly is something you can manage. You often get agreement among readers about what a reason is and what supports that reason, even though they can't agree on how persuasive the reason is."

When considering an argument's main claim, Elbow and Belanoff suggest you look to see if the claim is ambiguous, or if it "slips" or shifts from the beginning of the paper to the conclusion, where it is restated.

This is often a time to consider some of the logical fallacies introduced in the telecourse program; if the main claim is an example of jumping the bandwagon, name calling or a straw man fallacy to begin with, you know the rest of the essay is going to have problems.

Elbow and Belanoff suggest you read through the essay and summarize each "reason" that supports the main claim in a simple short sentence. In essence, you are being asked to create a skeleton outline that will reflect the bare bones structure of thesis and topic sentences. In evaluating these reasons, you may again consider the logical fallacies.

Elbow and Belanoff also ask you to look at and evaluate the support for each reason or topic sentence. How reputable are the sources for the evidence, examples, quotes, and statistics used to back the claims? If the evidence comes from a shaky source (nobody knows who built the Web site? A magazine with a clear editorial prejudice?), why does the writer assume the evidence creates a sound argument?

Elbow and Belanoff ask you to consider assumptions, with this warning: "Assumptions are often slippery and insidious, because the writer gets them into the reader's head without saying them." One way to identify (and evaluate) assumptions is to ask the two questions: What did the writer take for granted? Will the readers agree, up front, to take the same things for granted – or is the manipulation of assumptions part of the persuasive process?

This brings us to Elbow and Belanoff's final recommendations for evaluating an argument: Consider what kind of person is making the argument, and consider the implied audience. Is the writer adversarial, or is he or she preaching to the choir? Evaluate the writer's tone, attitude, and voice as it is directed to the audience.

In wrapping up this section, Elbow and Belanoff discuss the process of evaluating and assessing each stage of the argument that you have identified. They encourage you to consider counterevidence, counterarguments, and attacks that could be made against each bit of evidence and each assumption, claim, or reason.

This is, of course, the essence of academic debate and critical thinking. Your goal, after all, is not to be adversarial purely for the sake of being argumentative – but, through mutual inquiry, to move all parties in the discussion as close to common ground as possible.

In fact, Elbow and Belanoff end Workshop 11 with an essay that inspires critical thinking about the very act of an argument essay. In "Exploring Theory: Nonadversarial Argument, Reasoning and Grammar" (pp. 287–291), they suggest that most traditional argument/persuasion essays that "construct a thesis, state it forcefully, line up evidence to prove the thesis is correct; prove that contrary opinions are wrong" create a false model of right/wrong, good/evil stances that are "exercises in wasted energy and tend to become mere displays of the ability to follow a prescribed form."

Exercises

Check with your instructor for your formal assignments. You will be asked to do exercises from the *Telecourse Study Guide*.

Exploring critical thinking further
Exercise 1

Listen to one installment of Rush Limbaugh's show. (Any similar political radio talk show will do. We chose the Limbaugh show as an example because, as we were writing this book, the Internet had so many Web sites debating the logic of each day's program.) After listening to the show, you can easily find at least two or three sites on the Internet dedicated to counterarguments of his assertions for that day. (Sometimes, these "Flush Rush" counterarguments are up on the Internet Web sites less than an hour after broadcast.)

As you assess the credibility of arguments and thinking on each side,

look for lapses into name calling, jumping on the bandwagon, hasty gener-
alizations, false dilemma, anonymous authorities, false analogies, statistical
fallacies, and other logical fallacies. Note which side uses facts to back up
the arguments – and judge how credible the "sources" for these facts are.
Note which side uses emotional issues to persuade, rather than logical argument. Consider the balance of both sides, in their presentations of logical,
ethical, and emotional arguments.

EXERCISE 2
For this assignment you need to find some writing that has been created
with the definite purpose of advocating a certain viewpoint. (The more
extreme, the better.) Examples of this type of writing may be handed to you
daily by strangers as you walk across your campus to class. The Internet is
also a good place to find this kind of writing. Once you've found such a
piece of writing, your assignment is to think on your own and identify the
faults in the author's logic. Make a list of the faults you find, and write an
explanation for each.

Exercise just for fun
Try to find a textbook, a book in the library, or an Internet site that lists log-
ical fallacies, with both Latin names and common English descriptions.
   After identifying the names and meanings of these fallacies, make a list
of how many you hear used in a given day, during conversation, on the
Internet, on television – or by one of your instructors in a lecture.
   Here are just a few common names you should be aware of:

COMMON LOGICAL FALLACIES

False dilemma	Attacking the person
Slippery slope	Statistical fallacies
Appeal to authority	Straw man
Anonymous authority	Begging the question
False analogy	

Exercise related to A Community of Writers
In Workshop 16, "Autobiography and Portfolio," Elbow and Belanoff state
the following premise:

> Examining one's writings and the processes that went into composing
> them is a valuable learning process that can lead to improved writing and
> thinking.

   The following reading and writing exercise is aimed at helping you reach
the goal stated in that premise. Carefully read the main assignment for

Workshop 16 in *A Community of Writers* (pp. 417–427). Read Jean Shepherd's "From a Case Study of Myself as a Writer" (pp. 438–439) or any of the other "Case Studies" or "Autobiographies of Myself." That might appeal to you more in this section of the book. (There are several different styles, including a poem and an e-mail to a friend.)

Quick writing exercise

Throughout the course, you may have been asked to keep a process journal or to do a series of quick writing exercises. Some of you may have been asked to post focused freewriting responses to Internet bulletin boards or discussion threads. As explained in the first week of the course, those quick exercises were designed to help you build up to a longer document.

Look at the entries you have accumulated throughout the semester while responding to the Quick Writing exercises. The entire collection of brief, individual freewriting entries will add up to a substantial draft of an essay about your experiences as a writer.

Some students use the following approach: Copy and paste all of the responses into one long word-processing document. Look for themes, central ideas, or potential topic sentences. Create a skeleton outline. Arrange your paragraphs to roughly conform to the outline by cutting and pasting the entries so they will approximate the shape of the outline. Add new insights and fashion transition passages, so each section moves smoothly into the next. Massage the copy and revise the document so it has flow and coherence. Proofread and edit so that you have eliminated grammar, punctuation, and spelling problems.

Notice that the approach described above is parallel to the process of composition studied throughout this course: invent, draft, revise, and edit.

As you finish this document, consider Chitra Divakaruni's statement in the telecourse program: "Critical thinking is when you look at the information available, and you can see past a group of disconnected events or a group of disconnected facts. You see the connections and you begin to see how things fit together."

Additional reading

The excerpt in the appendix from *Everything You Need to Know About Latino History*, by Himilce Novas, contains several statements that could be considered persuasive or even controversial. As a critical thinker, how did you react to this short passage as you read it?

Why is critical thinking necessary for composing a process analysis essay, like the article by Steve Shanesy, editor of *Popular Woodworking*, that is featured in the appendix?

In the telecourse program, instructor Lynn Troyka makes a point that critical thinking is not a concept unique to academic circles. Though most of us would not consider the thought process of sports fans very "scholarly," Troyka maintains that they often make use of critical thinking. Given this assertion, can you spot elements of critical thinking in the essay, featured in the appendix, by Bill Walsh?

How is the critical thinking practiced by the sports fans and professionals different from or similar to the academic pieces by students Francine Taylor and Corie Cushnie, also featured in the appendix?

How would a student who practices critical thinking react to the politically oriented essays in the appendix by Kalle Lasn and Rush Limbaugh?

Quick Review

1. In academia, critical thinking is important in:
   a. the reading process
   b. the process of forming a thesis
   c. the research process
   d. all of the above
   e. none of the above

2. The following is a recognized logical fallacy in academia:
   a. the post-hole fallacy
   b. jumping on the bandwagon
   c. the fallacy of the ex-wife
   d. all of the above
   e. none of the above

3. When evaluating strong evidence, instructors quoted in this chapter said:
   a. They prefer strong statements that start with "In my opinion."
   b. Very emotional statements.
   c. Logical, fact-based arguments.
   d. All of the above.
   e. None of the above.

4. The recommended way to approach a thesis is
   a. Stick to your guns, and pull every trick you can to prove the thesis.
   b. To always change your thesis, if you find any evidence that questions your original ideas.
   c. Start with a working thesis that might evolve as you learn more.
   d. All of the above.
   e. None of the above.

5. Synthesis and analysis involve
   a. a discussion of chemical reactions in a laboratory and have nothing to do with English composition
   b. mentally digesting and blending ideas gathered from research and reading with your own ideas
   c. refusal to change your thesis
   d. all of the above
   e. none of the above

"It's so essential for students to realize that proofreading is abnormal reading. Good readers will chunk what they're reading; in other words, they read in phrases for meaning. But when you proofread, you have to pay attention to words – even to letters – watch for that *s* ending on the verb. That *s* could make the difference in terms of subject-verb agreement. And a subject-verb agreement error could be extremely stigmatizing."

TERESA REDD, Howard University

Introduction to the Topic

Excellent writers consider word usage at all points – during the brainstorming, while drafting, and, certainly, at the proofreading stage.

Incorrect vocabulary choices and bad spelling discombobulate the meaning. Bland phrasing bores the reader. Luxurious lingo can lapse into a jargon overdose of puffy prose.

In the final stages of composition, the student writer must become part dictionary, part thesaurus, part critic, and part savant. You must learn how to read your own work dispassionately, as if you were an instructor wielding a red pen – or a target-audience member with droopy eyelids, ready to nod off if the words don't inspire.

This telecourse unit chapter will introduce you to word usage decisions. Those decisions range from strategies for spotting and correcting word usage errors to suggestions for improving word choices that are technically correct but literally uninspiring.

Entire books have been written about this subject. Do not get discouraged if you haven't mastered word usage by the end of this course. You will have at least made significant progress.

There are many shades of "correctness" in this area of language use, and no one writer or instructor knows all the correct answers. It would be absurd to expect students to fare any better.

It is realistic to expect, however, that students will become inspired to think carefully about, and perhaps even start to *enjoy*, the process of using and selecting words.

Learning Objectives

In this chapter, you will learn proofreading strategies to identify and correct the most common word usage errors. You will develop strategies for detecting and correcting problems with pronouns and for identifying and fixing subject-verb disagreements. You will also learn the difference between active and passive voice and how to improve sentences that have passive verbs. Finally, you will examine how to make a bland but "technically correct" word choice more interesting with careful and appropriate selection of verbs, nouns, adjectives, and adverbs.

Before Viewing

Determine whether you have had a recurring pattern of word usage errors that instructors have detected – or that peers have detected. Many of the topics you will study in this program, including subject-verb disagreement, pronoun-antecedent disagreement, and passive voice, may sound familiar.

While Viewing

Draw a single line down the middle of a couple of pages in a notebook – creating two columns. In the first column, list the types of word usage problems that are explained in the program. In the second column, list techniques you can use when editing a paper that has word usage problems.

After Viewing

Create a personal editing checklist that features the word usage errors you commonly make in the early draft of a paper. Use this checklist the next time you proofread an important assignment. Using the exercises in this *Telecourse Study Guide* chapter, practice detecting and correcting errors in word usage.

Viewing Guide

In the telecourse, novelist and former English teacher David Guterson (author of *Snow Falling on Cedars*) explains that the professional writer's entire day is spent considering word choice.

"I have nothing else to work with except words," Guterson says. "Without them, the page is blank. So I have to use them carefully and use them well and get as much work done as I can with each word."

Though it is unrealistic to expect you, as an English composition student, to spend your entire day with such matters, we hope you will be inspired to spend a fraction of the time thinking about the lessons covered in this unit. If you do, you will fare better in a number of areas – from the marks you get in a grade book to the effectiveness of your communication on the printed page in *any* writing situation.

Subject-verb disagreements

(Correction symbols: vb = use correct verb form; agr = correct agreement problem)
In the telecourse, writer and English instructor Geoffrey Philp suggests that a poorly edited essay makes a first impression on an instructor, much like a rude young man on a first date might make a bad impression on his girlfriend's father.

A professor won't give you much more of a chance, Philp says, if your essay starts with a sentence that contains an obvious subject-verb disagreement – in other words, a sentence in which both the subject and verb are not singular, or in which both the subject and verb are not plural.

He is. They are. (CORRECT)

He are. They is. (INCORRECT)

Your paper may be filled with original ideas, but if you start an essay with such an obvious error, the instructor will now be thinking, "How many more mistakes are you going to make?" The natural inclination is to start correcting for mistakes, instead of seeing what the student has to *say*.

Author and humorist Dave Barry jokes, "Subjects and verbs often disagree, and it's why you should put them as far apart as you can in a sentence. You have many buffer words in there to keep the subject and verb from coming to blows – you can just put the words *buffer buffer buffer buffer* right in there. And now you can say, 'Three boys *buffer buffer buffer buffer* is walking down the street.' No one will notice there that the subject [boys] and verb [is] really don't get along at all."

Barry's intent, of course, is to make fun of the problem. However, there's a bit of wisdom hidden within the joke. The distance between the subject and verb is usually the cause of subject-verb disagreement. Sentences that introduce a noun (such as the word *boy* in Barry's example) followed by a lengthy clause (such as Barry's absurd example of *"buffer buffer buffer buffer"*) can cause confusion when the writer finally gets to the verb.

Most students would not compose a phrase such as the following:

> Three *boys* is walking down the street.

They might, however, write a sentence such as

> Three *boys*, all members of a successful basketball team, *is* walking down the street.

Most students would also not compose a phrase such as the following:

> The teacher said the grade *averages is* discouraging.

Since this sentence sounds wrong to the ear, fixing the subject-verb disagreement problem in the previous sentence is a simple matter:

> The teacher said the grade *averages are* discouraging.

The next example is a little more difficult. It would not be unusual to hear a sportscaster on television say something incorrect like

> Batting *averages*, long the obsession of the professional hitter, *is* today's subject.

Instructor Donald Pharr explains how mistakes like this usually happen: "We have the word *hitter* right there, right up against the upcoming verb, and *hitter* – well, the verb seems as if it has to be *is*. Except we're forgetting, if we do that, the word *hitter* is not the subject."

The problem, Dave Barry would say, is all those buffer words. The correct version of the sentence is

> Batting *averages*, long the obsession of the professional hitter, *are* today's subject.

Consider the following example of subject-verb disagreement:

> The *temptation* of colorful and exotic candies *are* difficult to resist.
> (INCORRECT)

The sentence is incorrect. It is easy to overlook that the object of the verb is the word *temptation*. While the casual eye might see the phrase "candies are difficult to resist" as correct, the careful eye, in proofreading and editing mode, will take out all of the nonessential words (the "buffer words"). The proofreading eye will then see that the correct combination should be "temptation is."

INDEFINITE PRONOUNS

Students often have trouble with subject-verb agreements in sentences that contain indefinite pronouns.

Indefinite pronouns (words such as *each, every, either,* or *neither*) refer to nonspecific persons or things. Even though they may seem to have plural meanings, they should be treated as singular nouns.

Consider this sentence:

> *Each* of the tempting chocolates and colorful hard candies *are* a delight. (INCORRECT)

Take out the nonessential words, and you get:

> *Each are* a delight (INCORRECT)

Clearly, this sounds uncomfortable. The writer should select the word *is* as the correct verb:

> *Each is* a delight (CORRECT)

Therefore, the *correct* sentence would read:

> *Each* of the tempting chocolates and colorful hard candies *is* a delight. (CORRECT)

Pronoun problems

(Correction symbols: case = use correct pronoun case; agr = correct agreement problem; ref = correct pronoun reference problem)

Pronouns, in general, cause many problems for beginning writers. One of the most common of these problems – pronoun-antecedent disagreements – is very similar to subject-verb disagreements. The pronoun does not agree in "number" with the antecedent it refers to. In other words, the antecedent is singular and the pronoun is plural, or the antecedent is plural and the pronoun is singular.

For example, the pronoun *they* is a plural word; the word *person* is singular.

Still, many students will write the following incorrect sentence:

> A person should study their pronouns. (INCORRECT)

To correct the pronoun-antecedent disagreement, the writer should either make both words singular or both plural.

> A person should study his or her pronouns. (CORRECT)

> People should study their pronouns. (CORRECT)

Instructor Santi Buscemi suggests that the root of the problem is that many students do not understand the function of a pronoun or an antecedent.

"The word *antecedent* is a fancy word which simply means the word that the pronoun refers to," he explains.

"Think about pronouns for a minute," Buscemi continues. "Pronouns really don't mean anything. If you say *he* or *she*, you've got to be thinking about a person to whom that pronoun refers. That person is the antecedent.

If your pronoun is singular, the antecedent must be singular – and you must use plural pronouns with plural antecedents."

Instructor Michael Bertsch suggests that students don't even need to know the terms *antecedent* or *pronoun* to learn how to detect and correct the problem.

"I never use the word *antecedent* in the class – that's a teacherly word that just goes right past students. I just take an arrow and I draw from a singular subject to the plural antecedent and I say, 'These disagree in number.'"

Bertsch gives this example, which is incorrect:

> The band played most of their favorite songs in the concert. (INCORRECT)

The *band* is a singular subject – and, as the antecedent for the pronoun *they*, it is incorrect. This could be fixed one of two ways:

> The band members played all of their favorite songs in the concert. (CORRECT)

> The band played all of its favorite songs in the concert. (CORRECT)

Following are some examples of pronoun problems, and suggestions for fixing the problems.

SINGULAR PRONOUN / PLURAL ANTECEDENT

Often, a student will use a plural pronoun with a singular antecedent as in this sentence:

> Each of the players will know, instinctively, how much *they* are getting paid per game. (INCORRECT)

The antecedent is the word *each*, not the word *players*, so the correct pronoun would be *he*.

> Each of the players will know, instinctively, how much *he* is getting paid per game. (CORRECT)

AMBIGUOUS PRONOUNS

This is a problem that occurs when more than one noun could be the antecedent for the pronoun. It is difficult for the reader to determine *which* antecedent the pronoun is supposed to refer to.

> Jerry told Steve *he* should have the ball on every play.

Who should have the ball on every play? Jerry or Steve?"

The cause of this problem is clear: The author knows but assumes – mistakenly – that the reader will also know. This sentence should be completely rewritten to avoid confusion. Here is a variation that will work:

> Jerry told Steve, "*I* want the ball on every play."

This would also work:

> Jerry complained to Steve about not getting the ball on every play.

Collective nouns

Collective nouns are words that "collect" a number of items together: a herd of horses; a team of players; a school of fish; a gaggle of geese. These collective nouns represent a *number* of things, but they are still considered to be *one* thing – or, in other words, a singular noun. For example, the word *team* is singular, even though it refers to many members. The correct pronoun for the antecedent *team* is the word *it, not* the pronoun *they*.

Examples:

The team celebrated *their* victory. (INCORRECT)

The team celebrated *its* victory. (CORRECT)

The team members celebrated *their* victory. (CORRECT)

Pronoun case

Pronoun case, Buscemi says, "Simply means that some nouns and pronouns take a different form when they are used as subjects, as opposed when they are used as objects."

Though knowledge of words like *subject* and *object* are helpful to explain sentences, from a grammar instructor's point of view, most students can "hear" correct usage, simply from being exposed to the language. Use your ear, and listen to the following examples:

We live in Chicago.

In this sentence, the word *we* is used as a subject.

The objective form of the word *we* is the word *us*. The objective form receives an action and therefore is called a *direct object*.

For example:

They called *us* from Chicago. (OBJECTIVE FORM)

Most student writers usually have no problem with pronoun case, unless a pronoun is followed immediately with a noun – such as in this incorrect sentence:

Us students *want* better computers. (INCORRECT)

The correct version of the sentence would be:

We students *want* better computers. (CORRECT)

There's an easy way to correct this problem and to determine whether the word should be *we* or *us*. Simply remove the words that sit between the pronoun and the verb. Ask yourself, is this correct?

Us want better computers. (INCORRECT)

Of course not.
You would say, "We want better computers."
The telecourse program provides a similar example.

Which of these sentences is correct?

The police called *we* students at midnight.

The police called *us* students at midnight.

Take out the word "students" and see how it sounds ...

The police called *us* at midnight.

The police called *we* at midnight.

The student writer can use the ear to "hear" the correct version or can use the rules of grammar for pronoun case. The correct version is, "The police called us ..."

PRONOUNS AND COMPOUND OBJECTS

Many students also have problems with pronouns that are combined with other nouns to create a subject or object in a sentence. For example, a person and a pronoun may be grouped together after a verb – and the writer may have trouble deciding which pronoun to use:

The government gave Sonia and *they* a free pass to Chernobyl.

The government gave Sonia and *them* a free pass to Chernobyl.

Which sentence sounds right? One way to find out is to use a technique similar to that described in the section about pronoun case. Take out the confusing noun (*Sonia*) and let's hear how the pronoun stands by itself:

The government gave *they* a free pass to Chernobyl. (INCORRECT)

The government gave *them* a free pass to Chernobyl. (CORRECT)

Additional exercises to study strategies for editing with pronouns are included toward the end of this *Telecourse Study Guide* chapter. If you generally have few problems with pronouns, just take enough time to refresh your knowledge of these rules. If you notice the instructor is marking a large number of pronoun errors in your early drafts, it is a good idea to read all of your course assignments once through, just to check the pronouns.

Word choice: beyond "just correct"

(Correction symbol: wc = check word choice)

Not all word choice decisions are based on correct or incorrect choices. Sophisticated writers learn to determine the difference between a perfunctory or technically correct word and one that is more eloquent.

In other words, you have the choice of writing just well enough to get a passing grade or actually saying something that rocks your instructor.

David Guterson explains how much thought a professional writer puts into the choice of just one word: "Earlier today I had a three-hour phone conversation with my editor at *Harper's* magazine, working through a story that I'd done – a work of nonfiction. And we were talking about verbs like *represent* and *signify* and *evoke* and *conjure* and *elicit* – all of which are permutations of the same notion. All of those words are slightly different enough that it was worth our time to consider which ones were precisely right.

"That is – Does the apple *signify* Washington State in the way that the pineapple *signifies* Hawaii? Does the orange *represent* Florida in the way the apple *conjures* Washington?

Conjure, evoke, signify, elicit, represent – all five verbs are close in meaning but different enough in their shades of meaning to deserve our careful consideration. And this happens at every juncture and every sentence. There are a lot of choices, and we want to make them carefully, both in terms of their denotation, what the individual word means, and also in terms of how they work rhythmically, in terms of tone, with the rest of the sentence."

Novelist Tom Robbins puts it this way: "You can't write a good story if you can't write a good sentence. But you can't write a good sentence if you can't find good words. So really it all boils down to choice of individual words."

ADJECTIVES AND ADVERBS

Many inexpert and uninitiated students attempt to impress an unsuspecting instructor with their impressive and majestic vocabulary by copiously throwing mellifluous adjectives and superlative adverbs into a sentence to make it more descriptive.

Better writers communicate with fewer words.

Carefully used adjectives and adverbs, as we discovered in the unit about description, can add a touch of flavor to a passage that is about as interesting as cafeteria food.

But the inexperienced writer can also overseason the stew with too many modifiers.

Novelist and writing instructor Charles Johnson gives this advice about selecting adjectives: "Adjectives won't give that specificity; that's just piling up words in front of a noun. Think like a painter. You must have a sort of facility with language to find just the right words to render it." He also recommends looking for just the right verb, instead of piling up adverbs.

"How do you get just the right words?" Johnson asks. "You sit down with a dictionary. And you go through it from A to Z. I did that with Webster's *Twentieth-Century Dictionary*; it's, like, two thousand pages. Our potential vocabulary of words is much greater than our spoken vocabulary. If you just rely on the way that we speak, you're not going to have that richness."

VERBS
(Correction symbol: v = correct active/passive voice)
Throughout this telecourse, you've heard many writers and instructors

express their preferences for active verbs over passive verbs. Though technically correct, passive verbs can bog down a sentence. When editing for word usage, many of the best writers read one more time through the text, checking all of the verbs.

Passive verbs put the wrong emphasis on the subject of the sentence. In the telecourse, Michael Bertsch explains passive voice this way: "The star of the sentence is being acted upon, instead of doing the acting."

> The ball was kicked between the uprights.

"We don't really see who's doing the acting until we get to the very end of the sentence," Bertsch says. "This is called passive construction; the actor is removed from the action by several words."

The same sentence, in the preferred active voice, would be:

> The player kicked the ball between the uprights by the player.

NOUNS

The telecourse program on description introduced you to the difference between concrete nouns and abstract nouns. A noun is a word that names a person, place, or thing. A concrete noun is a more specific name and is preferred over a vague, general, abstract noun. In the program on description, writer and instructor Duff Brenna gives the following example, which starts at the most abstract and ends with the most concrete:

> Animal; dog; poodle; FiFi

The best writers consider nouns as carefully as they do their verbs and adjectives.

"Nouns are the fabric of experience; they are the nature of reality," says David Guterson, who observes that a huge part of our vocabulary is "names for things, and we need them all!"

"Supposing you're a writer, and you're standing in front of a courthouse, and you want to describe what you're seeing," Guterson says. "Do you know the names of things? Do you have the language of architecture at your disposal, so that you can name the particular components of the building? Do you have the raw quality of the world, the specific names, the nouns – the hard reality of things at your disposal to use? If you don't, then you'd better do a little research, and learn them."

Summary

Most students have tendencies to make mistakes with word usage – especially in the final drafts. If you don't make many mistakes, you can always read your paper during the editing stage to find better choices – looking for words that could be improved, even if they *are* technically correct.

The best approach is to learn your tendencies and to make the commitment to take the time to proofread one last time, before you submit your work for evaluation.

Instructor Thomas Fox explains his approach to teaching proofreading techniques:

"I say, 'You have these three errors.' They're usually pretty similar, and I say, 'Make a list; it's your own personal editing checklist. You know you're likely to make those kinds of errors.'

"I do have a list for myself. I make subject-verb disagreement errors," Fox says. "I check my text for that. I think every student could create a list.

"Once you make a list, there really aren't a whole lot of excuses to make the mistake again. You know how to fix the mistake. Once I know that a student understands the rules, I just don't accept the mistakes."

Integrating the Text

Mini-Workshop L, "Copyediting and Proofreading" (pp. 502–504) in *A Community of Writers* suggests an approach to editing for errors that is in perfect harmony with advice given by instructors in this telecourse program. Compare the advice from Elbow and Belanoff to the advice in the telecourse program.

Exercises

Check with your instructor for your formal assignments. You will be asked to do exercises from the *Telecourse Study Guide*.

Exploring editing for word usage further
EXERCISE 1
Each of the following sentences features a problem with subject-verb agreements. Write a version that makes more sense.

Careful monitoring and regulating is the role of the inspector.

There is milk and cookies in the kitchen.

Hair styles, a subject of importance for a teenager, is of no concern to an old, bald guy like me.

EXERCISE 2
Each of the following sentences is written in passive voice. Write a version in active voice.

The errant pitch was thrown into the stands by the nervous rookie.

The coffee was spilled on my laptop computer by the spaced-out waiter.

The passive sentence was written by the first-year student.

EXERCISE 3

Each of the following sentences features a problem with pronouns. Write a version that makes more sense.

Her and the guys thrilled the crowd.

Us and the band had a rocking time that night.

The band played songs from it's great CD.

They're original songs inspired the crowd to dance.

If you're favorite type of music is the blues, your still not going to use an apostrophe in the possessive form of the pronoun you.

Exercise just for fun

Using a computer or a marking pen, highlight every verb you have used in a paper. Using your imagination, your dictionary, and your thesaurus, try to find stronger verbs that communicate your idea more specifically in every sentence.

Revision exercise

Using a computer or a marking pen, highlight every adjective or adverb you have used in a paper. Using your imagination, your dictionary, and your thesaurus, consider whether you can eliminate the adjectives and adverbs by using stronger, more specific verbs and nouns.

Quick writing exercise

Your instructor may ask you to do a quick focused freewrite about the topic you are studying in this unit. Those of you who are taking the course through a distance-learning system may be encouraged to share your thoughts in a discussion thread or to post your ideas on an Internet bulletin board. If you are writing your thoughts out by hand in a process journal, you might use these questions to get started. This is a freewriting exercise that will not be graded. You can use any of the following questions to stimulate your thoughts about editing and proofreading for the best vocabulary choices:

What is the difference between a merely adequate word choice and an expression that makes your writing sing? Do you ever use a dictionary or a thesaurus to find a better word, or do you habitually use the first word that comes to mind? Did any of the word usage problems mentioned in this program sound familiar? Have you seen correction marks on your papers for similar errors? Why is the study of editing and proofreading boring to so many students? If you were in charge of the English department, how would you make the study of grammar and syntax more interesting?

Exercises related to *A Community of Writers*

In *A Community of Writers*, Mini-Workshop L, "Copyediting and Proofreading" (pp. 502–504), Elbow and Belanoff recommend an approach to proofreading that is in perfect harmony with the techniques recommended by instructors in all three telecourse programs about proofreading and editing.

Mini-Workshop L is an exercise that requires students to analyze their own work or to work in a peer-feedback environment. Read this workshop, exchange a paper with a classmate, and see what happens.

Additional reading

Several student essays are featured in the appendix. They reflect different levels of writing ability, and they have been published in early draft form without final editing. How would you help Gregory Andrus, Corie Cushnie, Ethlyn Manning, and Francine Taylor, if they were in your own class and they were asking for help in spotting problems with word usage?

When you read the excerpt in the appendix from *Everything You Need to Know About Latino History*, by Himilce Novas, what did you do when you came to the word *fulminant*? Writers who care about word choice often read with a dictionary close by. When they come upon a word they don't know, they look it up and build their vocabulary. Do you do this, or did you just skip by difficult words? What do you think of the other word choices used by Novas in this excerpt?

Quick Review

1. Which of these sentences does *not* have a subject-verb agreement problem?

   a. The problem, Dave Barry would say, are all those buffer words.

   b. Dave Barry, in his twin roles as Pulitzer Prize–winning columnist and as grammar's "Mr. Language Person," are making a joke.

   c. Dave Barry, buffer, buffer, buffer, are making a joke.

   d. The problem, Dave Barry would say, is all those buffer words.

   e. None of the above.

2. Which of these sentences does *not* have a subject-verb agreement problem?
   a. Each of the players knows their batting average at the end of the day.
   b. Each of the tempting chocolates and colorful hard candies is a delight.
   c. Each of the tempting chocolates and colorful hard candies are a delight.
   d. All of the above.
   e. None of the above.

3. Which of the sentences does not have a passive verb?
   a. To be, or not to be: that is the question.
   b. The batter is killing the ball.
   c. The batter bunted.
   d. All of the above.
   e. None of the above.

4. Which of the pronouns refers correctly to the collective noun in the sentence?
   a. The band played a hit from their chart-topping CD.
   b. The team partied all night long on its bus.
   c. The bank could not pay competitive interest rates to their customers.
   d. All of the above.
   e. None of the above.

5. Which sentence is correct?
   a. We students want better computers.
   b. The police called us students at midnight.
   c. The police gave Sonia and they a free pass to Chernobyl.
   d. All of the above.
   e. None of the above.

"You have to ask, 'Are the values within each English department applicable to all the different academic languages across the curriculum?' I would say that there are commonalities, but there are definitely differences. The English department has its own academic language, and it can't be teaching writing for all the other academic languages. For instance, if you had the biology department be responsible for teaching writing for all of the other academic languages, would that be fair to the English major?"

MARIA MADRUGA, Shasta College

Introduction to the Topic

Think of this chapter and unit of the telecourse as a review of the entire composition course – or as a preview of the writing you will practice for rest of your life.

To revisit the skills of writing we have studied throughout the class, you will hear from instructors who are *not* specialists in English or writing. It is our intention to show that these are the types of folks who will pick up where this course leaves off.

It is, after all, not the sole responsibility of the English department to teach how language is used across the entire campus. Though most colleges and universities encourage (or require) all students to complete an English composition class, this first-semester writing course can only introduce you to the writing skills that are needed in college. Along the way to earning your degree, you'll encounter mentors who will show you how to grow even more as a scholar and a writer.

You will continue to study composition and refine your writing skills as you learn from excellent instructors of engineering, political science, chemistry, art, agriculture, history, and other academic disciplines in your upper-division classes.

In our early evaluations of this course, we noticed that the students who embraced the main points of this course and learned to take them to other classes (or to their occupations beyond school) achieved a high level of success.

Nothing will please us more than to know we have been some small part of helping you achieve that success.

Learning Objectives

After viewing this television program and reading the chapter in the *Telecourse Study Guide*, you will learn how to apply the writing processes and rhetorical strategies learned in an English composition course to various disciplines across the campus. In the process, you will review key instructional points from the previous twenty-four chapters of the *Telecourse Study Guide* and units of the telecourse, and you will consider how you will use those skills in the discourse community that you have chosen for your academic major and future profession.

These objectives are in harmony with the essential premises of Workshop 15, "Listening, Reading, and Writing in the Disciplines," in *A Community of Writers* (pp. 385–416).

- Although there are traits essential to all good writing, each discipline has its own additional standards.
- Writing can serve as a way to learn something as well as a way of explaining what you already know.

Before Viewing

Before viewing this program, think about how the techniques studied in this course will apply to challenges in other classes across the campus. Do the instructors in those courses ask you to respond in brief essays on exams? Do they expect you to participate in group projects that produce collaborative documents? Are research papers required? Do the instructors in those course judge you on the ability to edit and proofread your basic work? Consider your answers to these questions as you prepare to wrap up this course.

Read the main assignment in Elbow and Belanoff's Workshop 15, "Listening, Reading, and Writing in the Disciplines" (pp. 385–391).

While Viewing

Think about the skills you are reviewing in this unit, and imagine what will be valuable to carry forward to your upper-division classes. Pay careful attention to how the professors in various disciplines talk about the way narration, description, comparison, persuasion, definition, argumentation, and process analysis are used in their courses. Notice what these instructors say about the writing process, including their views on drafting, revising, and editing. Compare the attitudes expressed about collaborative writing, research, and reading.

Keep in mind the section "Examining Differences" in Workshop 15 (pp. 389–391), where Elbow and Belanoff offer an exercise to analyze the reasoning, structure, purpose, audience, and language of writing samples that represent different types of discourse communities.

After Viewing

Ask your English composition instructor about follow-up courses in your academic major. Most academic disciplines offer writing courses that build on the skills learned in English composition, teaching specialty-related approaches to research, collaborative writing, and other writing skills necessary for that discourse community. Consider asking professors in your academic major which of the thinking/writing strategies you should brush up on before taking upper division classes. Create a list of the most common errors you make in early drafts, and keep this list for proofreading papers in other classes.

Read the section "An Argument for Freshman Composition" in Workshop 15 (pp. 394–396). After viewing this telecourse program, do you agree or disagree with Elbow and Belanoff's argument advocating separate writing classes?

Viewing Guide

We sometimes take it for granted that English instructors – who are usually concerned with analyzing poems and serious literature – should teach *all* students, not just English majors, the language skills needed for academic writing in all the disciplines. The skills learned in English composition *are* helpful to engineers, political science majors, chemists, artists, agriculture majors, and nursing students. However, it's important to recognize that the individual writing styles of many academic discourse communities vary greatly from the writing favored by English majors. In this unit, we'll explore what you can take along from this class to help you succeed in future writing challenges.

Discourse communities

Early in the telecourse we introduced the concept of discourse communities – groups of people who have similar attitudes and rules regarding the use of language.

The notion of discourse communities is relevant in this summary unit of the telecourse. "There is no such thing as a universally-agreed-upon, campuswide academic discourse," says Beverly Moss of Ohio State University. Rather, there are a wide variety of academic *discourses*, and students need to learn to write appropriately for the different types of classes they will encounter.

This might seem like a daunting task, but Moss says that her students eventually figure out how to write for each instructor and each class. "You need to consider what your message is and how you shape that or craft that message in an appropriate style or tone for that audience," she says. "You have to consider, what are the acceptable conventions for this particular discourse community?"

In this unit, we'll revisit other chapters of the *Telecourse Study Guide* to see how the skills studied in this course apply to all fields of study. We can't possibly consider every single academic major on campus; however, we can give you an idea of how to explore the writing of your own discourse community by seeing how students and professors in several disciplines apply the lessons of English composition to their own writing.

"The main charge in the first year of writing is to prepare students to write academic discourse," says English instructor Joe Harris. You'll find, as we review, that this course has been designed to do just that.

Agriculture instructor Dave Daley speaks for instructors in many other disciplines when he observes that students who were effective creative writers in *some* English composition courses have yet to practice the writing skills needed to succeed in *his* courses.

"Creative writers come to a science course, and I say, 'Well, wait a second, I don't want that – I want the evidence. I want it clear; I want it stated; I want to be able to follow the paper. So we do have to look at how we train them differently for different disciplines, once they pass English One and move beyond that. They need to start thinking, 'Who is my community?' '"

How does an English composition course address this need?

Cindy Selfe of Michigan Technical University has a partial answer: "A computer scientist needs to know how to make a difference with language in the world of computer science. And an engineer certainly needs to know how to make a difference through language in the engineering world. So I do think that we're teaching students what they need to know if we're teaching them to think critically about the uses of language in their own environments."

The programs of this course are divided into two broad categories: "Thinking/Writing Strategies" and the "Writing Process." In other words, roughly half of the programs emphasize learning *how* to get mere words on a page to communicate the complex thoughts in your mind. The other half of the programs focus on the patterns of thinking that go along with the process. That's where this review will start.

Thinking/Writing Strategies
READING AND THINKING CRITICALLY
One of our assumptions is that the most important thinking/writing strategies in any discipline on campus are linked to an ability to read and decipher difficult text and to think critically about the information being processed.

Instructors from every discipline surveyed for this course agree with this premise.

Agriculture instructor Daley notes: "The ability to read and interpret is essential in the information age. In agriculture, it's particularly true; changes come so rapidly, if you aren't capable of interpreting that information, you're left out."

Instructors also agree that merely soaking up the information is not as important as learning how to *think critically* about it.

Art instructor Sheri Simon puts it this way: "What we really are training here are critical thinkers. And a critical thinker is somebody who is very comfortable living in that realm of the unknown."

Julia Shovein, an instructor of nursing, defines the process somewhat differently for her discipline: "When we're talking about critical thinking, we're kind of talking about assessment, problem identification, goal setting, and evaluation." The goal, she says, is to determine as quickly as possible, through critical thinking, what will heal the patient.

RHETORICAL MODES OR GENRES

One of the most important critical thinking skills you will encounter is learning how to apply the rhetorical modes studied in this course to the writing challenges you will encounter in other classes.

Shovein points out, "The rhetorical modes are used in any level of writing; it helps if the student has had a background, for instance, in describing patients."

Instructors use a variety of phrases (including "genres," "rhetorical modes," and "thinking/writing strategies") to talk about these various forms of writing and thinking, including description, narration, definition, persuasion, and argument.

Mike Rose of UCLA points out that after studying these genres abstractly in an English composition course, students always find themselves *applying them practically* across the disciplines. "The more that students try out these thinking/writing strategies with different kinds of disciplinary material – when they're actually trying these strategies in real, honest-to-god academic contexts – I think that is when they get more proficient at and comfortable with using them. They're able to leave that writing classroom and move into the world of the lower-division curriculum."

In *A Community of Writers*, Elbow and Belanoff explain, "A genre is a widely recognized *form* of writing." They discuss the rhetorical modes as forms of "expository essays" (pp. 48–49). However, the authors caution teachers and students to think carefully about genres by asking: "Are genres form, or content?"

In other words, they ask, "Do you usually start writing by thinking mainly about what you want to say, or how you want to say it? That is, are you thinking about content or form?"

In an "Exploring Theory" segment (pp. 53–55), Elbow and Belanoff consider the difference between starting with content and starting with form.

It is an important contradiction to ponder. For decades, students have been emphasizing form over content when writing comparison essays, description essays, argument essays, and other types of essays. When genres are seen as formulas for perfectly completing course assignments that have no connection with real-life writing challenges, the unfortunate result can be essays that are correct in form but curiously devoid of substance. Finding a genre that fits your content will enhance the quality of your work and help you see how genres can help you in your writing outside of college.

As agriculture instructor Dave Daley notes in the video, "When you say, 'comparison/contrast or argumentation,' I don't think they connect with a student [who is not an English major]."

Daley and others suggest that to truly understand why we study these genres, each student must see the practical application in his or her own area of study.

In the next few scenes of the telecourse, we discover that the content of each discipline often *determines* the form – and that, indeed, the genres are used heavily in each discipline.

COMPARISON AND CONTRAST

Every discipline surveyed for this course used comparison and contrast.

Julia Shovein says that nurses, who must be able to recognize (and document in writing) the contrast between normal and abnormal conditions, use comparison every day. "The background, in terms of English composition, can help," Shovein says. "You want someone to be grounded in many different ways of comparing and contrasting similarities and differences, so that they can build on that when they're in the professional setting."

Political science instructor George Wright emphasizes the academic applications in his discipline, noting: "A comparison-and-contrast paper is a very effective device in writing a political science assignment."

Wright explains two different approaches, giving the example of a student who is comparing two different countries. The first half of the paper can be about one country, and the second half of the paper can be about the other; or the writer can weave in comparisons of the two countries throughout the entire paper.

This example effectively reviews the strategies of subject-by-subject comparison and point-by-point comparison that were explained in Chapter 13 of this book and in the related telecourse program, "Comparison and Contrast."

NARRATIVE WRITING

The most useful narrative writing technique to learn is how to structure a document by using the typical narrative arc (with a satisfying beginning, middle and end) – the classic "shape" that has been used by storytellers ever since Aristotle described the style thousands of years ago.

Many English composition classes start with writing the personal narrative and show how the skills can be eventually adapted to formal academic arguments and research papers.

The related telecourse program, "Narrative Writing," also connects the narrative skills of short story writing to academic and professional writing situations.

In this program, we now see how instructors and students use narrative writing within their discourse communities, beyond the English composition classroom.

Julia Shovein explains that the narratives in personal journals kept by nurses help them on a number of different levels. Student nurses are encouraged to keep track of what they are experiencing and learning in these free-form diaries. As nurse Alicia Rapp points out, the skills of narrative writing carry over to professional writing with shift reports that are "a story of eight hours of what we did and how the patient responded."

Graduate student Larry Thompson explains that narrative skills are also important in technical writing, such as an engineering school research paper; he uses storytelling techniques to get the reader's attention and to elaborate upon the dry facts and figures contained in the document. And Wright explains that political science instructors appreciate papers with a good narrative structure. It makes for good storytelling within a paper, Wright says, and "clearly, the teacher who's grading the material will wake up and say, 'This student *got* it.' "

DEFINITION

Definition writing – using writing to interpret and illustrate the meaning of a word or concept – is extremely important in the sciences. Graduate student Marty Wallace explains in the video that first-year chemistry students learn more new words than students studying a foreign language.

Dave Daley agrees, pointing out that most of his agricultural science textbooks are little more than a series of definitions. "Clearly, that's an ability that a student has to have, to explain those in an exam," he says.

As Larry Thompson explains his use of definition in a research paper about industrial cutting fluids, he reviews several of the key techniques introduced in the program "Definition."

Thompson uses negative definition (also called definition by negation) by telling the reader what cutting fluids are *not*. He also defines using figurative language, examples, description, and comparison.

DESCRIPTION

Though the techniques of description in scientific writing are related to those studied in an English course, Dave Daley says the emphasis in agriculture is on a stark, no-frills style.

Still, many of the techniques explained in Chapter 3 of this book (and the related telecourse program "Description") can be adapted to scientific writing and to other disciplines. For example, Julia Shovein says that many of the passages in a well-documented nursing report are as thorough as descriptions in a well-written mystery novel by author Sue Grafton.

Shovein's summary of techniques is an almost perfect review of the telecourse program on description. Nurses use the senses (sight, touch, smell, and sound) to describe; they describe by analogy; they describe with concrete details instead of generalities.

PROCESS ANALYSIS

Process analysis – writing to explain how to do something – is essential in science and industry, where it is important to be able to explain technical procedures.

Chemist Marty Wallace explains that much of the writing in his discourse community is designed so that another scientist can replicate the results of an experiment. Larry Thompson emphasizes that an engineer must know how to explain a manufacturing process, with clear warnings about safety procedures built into the technical writing.

Daley reviews one of the key points of the telecourse program "Process Analysis," when he says he expects students to write "a step-by-step process with no questions [in terms of a peer review] of how to do that process again – how to duplicate those results."

ARGUMENT

Argument and persuasion writing are so common in college that the formal "academic argument" can actually be seen as a genre separate from all other types of argumentative writing.

Artist and instructor Sheri Simon reviews the key points of this instruction unit, noting, "The argument, the thesis, the development of the thesis, and then the concluding remarks is a paradigm [or model formula]. Paradigms are really good for initial grounding, initial learning."

According to Simon, many instructors in the creative arts are willing to "tear down the paradigm" and experiment with new models of argument writing.

However, instructors in most other disciplines expect their students to be able to communicate quickly and accurately with the rigid form of the academic argument. The "research paper" or "term paper" that most first-year students learn to write (usually over an entire term or semester) is just a practice run for the type of writing they will be expected to turn out at a rapid pace in upper-division courses.

Dave Daley explains that in his advanced class, "Students in the 'Agricultural Systems and Issues' course actually have to write six papers. They identify key issues, and the expectation is that they can validly research pros and cons to that argument and arrive at some reasonable summary and conclusion based on what they have read."

The academic argument is just as important in the social sciences. George Wright explains that the research papers he expects from all political science students are essentially extended academic arguments.

RESEARCH AND USING QUOTES

"The focus of my teaching is on what I call research papers," Wright says. He wants students to pick a topic, become an expert on the subject (through reading), and develop an argument built on a statement about the topic.

This type of paper, which is very common in the social sciences, is the most direct application of lessons learned in Chapter 21 and the telecourse program "Research." In *A Community of Writers*, Elbow and Belanoff lead students through formal argument and the research process in Workshops 11 and 12.

Along with those skills, you will need to learn how to cite sources correctly, to properly show your instructors the sources of your evidence, and to avoid unintentional plagiarism. These skills were studied in Chapter 20 of this *Telecourse Study Guide* and the telecourse program "Quotes and Citations." Elbow and Belanoff explain documentation procedures on pages 314 to 322.

One of the biggest issues these days in academic circles is how students handle research and the Internet. (The telecourse program "Computers in Composition" addresses these issues.) In *A Community of Writers*, Elbow and Belanoff address these issues as well in the Mini-Workshop F, "Doing Research on the Web." Though the Internet is a quick and easy place to get ideas, instructors often frown upon papers that ignore more traditional sources. Many instructors still feel the evidence with the highest level of credibility is usually found in peer-reviewed, academic journals that are not found for free on the public Internet.

Dave Daley expresses the feelings of many instructors: "I allowed students to use the Internet to research the information this semester, but I didn't force them to back that up with a refereed journal. I *should* have, because I found mostly opinions that had a citation [from the Internet] – so students thought it was fact. Quality control is severely lacking in terms of Internet research, at this point."

We see, at the conclusion of this section, that students will need to continue to refine and build on their thinking/writing strategies, including their relationship with the research process and the formal academic argument. These are skills that will be required in every class they take after the introductory English composition course.

Writing process

The *process* of writing learned in this telecourse should also apply outside of the English composition class. You should be able to assemble a document by inventing, drafting, revising, and editing your work – and then, by re-inventing, re-drafting, re-revising again, and re-editing the document, until it is acceptable to your instructor, your boss, and, most important, to you. Each of these aspects of the writing process was the focus of an individual chapter in the *Telecourse Study Guide* and a program in the telecourse; in this program, you will review the concepts and see how they work as a whole in the writing process.

As you do, you should also review how *A Community of Writers* explains the writing process. Many of you will be asked to provide a portfolio of your best work to your instructor at the end of the semester. This is a good time to examine your own relationship with the writing process by writing an "Autobiography of Myself as a Writer." This type of essay is explained in Elbow and Belanoff's Workshop 16, "Autobiography and Portfolio" (pp. 417–444).

DRAFTING

Julia Shovein recommends that her nursing students practice a form of freewriting in a diary or journal as a way to think about what they are learning on the job. This is similar to the type of freewriting studied in the telecourse program "Freewriting and Generating." In Workshop 1, "An Introduction to the Variety of Writing Processes," in *A Community of Writers* freewriting and generating are explained on page 323.

"Sitting down and just freely writing helps you clarify not only what actually happened in the professional nursing process – [it helps you, the student] clarify in your own mind the feelings and anxieties about what happened – and that helps you learn," Shovein says. Though this type of freewriting is not intended to create a finished document, it is a technique many use to invent ideas, overcome writer's block, or explore what's going on in the subconscious.

Some students might assume that freewriting and generative writing are helpful only in "creative writing" situations. However, instructors in every department surveyed for this course talked about using an unedited prewriting process to get ideas flowing. A brainstorming/drafting stage was even recommended for the type of writing where the end result was expected to conform to a very rigid, technical form.

All of these techniques are related. Though instructors use different names, and students practice writing freely in different ways, the goal is to generate a jumble ideas that can later be organized into a coherent, carefully-structured document.

ORGANIZING

In every department across campus, teachers expect students to know the basic skills of organization, as studied in Chapter 12 and the telecourse program "Organizing Devices."

The process of finding a topic, reading as much as possible, narrowing the ideas down to a clear thesis, and locating evidence to prove the thesis will be used in course after course. Your instructors will also expect you to know how to organize by unifying subsections of each paper with topic sentences and creating some sort of outline, either before writing or in the middle of the drafting process.

You can expect to repeat variations of this organizational process in the courses you take after this one and to continue to refine the process up until the highest level of graduate school courses.

REVISING

Most instructors see the processes of drafting and revising as overlapping. They also recommend using outlines at various stages of the writing process, including revision.

George Wright tells his political science students to create an outline after the first draft – and after the second, third, fourth, and fifth drafts, too. "It is the outline that is revised, as much as the paper," Wright says. In "Skeleton Feedback" (p. 544), Elbow and Belanoff recommend a technique of revision through peer feedback, where one student attempts to impose a skeleton outline of topic sentences on another student's draft.

These techniques are consistent with expectations of all the instructors interviewed for this program; across the campus, instructors in upper-division classes assume that the revision of the scholarly paper is a normal part of the composition process. A draft-quality document will not be accepted as passing work.

In *A Community of Writers*, Workshop 6, "Drafting and Revising," illustrates three levels of revision, including rethinking the "bones," reshaping the "muscles," and copyediting to treat the "skin" of the document.

EDITING

Instructors from all the departments urged students to bring along the lessons they learned in English composition about proofreading and editing for surface errors.

When you have submitted serious work for a grade, absolutely the last thing you want is for the instructor to be giggling at your grammar. But, it happens. As Dave Daley puts it, "I laugh as I grade these papers and I say, 'If you had just read this out loud – it's not what you thought you were saying.'" Daley recommends the simplest proofreading technique of all: Read your work out loud or have a friend read it to you. More than half the mistakes will usually surface.

"Everybody has weaknesses, such as run-on sentences or sentence fragments or misplaced modifiers," says Larry Thompson. He recommends a personal editing checklist similar to the approach recommended in Chapters 22, 24, and 26 of this *Telecourse Study Guide*.

Know your tendencies, Thompson says. Learn to detect and correct your most frequent mistakes. It's good advice – about the same you'd get from any English composition instructor.

PEER FEEDBACK AND COLLABORATION

In *A Community of Writers*, Elbow and Belanoff emphasize that revision through peer feedback is an essential part of the writing process. And, it is no coincidence that the title of this telecourse is "Writing for an Audience." We learn how effective our writing is by seeing what it does to an audience.

Peer feedback is the first step toward learning how to create a collaborative document, and collaboration plays an increasingly important role in the composition process as you progress from an undergraduate curriculum to graduate school.

The telecourse programs on these subjects emphasize that peer feedback and collaboration are very common in the business world, in the scientific community, in the law community, and in just about every career you might pursue.

Every department surveyed for this telecourse assigns collaborative writing tasks to upper-division students. As Larry Thompson observes, "That's part of what current learning is about – working with other people, helping people learn, and learning how not to degrade or embarrass other team members. With the way that the trends are going currently in the industrial world, I think that collaborative writing is the only way to go."

As Thompson explains the team writing process in the discourse community of engineers, he effectively reviews the key points made in both telecourse programs about peer feedback and collaboration.

He advocates a variation on the "division of labor" model and explains how the teams of engineering students in graduate school learn to research, draft, edit, and learn collaboratively. Students do better with collaborative writing challenges at his level, Thompson says, if they have been exposed to some sort of collaborative writing in writing classes before they reach their upper-division courses.

Summary

Instructors in science, art, engineering, agriculture, and political science agree that writing is an essential skill for success in their discourse communities and that the study of writing should not be terminated after a one-semester course in composition.

Julia Shovein summarizes their views effectively in the final segments of the program, when she says, "Learning to write isn't just the English department's responsibility. All of us have to help students learn to hone their skills, whether they're verbal or written. Still, the earlier they have the building blocks to learn writing skills, the better. So they *have* to have English composition early in their careers – *before* they get to us."

Integrating the Text

WORKSHOP 15 Listening, Reading, and Writing in the Disciplines
(pp. 385–416)

Several sections of *A Community of Writers* support a main premise of this program. In order to write in every discipline across campus, it is important to know how to adapt the skills you have started to learn in this course to the writing style of your academic discourse community.

Elbow and Belanoff's Workshop 15, "Listening, Reading, and Writing in the Disciplines" (pp. 385–416), starts with the premise that, "Although there are traits essential to all good writing, each discipline has its own additional standards." Its second premise holds that writing serves as a way to learn and explain something you already know. In other words, in order to prosper in your academic major, you need reading and writing skills to absorb the knowledge in a discipline and demonstrate to the instructor that you have mastered the intellectual challenges central to the discipline. The workshop ends with this thought: Writing classes can get you started, but in the long run, the writing you do in your discipline "may be the kind of writing that matters to you the most and that you do the most of for the rest of your life" (p. 396).

The main assignment of the workshop is designed to "get you to do some thinking about the differences between writing for a general audience and writing within a specific discipline." The workshop guides students through a process of listening and taking notes, drafting, and eventually examining the differences between the writing you produce in composition courses and the writing you will be asked to produce in other courses. (See Exercises related to *A Community of Writers*.")

The section "Exploring Theory: Writing (and the Teaching of Writing) in the Disciplines" (pp. 392–396) explains that most of your learning about how to use the methods (and writing conventions) of different academic disciplines does not occur until after your freshman year, and that "the real and essential 'knowledge' in a discipline is the language and thinking" rather than a memorized list of facts. In other words, Elbow and Belanoff explain, your professors will expect you to demonstrate not only what you know but also how skilled you are in the ways of writing in that discipline.

The essays in the "Readings" section (pp. 397–416) may have already been assigned in previous weeks of this course. It is a good idea to read them again to see the similarities and differences in the ways writers from each discipline use language to make a point.

Exercises

Check with your instructor for your formal assignments. You will be asked to do exercises from the *Telecourse Study Guide*.

Exploring writing across the disciplines further
EXERCISE 1
This exercise requires you to find and read a piece of writing from another one of your classes. The answers you end up with at the end of this exercise will help you identify and understand the characteristics of the discourse community from which the piece comes.

1. As you read, take notes about any ideas the piece inspires. Next, organize these notes using whichever organizational method you prefer.

2. Now go through your organized notes, and consider how each of the points you've identified fits within these topics:

   What kinds of arguments or reasoning is the author using?
   - How does the author back up his or her statements?
   - What kind of evidence is valued in this discipline?
   - Does the author make assumptions about your level of understanding or about the context within which the piece will be read?

   What do you think was the author's purpose in writing the piece?
   - Explanation?
   - Persuasion?
   - Entertainment?

   What thinking/writing strategies are valued by this discourse community?
   - Is there a strong narrative?
   - Is description important?
   - Does the paper use comparison/contrast?
   - Does the paper use process analysis?
   - Is persuasion, definition, or argument used in the thinking and writing?

   Who is the intended audience of the piece?

   How is the paper organized?

   What sort of language does the author use?
   - Personal and informal?
   - Impersonal and formal?
   - Everyday words or specialized jargon?

EXERCISE 2

This exercise requires that you find a piece of writing that has roughly the same subject matter as the one you used in Exercise 1. This piece, however, should be written in the style of a different discourse community than the first. Examples might include two reviews of a movie: one from a studio public relations Web site and one from a technical cinematographer's journal. While reading this second piece, repeat the steps you performed in Exercise 1. Write a brief analysis of the aspects you've identified from these two essays and explain the differences.

Exercise just for fun

Look in your college's course catalogue and find the description of your English composition class. Write a version of this short description in the style of a physical education instructor, an engineering instructor, or a biology instructor. Check the course catalogue to get a feeling for the style that instructors from another discipline might use.

Revision exercise

In this exercise you can use the essay from either Exercise 1 or Exercise 2 as a starting point for revision.

Write a version of the essay with your writing class as the target audience. Afterward, write an explanation of the choices you made; explain how your "voice" for the other class differs from the writer's voice you would use in an English course.

Quick writing exercise

Your instructor may ask you to do a quick focused freewrite about the writing in your discipline of choice. Those of you who are taking the course through a distance-learning system may be encouraged to share your thoughts in a discussion thread or to post your ideas on an Internet bulletin board. If you are writing your thoughts out by hand in a process journal, you might use these questions to stimulate ideas. This is a freewriting exercise that will not be graded. You can use any of the following questions and statements to provoke your thoughts about writing beyond this English composition course:

Every telecourse program in this PBS series features people who use writing in their academic disciplines or in their jobs. Before taking this course, what was your impression of English classes, as they related to your personal life? Try to list at least three pieces of wisdom that you will take from this course to help in your future writing challenges. If you can think of more than three lessons, list them. If you can, think of one moment of the telecourse that you will remember for the rest of your life.

You may use the questions in the "Process Journal" section of Workshop 15, "Listening, Reading and Writing in the Disciplines" (p. 392) in *A*

Community of Writers as an additional source of inspiration for this quick writing exercise.

Exercises related to *A Community of Writers*

EXERCISE 1

The section "Examining Differences" in Workshop 15 (pp. 389–391) features an exercise to help analyze the reasoning, structure, purpose, audience, and language of various pieces of writing that represent different types of discourse communities. The original version of this exercise is built around sample essays from representative disciplines, published in *A Community of Writers*. The same analysis should be applied to samples of writing from the academic major you intend to pursue. To ensure success in that field, here's an important follow up exercise: Approach an instructor of upper-division courses related to your career choice. Ask for examples of excellent writing in that discipline, and use the same criteria to evaluate the work.

EXERCISE 2

In *A Community of Writers*, Elbow and Belanoff explain, "A genre is a widely recognized *form* of writing." They discuss the rhetorical modes as forms of "expository essays" (pp. 48–49). A simple way to explore the writing you will practice beyond English composition is to list examples of how these various genres might be used in your academic major and for on-the-job writing in the career in which you are interested. As you make this list, think of the genres, not just as academic exercises, but as thinking/writing strategies to solve real-life writing situations. You should also consider the different types of audiences you will be writing for within the discipline. For guidance on this analysis, see the section "Exploring Theory: More on Purpose and Audience" (pp. 200–206).

EXERCISE 3

The main assignment in Workshop 8, "Writing in the World: An Interview About Writing" (pp. 213–231) is a more ambitious extension of the exercise described above. Instead of just imagining or analyzing how the writing is different in your field, follow the guidelines in this assignment and interview a professional who writes in the style of your academic discourse community.

Additional reading

How is the excerpt in the appendix from *Everything You Need to Know About Latino History*, by historian Himilce Novas, different from the writing in other disciplines? Compare this writing to the excerpts of books by David Ellefson (bass player from Megadeth) and Bill Walsh (former football coach of the San Francisco 49ers). How does each writer address the audience differently? What are the similarities in the styles?

How is the article by Steve Shanesy, editor of *Popular Woodworking*, similar to or different from the type of writing that an engineering major might practice?

Quick Review

1. The various types of essays you have practiced in this course, including narration, description, persuasion, definition, and comparison, are called by some instructors
    a. thinking/writing strategies
    b. genres
    c. rhetorical modes
    d. all of the above
    e. none of the above

2. Argumentative essays in social sciences, hard sciences, and other disciplines
    a. require skills in quoting and citing sources learned in this telecourse
    b. require skills in evaluating quality of evidence gained from Internet sources or peer-reviewed journals
    c. require skills in selecting a topic and creating a premise or thesis statement
    d. all of the above
    e. none of the above

3. Instructors from the following departments said they would value papers from students that contained pure freewriting:
    a. agricultural sciences
    b. political science
    c. engineering
    d. all of the above
    e. none of the above

4. The writing process most students use in classes beyond English composition will likely include
    a. drafting
    b. revising
    c. editing
    d. all of the above
    e. none of the above

5. The overall thrust of this program is that
    a. English instructors are the only instructors across the campus qualified to teach students about language issues.
    b. Writing is much less important in other disciplines than it is in the English department.
    c. The lessons of English composition are used by students in every discipline.
    d. All of the above.
    e. None of the above.

"Psychology is the study of the way people behave. Grammar is the study of the way language behaves. There are rules, but they weren't created by English teachers. They emerged from the way language behaves. Make a loud noise and people will wince. That's a rule. Stay underwater for a while and you'll drown. That's a rule.

"When I was teaching, we reproduced a page of pre-Elizabethan prose. There was no grammar at all – no punctuation. It was just random sentences that ran on and on and on. And the reader would have to figure it out for himself or herself. Punctuation? It came fairly late in prose; things weren't always the way they are now. Where did an apostrophe come from? What is a quotation mark? What is an exclamation mark? Did you ever look at an exclamation mark in Spanish prose? It's upside down. There are rules. But the rules are not created by teachers or English professors. They come down through the centuries. They belong to the people."

FRANK MCCOURT, novelist/English teacher

Introduction to the Topic

Editing for problems with sentence mechanics sounds like a job that should be left to someone in a work uniform covered with engine grease. This mythical "word mechanic" could fix any sputtering sentence or paragraph with just the right chrome wrench grabbed from a red toolbox.

Perhaps this isn't such an absurd image. There are those (including instructors) who swear that many grammar and punctuation rules were invented by Johannes Gutenberg's slowest printing press intern – just to make life easier for those who were setting the type.

Many of the rules of grammar have been passed down over the centuries through a series of similar accidents.

Now it is up to you, the student, to make sense of these rules.

You can start by proofreading each sentence out loud. Better yet, get a friend to read it. Try to remember that those dots of ink on the page are supposed to communicate a cadence, tone, and pace. If you or your reader do not pause at the correct places, you know there is something wrong; it's time to reconsider your use of commas.

If the reader hyperventilates and gasps while reading convoluted passages, look up the rules about periods and semicolons. It is quite possible you have used fused sentences or run-ons.

And if you are starting to waist (or is it waste?) time guessing which version of *they're, their,* or *there* is needed – haul out the old dictionary, and figure it out. (Your computer spellchecker is too stupid to differentiate between homonyms.)

It beats being perceived as an illiterate.

Learning Objectives

In this chapter, you will learn proofreading strategies to detect and correct common mistakes in language mechanics. You will learn how to proofread for misused commas, semicolons, and apostrophes in your own early drafts. You will also consider the source of most spelling errors in the student papers produced in the computer age: homonyms that spelling checkers approve, in spite of incorrect meaning.

These learning objectives work in harmony with Part II, Editing, in *A Community of Writers* (pp. 479–504), particularly with: Mini-Workshop G, "The Sentence and End-Stop Punctuation" (pp. 481–485); Mini-Workshop H, "Commas," In *A Community of Writers* (pp. 486–489); Mini-Workshop I, "Apostrophes" (pp. 490–493); Mini-Workshop K, "Spelling" (pp. 497–501); and Mini-Workshop L, "Copyediting and Proofreading" (pp. 502–504).

Before Viewing

Consider the errors you have had pointed out in various papers throughout the semester. Pay careful attention to problems with mechanics. These errors might include understanding how to use commas, semicolons, and apostrophes. Try to remember if you have had problems with spelling, or with homonyms that were not corrected by your computer's word-processing program.

In *A Community of Writers*, read Mini-Workshop L, "Copyediting and Proofreading" (pp. 502–504) and Mini-Workshop H, "Commas" (pp. 486–489), which will help make the passages in the telecourse program about comma rules easier to understand. Read Mini-Workshop K, "Spelling," on homonyms (p. 501) and also think about whether you are too dependent on computer spellcheckers. Read Mini-Workshop I, "Apostrophes," in *A Community of Writers* (pp. 490–493).

While Viewing

Draw a single line down the middle of a couple of pages in a notebook – creating two columns. In the first column, list the types of common problems in mechanics that are explained in the program. In the second column, write some techniques you can use to proofread for such errors.

Compare what Elbow and Belanoff have said particularly about homonyms and apostrophes to the advice given by instructors in the telecourse program.

After Viewing

Create a personal editing checklist that features the errors in mechanics that you are most likely to make in a paper. Use this checklist the next time you proofread an important assignment. Using the exercises in this *Telecourse Study Guide* chapter, practice detecting and correcting errors in language mechanics. For additional practice, see the exercise on copyediting and proofreading (p. 502) in *A Community of Writers*.

Viewing Guide

Marty Wallace, a graduate student in chemistry, starts off this unit by observing that grammar is not just a concern for English instructors. "It's unprofessional and it's amateurish to submit something that's not proofread – something that has a typo or grammatical error. I'm afraid that you start to lose credibility. The reader says, 'Wait a minute. You're telling me that you're discovering this compound or you've come up with this great synthesis, but you can't spell?'"

Sentence mechanics – punctuation, spelling, and the other physical details of getting written language right – affect much more than the credibility of a writer. These aspects of composition can influence the basic content of communication as much as the sounds we make control the emotion, intensity, feeling, and *meaning* of the words we speak.

Butte College English instructor Michael Bertsh offers this view: "When we talk back and forth, about seventy percent of the communication we do is nonverbal. My facial expressions, my vocal intonations, my body language, my hand gestures – that's part of the communication. But in writing, that is removed.

"All you can do is decode these arbitrary symbols. You have to replace that seventy percent (of nonverbal communications) with word choice, diction, and punctuation."

Bertsch offers one of his favorite examples of the importance of punctuation with the following sentence:

Let's eat, Adam.

What happens to the meaning when the comma is removed?

Let's eat Adam.

"This is an invitation to an entirely different meal," Bertsch explains. "So the comma makes meaning."

As a student writer, you certainly don't want errors that cause similar miscommunications in your work. This unit concentrates on sentence mechanics that allow a writer to communicate aspects of verbal language. Commas, apostrophes, semicolons, and even spelling help to replace some verbal *and* nonverbal elements that are missing on the printed page.

Our strategy will be to review the *most common* mechanical errors. You won't learn all the rules or all of the exceptions to those rules. However, you will be given the tools to develop your own personal strategy to proofread. Your goal, during editing, should be to detect and correct a high percentage of such mistakes in your early drafts *before* you submit the writing to a teacher or an audience.

Commas

Dave Barry, humor columnist at the *Miami Herald*, offers this oversimplification of all comma rules:

"The comma: The simple way to remember it is that wherever you just take a breath, you put a comma in. So people who are in good aerobic shape hardly ever use commas; they don't need them at all. Whereas, a heavy smoker is [gasps] going to have [gasps again] a comma about every other word. That's probably the simplest way to learn where to put a comma."

As absurd as Barry's explanation is, the most frequent use of the comma is to create a pause. However, there are so many other rules, exceptions to rules, additions to the exceptions to the rules, and exceptions to the additions to the exceptions of the rules that a grammar rule book often takes pages and pages to explain them all.

Rebellion against these rules often leads students to either never use commas, for fear of using them incorrectly; or, use, commas, incorrectly, in, every, possible, situation, because, they, are, afraid, of, leaving, them, out.

English instructor Santi Buscemi suggests that it is incorrect to tell students to use commas *only* when they want a pause. However, for most purposes, he says, it *would* be better to simplify the other uses to five relatively simple rules. Also see, "Commas and Pausing" (pp. 487–488) and "Rules for the Use of Commas" (pp. 486–487) in Elbow and Belanoff's *A Community of Writers.*

BUSCEMI'S FIVE BASIC COMMA RULES

Rule 1: After an introductory word, phrase, or clause, use a comma to create a pause.

According to Buscemi, "Many people will tell you, 'If it's a short introductory phrase or just maybe a word, you don't really *need* a comma.' Forget that; put a comma in anyway. You'll never be wrong. You *can* put a comma after a short phrase. You *can* put a comma after a single word. And you certainly *have* to put a comma after a normal introductory phrase."

The following sentences use a comma to create a pause after a long introductory clause, a shorter clause, and a single word:

> Because the state has budget problems, many communities are faced with a loss of service.

> After balancing the budget, the governor asked that the sales tax be increased.

> However, the legislature refused to go along with the increase.

Rule 2: Use commas to separate items in a series.

Usually, the use of commas in a series is fairly easy to understand. In *A Community of Writers*, p. 487, Elbow and Belanoff note that, "A series can be made up of any items that are parallel: sentences, clauses, phrases, or words." They add that, "The final comma – the one after *phrases* – is optional, but you should be consistent." For more on commas, see Elbow and Belanoff's Mini-Workshop H, "Commas."

There are complications to this rule that students must be aware of. A misplaced or omitted comma can *completely* change the meaning of a sentence, especially if items in the series are in pairs.

Santi Buscemi explains that two items in a series normally don't require a comma. This is especially true for items that are connected with an *and* or the word *or*.

However, a sentence with more than two items in a series should probably have a comma after each item, including the word before the conjunction. Notice we use the word *probably*. The style varies from profession to profession. Journalists do not put a comma after the word that comes before the word *and* in a series; English instructors almost always insist that the comma be used after the word that comes before *and* in a series.

For example, a journalist would write:

> The senator talked about taxes, crime and campaign reform.

An English instructor would ask for the comma to be added after the word *crime*:

> The senator talked about taxes, crime, and campaign reform.

The rule, as followed by English instructors, can help avoid confusion if a comma is omitted. Buscemi uses this absurd example:

"Let's say you're a Martian, and you come down to Earth and somebody wants to tell you about what she had for breakfast. And she writes:

> I had for breakfast French toast, orange juice, ham and eggs (NO COMMA) and stewed prunes.

"OK. What are eggs and stewed prunes? What kind of dish is that?"
The solution to the problem is more careful comma placement.

> I had for breakfast French toast, orange juice, ham and eggs, and stewed prunes.

Now the reader knows that ham and eggs are a unit in and of themselves; the eggs are *not* mixed in with the stewed prunes.

Rule 3: When two independent clauses are placed together, make sure you put a comma after the first main clause, followed by the coordinating conjunction. (Coordinating conjunctions are words such as *for, and, nor, but, or, yet,* and *so.* Some instructors suggest you remember them as FAN BOYS.)
Here are some examples:

> The prisoner was about to go to the gallows, so he ordered a twelve-course meal.

> The musicians lost their instruments on the way to the show, and they arrived late.

> The band is a bit frazzled, but the show must go on.

Rule 4: Use commas around a word, phrase, or clause that adds information to a sentence but is not essential to the meaning of the sentence.
Here is an example:

> My brother, Tim, is a doctor.

Buscemi asks students to consider: "If you take the word *Tim* out of the sentence, does the sentence still say what I want it to say? Yes it does, assuming I have *only one* brother.

If the writer has *more* than one brother, however, the word *Tim* becomes an *essential* part of that sentence:

> My brother (NO COMMA) Tim (NO COMMA) is a doctor.

Buscemi explains: "It identifies which brother I'm talking about. I'm talking about my brother Tim, not my brother Jack and not my brother Frank. Get it? You can actually even hear it, if you say it out loud. So the rule is, you put commas around words, phrases, and clauses that add information but are not essential to the understanding of the sentence."

Rule 5: Use commas to set off sentence interrupters. Here are some examples:

> He has reading problems, they believe, because he needs glasses.

> Most people, claims my father, are worth knowing.

The phrases "they believe" and "claims my father" are off the main thought of the sentence. Therefore, they should be set off with commas. This rule becomes very important in cases where the meaning can be confusing without a comma.

> Roberta said Jill is an excellent skier.

In this sentence, Roberta is saying that *Jill* is the excellent skier. Add commas, and Jill is saying that *Roberta* is the excellent skier.

> Roberta, said Jill, is an excellent skier.

There are numerous other rules about commas (including rules about using commas with names, addresses, numbers, and dates) and rules about how *not* to use commas. Though these five rules don't cover all conventions and exceptions for using commas, knowing them (and applying them in editing) will cure most of the comma errors made in a first-year college writing course.

Apostrophes

Students (and other writers) often get so confused by apostrophe rules, that they simply put an apostrophe on every word that ends with the letter *s*. This is partially due to the fact that apostrophes are frequently misused in newspaper advertisements, on billboards, on store signs, and just about anywhere else you will see the written language. This phenomenon leads to Dave Barry's observation about sign painters: "You would think that a group of people who are being paid a lot of money to put a sign up would learn where to use an apostrophe and where not to. The only thing I can conclude is the sign painters got a deal on apostrophes. At some point along the line, the sign makers bought millions of apostrophes and they need to unload them. And so they're just putting them [after every *s*] in every sign they can."

Again, more than 90 percent of apostrophe problems can be caught in proofreading by just remembering a few simple rules. Here are the three most important things to know about apostrophes when editing your work:

1. Use the apostrophe to show the possessive.

   > The player's bat broke when he hit a foul ball.

2. Do *not* use an apostrophe if the possessive form is not required.

   > The player's went to the team bus immediately after the game. (INCORRECT)

   > The players went to the team bus immediately after the game. (CORRECT)

3. Put the apostrophe *after* the letter *s* if the possessive is for a plural word that ends in an *s*.

> The players' uniforms were sent ahead in another vehicle.

4. Use commas in conjunctions to show that some letters have been left out when two words have been combined.

> Can not = can't
>
> I have = I've

Many students become confused by the most common *exception* to the rules. The apostrophe is *not* used to show the possessive with the word *its*. The apostrophe is used only in the contraction for *it is*.

The rule is this simple, but easy to forget:

> The contraction of *it is* = *it's*
>
> The possessive form of the word *it* = *its*

Here are examples.

> Even in heavy rain, the stream never wandered from it's path. (INCORRECT)

No apostrophe is needed.

> Even in heavy rain, the stream never wandered from its path. (CORRECT)
>
> Its beginning to look a lot like Christmas. (INCORRECT)

The apostrophe is used in the conjunction that combines the words *it* and *is*.

> It's beginning to look a lot like Christmas. (CORRECT)

This is only a quick summary to help you proofread for the most common apostrophe errors. There are many more exceptions, additions, and subtleties to the rules about apostrophes. For example, *it's* can also mean "it has," and some style guides recommend using an apostrophe with numbers, as in: Disco was big in the 1970's. The best advice, when editing for more complex uses of apostrophes in an important document, is to look up confusing rules regarding apostrophes in a grammar handbook.

For additional study of apostrophe rules, see Mini-Workshop I, "Apostrophes" (pp. 490–493), in Elbow and Belanoff's *A Community of Writers*.

Spelling and homonyms

Spelling has become less of a problem in the modern academic paper with the advent of word-processing programs that contain spellcheckers. However, spellcheckers are not able to differentiate between homonyms – words that are spelled alike but mean different things. In other words, you may have a word that is spelled correctly but means something completely *wrong* for your sentence.

Dave Barry observes, "The spellchecker doesn't have a clue which version of *there* [or *their* or *they're*] you mean. Basically, because we have so many variations of *their* in our language, whatever random series of letters you write down probably is a form of the word *they're*. And the spellchecker says, 'Fine.' It doesn't have a problem with it. To be honest, I'm not sure spellcheckers are such a great idea."

The following examples are absurd, but they illustrate how contorted a sentence can become if the wrong homonyms are used. (You can be assured *every* one of these homonyms has been used incorrectly in student papers.) Read them allowed (or is that aloud?) to see how poor editing for homonyms can make a paper seem silly.

Example 1: The coach and I *disgust* how *they're currant* running back would always *faint too* the *write*.

Example 2: If *your* going to ask *you're* girlfriend to walk down the *isle* to the marriage *alter*, *nun* of your *bier* buddies should be *aloud*. Of *coarse*, when *your build* for the *ail*, and other *boos*, you'll be glad you paid for fewer *bruise*.

Here is just a short list of homonyms that cause common errors in student papers.

affect, effect	insight, incite	quartz, quarts
billed, build	juggler, jugular	rays, raise, raze
capital, capitol	knight, night	sight, site, cite
due, do, dew	lightening, lightning	too, two, too
elicit, illicit	mussel, muscle	vary, very
facts, fax	navel, naval	waste, waist
gorilla, guerrilla	overdue, overdo	your, you're
heroine, heroin	passed, past	

If you have frequent problems with these types of words, there are many textbooks and Internet sites that give much longer lists for you to consider.

For additional study of spelling rules, see Mini-Workshop K, "Spelling" (pp. 487–501), in Elbow and Belanoff's *A Community of Writers*.

Semicolons

Understanding the correct use of the semicolon is another important aspect of learning how to edit for surface errors in sentence mechanics. As Mr. Language Person (Dave Barry) points out, it's not an easy punctuation mark to master.

According to Barry's absurd theory, "The semicolon is what happens when you have a period and a comma, and the sentence got too long, so you just sort of shoved them together, and now you have a period on top of a comma. Modern science has spent years trying to figure out how to use that phenomenon, but nobody really has a clue."

Though there *are* a few students (and, sometimes, instructors) who know every semicolon rule, you can catch most of your errors by just understanding a few of the *most common* uses.

1. The semicolon is used as an internal pause within a sentence, usually to join two complete sentences. In other words, each of the two sentences joined by the semicolon has a noun and a verb. Some instructors would call each of the sentences an "independent clause," because each has a subject and verb and expresses a complete thought. Here are some examples:

   The Democrats won the election; taxes went up.

   The Republicans won the election; the stock market crashed.

2. The semicolon is used to separate two complete sentences (or independent clauses) joined by conjunctive adverbs or transitional phrases. Here are some examples:

   Don't come late; otherwise, you will miss dinner. (CONJUNCTIVE ADVERB)

   In some schools, classes are small; *as a result*, teachers can give students individual attention. (TRANSITIONAL PHRASE)

3. The semicolon is used to separate items in a series, under certain circumstances. (Usually, this is when some of those items contain commas, and attempts to separate those items with additional commas only cause confusion.) This use of the semicolon is rare. Here is an example:

   In the telecourse program, we heard Dave Barry, a humor columnist and grammar expert; Rush Limbaugh, a conservative radio-talk show host and author; Al Franken, a professional comic and harsh critic of Limbaugh; and Frank McCourt, a novelist and former schoolteacher.

FIXING FUSED SENTENCES AND COMMA SPLICES

First-year writing students find they are most often encouraged to use a semicolon to fix one of two problems: the comma splice and the fused sentence. These uses of the semicolon fall under the first of three most common uses on our list.

- A fused sentence is two sentences (or independent clauses, each complete with a subject and verb) jammed together (incorrectly) without punctuation.
- A comma splice is two sentences (or independent clauses, each complete with a subject and verb) jammed together (incorrectly) with a comma.

English instructor Donald Pharr of Valencia Community College explains: "The structural use of the semicolon is to prevent the comma splice and the fused sentence; you use them to correctly connect independent clauses into compound sentences. In other words, you can simply run two independent clauses together [two sentences together] if you use a semicolon."

Santi Buscemi adds this view: "Fixing a comma splice is really about one little tiny dot. But that one little tiny dot is very important, because it makes your writing easier to read. It's also a way to add emphasis to separate two main clauses or two complete ideas. The reader can see that one idea is separate from the other and can more easily digest those ideas." The telecourse offers these examples:

> Democrats won the election taxes went up. (INCORRECT: fused sentence)

> Democrats won the election, taxes went up. (INCORRECT: comma splice)

Notice that by careful placement of the semicolon, the writer communicates very important implications. In this sentence, the writer expresses surprise that taxes went up:

> Republicans won the election; still, taxes went up. (CORRECT)

In this sentence, the semicolon implies there is a connection between the results of the election and the tax increase.

> Republicans won the election; taxes went up. (CORRECT)

AVOIDING OVERUSE OF SEMICOLONS

Donald Pharr warns that students should not get "semicolon happy," tossing the punctuation mark into sentences without knowing what the semicolon is actually supposed to do.

"Students will frequently overuse the semicolon because they think it's an insurance device. If the comma causes the comma splice and the semicolon fixes it, well [they figure], why don't you just dump that semicolon in there. It can't hurt, right?

"Well, it *can*! It causes a fragment and causes a weird sort of nineteenth-century British punctuation that teachers hate. An example:

> Click County was named after Major Ezikiel Click; who was born in Chattanooga, Tennessee; and joined the military during the Civil War. (INCORRECT)

"There is no logical, rational, or structural reason to use that semicolon," Pharr says. "But this writer got a little bit scared."

Buscemi adds: "Many of my students, once they learn how to use semicolons, sort of sprinkle them everywhere. I have to say, 'Hold back for a second. I'm glad you're experimenting with semicolons, but remember that semicolons connect sentences that are *related* to one another.'"

Summary

No matter how much mastery you have over sentence mechanics and punctuation, it's always good to know your tendencies and to save time for one last proofreading for your most common blunders before you hand in the paper for evaluation.

Many instructors interviewed for the telecourse recommended similar techniques for proofreading:

- Write down a list of the most common errors from your recent papers, and take the time to check one time through new assignments for each of those errors.

- Read your paper out loud to see if it sounds right. If you have trouble separating meaning from mechanics, start at the end of the paper and read the document one sentence at a time.

For example, if you tend to forget about apostrophes or possessive words, check once for all words that end with the letter s. If you have problems with spelling, haul out a dictionary and take an extra ten to fifteen minutes to try to spot the homonyms that the spellchecker missed. If you tend to forget commas with introductory phrases, spend a little more time reading the sentences out loud to see if you need to use a comma to indicate a pause.

Though you many not know all the rules and exceptions to the rules of English grammar, if you focus on the most common errors that have been summarized in the three telecourse programs about editing and proofreading, you will catch a very high percentage of the errors that demolish the grades (and effectiveness) of first-year college papers.

Integrating the Text

Mini-Workshop H, "Commas," in *A Community of Writers* (pp. 486–489) is an excellent companion to the passage in the telecourse program about comma rules. Mini-Workshop I, "Apostrophes" (pp. 490–493) is also an excellent supplement to the study of apostrophes in the telecourse program. If you are a student who has problems with either of these issues, read the workshops very carefully.

Students who have frequent problems with spelling should pay careful attention to Mini- Workshop K, "Spelling" (pp. 497–501).

Exercises

Check with your instructor for your formal assignments. You will be asked to do exercises from the *Telecourse Study Guide*.

Exploring editing mechanics further

Punctuate this sentence so it says that *only* women who work hard should be promoted.

> Women who work hard should be promoted.

Punctuate this sentence so it implies that all women should have the right to be promoted.

> Women who work hard should be promoted.

EXERCISE 2

Each of the following sentences features a problem with apostrophes. Write a version that makes more sense.

> The river's and stream's are fed from melting snow.

> The stream on the farmers land was fed with melting snow.

> The dog chased it's tail.

> The sink in the mens room was overflowing.

> I went to see the San Francisco Giant's play against the Los Angeles Dodger's.

> The Dodgers shortstop broke his leg.

EXERCISE 3

Each of the following sentences has a comma splice. Write a version that makes more sense.

> The ship buzzed close to the planet, it left turbulent waters in its wake.

> Winter came early, we had a great season for snowboarding.

> The teacher asked for a complete revision, the student only edited the mechanical errors.

Exercise just for fun

Pair up with another student. Take two essays you have written. Using a computer, take out all of the punctuation marks. Swap the unpunctuated essays. See how easy or difficult it is to punctuate the other student's essay; compare how your partner decides to use apostrophes, commas, periods, and semicolons to the way you punctuated your own essay, before you started this exercise.

Quick writing exercise

Your instructor may ask you to do a quick focused freewrite about the topic you are studying in this unit. Those of you who are taking the course through a distance-learning system may be encouraged to share your thoughts in a discussion thread or to post your ideas on an Internet bulletin board. If you are writing your thoughts out by hand in a process journal, you might use these questions to come up with ideas. This is a freewriting exercise that will not be graded. You can use any of the following questions to stimulate your thoughts about editing for mechanics:

After seeing three programs on proofreading, do you feel competent to help edit the work of other students? Do you feel these skills will be helpful at any point in your career? How do you personally react when you read professional documents that have errors in spelling and grammar? What are your tendencies for errors? What types of things would you put on a personal editing checklist for a very important document, such as a job application, or a letter written to the governor, asking for a stay of execution?

Exercises related to *A Community of Writers*

Mini-Workshop H, "Commas," in *A Community of Writers*, reviews the rules of comma usage (pp. 486–488) and concludes with an exercise that includes a passage in need of commas (pp. 489). The rethinking of this passage (which is published with correct punctuation in another part of the textbook) is a perfect complement to the study of comma rules in this telecourse program.

Mini-Workshop I, "Apostrophes" (pp. 490–493), reviews the rules for apostrophe use. Three paragraphs are published twice – once without apostrophes in the correct places, and once with apostrophes inserted where they belong. This exercise is a good review of the lessons learned in the telecourse.

Mini-Workshop K, "Spelling" (pp. 497–501), features several exercises to help students who have severe problems with spelling and homonyms, a topic that is covered briefly in the telecourse program. Though many students at this level of college composition are not in desperate need of this final workshop, many good writers still find the brief review of spelling rules helpful.

Additional reading

You will get an assignment from your instructor to read a passage in the appendix. This assignment will be tied directly to this instructional unit.

Several student essays are featured in the appendix. They reflect different levels of writing ability, and they have been published in early draft form without final editing. How would you help Gregory Andrus, Corie Cushnie, Ethlyn Manning, and Francine Taylor, if they were in your own class and they were asking for help with finding problems in mechanics?

The excerpt from Frank McCourt's *Angela's Ashes* (featured in the appendix) is punctuated unconventionally, because the writer is trying to create an effect. How would you approach this passage, if you were trying to make it conform to standard written English? Why can some writers (such as McCourt, who is an expert in English grammar) get away with nonstandard punctuation in certain styles of writing, while college students are expected to punctuate perfectly?

Quick Review

1. Which sentence needs a comma to create a pause at the introductory phrase or clause?
   a. Because the state has budget problems, many communities are faced with a loss of service.
   b. When a sentence starts off with an introductory word or clause use a comma to create a pause.
   c. After balancing the budget, the governor asked that the sales tax be increased.
   d. However, the legislature refused to go along with the increase.
   e. When a sentence starts off with an introductory word or clause, use a comma to create a pause.

2. Which sentence uses the apostrophe incorrectly?
   a. The player's bat broke when he hit a foul ball.
   b. The player's went to the team bus immediately after the game.
   c. The players went to the team bus immediately after the game.
   d. The players' uniforms were sent ahead in another vehicle.
   e. None of the above.

3. Which sentence uses the apostrophe incorrectly in contraction or possessive form?
   a. The dog hid it's bone.
   b. "They're going to have to launder their own uniforms," the ballplayers' manager said.
   c. When you finish your algebra, you're going to have to do your biology homework.
   d. It's beginning to feel a lot like Christmas.
   e. None of the above.

4. Which sentence is correctly punctuated?
   a. The Democrats won the election, taxes went up.
   b. The Democrats won the election taxes went up.
   c. The Democrats won the election; taxes went up.
   d. All of the above.
   e. None of the above.

5. Which of the sentences uses a homonym with a correct spelling?
   a. The Seattle Mariners were happy to raise their abandoned stadium to make room for a new one.
   b. The drug enforcement agent was hired to stop the flow of elicit drugs.
   c. The gorilla warfare waged by the revolutionaries helped overthrow the government.
   d. The bad test score will not affect my overall grade.
   e. The heroin of the novel was a girl my age.

Appendix

Student Essays

Gregory Andrus
Middlesex County College, Edison, New Jersey

"MY MOTHERS SOUL"

The following is a draft of an essay by Gregory Andrus, of Middlesex County College. In the telecourse, we see Andrus presenting portions of this essay to his classmates for peer feedback in the programs "Narrative Writing" and "Description." The essay is reproduced – with permission from Andrus – complete with a few of the errors that remained before the final draft was edited. The video shows how his classmates point out the strengths (as well as a few minor flaws) before Andrus presents the final, edited draft to his instructor, Santi Buscemi. This essay will be used to study instructional points made in the telecourse programs "Narrative Writing," "Description," "Voice," "Editing," "Revision" and "Peer Feedback."

Of all the memories of my childhood, it is the memory of my mother's smile that remains the strongest. Unfortunately, it was the absence of her smile, and of her piano, that has haunted my soul to this day. My mother was her music, and music was my mother.

When I was a young boy, there was absolutely no separation between what was beautiful, what was pure, what was brilliant and warm, and what was my mother at her piano. She was not unlike some exquisite, exotic animal perched on her bench when she played at her piano. Her long hair cascaded down her back. Her eyes, proud and dignified as if she were royalty, looked straight ahead at her sheet music, and her long slender arms extended to the keyboard where her elegant, tiny fingers would almost seem to caress the very keys they depressed.

I know this is my mother that I speak of, and I was very young. But I still couldn't help feel something sensual, something seductive about the way she played the piano. I would even bee remiss in saying she "played" the piano. For my with mother, it was clear that she seduced, she conquered, and then she made love to the piano. Every piece she played, whether it was Mozart or Rachmaninoff, was played with such passion that the very notes seemed to have been individually written by these master composers for her fingers, and her fingers only.

I think the sensuousness of her playing, and the effect it had on the men at the parties she played at, paid a heavy toll on my father's psyche, for many times after a party, we left with my father sulking. My father never had much appreciation for for my mothers talents, and he even seemed to feel threatened by them. The obvious adulation she received from her male admirers at these parties caused many bitter arguments between my parents.

It was quite apparent to me at seven years of age that my mother was most indifferent to these admirers. So why couldn't my father see that ? It was obvious to everyone at these parties that my mother didn't even notice her audience when she played. She could have just as easily been playing in a tiny cellar as in a packed house with dozens of people watching her, mesmerized. As soon as she finished each piece, a crescendo of thundering applause reached her ears, and, startled, almost seeming embarrassed, she became human again, turned to the audience, and flashed that brilliant smile, a smile that reflected the very gleam of everyone's approving eye.

I have said that she lost herself everytime she played the piano. Everytime, that is, except for when she played solely for me. When playing she didn't even look at her sheet music, she just looked down upon me lying at her feet in adoration and smiled at me with that enchanting, loving smile of hers that seemed to span the whole room. It brought a holy place, where not even angels or saints nor even gods who had blessed her with her talents dwelt. Only my mother and I shared this place when she played the piano for me.

Then one day, disaster struck. My father had just gone bankrupt, and one day I came home from school and found a gaping hole where the piano had been. My father's threat, now gone forever, had been liquidated to pay his bills. Feeling outraged, I began trembling. With tears in my eyes, I walked quietly into my mother's room. She was there, but my Mother, my glorious smiling angel, was far away. She looked at me, attempted a weak smile, then just broke into tears. "Never let your father know that I'm crying, Gregory." She whispered to me as we held each other. I quietly agreed.

Never again was there to be adoring audiences watching my mother bare her soul on the ivory keys. Never again would she play "Moonlight Sonata" until I fell asleep. And never again would I see that smile, which would make the sun itself feel inadequate, fall upon my face, nor anyone else's. For playing the piano was my mother's soul, and my mother's soul was now just a memory.

Francine Taylor

"Are Manufacturers of Caffeinated Beverages Targeting Children?"

The following essay is reprinted with permission from student Francine Taylor, in the form she presented to her teacher at Shasta College, just before the final draft was due. This essay was written as the first stage of developing a much longer research paper – just after Francine viewed telecourse the programs titled "Persuasion," "Quotes and Citations," "Argument," and "Critical Thinking." The essay will be an excellent sample for class discussions and personal analysis in those units, as well as the units called "Research," "Reading as a Thinker" and "Voice." This sample can also be used as a practice essay, as if you were a student in Taylor's class, and you were asked to give peer feedback.

Children are drinking more soda per capita than they did twenty years ago. Conservative estimates, from a study done in 1994 by the U.S. Agriculture Department, show children are drinking more than sixty-four gallons of soda a year. Alarmingly, these figures indicate increased consumption amounts of 25% for tots (ages 5 and under), 50% for kids (ages 6 through 11), and 75% for teenagers (Cordes 11). A soda swell is taking place.

Soda barons and makers of other high caffeinated beverages are using clever marketing schemes, similar to those used by the tobacco industry, to promote their addicting products. Their strategy: Younger consumers create more of a demand. I quote Terry Barker, owner of Interstellar Beverage Company, who manufacturers Krank 20, a caffeinated bottled water, "The goal is to perpetuate the market." Barker adds, "The only market available is to start them out younger and younger." (Cordes 12).

Kids are easy prey for caffeine lords. Drinks (with their caffeine content per 12oz) such as: Coke (46mg.), Pepsi (38mg.), Mountain Dew (54mg.) and Sunkist Orange (41mg.) are aggressively advertised to juveniles everywhere. Refreshments containing increased amounts of caffeine with powerful names, such as: Surge (51mg.), Josta (58mg.), and Jolt (72mg.) are also attracting youthful attention by flooding the marketplace.

To expand their promotional horizons, soda empires are targeting children's havens. Schools are now main objective areas for promoters. Here, boys and girls spend the majority of their time away from home and are a captive audience for these legal substance peddlers. On campuses across the nation, logos appear on walls, school buses, textbook covers, computer screensavers, and mousepads (Cordes 11). Coke and Pepsi pay a commission to school districts who display ads and install soda machines on school grounds (Watson). Pupils may purchase 21 ounce bottles, rather than 12 ounce cans, multiplying the caffeine intake for students. What's wrong with this equation?

Recently, Pepsi has started an incentive program that provides educational facilities with computes, musical instruments, and other expensive equipment. Families are swayed into buying products with "Pepsi purchase points" to contribute to this fund raising effort. "Schools are selling off students to soda," charges Marianne Manilov of the Center for Commercial-Free Public Education in Oakland, CA. "Is this what we really want in public schools?" she adds (13).

Other aimed sites, populated with children, are fast food restaurants. Places like Wendy's, McDonald's, Burger King, and Carl's Jr. are where many kids get up to 40% of their meals. Soft drink companies use junk food establishments as vehicles to promote sales. They empower franchises with "a license to fill." Refillable soda stations offer limitless quantities of caffeine to kids at a price cheaper than milk. One megadrink can equal three cups of strong coffee (approx. 350 mg.) (Cordes 11). This is enough caffeine to rev up an adult's nervous system, not to mention a smaller child's. Maybe on-site playgrounds are bouncing zones for the little ones under the influence of caffeine.

Neighborhood athletic fields are also targeted play areas where children can be found. Large numbers of youth participate in different sports, such as baseball, football, and soccer. Packets of caffeine-packed "Sports Goo" and caffeinated water, such as "Krank 20" (70mg), are being guzzled by young athletes (Cordes 11). Advertisers claim these potent potables provide "a winning edge." In Boston, a soccer coach undermined one mother's efforts to keep her child caffeine-free. He supplied his team with caffeinated beverages between matches. When questioned, he recalled an earlier game played with an opposing team who was "jolted" up on something. He answered "Pharmacology is a fair weapon" (Feldmann 1). Isn't there anyplace where children can be safe from caffeinated firearms?

At home, soda sovereigns spend millions of dollars on commercial campaigns. Coca Cola's cutesy polar bears are appealing to youngsters and are pictured on children's clothing. Pepsi's latest commercial spokesperson, Hallie, a young and innocent actress, is becoming a cola quenching exemplar for other children to imitate. Kids are also being tempted with popular giveaways. For example, Mountain Dew is distributing half a million free pagers to kids, who can use them to call friends – but only after they read a promotional ad (Cordes 11). Is the soda hierarchy making profit a priority, rather than children's well-being?

Another major producer of caffeinated beverages, who is putting profit before children, is Starbucks. At any of their local cafes, you'll find an assemblage of giggling kids, ranging from pre-teens to teens. Adolescents are sipping frothy lattes and frosty frappes, soaking up the ambience at these sweet drink saloons. Sugary coffee mixtures appeal to younger palates and contain approximately 60 milligrams of caffeine per 8 ounces. Starbucks' coffee contains about 140 milligrams per cup. Chris Gimbl, spokesman for Starbucks, says "We don't market to teenagers. However anyone is welcome at our stores." (12) Author of Trends 2000, Gerald Celente, states, "Coffee bars are the only legal places for kids to hang out." (12). Hanging out makes kids feel more grown up. And for kids who don't hang out at the local coffee joint, Starbucks, in partnership with Pepsi, is making a new bottled creamy coffee drink called Frappuccino. They are also test marking Power Frappuccino, a cold coffee and carbo drink, to entice younger consumers. Extreme caffeine vending in grocery stores is another snare for youth to dodge.

There are few places left where children are not exposed to caffeinated beverage propaganda. They are bombarded with blurbs, whether by their own choice or not. Caffeine might have been the drug choice for kids in the '90s (Feldmann 1), but it doesn't have to be their choice in the new millenium. As adults, we can take action to educate other and safeguard children against becoming future addicts.

We can demand that public school districts restrict the sale of beverages containing caffeine on their premises. Coffee bars can enforce an age limit for their patrons. The FDA can be petitioned to place labels of caffeine quantities, along with hazardous health warnings, on goods. Cautions may heighten consumer awareness about what they are drinking. We can take an approach, similar to Canada's, where it's against the law to add caffeine to non-cola soft drinks (9). Tougher laws would help decrease the amounts of caffeine made available to youngsters. If these protective measures are practiced, we can help keep children safe from this habit forming drug. If we don't take heed now, caffeine will harm our "Generation Next."

WORKS CITED

Cordes, Helen. "Generation Wired – Caffeine Is the New Drug Choice for Kids."
Nation 266.15
27 April 1998: 11 MasterFILE Premier Database. EBSCO. 26 October 2000

Feldmann, Linda. "Caffeine's Cool Image Appeals To Kids, Perks Adult Concern." Christian Science Monitor 89. 139
13 June 1997: 1. MasterFILE Premier Database. EBSCO. 30 October 2000.

"Kids and Caffeinated Sodas"
<u>Consumer Reports</u> 65. 3
March 2000: 9 <u>MasterFILE Premier Database.</u> EBSCO . 29 October 2000

Watson, Robert. Personal interview with Superintendents of Grant School.
15 November 2000

"What's Wrong with Caffeine?"
<u>Current Health</u> 23.5
1 January 2000: 14-17 <u>MasterFILE Premier Database.</u> EBSCO . 30 October 2000

Ethlyn Manning
Middlesex County College

"COUNTRY LIFE"

The following is an early draft of an essay by Ethlyn Manning, an English student from Middlesex County College in Edison, New Jersey. The essay is reproduced – with permission from Miss Manning – complete with the original errors. This essay will be used to study instructional points made in telecourse programs entitled "Voice," "Editing," "Revision," "Peer Feedback," "Description," and "Narrative Writing."

Growing up in Ashley was the most pleasurable experience I have ever had. I know many would like to differ, saying that living in the country was too dull, but it never was to me. This was my world my beautiful world.

Ashley is a small town in Clarendon, the most southern parish in Jamaica. The major jobs were fishing and farming. Even though most of the coastal lands in Jamaica served as a tourist attraction, our little world somehow did not and remained unspoilt.

The sea was gorgeous, blue, clear. No matter what time of day or season of the year, there was always someone taking a swim. Swimming became a part of our lives from the youngest baby to the oldest. I remember when we came from school especially during the summer time my friends and I would have to go take a swim before we did anything else.

Summertime was the best time of the year for us because this was when most of the fruits were ready to be harvested. There were so many fruits we did not know which one to start eating. In my town everyone's food was everyone's. If we did not have bananas one day then we could go next door and get some. Reaping the fruits was so much fun for us no matter how hot it got. Just looking a the yellow mangos and bananas and the orange tangerines made us happy, even though picking them was not so much fun, since it was such hard work reaping for the market. I remember getting so sticky with the sweet juices that there were bees following me all around.

We really did not have much of a season change, so winter time was when we had most of our outdoor activities, as the temperature was so comfortably cool during the days. There was this breeze that could be experienced only in the Caribbean. It was a big ritual for us on Christmas eve to go carolling through the night around the community. This would flow right into the next day, when all our relatives would gather together and we would have the biggest feast in our back yard. almost everybody praying for a white Christmas. Our Christmas was always warm and cozy. We never had a white Christmas.

The people in my town did not believe in sparing the rod and spoiling the child. The would not hesitate to scold a child who was misbehaving. I remember getting a spanking from some lady I hardly knew and my parents thought it was just as good as I deserved it. These were very hard working people and they had a fear for God about all and going to church on Sundays was mostly obeyed. Whenever someone was not in church because of sickness the pastor would go himself or some other member of the church to visit that person and say a prayer together. Church was not just a place of worship for us. It was a place where we discovered and paraded our many talents in Christ-like manner. We would always have a talent parade at least every Easter and Christmas time.

Our Government did not spend a lot on Education especially in the country areas. However education was very important to us, so all the all the older people would make sure we all went to school whether we had the money to go or not. We all had to pay for lunches at school and if anyone couldn't, then there was always seem to be someone there to help out. Our elementary school always seemed to be over-populated. There were at least forty students to a class with one teacher. Even though there were so many children, we all aimed for a common goal; attend high school which was in the city. Class was packed but our fun time came at break time We would all run to our little snack counter, which was just one old lady selling her home made goodies. She was very kind and would sometimes gives us a little bonus on what we could afford to buy.

There were basket ball, baseball, cricket, soccer, swimming and many more games to entertain us. I am really thankful for all the entertainment we had and now know why our parents tried so hard to keep them going, so that there would hardly be any time to do bad things like drugs. I can remember this group of girls in my town who hung out with these other guys from out of town and thought our games were too silly and childish for them. We called them the "up town girls", as they thought our little town was too local for them; they wanted to go and live in the big city.

It was customary for us to bury our dead ones in our back yards or wherever we had enough space. Many people may think this really weird, but there were generations of our people buried like this and we just somehow thought this was the right way. I guess this was our way of preserving the memories of our loved ones.

Our transportation system was less than acceptable. The journey to any bus stop was at least a mile long, and then as if that walk wasn't long enough, we had to stand in the bus. The early ones were lucky to get a seat. Just when we thought that there was no way the conductor would pick up anybody else: we heard him say "Go down in the bus, there's two more people standing outside." It would seem frustrating now but we knew everyone needed to get to their destination. We grew to accept it and came to find it hilarious.

This was, and is my world, my backbone. It certainly was not perfect, but definitely not dull.

Corie Cushnie

The following essay is reprinted with permission from student Corie Cushnie; it is an early draft form she presented to her teacher at the University of Hawaii. This essay was written as the first stage of developing an essay designed to explore personal identity. The essay will be an excellent sample for class discussions and personal analysis in the units entitled "Voice," "Narrative Writing," and "Definition." This sample can also be used as a practice essay, as if you were a student in Cushnie's class, and you were asked to give peer feedback before the final draft was due.

"What's your name?," this cute guy at a party asks me. "What do you think?," I ask him. He starts to guess all these really feminine names like Jessica, Nicole, Jennifer, and Lauren. "Not even close," I tell him. My name is Corie." "Really, I never would have guessed that," he tells me. It's funny how I get this a lot when I ask people to guess my name. I guess I just look more feminine that my name suggests. But, what's in a name, anyway? I think a lot has to do with it. Throughout the years of my life I have been given all sorts of nicknames that sort of reflect me in some way. And so, I think that the names a person is given reflect who a person is.

First of all my full legal name is Corie Kimiko Cushnie. My parents didn't know if I was going to be a girl or a boy so they made a deal with each other: If I was a girl, my dad would name me. If I was a boy, then my mom would name me. Well, I turned out to be a girl so my dad named me. The only problem was that my mom didn't want me to be another Jessica or Jennifer, because at that time everybody was naming their daughters those names. She wanted me to have a name that stood out from the norm. She didn't want me to be like everyone else. That's why when my dad thought of Corie she was all for it. Then they looked it up in a name book to see if there was anything negative about it because they didn't want me to have a name with a black cloud hanging over it. I guess they believed that "good or bad names impressed a certain kind of character and conduct on a person" (Kaplan, Bernays 104). They found nothing wrong with it, so I was named Corie. But then there was ways of spelling of my name that had to be considered since there are so many ways of spelling it. My dad wanted to spell it the boy's way: Cory, while my mom wanted something more unique like Corie. Of course, my mom won because she gave birth to me. She also told me that it just sounded good when she put my name together. Kind of like in "Naming the Possibilities," where it says that "People associate harmonious sounds with good things" (Cook 57), meaning that when things sound good together it seems more positive. I think that's how my mom felt about my name.

My middle name is Kimiko. It's a Japanese name that was given to me by my mother. I asked my mom what it meant but she didn't know. Kimiko is also my mother's middle name so I am sort of named after her. I think that because I was named after her, I have a lot of her traits. I'm glad I was named after her because I hope to be a good mom like she is when I have kids. I look up to her and I hope that sharing the same middle name as her will give me some of her qualities. I also have a nickname because of it. My dad wanted to name me Kimi but my mom thought it was too common. So because my middle name is Kimiko, he can call me Kimi for short. I think he calls me that because it sounds like a little girl's name and that's the way he wants to see me for the rest of my life. He always calls me that when he scolds me or praises me for something I did. It makes me feel like a little kid so I don't like it too much.

My last name is Cushnie. It is a Scottish name and it's also a little town in Scotland. I am related to all of the Cushnies in the state of Hawaii, but I haven't met all of them yet. Because my last name is so uncommon, I get a lot of comments about it. I even got some of my nicknames from it such as Cushining and Cushball. A lot of times people pronounce it wrong. The most common way they say it is Cushini. I get so annoyed at that, I always ask myself why can't they just say it how it's spelt.

I have tons of nicknames. Some have to do with what I have done, what I look like, or just based on my name. One nickname from my name I haven't mentioned yet is Cor. Usually it's my mom who calls me this but sometimes one of my friends will call me this. I guess people who call me this feel close to me and that's why not too many people use it. "People normally call you by a shortened version of your name if they want you to feel friendly towards them" (Ashley 51). I guess people who call me Cor feel comfortable enough with me to shorten my name.

I have a bunch of names from things that I have done or because of how I have acted. The weirdest nickname I have has got to be Spicy, Crispy ... daruma. The name is so long I can't remember it. It was given to me by my friend Andrew and my boyfriend Rob. We hang out a lot and I always like to sit in the back seat of the car wherever we go. My friend Andrew always drives and he drives kind of wild. He's always making really fast turns that make you hold on to your seat. One night, we were somewhere where he had to make a lot of turns, so I was flying from one side of the car to the other. Everytime I went to one side I would go back to where I was sitting. He noticed that and was trying to describe how I looked doing that, when my boyfriend said I was like a daruma (a daruma is something like a punching bag, everytime it gets knocked down, it comes back to its original position). Andrew agreed with that so they kept calling me Daruma for the rest of the night. Then we were at a stop light. It was two o'clock in the morning so there weren't too many cars on the road. Andrew called out "Chinese firedrill" and then he and my boyfriend got out of the car in the middle of the street, ran around the car, and then came back in. I didn't want to do it so I stayed in the car. When they got back into the car they said that I was burnt because I didn't get out of the car. It just so happened that we were by a Jack in the Box where they were advertising their Spicy Crispy Chicken Sandwich. When they saw it, they said I was like that sandwich and added it to daruma. There's more to the name but we can't remember what it was. Now they call me Dizzy Spice because they think I'm a lost Spice Girl. They figure because I act dizzy all the time and I like the Spice Girls, that Dizzy Spice suites me.

When I was in high school, one of my friends gave me the nickname Hybrid. My friend Angie always called me this and still does. It all started one day when my friends and I were talking about some science thing that had to do with cross breeding plants making them hybrid. That's when Angie said that hybrid was what my friend and I were because we we're hapa (hapa means half Caucasian, half local). So ever since that day I've been known as Hybrid. Another nickname I got in high school was Valley Girl. It was given to me because my friend Lori said that when I put my hair up in a ponytail I look like a cheerleader. When she told me I looked like a cheerleader I said something a cheerleader would say in a tone that sounded like a Valley Girl.

Because she thought that I fit the part so well, she called me Valley Girl and it just stuck. So now when I put my hair up I a ponytail she calls me Valley Girl.

A nickname I got just recently is Elf. My friend Myka insists that I look like an elf because I have pointy ears and I look like one of the elves in *The Santa Clause*. Even though he knows I hate it when he calls me that, he still does. Another nickname that I hate is when people call me Punky Brewster. I admit that I do kind of look like her, but I am nothing like her. She's this character that was on a cartoon a long time ago., She had a friend that was a furry leprechaun creature from the other side of the rainbow and was always getting into trouble. I have always had someone calling me that, ever since I can remember and I hate it. It makes me feel like a little kid and I'm not. There's one more nickname that I can't stand. It's when my dad calls me Victoria. Victoria is the name of this character on "The Young and The Restless" (a soap opera on CBS) that I absolutely cannot stand. She's this really mean and manipulative character and she just absolutely annoys me everytime she comes on the show. My dad insists that I act just like her but I really don't agree with that. He knows I hate her and that's why he calls me that, just to annoy me.

Although I have many nicknames, I would never change my real name. I think that my name kind of hides me because it could also be a boy's name. A lot of times when teachers have gone through roll call and call my name, they look at the boys in the class expecting it to be one of them. Then when I answer, they kind of make this funny facial expression that's half surprised and half "oops, I made a mistake." I think it's funny and I like that I surprise them. My name gives the impression that I'm one way, when I'm really not so it hides who I really am. I don't always show who I really am or how I really feel about things either. I think that my name describes that mysterious hidden side to me. I am also kind of a trickster because I am always playing tricks on my boyfriend. Since my name tricks people into thinking that I'm a boy, it kind of shows the trickster part of my personality. I think that if someone were to look at my name including all of my nicknames they would get a sense of who I am. They would be able to see the fun loving, cheerful, and unique person that I am just by looking at all the interesting and sometimes weird names that I have. "Nicknames are tools that let you see into what a person is all about." (Leslie, Skipper 274–275). They tell a story about you without you even knowing it. The reasons why you got the different names show parts of your personality that may not always be obvious to people. Names are like the stories of a person. You get different names in different parts of your life, like chapters in a book. Those names may not always be true to the person, but they do show different things about the person's character.

Professional Writing Samples

David Ellefson
From *Making Music Your Business*

"Getting Started"

I will always remember a saying I heard years ago: Musicians must eat crow, smile, and ask for more. After playing in many short-lived bands early in my career, I realized that my quest for the big time was not going to be an easy one – and that perhaps there was some truth to this quote!

The early stages of building a musical career can be a very trying time, and they may teach you more about your breaking point than you care to know. It's quite a juggling act to write, rehearse, and record your music while trying to learn the business aspect of music and stay sane. (Sanity is, of course, an option in the music industry.)

When talking with aspiring players, I'm often asked how they can get started in the music business. Well, I've got to be honest with you – when I started out, the whole thing seemed like a big mystery to me, too. So the first thing I say is: "You don't wake up one day and realize you've made it." It doesn't just happen; you must work diligently and hope your talent and persistence (plus a little luck) will eventually lead to the breaks that are needed to have a professional music career.

If you're searching for the secret to success, I suggest you stop right now and realize there's no such thing. In fact, all I can really do in this book is share my experiences – as well as those of some of my fellow professionals – in the hope that you will learn enough to be able to create your own niche in the world of music. So if anyone tells you he has it all figured out, I suggest you walk away and save yourself from an earful of B.S.

While being in the right place at the right time can be extremely helpful, I feel that individuality, charisma, and integrity are the real keys to any artist's survival. Hey, I'd love to spell out a magical plan for overnight success, but there just doesn't seem to be one. The good news is that most of us use a similar approach in piecing together the essentials of a music career, and those essentials are what I've tried to put in this book.

For starters, put things in perspective and figure out what it is you want from playing music. Do you want to make music a full-time career, or is it just a leisure pastime reserved for special occasions? Then ask yourself how much you're willing to sacrifice in order to achieve your goal. The answers to these questions may seem obvious, but you'd be surprised to know how many musicians have become distracted by their lifestyles and completely lost sight of their original goals. By establishing a game plan, you can focus your energies and not squander valuable time and money.

In the early stages of your career, a few simple steps will get you off to a good start. First things first: Write your own music. Second, seek out all performance opportunities; consider playing parties, dances, and nightclubs to be basic training. These gigs are great jumping-off points for tightening up your act and learning to read an audience's response.

If you're already in a band and making live performances, it's crucial to be on the scene and regularly networking through word of mouth. Believe it or not, this can be just as important as your actual talent. If you think someone will knock on your door one day and invite you to become rich and famous, you'd better think again. In Minnesota, where I grew up, my earliest bands spent a great deal of time hanging up flyers in our hometown and the neighboring cities. We played all the usual high school dances and keg parties, and we took slots opening for established acts, hoping that someone would "discover" us. We didn't become instantly successful, but I learned that the more you make your presence known through your own efforts, the more you improve your chances of succeeding.

This leads us to the next step: putting together a team of people who will help to further your career. A reliable team of professional managers and agents can take your musical vision to new heights. My experience has been that without the guidance of these key people, it's virtually impossible to be a real contender in the music business.

Young musicians are especially vulnerable to the "sharks" who feed on naïveté. I suggest meeting with as many managers, agents, and record-label executives as possible – find out what they're about and what they have to offer. There's nothing wrong with absorbing as much information as possible, but before you sign any long-term agreements with anyone, you must be very clear on how the vision of these people is going to fit in with yours.

One good way to investigate managers, booking agents, and record companies is to talk with artists who have already worked with them. It may be worthwhile to set up a showcase and invite as many of these people to the performance as possible. This can be done either publicly in a nightclub or privately at a sound stage. A showcase is a great way to create a "buzz" about your act – but if you live in a remote part of the world, it may mean considerable travel and expense. It might be better to send a representative of your group to a major music metropolis to generate interest within the industry. That way, you can develop local contacts – and it's a whole lot cheaper than moving the whole band!

Teamwork

Teamwork is the foundation for success in all successful organizations. It's probably mentioned most often in the world of sports – it's hard to listen to a sports broadcast without hearing a discussion of team "chemistry" or some comments about how the sum of the parts is greater than the individuals. Consider the position of a football quarterback: He's often regarded as the star player, but he can't win the games by himself. The quarterback relies on the expertise of the coaching staff and the efforts of the linemen, receivers, and other players. All these components working together are what makes a football team successful. By working together as a team, everyone shares in the efforts and the rewards.

There are many similarities between sports and music. In the music business teamwork operates at many levels, some of which may not be obvious. The members of a band must get along with each other musically and personally in order to survive, and they must also have good working relationships with their manager, agent, record company reps, and road personnel. All of these people together make up your musical team.

The same principle applies for session players, too. Prominent session bassist Dave Pomeroy says the team mentality is a strong factor in Nashville, where he does most of his work. "As the leader of a session, it's important to be aware of the fine line between offering helpful direction and being a control freak," says Dave. "There are few things more satisfying than a job well done, especially when the combined efforts of a number of people result in far more than you could have done yourself."

Some people refuse to be team players, and most of them suffer the consequences sooner or later. An artist with a raging, out-of-control ego may think that if it weren't for him, nothing would matter – so whatever he says goes, despite other opinions. He's likely to learn otherwise. Arrogance and an over-inflated sense of self-importance are rarely conducive to a team mentality. These qualities don't contribute to the success of a team – and they'll alienate you from people faster than a speeding bullet.

How do you start to piece together the members of your team? First, every group needs a leader. Someone needs to be accountable for the project, unless you're a solo artist (in which case you've pretty much designated yourself as your own leader). With one key person at the helm, it's easier to put the team together and spell out each member's role right from the beginning. Let's face it – in most cases, one person (possibly two) has the vision and foresight to guide the project. It's important to consider feedback from everyone in the group, but having a leader will help the operation to run more efficiently.

Allow me to share a simple yet important piece of business etiquette: It's to your advantage to align the members of your team to work toward the common goal of the organization. In other words, share the work and you will all share the wealth. Let everyone do the job he was hired to do. This helps to dispel mutiny, which may manifest itself in the form of private agendas. Once these agendas get started, they can quickly undermine the team's well being. But if everyone feels he's getting a fair deal, then everyone will be motivated to help achieve the team's overall success. Remember, as the team succeeds, so do all the individuals.

Of course, not all working relationships turn out to be as successful as we'd like them to be. Sometimes a change is necessary. Having had the experience (more than once), I dislike being in a situation where there's a "revolving door" for employees. But if someone's motives have strayed, or if he's lost the passion for the job, a change may be the best course of action. For obvious reasons, the most direct and honest approach is usually best for everyone involved. That's why it's important to be clear about job descriptions. It's always good business practice to establish comfortable boundaries within the team. Teamwork requires compromise and commitment – but never forget that there is strength in numbers.

Rush Limbaugh
From the *Limbaugh Letter*

"Newsletter"

The media tells us George W. Bush has two problems. Problem One is a 50–50 split of the voters. Problem Two is a thumbs-down from the African-American community. But I think that these are not two problems, it's one problem buried in media clichés and oversimplification – and that there has to be a way to do race-free election analysis.

Let's look at this "all-but-tied," 50-million-to-50-million, vote on Election Day. Ninety percent of the African-American vote, 12 million people, went to Al Gore. So if you take out the black vote from the election total (I'm not suggesting that we do so. Don't misunderstand me as advocating disenfranchisement. I'm saying pretend that they didn't show up that day, then do a statistical analysis) and what happens? You leave George W. Bush with 49 million votes and Algore with 38 million. W won a staggering 55.6% of the non-African American vote to Gore's 44.4%!

If you're an African-American voter, you could look at this Bush landslide and say, "Oh, man. We have serious reasons to fear George W. Bush, because he doesn't owe us anything." In fact, you don't have a thing to fear in George W. Bush, because he's not a vindictive guy – despite the leaders in the black community who may use this fear to manipulate their flock.

Of course, if George W. Bush looked at life the way Bill or Hillary Clinton does – or the way some of these vindictive Democrats do – then, yeah, you would have something to fear and he would be looking around for payback.

He would say, "I've got a mandate" when he doesn't. But Bush isn't that way, and his cabinet selections prove it.

You could also look at this Bush landslide from the other side and ask, "What does he owe people who didn't vote for him? It's sort of like Reagan and Bush, in a way, who were just over the top with their support for Israel but didn't get anywhere near a majority of the Jewish vote. Why should he be naming black people to positions when he didn't get any support from them?"

In a strictly political sense – and that's the umbrella under which all this takes place, a political one – it cannot be said that Bush owes the African-American community anything. But Bush isn't seeking revenge for that lack of support, nor is he ceding those votes to the Democrats. What Bush is doing is attempting to redefine the Black Leadership in America. This tactic is not only brilliant; it's great for America as a whole and African Americans in particular.

I saw a fascinating interview on *Fox News Sunday* with John McWhorter, professor at U.C. Berkeley and author of *Losing the Race: Self-sabotage in Black America*. As a lead-in to the McWhorter segment, Fox played video from the Congressional Black Caucus in the House of Representatives. They raised a little hell during the official tabulation of the electoral votes for the presidency in this election.

McWhorter – who happens to be black – said George W. Bush did everything he should have done, but that nothing will change until "African-American leaders and thinkers can learn to wean this race off of obsessing with victimhood." McWhorter says change will only come "if more and more African-Americans start speaking out for the sorts of things that I and many people who have come before me believe in. We will know we've gotten there when, for example, in the media we see both sides of the African-American question portrayed without people like Shelby Steele or Thomas Sowell or myself being portrayed as novelties or freaks."

This is what Bush is trying to make happen by appealing to African-American leaders outside the Jackson / Sharpton crowd. He doesn't have to reach out like this, but he is – and that scares the heck out of the Democrats.

the big white bridal pillow I had embroidered with a pair of doves for married harmony, and Somesh would describe how the store's front windows were decorated with a flashing neon Dewar's sign and a lighted Budweiser waterfall *this big*. I would watch his hands moving excitedly through the dim air of the bedroom and think that Father had been right, he was a good man, my husband, a kind, patient man. And so handsome, too, I would add, stealing a quick look at the strong curve of his jaw, feeling luckier than I had any right to be.

The night before he left, Somesh confessed that the store wasn't making much money yet. "I'm not worried, I'm sure it soon will," he added, his fingers pleating the edge of my sari. "But I just don't want to give you the wrong impression, don't want you to be disappointed."

In the half dark I could see he had turned toward me. His face, with two vertical lines between the brows, looked young, apprehensive, in need of protection. I'd never seen that on a man's face before. Something rose in me like a wave.

"It's all right," I said, as though to a child, and pulled his head down to my breast. His hair smelled faintly of the American cigarettes he smoked. "I won't be disappointed. I'll help you." And a sudden happiness filled me.

That night I dreamed I was at the store. Soft American music floated in the background as I moved between shelves stocked high with brightly colored cans and elegant-necked bottles, turning their labels carefully to the front, polishing them until they shone.

Now, sitting inside this metal shell that is hurtling through emptiness, I try to remember other things about my husband: how gentle his hands had been, and his lips, surprisingly soft, like a woman's. How I've longed for them through those drawn-out nights while I waited for my visa to arrive. He will be standing at the customs gate, and when I reach him, he will lower his face to mine. We will kiss in front of everyone, not caring, like Americans, then pull back, look each other in the eye, and smile.

But suddenly, as I am thinking this, I realize I cannot recall Somesh's face. I try and try until my head hurts, hut I can only visualize the black air swirling outside the plane, too thin for breathing. My own breath grows ragged with panic as I think of it and my mouth fills with sour fluid the way it does just before I throw up.

I grope for something to hold on to, something beautiful and talismanic from my old life. And then I remember. Somewhere down under me, low in the belly of the plane, inside my new brown case which is stacked in the dark with a hundred others, are my saris. Thick Kanjeepuram silks in solid purples and golden yellows, the thin hand-woven cottons of the Bengal countryside, green as a young banana plant, gray as the women's lake on a monsoon morning. Already I can feel my shoulders loosening up, my breath steadying. My wedding Benarasi, flame-orange, with a wide *palloo* of gold-embroidered dancing peacocks. Fold upon fold of Dhakais so fine they can be pulled through a ring. Into each fold my mother has tucked a small sachet of sandalwood powder to protect the saris from the unknown insects of America. Little silk sachets, made from *her* old saris – I can smell their calm fragrance as I watch the American air hostess wheeling the dinner cart toward my seat. It is the smell of my mother's hands.

I know then that everything will be all right. And when the air hostess bends her curly golden head to ask me what I would like to eat, I understand every word in spite of her strange accent and answer her without stumbling even once over the unfamiliar English phrases.

Dave Barry
From *Claw Your Way to the Top*

"Business Communications"

No modern corporation can survive unless its employees communicate with each other. For example, let's say that Stan, who works in Building Administration, notices that the safety valve on the main steam boiler is broken. If he doesn't communicate this information to Arnie, over in Maintenance, you are going to have little bits and pieces of the corporation spread out over three, maybe four area codes. So communication is very, very important. It should not, however, be confused with memos.

What makes a good business memo
Ask any business school professor, and he'll tell you a good memo is clear, concise, and well organized. Now ask him what his annual salary is. It's probably less than most top executives spend in a month on shoe maintenance. What you can learn from this is that in your business correspondence, you should avoid being clear, concise, and well organized. Remember the Cardinal Rule of Business Writing (invented by Cardinal Anthony Rule, 1898 – 1957): "The primary function of almost all corporate correspondence is to enable the writer to avoid personal responsibility for the many major bonehead blunders that constantly occur when you have a bunch of people sitting around all day drinking coffee and wearing uncomfortable clothing."

There are big balloons of blame in every corporation, drifting gently from person to person. The purpose of your memos is to keep these balloons aloft, to bat them gently on their way. This requires soft, meaningless phrases, such as "less than optimal." If you write a direct memo, a memo that uses sharp words such as "bad" to make an actual point, you could burst a balloon and wind up with blame all over your cubicle.

Standard format for the business memo
1. Always start by saying that you have received something, and are enclosing something.

   These can be the same thing. For example, you could say: "I have received your memo of the 14th, and am enclosing it." Or they can be two different things: "I have received a letter from my mother, and am enclosing a photograph of the largest-known domestically grown sugar beet." As you can see, these things need have nothing to do with each other, or with the point of the memorandum. They are in your memo solely to honor an ancient business tradition, theTradition of Receiving and Enclosing, which would be a shame to lose.

2. State that something has been brought to your attention.

   Never state who brought it. It can be virtually any random fact whatsoever. For example, you might say: "It has been brought to my attention that on the 17th of February, Accounts Receivable notified Collections of a prior past-due balance of $5,878.23 in the account of Whelk, Stoat, and Mandible, Inc." Ideally, your reader will have nothing to do with any of this, but he will think he *should,* or else why would you go to all this trouble to tell him? Also, he will get the feeling you must be a fairly plugged-in individual, to have this kind of thing brought to your attention.

3. STATE THAT SOMETHING IS YOUR UNDERSTANDING.
This statement should be firm, vaguely disapproving, and virtually impossible to understand. A good standard one is: "It is my understanding that this was to be ascertained in advance of any further action, pending review."

4. END WITH A STRONG CLOSING LINE.
It should leave the reader with the definite feeling that he or she is expected to take some kind of action. For example: "Unless we receive a specific and detailed proposal from you by the 14th, we intend to go ahead and implant the device in Meredith."

The beauty of this basic memo format is that it can even be adapted for sending personalized communications to your subordinates ("It has come to my attention that your wife, Edna, is dead.").

In addition to writing memos, every month or so you should generate a lengthy report. This is strictly so you can cover yourself in case something bad happens.

Standard format to use for lengthy reports to insure that nobody reads them

I. SUBJECT: This is entirely up to you. If you follow the format, it will have virtually no impact on the rest of the report.

II. INTRODUCTION: This should be a fairly long paragraph in which you state that in this report, you intend to explore all the ramifications of the subject, no matter how many it turns out there are.

III. STATEMENT OF PURPOSE: This is a restatement of the Introduction, only the sentences are in reverse order.

IV. OBJECTIVES: This is a restatement of the Statement of Purpose, only you put the sentences in a little numbered list.

V. INTRODUCTION: By now, nobody will remember that you already had this.

VI. BACKGROUND: Start at the dawn of recorded time.

VII. DISCUSSION: This can be taken at random from the *Encyclopedia Britannica,* because the only people still reading at this point have been able to continue only by virtue of ingesting powerful stimulants and will remember nothing in the morning.

VIII. CONCLUSIONS: You should conclude that your findings tend to support the hypothesis that there are indeed a great many ramifications, all right.

IX. INTRODUCTION: Trust me. Nobody will notice.

X. RECOMMENDATIONS: Recommend that the course of action outlined in the Discussion section (Ha ha! Let them try to find it!) should be seriously considered.

Bill Walsh
From *Finding the Winning Edge*

"ESTABLISHING EVALUATION TOOLS"

In February each year, coaches, scouts and personnel department members from every National Football League team gather in Indianapolis for a pre-draft NFL-style ritual of sorts – to watch the top collegiate football draft prospects in the nation take a series of tests designed to evaluate the potential of these individuals to play at the pro level. Each prospect is evaluated on a diverse array of measures, including the 40-yard dash, the vertical jump, the standing long jump, the bench press, an intelligence test, a personal interview and several position-related skill tests (e.g., passing, catching, agility, runs, etc.).

The scores and marks that the prospects achieve on these measures are subsequently recorded, scrutinized, and used as input in each team's evaluation process. In a few instances, players are sometimes linked with their "Indy" results for the rest of their careers. Astute teams, however, keep the results of these evaluative measures in perspective, using them as reference guidelines, rather than as absolute criteria.

For example, a player's time in the 40-yard dash doesn't really tell you how fast he will be in a game. His scores on either the vertical jump or the long jump may only indicate that he is out of shape (rather than lacking leg power). Even a player's marks on an intelligence test may have limited value. They may have less to do with an individual's innate instincts that enable him to play "smart" in the game than with his ability to take written tests.

On the other hand, value exists in the process, if you keep the results in perspective and you know how to properly utilize the collected data. It is important to remember that functionality is the most important indicator of a player's ability to perform.

No matter how fast an athlete runs, how high he jumps, or how well he scores on a written test, his value can only be related to how functional he is on the field. In reality, functionality is usually something that cannot be precisely measured any place except on the practice field or in a game situation.

Many teams feel that the most valuable evaluative measure is not the one that yields precise marks, but rather one that must be evaluated with a great deal of subjectivity: the personal interview. It seems ironic that, after going through all the existing intricate tests and procedures, teams often reach their final judgment on a player based on a good, old-fashioned face-to-face discussion. The 49ers utilized the accomplished services of Dr. Harry Edwards, a renowned expert in the interview process, to help in this area.

Another issue that has increasingly become a problematic factor in assessing the usefulness of the Indy testing results involves the fact that many coaches and scouts use the Indy data to inject a self-protective mechanism into the evaluative equation. "This player has good size, speed and plays with lots of heart, *but* he only had a 28-inch vertical jump at the combine." This type of qualifier is often put in the evaluation report to cover one's backside if the evaluation proves inaccurate and the player does not pan out (i.e., "I told you he didn't have a good vertical jump.").

Eventually, each team must decide for itself how to use the information obtained at the

Indy combine. One of the initial steps in deciding what to do with the Indy results should be to thoroughly review each testing measure for its application to the team's needs and interests. How well teams perform this task will have an impact not only on the effectiveness of their process for evaluating players, but also on their ability to be successful where it counts – on the field....

Evaluating players who are currently on the roster

As the head coach, you must ensure that a process is established to evaluate your players on an on-going basis even after they have joined your team. This evaluation is typically performed by members of your coaching staff as part of their responsibility to help develop a projection of the team's needs for the upcoming year. Among the steps that you can take to make sure that such an evaluation is conducted in an appropriate way are the following:

- Make sure that the evaluation is completed with both a short-term and a long-range–appraisal in mind.

- Project the maturation of younger players how their skills and abilities may improve and how those capabilities will affect the make-up and overall production of your team. As part of this effort, individual and collective talent must be continually reassessed, with projections three to five years in the future.

- Develop a plan for dealing with free agency as it affects your team's roster. Such a plan is critical, given the high priority that many teams place on maintaining the continuity of their existing rosters and the fact that most players are eligible for free agency in a relatively brief period of time (i.e., if otherwise unrestricted, five years or four years with a capped year).

Himilce Novas
From *Everything You Need to Know About Latino History*

The history of Mexico and that of the United States are so closely intertwined that they have been compared to Siamese twins who, before suffering a radical and painful separation, shared the same heart. When we speak about Chicanos, we do not speak of a cultural minority who crossed our borders and then by slow assimilation became part of the great American melting pot. We refer to a cultural minority who have lived within the boundaries of the present United States since long before the first English settlement at Jamestown.

Who are Chicanos?

"Chicanos" (the name is an abbreviation of "Mexicanos," Spanish for "Mexicans") was originally used as a pejorative term by both Anglos and Mexican-Americans to refer to unskilled workers born in Mexico, particularly recent immigrants. But since prejudice seldom makes fine distinctions, all Mexican-Americans, no matter how many centuries they may have been living in the territory that is now the United States, are often labeled Chicanos.

Although for years many Mexican-Americans objected to the term, more recently, starting with the labor revolt led by César Chávez in the 1960s, Mexican-Americans have chosen to call themselves Chicanos as a symbol of pride and solidarity with *la raza* – the people.

Who are Anglos?

To Chicanos, "Anglos" originally meant Americans of Anglo-Saxon descent. Today Anglos are more broadly defined as Americans who are neither African-American, Latino, Native American, Asian, or Brown. An Italian-American or a Hungarian-American, for instance, could qualify as an Anglo, even if she or he doesn't have a drop of Anglo-Saxon blood coursing through her or his veins.

Who's a Gringo?

"Gringo" is the Latin American term for a foreigner of English or Anglo-American descent. Although the term is sometimes interchangeable with "Anglo" among Mexican-Americans, it seems to be slowly falling into disuse. There are many theories on just how gringo became a word, since it's not of Spanish origin. Some historians have argued that it was part of a phrase Mexicans used repeatedly during the Mexican-American war, when U.S. soldiers wore green uniforms – "green go" home or "green go" away.

THE CONQUISTADORS IN MEXICO
How long did it take the Spanish to conquer Mexico?

From the time Hernando Cortés and his 550 men landed at the Gulf of Mexico near present-day Veracruz in the year 1519, the Spanish *conquista* of Mexico took only two and a half years.

The reason for this fulminant takeover can be attributed in part to Montezuma II's belief that the *conquistadors* were gods and that their takeover had been divinely preordained to punish the Aztec for having previously conquered and enslaved the Toltec and other Indian groups. But success of the takeover had several other causes. The Spanish army, with its cannons, horses, and harquebuses, was decisively superior to the Aztec arrows, which, incidentally, were not poisoned. The Spanish introduced bacteriological warfare in the form of smallpox and other European diseases, which the Indians succumbed to by the thousands. Finally, the native Mexicans were themselves divided into many warring factions, among them the Tlaxcalans, whom the Spanish enlisted as powerful allies against Montezuma.

Did Mexico become Spanish right away?

In name, yes, but, in practice, no. Cortés conquered and settled Tenochitlán (present-day Mexico City) after a fierce war with the natives, but the rest of Mexico, which was conquered only gradually, remained much the same after the arrival of the Spanish. The Maya in the south, for instance, were almost impossible to subdue, and the Spanish left them alone for quite a while. Similarly, the Chichimec of the north continued in their traditional ways almost uninterrupted by the Spanish.

Kalle Lasn
From *Adbusters*

"MERGER MANIA: FILTERING OUT DISSENTING VOICES"

Time Warner swallows up CNN. AOL swallows up Time-Warner. BCE snaps up Canada's premier television broadcaster CTV. The media mergers keep coming and the conventional wisdom says that they are good. They wake up snoozing CEO's, shake up company boardrooms and most importantly, they marry industries like broadcasting, telecommunications and computers into efficient new digital age corporations.

The downside, of course, is that with each merger, media power is concentrated in the hands of fewer and fewer corporations. We know what it means when two companies (Coke & Pepsi) dominate the world's soft drink market, or when one corporation (Microsoft) has a near monopoly on the world's operating systems, or when half a dozen companies (Exxon, Chevron, Texaco, BP, Total Fina and Shell) control the bulk of the global oil supplies. But what does it mean when a handful of media corporations gain control of the world's news, entertainment and information flows?

It means cultural homogenization. It means the same hairstyles, catchphrases, music and action-hero-antics perpetrated ad nauseam around the world. It means a world in which dissenting voices that challenge corporate interests and profitability are increasingly filtered out.

In all systems, such homogenization is poison. Lack of diversity leads to inefficiency, stagnation and failure. Just as this is true for physical systems, lack of infodiversity spells disaster for mental systems too. The loss of a language, tradition or cultural heritage – or the censoring of one good idea – can be as big a loss to future generations as a biological species going extinct.

Infodiversity is a word you'll probably keep hearing in the years ahead. Infodiversity is analogous to biodiversity. Both are bedrocks of human existence, and both are currently plummeting at alarming rates.

Thirty-five years ago Rachel Carson's *Silent Spring* evoked a future in which birds no longer sing. This book shocked us into realizing that our natural environment was dying, and catalyzed a wave of environmental activism that changed the world. What we need now is a *Silent Spring* of the mental environment – a book, a film, a charismatic media reformer who warns of a future in which corporations do the talking and dissenting voices no longer speak back.

Steve Shanesy
From *Popular Woodworking*

"BOATING BOOKSHELVES: RUSTIC SHELVING – WITHOUT CUTTING APART THAT OLD CANOE"

On a Sunday outing I wandered into a small town and came upon a handmade sign along the side of the road that simply said "FISH DECOYS, OPEN." What a discovery. First, I wasn't aware there were decoys used to attract fish. Second, it so happened that this modest little shop behind the owner's home was the studio of S. Robbins, one of the most highly regarded carvers and painters of fish decoys. As he worked at his bench, I browsed through the shop showroom and admired his beautifully detailed work.

In one corner were examples of what I thought was his most interesting work. They were displayed on shelves that had been fitted into an ancient canoe that had been cut in half at its midsection and stood on end. Not having a canoe to lop in half, I came up with this shelving project as a variation on his theme.

As a "Little Shop That Could" project the ship shelves offered some challenges that the limited equipment I had to work with wasn't prepared to overcome. I'll add that the hull geometry underwent a "midstream" change from how I had originally envisioned it. You see, I wanted the sides of the boat to curve not only bow to stern, but also top to bottom. In photo 2 you'll notice that the ribs (shelves) of the hull curve on the outside. I discovered, when trying to apply the "siding" to the ribs, that the compound curves created by the curve in the ribs caused the siding to head off in odd directions.

After scratching my head and reading about lapstrake boat building, I decided I could live with a hull that was straight from top to bottom. The rest was smooth sailing.

A word about materials

During a trip to the lumber yard I also learned that my initial plan to use clapboard siding to cover the hull was too expensive. My alternative was 1/8" thick tempered hardboard called Duron ™. It's great for this application because the material is dense so the sawed edges don't fuzz up. The yard also had 3/8" thick plywood that sported a bead board detail that looked appropriately "boaty" and so I bought it for the vessel's bottom.

Step 1: Lay out your bottom

Before cutting any other material, first make a full-size layout of the boat bottom showing the outside shape and the location of the shelves. Start by cutting the bead board plywood over-sized to 26" x 74". Strike a centerline on the back of the plywood from its top to bottom.

Next lay out the shelf locations. Use the diagram to establish the curve of the boat side and rip a piece of bendable wood to 1/4" thick and about 84" long (I used 3/4" clear pine).

To establish the proper bends, pound a small finish nail at the location of each shelf. Place the nail on the edge of the shelf line at the bottom shelf, then place the next nails at each shelf edge less the 1/4" thickness of the bending stick. Do this at all shelf end locations, and set the last nail at the bow on the center line. Then insert your bending stick into the nails as shown in the photograph.

Step 2: Cut out the shelves

Next, verify the shelf lengths on your layout against the lengths given in the Schedule of Materials. Use the degree settings given in the diagram for cutting your shelf ends. These angles will give you a better surface to nail and glue to when applying the siding for the hull.

With the shelves complete, cut out the bow stern piece from a short length of 2 x 4. The actual point of the stern piece turned out to be a 45-degree angle.

Now cut out the bottom following your drawing. Because you're cutting from the bottom using a jigsaw, there won't be any tear out on the good side. Speaking of the jigsaw, readers who have followed this series might notice that it's a new acquisition for the "Little Shop." After cutting more round and odd shapes than I care to remember using my muscle-powered compass saw, I treated myself to a $55 Skil Classic Jigsaw. It is the first substantial new tool I've added to my initial $498 tool investment.

Step 3: Begin assembly

Before attaching the shelves, apply veneer tape to the shelves' front edges. This will cover the plywood edge, giving it the appearance of solid wood. Veneer edging is available pre-glued and is easy to apply using an ordinary iron. Trim any veneer overhang and presand the shelves. Next, drill and countersink holes through the boat bottom and screw the shelves in place.

Step 4: Cut the skin

To prepare the 1/8" hardboard siding, first rip 16 pieces to 1 7/8" wide. To make this task easier, I first ripped two 9" widths off the big 4' x 8' sheet. I then crosscut the pieces to about 78" in length, leaving enough to cover the side and trim to length when done. The last step in preparing the pieces is sawing a bevel on one edge to allow overlapping pieces to seat together without producing a gap (see photo).

Step 5: Attach the siding

To apply the siding, set your craft upside down on a level surface so you can nail the first piece starting at the bottom. Because the hardboard is too dense to nail through without splitting, first drill clearance holes. I didn't use a lot of nails, just enough to keep the strips in place, but I did use a modest dab of Liquid Nails™ at each fastening point for each strip. Start nailing at the bow with the strip length overhanging slightly.

When one side is completely covered, trim any overhang at the bow so it doesn't interfere with attaching the siding on the next side. It need not be a pretty cut because the bow will eventually be capped. For now, leave any excess at the stern. Proceed with covering the second side. When done, let your project sit for a couple hours to allow the adhesive to cure.

Before trimming the siding at the stern, use some scrap to make a 3/4" build up and apply it with glue and nails to the front edge and sides at the stern. With the build-ups in place, use its edge to guide your saw to trim the overhang.

Step 6: Laminating the top rails

Because you can't bend a piece wide enough to cover the top edge of the boat's sides, it's necessary to laminate the wood into the required shape. This is done by cutting thinner, bendable strips, then gluing them back together on a form using clamps. While this can be a lot of trouble, we're in luck because the necessary bending form is already made – it's the bottom of the boat!

Start by cutting 3/4" thick pine into 3/8" wide strips that are about 72" long. Cut six strips in all. Before gluing up, have three clamps ready and make two clamping cauls each for the stern and bow end. The caul's face that contacts the wood strips should closely match the contour of the boat's shape, while the edge that goes against the clamp should be square to the clamp face (see diagram). These are easy to make and need not to be perfect. Make two cauls for the bow end that match the bulkhead, and another two cauls that match the side shape at the stern.

After both strips have dried, clean them up by sanding, then cut them to length. So that the top rails butt to the top plate at the bow, the rails are cut at an angle, and should overlay the front edge of the forward bulkhead by 1/2". This will give you enough surface to nail the rail to the bulkhead. The other 1/4" gives you room to glue the top plate in place. Nail the top rails in place by fastening them to the shelves.

Make the top plate by setting a slightly oversized piece of plywood in position on the bow. Mark the bow shape on the underside of the plywood with a pencil. Then measure the overhang on the top rail on the outside of the boat, and add that dimension (approximately 5/8") to the pencil lines to determine the necessary overhang of the top plate. Use your jigsaw to cut the shape, then use the edge tape veneer to cover the plywood edge. When done, nail and glue the top plate in place.

Stem cap and stern rail

Only two more pieces, and the hard work will be done. Fashion the stem cover following the diagram. I shaped the outside to a rough form using a block plane. When done, nail it in place. The stern rail bridges the two side rails at the bottom. Match the angles at the ends formed by the rails and nail in place.

Before sanding and finishing, set the nails and fill with putty. Sand only the wood parts and the Duron where you have used putty. I finished the wood parts with one coat of polyurethane to protect it from my green paint, then painted the hull with two coats. Lastly, I lightly sanded the first coat of polyurethane and brushed on a final coat.

Now, if only I had some of those fabulous looking fish decoys to display in my "boat" shelf.

Mad TV

"Spishak Home Theater Experience Sketch"

INTERIOR. LIVING ROOM – NIGHT

MOM, DAD, TEEN GIRL (JILL), AND TEEN BOY (JACK) PUT THEIR COATS ON.

CHYRON: (POST) SPISHAK PRESENTS TYPICAL AMERICAN FAMILY, USA

SPISHAK SPOKESPMAN (V.O.) (SOT): Hey, typical American family! How many times has this happened to you?

DAD: Come on! We're gonna be late for the movies!

JILL: We're going to miss the commercials.

DAD: And you know how it is with those Meg Ryan movies. If you miss the first five minutes, you're lost. Is she cute in a pet shop? Is she cute in a bookstore? Please hurry!

MOM: (TO CAMERA) Why does going to the movies have to be such an ordeal! I wish there was some way to bring the movies to us!

DAD: Who the hell are you talking to?

SPISHAK SPOKESMAN: Well now there is!

> SUDDENLY IN THE MIDDLE OF THE LIVING ROOM ARE TWO ROWS OF SEATS WHERE THE COUCH USED TO BE. THE SPISHAK SPOKESMAN IS SITTING IN THE BACK ROW.

SPISHAK SPOKESMAN: It's the Spishak Home Theater Experience!

MOM: What happened to my sofa?

SPISHAK SPOKESMAN: Now Spishak brings the complete cinema-going experience right to your living room.

MOM: No, really, what happened to my sofa?

> THE FAMILY BEGINS TO INSPECT THE SEATS.

SPISHAK SPOKESMAN: It begins with these actual theater seats seized from San Francisco's recently raided Adonis Theater.

> JILL AND MOM ARE LOOKING AT A STICKER ON ALL OF THE SEATS.

MOM: "Biohazard"?

JILL: "Seized by the Health Department"?

> THE FAMILY CLIMBS INTO THE SEATS. DAD FOLDS DOWN A SEAT IN THE FRONT ROW AND SITS, WHICH BREAKS ON ONE HINGE. HE FALLS OUT OF FRAME.

MOM: (TO CAMERA) Hear this. I want my sofa back!

DAD: (FROM THE FLOOR) Who are you talking to?!

> THE SPOKESMAN HOLDS UP TILE, WITH JUJU BEES, HAIR, CIGARETTE BUTTS, ETC. STUCK TO IT.

SPISHAK SPOKESMAN: Each system comes complete with authentic theater flooring.

MOM: Eeew, it's all sticky!

> DAD STRUGGLES TO GET UP FROM THE FLOOR, HIS LEFT SIDE HAS BEEN ENVELOPED IN GREEN GOOK.

DAD: This feels like the movies alright.

SPISHAK SPOKESMAN: But it doesn't <u>smell</u> like the movies!

THE SPISHAK SPOKESMAN IS NOW HOLDING A CAN THAT LOOKS LIKE A FLEA BOMB.

SPISHAK SPOKESMAN: It's Spishak's Cine-Aroma! Simply remove the safety.

HE DOES SO.

THE CAN BEGINS TO SPEW THE SPRAY VIOLENTLY ALA A HOUSEHOLD FLEA BOMB.

MOM: Oh my god, what the hell is that?

SPISHAK SPOKESMAN: That's Cine-Aroma's authentic movie theater scents.

<u>CHYRON</u>: (POST) RANCID BUTTER, B.O., STALE URINE, HOT BREATH, OLD PEOPLE SMELL, NACHO GAS, BURNT HAIR AND ROSEWATER.

SPISHAK SPOKESMAN: The authentic movie theater scent will permeate every nook and cranny of your home with authentic movie theater scent.

<u>CHYRON</u>: (POST) (FLASHING) CAUTION: DO NOT TOUCH DURING NINETEEN HOUR MISTING PHASE.

DAD: My throat is burning!

MOM: I'm calling the police, Spishak!

SPISHAK SPOKESMAN: But wait, it's time for Spishak Home Movie Theater Authentic Refreshments.

A SODA CUP APPEARS IN EACH OF THEIR HANDS, ONE AT A TIME.

<u>SFX</u>: (POST) PING!

MOM GETS THE CUP FIRST.

<u>EFX</u>: LOCK-OFF

<u>SFX</u>: (POST) PING!

DAD GETS A CUP.

<u>EFX</u>: LOCK-OFF

<u>SFX</u>: (POST) PING!

JILL GETS HER CUP, MOM VANISHES.

<u>EFX</u>: LOCK-OFF

<u>SFX</u>: (POST) PING!

JACK GETS HIS CUP, MOM REAPPEARS WITH HER CLOTHES ON INSIDE OUT. THEY EAGERLY DRINK, MOM LOOKS CONFUSED.

SPISHAK SPOKESMAN: Drink up! When at the movies, what's better than a cup of golden fla-
vored popcorn topping?

  THE FAMILY MAKE A HORRIBLE FACE, AND STOP DRINKING.

FAMILY: Eeew!

DAD: Ouch, my arteries.

  HE CLUTCHES HIS CHEST.

  A GROUP COMPOSED OF <u>ONE REALLY TALL GUY</u> (EXTRA) WITH BIG HAIR, A
<u>WOMAN</u> (EXTRA) WITH A CRYING BABY (DOLL), WEARING A HUGE HAT, A
<u>GANG MEMBER</u> (EXTRA), AND AN <u>ELDERLY WOMAN</u> (EXTRA) ENTER TOGETH-
ER, MUMBLING LOUDLY, AND SEAT THEMSELVES.

  <u>SFX:</u> (POST) BABY CRYING

DAD: Who are these people?

SPISHAK SPOKESMAN: They're your Spishak Home Theater audience ambience.

MOM: What?!

  <u>SFX:</u> (POST) MUFFLED EXPLOSION

  <u>EFX:</u> EVERYTHING SHAKES.

JACK: Mommy, I'm scared!

SPISHAK SPOKESMAN: No need to be! That's just the Multiplex Sound experience. Spishak
installed speakers in the next room blasting "Mission To Mars" so you know what's playing
in the next theater whether you like it or not.

MOM: Well I don't. And I'm not asking again. Sofa.

SPISHAK SPOKESMAN: Behold Spishak's Authentic Multi-plex Screen, and your Home
Theater Experience is complete!

  <u>EFX:</u> LOCK-OFF

  <u>SFX:</u> (POST) PING!

  THEIR T.V. DISAPPEARS AND LARGE THEATER CURTAINS APPEAR IN ITS
PLACE. THE CURTAINS OPEN TO REVEAL A SMALL SCREEN, MUCH SMALLER
THAN THEIR T.V.

  <u>LIGHT CUE:</u> THE LIGHTS DIM

SPISHAK SPOKESMAN: Now sit back and enjoy the –

MOM: That's it! Nobody leaves til I get back that TV, and my sofa.

SPISHAK SPOKESMAN: Fine.

EFX: LOCK-OFF

SFX: (POST) PING!

THE SPISHAK SPOKESMAN VANISHES, AND THE SOFA APPEARS ON TOP OF JILL. THE TV IS ON THE SOFA.

MOM: Way to go Spishak. Now you've killed Jill. Frank help me!

DAD AND MOM TRY TO GET THE SOFA OFF THE DAUGHTER AS THE THEME SONG PLAYS IN.

MUSIC: (SOT) STRANGE MUZAK – WITH BIRDS CHIRPING

SPISHAK SINGER: (V.O.) (SOT)

A RAINBOW, A KITTEN/
A UNICORN, A CARNIE/
BUY THE SYSTEM/
ENDORSED BY THE ESTATE OF JIM VARNEY/
(SLOWLY) IT'S SPISHAK'S AUTHENTIC HOME MOVIE THEATER EXPERIENCE, GIRL.

GRFX: (POST) (CURSIVE FONT) THE ESTATE OF JIM VARNEY'S (NON-CURSIVE FONT) AUTHENTIC HOME MOVIE THEATER EXPERINCE

FADE OUT.

Sue Grafton
From *I Is for Innocent*

The building that houses Rosie's looks as if it might once have been a grocer's. The exterior is plain and narrow, the plate-glass windows obscured by peeling beer ads and buzzing neon signs. The tavern is sandwiched between an appliance repair shop and an ill-lighted Laundromat whose patrons wander into Rosie's to wait out their washing cycles, chugging beer and smoking cigarettes. The floors are wooden. The walls are plywood, stained a dark mahogany. The booths that line the perimeter are crudely built, destined to give you splinters if you slide too fast across the seat. There are eight to ten tables with black Formica tops, usually one leg out of four slightly shorter than the rest. Mealtime at Rosie's is often spent trying to right the wobble, with the endless intervention of stacked paper matchbooks and folded napkins. The lighting is the sort that makes you look like you've been abusing your Tan-in-a-Bottle.

Dinner was uneventful once I knuckled under and ordered what Rosie told me. She's a formidable presence: in her sixties, Hungarian, short, top-heavy, a merciless enforcer for the food Mafia. The special that night was called *gulyashus,* which had to translate to "beef stew."

"I was thinking of a salad. I need to clean up my act after too much junk food."

"Salad is for after. The *gulyashus* comes first. I make very authentic. You're gonna love it," she said. She was already penciling the order in the little notebook she'd begun to carry. I wondered if she kept a running account of all the meals I'd eaten there. I tried to peek at the page once and she rapped me with her pencil.

"Rosie, I don't even know what *gulyashus* is."

"Just hush and I'm telling you."

"Tell me then. I can't wait."

She had to get herself all settled for the recital, like a concert violinist with her feet placed properly. She makes a point of speaking lumpy English which she apparently thinks contributes to her authority. "In Hungarian, the word *gulyás* means 'herdsman.' Like a shepherd. This dish originate in ninth century. His very good. The shepherd cook up these cubes of meat with ongion, very little moisture. No paprika then so I don't use myself. When all the liquid is boil out, the meat is dried in the sun and then stored in this bag made of the sheep's ... how you say ..."

"Balls?"

"Estomach."

"Previously digested. Very tasty. I'll take it. I don't want to hear the rest."

"Good choice," she said complacently.

The dish she brought was actually what my aunt used to call "galoshes," cubes of beef simmered with onion and thickened with sour cream. It really was wonderful and the tart salad afterward was the perfect contrast. Rosie allowed me to have a glass of mediocre red wine, some rolls and butter, and a cheese tray for dessert. The dinner cost only nine dollars so I couldn't complain. Dimly I wondered if, for total obedience, I'd sold out too cheap.

While I drank my coffee, she stood by my table and complained. Her busboy, Miguel, a sullen lad of forty-five, was threatening to quit if she didn't give him a raise. "Is ridiculous. Why should he get more? Just because he learned to wash a dish like I teach him? He should pay me."

"Rosie!" I said. "The man started washing dishes when Ralph quit six months ago. Now he's doing two jobs and he ought to be paid. Besides, it's nearly Christmas."

"Is easy work," she remarked, undismayed by the notions of fair play, justice, or seasonal generosity.

"It's been two years since his last raise. He told me that himself."

"You taking his side, I see."

"Well, of course I am. He's been a good employee. Without him, you'd be lost."

Her look was stubborn. "I don't like men who pout."

Acknowledgments

Dave Barry, "Business Communications: How To Write a Memo" from Claw Your Way to the Top Copyright © 1986 by Dave Barry. Reprinted by permission of Rodale, Inc; Emmaus, PA 18098

Chitra Divakaruni, "Clothes" from *Arranged Marriage* by Chitra Divakaruni, Copyright © 1995 by Chitra Divakaruni. Used by permission of Doubleday, a division of Random House, Inc.

David Ellefson, "Getting Started" and "Teamwork" from *Making Music Your Business: A Guide for Young Musicians* by David Ellefson, Copyright © 1997 by David Ellefson. Reprinted by permission of Backbeat Books & Miller Freeman Inc.

Sue Grafton, from *I Is for Innocent* by Sue Grafton, Copyright © 1992 by Sue Grafton. Reprinted by permission of Henry Holt & Co., LLC

Kalle Lasn, "Merger Mania" from *Adbusters* magazine, by Kalle Lasn, Copyright © 2000 by Kalle Lasn. Reprinted by permission of the author www.adbusters.org.

Rush Limbaugh, "African-American Vote" from *Rush Limbaugh Newsletter* and the Rush Limbaugh – National Radio Talk Show Host official Web site. Copyright © 2000 by Rush Limbaugh, reprinted by permission of the author

Mad TV script, "Spishak Home Theater Sketch" from *Mad TV*. Copyright © 2000 by Girl Group Company, reprinted courtesy of Girl Group Company.

Frank McCourt, from *Angela's Ashes* by Frank McCourt. Copyright © 1996 by Frank McCourt. Reprinted by permission of the author.

Himilce Novas, "Who are Chicanos – the Conquistadors in Mexico" from *Everything You Need to Know About Latino History* by Himilce Novas, copyright © 1994 by Millicent Novas. Used by permission of Dutton Signet, a division of Penguin Putnam Inc.

Steve Shanesy, "Boating Bookshelves" from *Popular Woodworking* magazine. Copyright © 1998 by Steve Shanesy. Reprinted by permission of the author.

Bill Walsh, "Evaluating Players Who Are Currently On The Roster" and "Establishing Evaluation Tools," from *Finding The Winning Edge* by Bill Walsh. Copyright © 1998 by Bill Walsh. Reprinted by permission of Sports Publishing Inc.